CONTEXTUALIZATION
IN THE NEW TESTAMENT
Patterns for Theology and Mission

DEAN FLEMMING

InterVarsity Press
Downers Grove, Illinois

InterVarsity Press
P.O. Box 1400, Downers Grove, IL 60515-1426
World Wide Web: www.ivpress.com
E-mail: mail@ivpress.com

InterVarsity Press® is the book-publishing division of InterVarsity Christian Fellowship/USA®, a student movement active on campus at hundreds of universities, colleges and schools of nursing in the United States of America, and a member movement of the International Fellowship of Evangelical Students. For information about local and regional activities, write Public Relations Dept., InterVarsity Christian Fellowship/USA, 6400 Schroeder Rd., P.O. Box 7895, Madison, WI 53707-7895, or visit the IVCF website at <www.intervarsity.org>.

Design: Cindy Kiple

Images: Portraits of Diversity/PhotoDisc

ISBN-10: 0-8308-2831-1
ISBN-13: 978-0-8308-2831-9

Printed in the United States of America ∞

Library of Congress Cataloging-in-Publication Data

Flemming, Dean E. 1953-
  Contextualization in the New Testament: patterns for theology and
mission / Dean E. Flemming.
    p. cm.
  Includes bibliographical references and indexes.
  ISBN 0-8308-2831-1 (pbk.: alk. paper)
  1. Bible. N.T.—Socio-rhetorical criticism. 2. Christianity and
culture
  —History—Early church, ca. 30-600. 3. Intercultural communication
  —Religious aspects—Christianity—History of doctrines—Early
church, ca. 30-600. 4. Missions—Theory. 5. Christianity and
culture. 6. Intercultural communication—Religious
aspects—Christianity. I. Title. BS2380.F54 2005 225.6'7—dc22

2005018512

| **P** | 18 | 17 | 16 | 15 | 14 | 13 | 12 | 11 | 10 | 9 | 8 | 7 | 6 | 5 | 4 | 3 | 2 | 1 |
| **Y** | 18 | 17 | 16 | 15 | 14 | 13 | 12 | 11 | 10 | 09 | 08 | 07 | 06 | 05 | | | | |

In honor of my father,
Floyd O. Flemming,
and in memory of my mother,
Barbara E. Flemming
(1927-2002)

CONTENTS

PREFACE

This book has been a long time in the making. It reflects a journey that began some thirty years ago when as a seminary student I was first exposed to the importance of contextualizing the gospel by a great missionary and mentor, Dr. Paul Orjala. It continued during my doctoral studies at the University of Aberdeen as I probed the issue of Paul as a contextual theologian under the able guidance of Professor I. Howard Marshall. In more recent years, I have shared the journey with many fellow travelers—especially students and colleagues at Asia-Pacific Nazarene Theological Seminary in the Philippines and at European Nazarene College in Schaffhausen, Switzerland, my current context of ministry. We have explored together what it means to sing the old gospel in new keys. Without their interaction, encouragement and prayers, this book could not have been written. To these travel companions I express my deepest thanks.

I am grateful to a number of colleagues and friends who have read and reacted to parts of the book in various stages of its development, including Phil Towner, Clinton Arnold, I. Howard Marshall, John Hall and Joel Scott. Thanks are especially due to John Nielson and Ayo Adewuya, who have graciously given of their time and insight to read and comment on the entire manuscript in draft form. In addition, I am indebted to Daniel Reid at InterVarsity Press for his patience, confidence and valuable suggestions throughout the preparation of this book. I could not have asked for a more helpful overseer of this project. I owe thanks as well to the editors of *Missiology: An International Review* for permission to use, in a revised form, material that first appeared in the article "Contextualizing the Gospel in Athens: Paul's Areopagus Address as a Paradigm for Missionary Communication," *Missiology* 30 (2002): 199-214. I also want to express appreciation to the library staff at Mount Vernon Nazarene University and to

Sylvia Locher at the Ashland Theological Seminary library for their invaluable assistance.

Finally, I gratefully acknowledge the unflagging love and support of my father, Dr. Floyd Flemming, and my mother, Barbara Flemming, who went to be with the Lord before this project was completed. Through the years these two people have been my models of what it means to authentically live out the gospel and my biggest encouragers. I gladly and lovingly dedicate this book to them.

LIST OF ABBREVIATIONS

AJT	*Asia Journal of Theology*
AsTJ	*Asbury Theological Journal*
ATA Journal	*Asia Theological Association Journal*
Bib	*Biblica*
BR	*Biblical Research*
BSac	*Biblioteca sacra*
CBQ	*Catholic Biblical Quarterly*
EMQ	*Evangelical Missions Quarterly*
EvRT	*Evangelical Review of Theology*
ExAud	*Ex auditu*
Hom. Act. (John Chrysostom)	*Homiliae in Acta Apostolorum*
HUCA	*Hebrew Union College Annual*
IBMR	*International Bulletin of Missionary Research*
Inst. or. (Quintilian)	*Institutio oratoria*
Int	*Interpretation*
IRM	*International Review of Mission*
JBL	*Journal of Biblical Literature*
JPT	*Journal of Pentecostal Theology*
JR	*Journal of Religion*
JSNT	*Journal for the Study of the New Testament*
JSNTSup	Journal for the Study of the New Testament Supplement Series
NovT	*Novum Testamentum*
NTS	*New Testament Studies*
RevExp	*Review and Expositor*
RSR	*Religious Studies Review*
TJ	*Trinity Journal*
TSFBul	*TSF Bulletin*
TynBul	*Tyndale Bulletin*
WesTJ	*Wesleyan Theological Journal*
WTJ	*Westminster Theological Journal*

INTRODUCTION

I was fresh out of graduate studies, ready to teach my first class on New Testament theology at an international seminary in the Philippines. Armed with the advanced critical weapons of my theological training in North America and Europe, I proceeded to articulate the message of the New Testament in the language and categories that were familiar to me. I expounded on matters like the development of biblical theology in the West, the historicity of Christ's resurrection and the assurance of personal salvation. But then something changed. I started to *listen* to my Asian and Pacific students. I soon realized that many of the "answers" I had been giving them did not fully connect with the questions *they* were asking when they read the Scriptures. Questions like, what is the New Testament perspective on suffering and oppression? What theological resources does the Bible provide for our encounter with spiritual powers? What is the relationship between the Christian Scriptures and the writings of Asian religions? Is it wrong to honor our ancestors? These were questions that had seldom been addressed or even considered in the contexts where I had learned to interpret Scripture and do theology. For my students, however, they were burning issues that needed biblical and theological answers. As a result, I was forced to go back to the New Testament texts. I began to listen, together with my students, for theological perspectives that had previously been mute to my ears. In the process, my own understanding of the gospel and its implications was expanded and enriched.

My experience is hardly unique. Today there is a burgeoning recognition among Christians around the globe that in order for the Christian message to be meaningful to people it must come to them in language and categories that make sense within their particular culture and life situation. It must be *contextualized*. Contextualization has to do with how the gospel revealed in Scripture authentically comes to life in each new cultural, social, religious and historical setting. At one time, discussions about contextualization tended to be confined to the circles of missiology and intercultural studies. But as reflection on the matter has entered its second generation, they have moved more and more into the theological mainstream. We have increasingly realized that it is not crosscultural missionaries alone who must grapple with these issues. Every church in every particular place and time must learn to do theology in a way that makes sense to its audience while challenging it at the deepest level. In fact, some of the most promising conversations about contextualization today (whether they are recognized as such or not) are coming from churches in the West that are discovering new ways of embodying the gospel for an emerging postmodern culture.

In reality contextualizing the gospel is far from an easy task. In spite of an explosion of literature on the subject in recent decades, there is still a great deal of confusion about what it means and how it should be practiced. Many sincere Christians are still suspicious that attempts to contextualize theology and Christian behavior will lead to the compromising of biblical truth. Christians throughout the world find themselves caught between the desire to communicate the Word of God in culturally relevant ways and the fear of giving away too much of the gospel in the process. In addition, emerging global realities pose new challenges to the task of doing contextual theology. What, for example, will it mean to contextualize the gospel in a world that is moving toward increased economic and cultural globalization on the one hand but faces reactionary nationalism and intolerance on the other? And how should the church inculturate its faith when increasingly its field of mission is not just a single target culture but a multi-faceted cultural mosaic? These questions, along with many others, demand our renewed theological reflection.

This book is an attempt to look at the issue of authentic contextualization through the lens of the New Testament. This is a different path to the question than is normally taken. True to the missiological roots of the modern conversation about contextualizing the gospel, most theoretical reflection on the matter has drawn upon models from the fields of linguistics, anthropology, crosscultural communication studies, or contextual theology.[1] As helpful as these discussions have been, the contributions of biblical scholars or students of herme-

---

[1]See, for example, Stephen B. Bevans, *Models of Contextual Theology* (Maryknoll, N.Y.: Orbis, 1992); Charles H. Kraft, *Christianity in Culture: A Study in Dynamic Biblical Theologizing in Cross-Cultural Perspective* (Maryknoll, N.Y.: Orbis, 1979); David J. Hesselgrave and Edward Rommen, *Contextualization: Meaning, Methods, and Models* (Grand Rapids, Mich.: Baker, 1989); Robert J. Schreiter, *Constructing Local Theologies* (Maryknoll, N.Y.: Orbis, 1985).

neutics have for the most part been missing from the dialogue.[2] In particular, we need to ask if Scripture itself can offer us a more adequate approach to the challenge of reappropriating the gospel. This book proposes that we must look to the New Testament for mentoring in the task of doing theology in our various settings.

But what does the New Testament have to do with a modern notion like contextualization? A great deal. Although the term *contextualization* was quite recently minted, the *activity* of expressing and embodying the gospel in context-sensitive ways has characterized the Christian mission from the very beginning. The New Testament itself bears witness to this process in at least two ways. First, it provides "stories of contextualization"—particularly in the Gospels and Acts—in which Jesus and the apostles tailor the gospel message to address different groups of people. The journey of the church from its beginnings as a Jewish sect to becoming a largely Gentile body that proclaimed a universal faith required the gospel to engage new cultural groups and circumstances at each point along the way. Second, the New Testament writings are themselves examples of the church's theological task. All four Gospels, we could say, are attempts to contextualize the story of Jesus for different audiences. Paul's letters are models of doing context-oriented theology for the diverse churches and situations he addressed. Indeed, each book of the New Testament represents an attempt by the author to present the Christian message in a way that is targeted for a particular audience within a given sociocultural environment. The New Testament documents show us the *process* as well as the product of this contextualizing activity.

The aim of this book, then, is twofold: first, to study the New Testament writings in order to discover how they demonstrate the task of doing context-sensitive theology; and second, to reflect on what these patterns and precedents

---

[2]Although a number of journal articles or book chapters look at biblical precedents for contextualization, none that I am aware of goes beyond a preliminary level of discussion. See Daniel von Allmen, "The Birth of Theology," *IRM* 64 (1975): 37-52; Norman R. Ericson, "Implications from the New Testament for Contextualization," in *Theology and Mission*, ed. David J. Hesselgrave (Grand Rapids, Mich.: Baker, 1978), pp. 71-85; Dean S. Gilliland, "New Testament Contextualization: Continuity and Particularity in Paul's Theology," in *The Word Among Us: Contextualizing Theology for Today*, ed. Dean S. Gilliland (Dallas: Word Books, 1989), pp. 52-73; John R. Davis, "Biblical Precedents for Contextualization," *ATA Journal* 2 (January 1994): 10-35; R. C. Hundley, "Towards an Evangelical Theology of Contextualization" (Ph.D. diss., Trinity Evangelical Divinity School, 1993), pp. 29-37, 167-88. See also the valuable work of Mbachu Hilary, *Inculturation Theology of the Jerusalem Council in Acts 15: An Inspiration for the Igbo Church Today* (Frankfurt am Main: Peter Lang, 1995). Mbachu, however, concentrates on one New Testament narrative (Acts 15) and relates it to the single context of the Igbo church in Nigeria.

teach us about how the gospel might become embodied within our diverse cultures and life settings today. It is my hope that this study will not only help to provide a stronger biblical foundation for the church's efforts to contextualize the gospel, but also contribute to the reader's understanding of the New Testament as a collection of books that have the church's mission to all sorts of people at their very heart. By applying the questions raised by the problem of contextualization to the New Testament, we may well discover examples of doing contextual theology in Scripture that are often missed by traditional ways of reading the text.

THE PLAN OF THE BOOK

The lion's share of this volume seeks to uncover the patterns of contextualizing the gospel we find within the New Testament.[3] Due to limitations of space the focus will be on representative writings which contain some of the clearest and most suggestive New Testament examples of doing context-oriented evangelism and theology. I begin with the book of Acts, where we encounter the story of the church's earliest efforts to tailor its witness to particular cultural settings and groups of people. Acts provides a fitting entrée into our study by showing that contextualizing the gospel was intrinsic to the church's mission. Chapter one looks at Luke's chronicle of a series of critical moments in that expanding mission. These offer precedents for how the gospel addresses new situations and cultural groups in fresh ways. In chapter two, I focus on Paul's missionary sermons in Acts as compelling examples of evangelistic contextualization for a variety of audiences.

The apostle Paul—missionary, theologian, interpreter of Scripture—is undoubtedly the key figure for an understanding of the process of doing contextual theology in the New Testament. Consequently, I will spend a substantial part of this study (chapters three through seven) in conversation with Paul and his letters. Chapter three considers Paul as a contextual theologian, exploring

---

[3]Some readers might object that I have not examined Old Testament patterns of contextualization in this book. This omission is not because that study would not be fruitful. Such an investigation, however, could in itself be the subject of another entire book (e.g., how does Deuteronomy recontextualize the laws of Exodus for a new life setting, or how does Chronicles reinterpret Kings?). What is more, since my focus is on contextualizing the gospel in the context of the church, the canonical New Testament obviously provides the primary record of that process. For preliminary discussions of the implications of the Old Testament for contextualization, see Gleason Archer, "Contextualization: Some Implications from Life and Witness in the Old Testament," in *New Horizons in World Mission*, ed. David J. Hesselgrave (Grand Rapids, Mich.: Baker, 1979), pp. 199-216; Arthur Glasser, "Old Testament Contextualization: Revelation and Environment," in *The Word Among Us: Contextualizing Theology for Today*, ed. Dean S. Gilliland (Dallas: Word, 1989), pp. 32-51.

what it is that is nonnegotiable about his thought and how he enabled his abiding gospel to flexibly address the diverse situations of his mission communities. The role of culture in Paul's contextualizing of the gospel is the theme of chapter four. I first reflect on Paul's own cultural identity and then look at the various ways in which the gospel interacts with Paul's cultural world in his writings. Since contextualization has an important hermeneutical dimension, chapter five observes Paul as an interpreter, both of Israel's Scriptures and of the gospel tradition he received. My treatment of Paul concludes in chapters six and seven with several case studies that demonstrate how Paul does theology in relation to specific concerns. First Corinthians is a treasure trove of contextual theologizing, and chapter six asks what we can learn from two concrete examples of how Paul enables the gospel to reshape both the Corinthians' lifestyle and basic worldview assumptions. In chapter seven the letter to the Colossians enters the spotlight as a classic case of how the gospel addresses a context of religious pluralism and syncretism.

The focus turns to the four Gospels in chapter eight. I approach them as four retellings of the one story of Jesus for different target audiences, with the goal of transforming those hearers and their worlds. Our studies in the New Testament conclude in chapter nine with a foray into the book of Revelation. John's Apocalypse proves to be a fascinating theological response to churches living in a world dominated by the oppressive power and idolatry of Rome. Although these nine chapters concentrate on how the missionaries and theologians in the New Testament contextualize the gospel for their worlds, in each case I also try to draw out some implications for the challenge of doing context-sensitive theology today. The book's final chapter addresses that concern in more detail. It asks how the patterns we have seen in the New Testament might help to shape the church's ongoing efforts to engage the tapestry of cultures and contexts that make up its field of mission. Also, how might these New Testament precedents inform the task of authentically incarnating the gospel in light of complex realities like globalization, pluralism, and postmodernism? My aim in addressing such questions is not to tell readers *how* to do contextual theology within their own location and culture. Only they can best determine that. My concern is rather to examine how the New Testament as Spirit-inspired Scripture might provide readers with exemplars and resources for the task.

In my treatment of the New Testament I seek to address two distinct but closely related aspects of contextualization. First, how do the New Testament theologians and writers tailor their theological reflections to particular audiences so that the Word of God becomes an appropriate word for each specific context?

Second, how does the gospel engage the cultural and social world of the readers in a way that both participates in that world and at the same time challenges and transforms it? In taking up these issues, I stand on the shoulders of many others. In particular, some of the more recent studies of the cultural, social and political environment of the first-century Roman world have opened up new vistas for sighting the intriguing interaction between the gospel and culture in the New Testament.

Before we embark on our exploration of the New Testament writings, however, there are two preliminary matters that need to be addressed: I will first try to give a more precise definition to what I mean by "contextualization" and then I will look at a foundational theological paradigm for the entire study—the incarnation of Jesus Christ.

A WORD ABOUT WORDS

There has been no shortage of terms used to describe the activity of relating the gospel to local cultures and contexts that this book is concerned with—*accommodation, adaptation, indigenization, incarnation, translation, transposition,* and *rereading of Scripture* among them.[4] A word that has gained much broader influence, particularly among Roman Catholic theologians, is *inculturation.*[5] Although it overlaps considerably with the notion of contextualization, inculturation, as I understand it, focuses more narrowly on the cultural dimension of human experience. In contrast, *contextualization* is better able to embrace the gospel's interaction with all kinds of contexts, including social,   political, economic, religious and ecclesial settings. I will therefore reserve   *inculturation* primarily for speaking of the encounter between the gospel and human cultures.

Unfortunately, *contextualization* has proved to be a slippery word. No doubt its very popularity has contributed to the fuzziness of its meaning. Today the term is used within a number of theologically related disciplines and by thinkers from a wide range of philosophical and theological perspectives. As a result,

---

[4]*Accommodation, adaptation* and *indigenziation* are older terms that for various reasons have been widely viewed as inadequate for the question of doing contextual theology. For *translation,* see Lamin Sanneh, *Translating the Message: The Missionary Impact on Culture* (Maryknoll, N.Y.: Orbis, 1989); for *tranposition,* see C. S. Song, *The Compassionate God* (Maryknoll, N.Y.: Orbis, 1982), pp. 5-17; for *rereading,* see William A. Dyrness, *The Earth Is God's: A Theology of American Culture* (Maryknoll, N.Y.: Orbis, 1997), p. 80.

[5]A helpful introduction to inculturation from a Roman Catholic scholar is Peter Schineller, *A Handbook on Inculturation* (New York: Paulist, 1990); cf. Alyward Shorter, *Toward a Theology of Inculturation* (Maryknoll, N.Y.: Orbis, 1988).

there are different perceptions of what it is about.[6] For example, some writers speak of contextualization as a hermeneutical activity that is virtually equivalent to what has traditionally been thought of as application of Scripture.[7] Others define it theologically as the process of developing local theologies in a context of rapid social and cultural change.[8] For still others, it is a missiological activity that involves the crosscultural communication of the gospel and various other functions of the Christian mission.[9] Adding to the flux, there is still no consensus regarding whether the gospel (or Scripture) or the cultural context should play the lead part in determining the shape of the contextualizing process. Consequently, before we can talk about patterns of contextualization in the New Testament, we need to clarify what is meant by that activity.

Any adequate understanding of contextualization should not simply prescribe what *should* be done, as if we were initiating something new. It should also describe what *has been* and *is* being done, recognizing that it has to do with something that has been ingrained in the Christian mission through the ages. I take contextualization, then, to refer to the dynamic and comprehensive process by which the gospel is incarnated within a concrete historical or cultural situation. This happens in such a way that the gospel both comes to authentic expression in the local context and at the same time prophetically transforms the context. Contextualization seeks to enable the people of God to live out the gospel in obedience to Christ within their own cultures and circumstances.

To speak of the gospel as the focus of this activity assumes, in the first place, that there is something normative and transcultural about the Christian faith that has been revealed by God in Scripture and which serves as the text. Precisely what we mean by the gospel that is being contextualized from a New Testament perspective will be an important concern of this study.

We must, however, not only ask, what is the *text* but also, what is the *context?* Some popular understandings of contextualization have equated *context* with human culture and the contextualizing process with the communication of the Christian message from a home culture to a different one. This is fine as far as

---

[6]On the origins of the term *contextualization,* which has roots in the conciliar movement, see Hesselgrave and Rommen, *Contextualization,* pp. 27-35.

[7]E.g., Grant R. Osborne, *The Hermeneutical Spiral* (Downers Grove, Ill.: InterVarsity Press, 1991), pp. 318-38; cf. Hundley, *Towards an Evangelical Theology,* pp. 19-25.

[8]E.g., Shokie Coe, "Contextualizing Theology in Mission," in *Mission Trends No. 3,* ed. Gerald H. Anderson and Thomas F. Stransky (New York: Paulist, 1976), pp. 19-24; Bevans, *Models,* pp. 21-22.

[9]E.g., Krikor Haleblian, "The Problem of Contextualization," *Missiology* 11 (1983): 95-111; Charles Taber, "Contextualization," *RSR* 13 (1987): 33; Hesselgrave and Rommen, *Contextualization,* p. 200.

it goes, but it is too narrow. Contextualization can occur *whenever* the gospel engages a new setting or a particular audience. As Gary Burge points out, any time one preaches a sermon, teaches a theology class, or shares one's faith with a group of university students, the message should be in some way shaped by the context of the people to whom it is being expressed.[10] A *context,* then, might be defined by a variety of boundaries: regionality, nationality, culture, language, ethnicity, social and economic status, political structures, education, gender, age, religious or theological tradition, worldview or values. It is the "life world" of the audience. This understanding is important for our study of New Testament patterns of contextualization. Paul, for example, frames the gospel differently for the Thessalonians than he does for the Corinthians even though both communities are situated in a predominantly Greco-Roman cultural setting.

Contextualization is also comprehensive. It must take place at many levels: evangelism, preaching, Bible translation, hermeneutics, theologizing, discipleship, Christian ethics and social involvement, worship, church structures and leadership, and theological education among them. In short, it has to do with the mission of the church in the broadest sense. Due to the limited scope of this book, however, I will concentrate on the tasks of doing contextual theology and biblical interpretation, which are central to both the New Testament witness and the ongoing debate over contextualization today.

THE JESUS MODEL

In a sense the example of Jesus is foundational to everything I will say in this book. The incarnation of Jesus serves as a key paradigm for a contextualized mission and theology. The New Testament declares that the eternal Word of God was enfleshed in Jesus of Nazareth (Jn 1:14). Through his incarnation, Jesus explained or "exegeted" *(exēgēsato)* the Father to us. Jesus was no Melchizedek figure, someone cut off from any cultural past (Heb 7:3). Rather, he embraced the human context in all of its "scandalous particularity"—as a male Palestinian Jew, "born of a woman, born under the law" (Gal 4:4)—in a specific time and place. He was thoroughly immersed in his Jewish culture; he participated in its celebrations and traditions; he spoke Aramaic with a Galilean accent; he had distinctive physical features and personality traits. As Charles Kraft reflects, "God in Jesus became so much a part of a specific human context that many never even recognized that he had come from somewhere else."[11] Jesus became one with the weak and the marginalized of his society. As a humble village artisan

---

[10]Gary Burge, *Interpreting the Gospel of John* (Grand Rapids, Mich.: Baker, 1992), p. 170.
[11]Kraft, *Christianity in Culture*, p. 175.

from Galilee, he lived outside the mainstream of religious, administrative and economic power. Paul describes Jesus' radical identification with humanity as a "self-emptying," a "self-humbling" and a "self-enslavement" on behalf of those he came to serve (Phil 2:6-8). In C. René Padilla's words, "It may be said that God has contextualized himself in Jesus Christ."[12]

Furthermore, when Jesus did theology, he consistently used local resources. Jesus' preaching of the kingdom of God, his teaching on the law and righteousness, and his use of life-specific parables drew upon language, thought categories and rhetorical traditions from the Jewish culture of his day. He communicated to people not in theological abstractions but through familiar, concrete forms—miracles, illustrations from common life, proverbs and stories, master-disciple dialogue and the example of his life among them. Although he offered a radically new teaching he did not coin a new language to express it. Instead, he used the earthy images of everyday rural life. Fishing and farming, weeds and wineskins, soil and salt became the "stuff" of his theological activity. From the beginning the gospel was voiced in local, culturally conditioned forms.

What is more, Jesus' message and method of doing theology were context-specific. He mediated the good news in ways that were appropriate to particular people and occasions.[13] A request from a centurion for a long-distance healing becomes an occasion to consider just who are the insiders and who are the outsiders in relation to God's kingdom (Mt 8:5-13). A rejection by a wealthy would-be disciple launches a reflection on how difficult it is for a rich person to be saved (Mt 19:16-26). A rebuke from Peter following Jesus' prediction that he would be killed and rise again leads Jesus to clarify that all true disciples are bearers of the cross (Mk 8:31-38). Jesus spoke differently to the crowds than he did to the Pharisees, differently to Nicodemus than to Peter. He tailored his exposition of the gospel to the situation at hand.

The incarnation of Jesus makes contextualization not just a possibility but an obligation. It establishes a paradigm for mediating God's redeeming presence in the world today. In a visit to the Basilica of the Annunciation in Nazareth, Israel, a number of years ago, I was struck by a series of full-length mosaics depicting Jesus that lined its walls: in one he is Asian, in another African, in another European, in another Latin American. Through the presence of the Spirit and the

---

[12]C. René Padilla, *Mission Between the Times: Essays on the Kingdom* (Grand Rapids, Mich.: Eerdmans, 1985), p. 83. Cf. the critique of appealing to the incarnation as a paradigm for contextualization in Hundley, "Towards an Evangelical Theology," pp. 168-73.

[13]See Clemens Sedmak, *Doing Local Theology* (Maryknoll, N.Y.: Orbis, 2002), pp. 29-31, 37-38.

ministry of the church, Christ must be enfleshed in every contemporary human culture and context. To be true to the nature of the gospel itself, we must enable it "to enter the bloodstream of the people."[14]

But at the same time, Jesus came to transform the human institutions he entered, and as a result the incarnation retained a universal significance. He prophetically challenged his Palestinian Jewish culture and sought to evangelize it from within. Jesus confronted the religious and political authorities of his social context; he reshaped people's distorted understanding of the law and its observances. He radically redefined cultural notions of purity and impurity by claiming that it is the defilement that comes from within the human heart, not external matters like foods and physical conditions, that makes a person unclean (Mk 7:20-23). Jesus' teaching subverted prevailing attitudes toward wealth and greatness (Mk 10:23-25, 42-45) and questioned the rules that governed social interactions like family obligations (Mt 8:22; 12:46-50) and divorce (Mt 5:31-32; 19:3-12). Jesus scandalized the dominant social norms by touching lepers, eating with tax collectors and zealots, and associating with sinful women (e.g., Lk 7:36-50). His message of the kingdom, although it was articulated in language and symbols thoroughly familiar to his Jewish hearers, had a boundary-breaking character and a cosmic eschatological vision that transcended his own social location and culture.[15]

Jesus' death and resurrection, which are inseparable from his incarnation, likewise point to this transformational aspect of contextualization. Alyward Shorter insists that the dying and rising of Christ function in an analogous way for contextualization, which demands conversion of cultures at their deepest level. There must be a dying to what is sinful and incompatible with the gospel and a radical renewal of human cultures into something new.[16] Furthermore, while Jesus in his earthly life functioned primarily within a Palestinian cultural setting and ministered to his own Jewish people, his sacrificial death and in particular his resurrection from the dead gave the incarnation a universal and intercultural thrust. Through the Spirit of the living Lord and his body the church, he can be present with people of every time and culture and nation.[17]

Jesus' incarnation, then, in its fullest dimensions points the way to both a rad-

---

[14]Emefie Ikenga-Metuh, "Contextualization: A Missiological Imperative for the Church in Africa in the Third Millennium," *Mission Studies* 12 (1989): 6.

[15]See Donald Senior and Carroll Stuhlmueller, *The Biblical Foundations for Mission* (Maryknoll, N.Y.: Orbis, 1993), 144-158.

[16]Shorter, *Toward a Theology*, pp. 83-85. Shorter prefers the term *inculturation* to *contextualization*. Cf. Peter Schineller, "Inculturation: A Difficult and Delicate Task," *IBMR* 20 (1996): 112.

[17]Shorter, *Toward a Theology*, p. 83.

ical identification with each culture in all of its specificity and at the same time to a conversion of cultures from within. Jesus our example was an insider who never relinquished his outsider status that challenged people to see their world from an entirely new perspective. We will see that this tension between "at-homeness" and prophetic transformation is the consistent pattern of biblical contextualization.

ON READING THIS BOOK

This book is integrative and interdisciplinary. In particular it tries to bridge the gap between the normal interests of biblical studies on the one hand and missiology and contextual theology on the other. Through such a conversation, I believe both can be mutually enriched. Because of its integrative character, this volume is intended to have relevance to readers who approach it from a number of perspectives. No doubt a reader's specific interests will be different if she or he comes to the work as a New Testament student or scholar, as someone engaged in intercultural ministry, as a Christian in the Third World living with a theology handed down from the West, or as a First World disciple grappling with how to engage a complex, rapidly changing cultural and religious landscape with the gospel. It is my hope that the biblical perspectives and precedents discussed in this book can speak meaningfully to all such interests and concerns. Further, I have attempted to minimize technical jargon to make it accessible to as many readers as possible. When I have included transliterations of Greek words from the New Testament, I have normally placed them in parentheses after the English translation. Discussions of some of the more technical issues raised by the study can be explored in footnotes. I would also encourage the reader to keep the Scriptures open, taking the time to read biblical passages being discussed and to look up the numerous scriptural references contained in parentheses. This additional effort will significantly enhance what can be gained from the reading.

I make no effort to hide that this book deals with two things about which I care passionately—the message of the New Testament and the church's calling to reflect on the gospel in authentic and context-appropriate ways. The impetus for writing this volume arises out of my own journey of faith and service. I am a North American whose academic training is as an exegete and teacher of the New Testament. The context in which I have fulfilled my ministry calling, however, has been primarily in communities of theological learning with immense cultural diversity—first in Asia and now in Europe. I have been privileged to teach and be taught by students in a wide variety of settings around the globe. I have also engaged in pastoral ministry in a multicultural setting in Asia. These experiences have compelled me to grapple firsthand with the issues addressed in this book. In the course of teaching both biblical and mission studies I have wrestled for the better part of two decades, in tandem with my students and ministry colleagues, with what it means to contextualize the biblical message within a diversity of cultural and church settings. This joyful journey has taught me not only that authentic contextualization of the gospel is complex and demanding work—and I have sometimes practiced it poorly—but also that there is a pressing need for solid biblical and theological moorings for the task.

If the New Testament does indeed show us that to appropriately engage our world with the gospel is essential to what it means to be the church, and if the contemporary global scene cries out for such an engagement, then these are matters that ought to be of genuine concern to every follower of Jesus Christ. I am keenly aware that I do not have the answers to all of the questions this book may raise. But it is my deep-seated hope that the following pages might challenge readers to hear the Scripture story afresh so that the church might learn to sing the gospel in new keys within the rich mosaic of contexts in our world.[18]

---

[18]I am grateful to Brad J. Kallenberg's reflection on what it means "to sing the gospel story in a postmodern key" (*Live to Tell: Evangelism for a Postmodern Age* [Grand Rapids, Mich.: Brazos, 2002], p. 13) for stimulating my own thoughts on how this metaphor expresses the task of contextualization.

1. CONTEXTUALIZATION IN ACTS
Bridging Cultural Boundaries

> *I truly understand that God shows no partiality, but in every nation anyone who fears him and does what is right is acceptable to him.*
>
> ACTS 10:34-35

Contextualizing the gospel is inherent to the mission of the church. The book of Acts tells the story of a church whose very identity involved expressing the good news about Jesus in multiple settings and among new groups of people. It is little wonder, then, that interpreters of the New Testament and missiologists alike have begun to ask whether the experience of the early church in Acts might serve as a crucial paradigm for the process of contextualization.[1] This chapter and the next will probe the extent to which we can uncover precedents for rearticulating the gospel in Luke's narrative.

There is more than one way to get at this task. One approach would be simply to focus on the events recorded in Acts, as well as the sermons of the apostles to different audiences, as examples of the gospel's encounter with Jewish and Greco-Roman culture. Another angle, however, would be to ask how Luke's way of telling the church's story is itself a fresh translation of the gospel for his audience and cultural setting. There is no need to choose between the two. I will begin by briefly considering Acts as a contextual document in its own right.

---

[1]See e.g., M. Dumais, "The Church of the Acts of the Apostles: a Model of Inculturation?" in *Inculturation: Working Papers on Living Faith and Cultures*, ed. A. A. R. Crollius (Rome: Pontifical Gregorian University, 1987), 10:3-24; Mbachu Hilary, *Inculturation Theology of the Jerusalem Council in Acts 15: An Inspiration for the Igbo Church Today* (Frankfurt am Main: Peter Lang, 1995); David K. Strong, "The Jerusalem Council: Some Implications for Contextualization: Acts 15," in *Mission in Acts: Ancient Narratives in Contemporary Context*, ed. R. L. Gallagher and P. Hertig (Maryknoll, N.Y.: Orbis, 2004), pp. 196-208. Cf. Stephen B. Bevans and Roger P. Schroeder, *Constants in Context: A Theology of Mission for Today* (Maryknoll, N.Y.: Orbis, 2004). pp. 10-31.

The major part of the chapter will then focus on patterns of incarnating the gospel that emerge from Luke's story.

ACTS AS A CONTEXTUAL DOCUMENT

Like all New Testament writings, Acts is a "cultural product" in that it participates in the particular first-century cultural and literary world that Luke shares with his readers.[2] This is nowhere more apparent than when we view Acts in light of the typical forms of literature of the ancient world. Although the debate over the specific literary genre of Acts goes on, it is likely that Luke's readers would have recognized this book as an example of ancient Hellenistic historical writing.[3] There is now widespread agreement that the prologue to Luke's gospel (Lk 1:1-4) functions as an introduction to a two-volume work, Luke-Acts. Not only does this preface follow the convention of Greek historical works, but in calling what he wrote a "narrative" (Lk 1:1), Luke "identifies his project as a long narrative account of many events, for which the chief prototypes were the early Greek histories of Herodotus and Thucydides."[4] What is more, a number of other literary features of Luke-Acts—travel narratives, speeches, letters, dramatic episodes such as Paul's shipwreck story (Acts 27:13-44)—would have reminded its audience of other Greco-Roman histories.[5]

In addition, Acts shows ample influence from the conventions and patterns of ancient rhetoric, the art of persuasion.[6] This is hardly surprising since Greco-Roman historical writing was intended not simply to inform but to *persuade* an audience. It was history with a message and a goal. Furthermore, ancient literary works, including histories, were meant in the first place to be read aloud and

---

[2]On the notion of a "cultural product," see Joel B. Green, *The Gospel of Luke* (Grand Rapids, Mich.: Eerdmans, 1997), pp. 11-12.

[3]See e.g., David E. Aune, *The New Testament in Its Literary Environment* (Philadelphia: Westminster Press, 1987), pp. 77-140; Darryl W. Palmer, "Acts and the Ancient Historical Monograph," in *The Book of Acts in Its Ancient Literary Setting*, ed. Bruce W. Winter and Andrew D. Clarke, The Book of Acts in Its First Century Setting (Grand Rapids, Mich.: Eerdmans, 1993), 1:1-29.

[4]Green, *Gospel of Luke*, p. 5.

[5]Joel B. Green, "Acts of the Apostles," in *Dictionary of the Later New Testament and Its Developments*, ed. Ralph P. Martin and Peter H. Davids (Downers Grove, Ill.: InterVarsity Press, 1997), pp. 8-9. This does not mean that Luke-Acts shares all of the formal and content features of Greco-Roman historiography. Luke's work shows certain similarities to Old Testament and Hellenistic Jewish historical writings as well. See Brian S. Rosner, "Acts and Biblical History," in *The Book of Acts in Its Ancient Literary Setting*, ed. Bruce W. Winter and Andrew D. Clarke, The Book of Acts in Its First Century Setting (Grand Rapids, Mich.: Eerdmans, 1993), 1:65-82.

[6]See Philip E. Satterthwaite, "Acts Against the Background of Classical Rhetoric," in *The Book of Acts in Its Ancient Literary Setting*, ed. Bruce W. Winter and Andrew D. Clarke, The Book of Acts in Its First Century Setting (Grand Rapids, Mich.: Eerdmans, 1993), 1:337-79; W. S. Kurz, "Hellenistic Rhetoric in the Christological Proof of Luke-Acts," *CBQ* 42 (1980): 171-95.

heard by an audience. Historians like Luke would have well understood the power of rhetoric to convince people to "give ear" to the case they were making.[7] In a valuable study of the rhetorical background of Acts, classics scholar Philip E. Satterthwaite argues that Luke seems to write as someone trained in Greek rhetoric, using familiar techniques of persuasion in his selecting and arranging of material as well as in his style of writing. "At point after point," Satterthwaite concludes, "Acts can be shown to operate according to conventions similar to those outlined in classical rhetorical treatises. There are some aspects which it is hard to explain other than by concluding that Luke was aware of rhetorical conventions: the preface; the layout of some of the speeches; and the presentation of legal proceedings in chapters 24—26."[8] We will have more to say in the next chapter about the evidence of rhetoric in the speeches of Acts, where Luke's persuasive skills are particularly on display. In addition, Luke follows the ancient practice of "writing in character" *(prosopopoiia),* in which he varies his style of writing to fit the specific subject and occasion. For instance, Luke seems to deliberately imitate the biblical rhythms of the Greek translation of the Old Testament (Septuagint) when the subject matter demands it (especially Acts 1—12; cf. Luke 1—2), in contrast with his more Greek style as the gospel moves out into the Gentile world (e.g., Acts 17:16-34).[9] Familiar literary and rhetorical forms become vehicles for communicating Luke's message in a way that would have a maximum impact upon his audience.

Acts also reflects the historical and cultural circumstances of the first century Mediterranean world. Chronological markers, such as the reference to a popular revolt led by an Egyptian during the rule of the Roman governor Felix (Acts 21:38; cf. Acts 5:36-37), anchor the narrative in a specific time and place. In other ways, too, Luke's book represents the social and cultural realities of his time. Thus, when a Roman tribune tells Paul that he has bought his Roman citizenship (Acts 22:22-29), it would have been common knowledge for people of the Greco-Roman world that this involved paying a bribe, since citizenship could not be legally purchased. Cultural insiders would also know that, according to the honor code of the day, if this tribune mistreated a more "honorable" Roman citizen like Paul—a citizen by birth—it would involve a serious breach of social norms.[10] At the same time Luke's narrative can subvert the conventions and values of the Jewish and

---

[7]Ben Witherington III, *The Acts of the Apostles: A Socio-Rhetorical Commentary* (Grand Rapids, Mich.: Eerdmans, 1998), pp. 41-42.

[8]Satterthwaite, "Acts Against the Background," p. 378.

[9]See Johnson, "Luke-Acts, Book of," in *Anchor Bible Dictionary,* ed. D. N. Freedman (New York: Doubleday, 1992), 4:408-9; Witherington, *Acts of the Apostles,* p. 44.

[10]Witherington, *Acts of the Apostles,* pp. 680-81.

Greco-Roman worlds. For example, Acts' description of the earliest Christian community's sharing property and food in order to care for all those in need (Acts 2:44-45; 4:32-37) tacks against the wind of the dominant culture. In the Roman world, extreme social inequalities, status hierarchies and giving in order to get a return benefit were the norm. Luke not only roots his narrative in the cultural context he and his readers share; he challenges it as well.

THE AUDIENCE AND PURPOSE OF ACTS

To ask how Luke contextualized his presentation of the Christian message in Acts inevitably raises the question of his intended audience. We have no good reason to doubt that Luke's addressee, Theophilus (Acts 1:1; cf. Lk 1:3), was a real person and that he represented the kind of reader whom Luke was particularly addressing.[11] The language and content of Acts suggest that Luke's primary target audience would have been Greek-speaking Gentiles, especially those familiar enough with the Septuagint to appreciate Luke's frequent allusions to the Scriptures and their fulfillment.[12] Most likely, Theophilus was already a believer but not yet fully integrated into the Christian way, someone who needed further understanding of the saving events that had taken place (Lk 1:1-4).

What, then, is Luke's contextual purpose in writing to Theophilus and his fellow Gentile believers? It is difficult to pinpoint a single answer to this question, and there is no reason that we must limit Acts to any one, exclusive aim. Clearly Theophilus has some knowledge of "the events that have been fulfilled among us" (Lk 1:1), that is, God's unfolding purpose in the history of Jesus and the early church. However, the "assurance" (Lk 1:4) that Luke wants to give Theophilus has to do not so much with confirming the historical truth of those events as in their *interpretation* for his audience.[13] In other words, Luke-Acts relates *theological* history from which its readers are intended to learn and to be "convinced."

---

[11]Joseph A. Fitzmyer, *The Acts of the Apostles* (New York: Doubleday, 1998), p. 195. While it is possible to distinguish between Luke's actual narratee, Theophilus, and the portrait of his "implied reader" that can be discovered within the narrative text of Acts, in practice the two cohere to a large extent.

[12]Johnson, "Luke-Acts," pp. 405, 408. Does this mean that all of Luke's Gentile readers would have been able to grasp the Old Testament nuances of Luke-Acts? This is highly unlikely. I like the suggestion of Max Turner that presumably "most Christian communities contained Jews and God-fearers who would contribute to the interpretive reading" ("Historical Criticism and Theological Hermeneutics of the New Testament," in *Between Two Horizons: Spanning New Testament Studies and Systematic Theology*, ed. J. B. Green and M. Turner [Grand Rapids, Mich.: Eerdmans, 2000], p. 63 n. 36).

[13]Joel B. Green, "Internal Repetition in Luke-Acts: Contemporary Narratology and Lucan Historiography," in *History, Literature and Society in the Book of Acts*, ed. Ben Witherington III (Cambridge: Cambridge University Press), pp. 287-88.

Acts is therefore targeted in the first place to the church. Only in a secondary sense is it meant to evangelize unbelievers or to offer a defense of Christianity to those outside the movement. It seeks primarily to build up an increasingly Gentile Christian community by showing them through the story of God's working in the past what it means to be the church and how they are to live in light of that pattern.[14] Given this aim, Luke spotlights the theme of God's plan to bring salvation in its fullness to all people, both Jews and Gentiles. Gentile readers of Acts would have been well aware of the Jewish heritage of the Christian movement as well as the largely Gentile context in which the gospel had spread. No doubt they wanted to know how a movement that centered around a Jew and began as a reform movement within Judaism became a church in which Gentiles far outnumbered Jews. According to John Squires, these Gentile Christians needed a cultural "translation" of a largely "Jewish" story for a new setting. Consequently, Luke-Acts attempts to explain and defend God's saving project to Hellenized Christians in a way that would speak to their needs and thought world. Squires shows that, in particular, Luke's emphasis on the unfolding plan of God allows him to contextualize the gospel for a Gentile world whose writings were already deeply concerned with the role of divine guidance in human affairs.[15] Acts could also provide the Gentile church with theological legitimacy by proclaiming that, in spite of Jewish rejection of the gospel, it stands in continuity with Israel and the ministry of Jesus as the fulfillment of God's plan promised in Scripture. In important ways, then, Acts is an intercultural document. It transposes a story that is grounded in the Hebrew Scriptures, as well as the Jewish identity of Jesus and the early Jerusalem church, into a Greco-Roman cultural setting.

At the same time, Acts would have offered encouragement and strength to Christians who were facing opposition, both by reminding them of the progress of the gospel in the midst of suffering in the past and by calling them to ongoing involvement in God's plan to bring salvation to the ends of the earth.[16] Through the stories of the preaching of the apostles and the church's Spirit-led witness to both Jews and Gentiles, Luke provides models for his readers as they explore

---

[14]I. Howard Marshall, *The Acts of the Apostles*, Tyndale New Testament Commentaries (Grand Rapids, Mich.: Eerdmans, 1983), p. 33; cf. John T. Squires, "The Plan of God in the Acts of the Apostles," in *Witness to the Gospel*, ed. I. Howard Marshall and David Peterson (Grand Rapids, Mich.: Eerdmans, 1998), pp. 38-39.

[15]John T. Squires, *The Plan of God in Luke-Acts* (Cambridge: Cambridge University Press, 1993), pp. 190-94.

[16]See Green, "Acts of the Apostles," p. 17; David Peterson, "Luke's Theological Enterprise: Integration and Intent," in *Witness to the Gospel: The Theology of Acts*, ed. I. Howard Marshall and David Peterson (Grand Rapids, Mich.: Eerdmans, 1998), pp. 540-44.

how to live out God's saving mission in their own contexts. Acts is therefore intended to be more than simply a description of the gospel's progress between Jerusalem and Rome. It is also an invitation. It beckons its readers to embrace God's saving purpose for the world. It calls them to enter into the story that continues beyond the open ending of the narrative in Acts 28:31. In short, Luke tells the story in such a way that it could build up and fortify the largely Gentile church of his day (including Theophilus), helping it to understand who it is, where it stands in God's plan for the ages and what it must do to fulfill its calling as a missionary community. The particular theological themes that Luke features—salvation, God's plan, the risen and exalted Christ, the Holy Spirit, the witness of the church in the face of opposition, the people of God comprised of Jews and Gentiles, and the like—contextualize God's good news for his audience in light of these aims. In this way, Acts becomes a "word on target"[17] for educated Gentile Christians in the Mediterranean world.

STORIES OF BRIDGING BARRIERS: ACTS 1—8

Part of Luke's reason for writing Acts, then, was not only to encourage Theophilus and other Gentile Christians to participate in God's universal mission but also to give them programmatic examples of the church's Spirit-empowered witness to various groups of people. If this is true, the patterns of contextualizing the gospel that emerge from Acts could be of particular value to the church, both in Luke's time and our own. We will consider a series of critical moments in the story of the church's mission which offers precedents for how the gospel speaks afresh to new audiences and circumstances.

First to the Jews. In line with the promise of Acts 1:8, Luke tells the story of the unfolding progress of the gospel from Jerusalem to the ends of the earth by way of Judea and Samaria. Like the rippling effect of a stone dropped into a pool of water, the witness of Jesus' disciples extends to ever-wider geographical areas and new people groups. In this account the church does not intentionally set out to contextualize its message. The focus in Acts is on *witnessing* to God's salvation in Jesus Christ, among Aramaic and Greek-speaking Jews, Samaritans, God-fearing Gentiles and finally pagans. The result is that fresh "translations" of the gospel occur under the guidance of the Spirit as the word of God spans cultural, linguistic and religious boundaries.

At the beginning of the story, however, the inclusive and transcultural dimensions of the gospel are far from obvious. In spite of Jesus' promise of a

---

[17]This is the apt phrase of J. Christiaan Beker (*The Triumph of God: The Essence of Paul's Thought* [Minneapolis: Fortress, 1990], p. x).

universal witness by his followers in Acts 1:8, chapters 1—5 describe a Christian movement that operates within the ethnic and religious borders of the Jewish people. The original articulation of God's new revelation in Christ was tailored for the Jews in the framework of their history, Scriptures, culture and religious experience. The gospel cannot exist apart from a concrete historical and cultural home. Luke portrays the Christian message in these chapters exclusively within the thought forms and images of the Judaism from which it emerges. Jesus is the Jewish Messiah who will restore the kingdom to Israel (Acts 1:6; cf. 5:31). Perhaps we could say that the Jerusalem believers unconsciously "inculturate" the newness of the gospel into their own Jewish heritage.[18]

Nevertheless, there are signs that the gospel is overcoming obstacles even during this early stage of close identification with Jewish culture. The outpouring of the Holy Spirit at Pentecost is accompanied by the miracle of languages, in which Jews and proselytes who represent "every nation under heaven" hear the apostles declare the mighty acts of God in their own vernacular languages (Acts 2:4-11). The miracle would not have been simply for the purpose of communication, since this audience of Jews apparently would have understood either Aramaic or Greek.[19] It also symbolizes that the good news is not confined to any single nation or to the Hebrew tongue. From the beginning, the gospel is translated into the various languages of people from all nations. Although the Acts 2 crowd is made up entirely of Jews and Jewish proselytes who have come to Jerusalem to worship, Pentecost foreshadows the church's universal witness that moves out from Jerusalem to the ends of the earth ("all flesh," Acts 2:17; "everyone," Acts 2:21; "all who are far away," Acts 2:39). The Spirit's bridging of the communication barrier caused by the diversity of languages signals that the word is able to address *all* people in the particularity of their own "language of the heart."

Stephen and the Hellenists. It is in Acts 6—15 that we see the actualization of the boundary-shattering work of the Spirit, as the gospel moves incrementally from a singularly Jewish to a multicultural sphere of influence. Harold E. Dollar observes that Luke deliberately highlights events that show the gospel's journey

---

[18]Francesco Rossi de Gasperis, "Continuity and Newness in the Faith of the Mother Church of Jerusalem," in *Bible and Inculturation*, ed. A. A. R. Crollius (Rome: Pontifical Gregorian University, 1983), pp. 63-64.

[19]Anthony T. Lincoln, "Pentecost," in *Dictionary of the Later New Testament and Its Developments*, ed. Ralph P. Martin and Peter H. Davids (Downers Grove, Ill.: InterVarsity Press, 1997), p. 905. This is supported by the clear impression given by Luke that the entire crowd understood Peter's sermon, which was likely delivered in Aramaic (Acts 2:14ff.).

from Jewish particularism to inclusivism. Consequently, "[e]ach episode in these chapters, with the exception of chapter twelve, advances this movement in the direction of the Gentiles until the leadership explicitly announces this accomplishment in chapter fifteen."[20]

In chapter six, Luke introduces the Jerusalem "Hellenists." This group is vital to the narrative, not least because they play a key role in the progress of the word to the non-Jewish world. There is a growing consensus that the term "Hellenists" (Acts 6:1) referred to Greek-speaking Jews from the diaspora, in contrast with the "Hebrews," whose primary language was Aramaic. Language, however, is a basic vehicle of culture, and the Hellenists appear to be a Jewish subculture within Jerusalem who had adopted at least some elements of Greek culture as well.[21] The response of a significant number of Hellenists to the earliest preaching of the church implies that the gospel message had already been translated into Greek for their benefit.[22] In addition, the Hellenists who spoke only Greek probably worshiped separately in Greek-speaking homes, with the Seven emerging as their functional leaders (Acts 6:5-6). From its infancy the Jerusalem church was characterized by linguistic and cultural diversity. Such differences no doubt contributed to the tensions between the Hellenists and Hebrews over the distribution of food (Acts 6:1-6).[23]

Did the Hellenists develop a distinctive interpretation of the Christian message, as well? Although the theological differences between the Hebrews and Hellenists have often been overblown, Luke's account of the preaching of Stephen, the leading Hellenist (Acts 6:8—7:60), suggests an advancement in the church's understanding of the implications of God's revelation in Christ, one which helps ultimately to open the door to the Gentile mission.[24] Indeed, Stephen's sermon in Acts 7 is a compelling example of doing contextual theology for a new situation.

In the narrative, Stephen's speech before the Jewish council is prompted by charges from other Hellenistic Jews that he blasphemes Moses and God and that

---

[20]Harold E. Dollar, *A Biblical-Missiological Exploration of the Cross-Cultural Dimensions in Luke-Acts* (San Francisco: Mellen Research University Press, 1993), p. 115.

[21]James D. G. Dunn, *The Acts of the Apostles* (Valley Forge, Penn.: Trinity Press International, 1996), p. 81; G. R. Stanton, "Hellenism," in *Dictionary of New Testament Background*, ed. Craig A. Evans and Stanley E. Porter (Downers Grove, Ill.: InterVarsity Press, 2000), pp. 468-70.

[22]Dunn, *Acts of the Apostles*, p. 82.

[23]Ibid., pp. 83-84.

[24]Heinz-Werner Neudorfer, "The Speech of Stephen," in *Witness to the Gospel*, ed. I. Howard Marshall and David Peterson (Grand Rapids, Mich.: Eerdmans, 1998), pp. 279-80; Bevans and Schroeder, *Constants in Context*, pp. 18-20.

he is constantly attacking the Jerusalem temple and the law (Acts 6:11, 13). In response, Stephen appeals to a shared story of God's dealings with Israel and the testimony of Scripture in order to call his Jewish audience to account. On one hand, Stephen's narrative shows his accusers that his message stands in continuity with Moses (Acts 7:35, 39, 44) and the law (Acts 7:38, 44). On the other, he gives Israel's history and traditions a messianic makeover. Retelling Israel's story allows Stephen to establish common ground with his listeners, drawing them into the narrative with repeated first person references (e.g., "our ancestor[s]," Acts 7:2, 11-12, 19, 38-39, 44-45; "our people," 7:17). At the same time, the sermon reconfigures the story of God's people in order to reshape his hearers' understanding and identity.[25]

Stephen's speech develops two main themes, both of which advance this contextual purpose. First, the Jews have over and over rejected God's agents of deliverance who intervened on their behalf. This grim pattern of rejection has continued even to the present in their opposition to Jesus, the "Righteous One" (Acts 7:52), and his servants. Second, God's presence is not tied to the Jerusalem temple. Throughout his retelling of the Jewish story, Stephen demonstrates that God was with his people *outside* of the Promised Land (Acts 7:1-38). As such, the speech gives short shrift to the settlement of Canaan and the Jerusalem-based monarchy. It focuses rather on the sojournings of the patriarchs and the wilderness wanderings, where the people encountered God in a mobile tabernacle. What is more, Stephen describes the temple "made with human hands" (Acts 7:48) in language daringly similar to that used previously for the golden calf (Acts 7:41). The implication is clear: his opponents' attitude toward the temple is tantamount to a form of idolatry. Stephen's targeted speech thus not only addresses the charge laid against him of criticizing the temple (Acts 6:13-14), but, more importantly, it challenges Jewish exclusivism. By freeing the Christian movement from the centrality of Jerusalem and the temple, Stephen the Hellenist cultivates the theological soil for the church's universal witness.

Bridges to peripheral people. The scattering of the Jerusalem disciples following Stephen's martyrdom allows the gospel to cross new cultural and geographical thresholds through the ministry of Philip, the Hellenist evangelist. First, he preaches to a group of people who were social, political and religious rivals of the Jews, the Samaritans (Acts 8:4-25). For Luke they were not Jews in the strict sense, although they remained on the fringes of Judaism. Rather, the Samaritans "stood as a halfway house between the Jewish and Gentile worlds

---

[25]See Robert C. Tannehill, *The Narrative Unity of Luke-Acts* (Philadelphia: Fortress, 1990), 2:88.

leading to a transition to the Gentile mission."[26] It is surely no coincidence that it was a Hellenist Christian, someone who would probably be more open to contact with outsiders, who becomes the catalyst for the church's initial mission to non-Jews. Philip proclaims "the Messiah" to this crowd (Acts 8:5), which may have been a calculated but courageous strategy since the Samaritans had a different messianic expectation from the Jews (later called the "Taheb" = "Restorer") based on Deuteronomy 18:18.[27] The link between the Jewish hope for a messiah and that of the Samaritans provides an evangelistic bridge for Philip. Yet that expectation must still be reframed in terms of Jesus as the Messiah. The Evangelist proclaims "the good news about the kingdom of God [cf. Acts 1:3] and the name of Jesus Christ" (Acts 8:12; cf. 4:17, 18; 5:28, 40), which underscores that Philip's ministry of the word stands in continuity with Jesus and the apostles.[28]

Luke's introduction of Simon the magician within the story of the Samaritan mission signals an early encounter between the gospel and syncretism (Acts 8:9-13, 18-23). Simon tries to incorporate Christianity into his already syncretistic concoction of heretical Samaritan Judaism and popular Greco-Roman magic. For Simon, religion is a fountain of power and self-promotion (Acts 8:10-11, 19). Initially, Luke describes the interaction between Simon and Philip as a kind of "power encounter," in which Simon's sorcery is bested by the authentic miracle-working power of the Spirit (Acts 8:6-7, 9, 11, 13). Impressed by Peter and John's access to the gift of the Spirit, Simon regards God's power as a form of magic to be manipulated for selfish ends. He looks at the Holy Spirit as a commodity that can be bought and sold (Acts 8:18-19). Luke, however, unequivocally denies that Christianity can be viewed through the lens of a magical worldview.[29] Peter condemns Simon with a curse formula threatening eternal destruction (Acts 8:20-23). The passage serves as a strong warning to Luke's readers against the dangers of syncretizing the Christian faith. This is a theme that would have had critical relevance within the religiously plural Greco-Roman world.

The account of Philip's divinely orchestrated encounter with an Ethiopian eunuch (Acts 8:26-39) enables the gospel to bridge further boundaries. The high-

---

[26]P. U. Maynard-Reid, "Samaria," in *Dictionary of the Later New Testament and Its Developments*, ed. Ralph P. Martin and Peter H. Davids (Downers Grove, Ill.: InterVarsity Press, 1997), p. 1076.

[27]Dunn, *Acts of the Apostles*, p. 108.

[28]Tannehill, *Luke-Acts*, 2:104.

[29]Clinton E. Arnold, "Syncretism," in *Dictionary of the Later New Testament and Its Developments*, ed. Ralph P. Martin and Peter H. Davids (Downers Grove, Ill.: InterVarsity Press, 1997), p. 1148.

status official whom Philip discovers on a desert road cuts an intriguing and somewhat mysterious figure. On one hand, he represents an outsider from a Jewish perspective. He is a dark-skinned African, a castrated male, probably a Gentile,[30] whose homeland was considered to be at "the end of the earth"[31] (cf. Acts 1:8). On the other hand, he is a pious Jewish sympathizer, returning from worship of the God of Israel in Jerusalem and avidly reading Isaiah the prophet. For Luke, this episode signals another step in the gospel's steady advance to peripheral people. In this Ethiopian's embrace of faith in the Messiah, the gospel overcomes racial, physical, cultural and geographical barriers and upends human power structures. The Spirit brings the word to someone from the world's outer borders, anticipating the fulfillment of the promise of Acts 1:8.

Philip tailors his evangelistic witness to the royal official's circumstances and spiritual need. Using the Scripture passage in Isaiah 53 that the Ethiopian is already reading as a bridgehead, the Evangelist interprets it as a prophetic testimony about Jesus the Messiah (Acts 8:35). Given that a eunuch would have a marginalized status within Judaism as someone dishonored and excluded from God's assembly due to his physical defect (Lev 21:18-20; Deut 23:1), the identification of Jesus with the humiliated and suffering Servant of Isaiah 53 would have been particularly relevant.[32] Philip uses the text at hand and the Ethiopian's sincere searchings as a point of departure for a fuller exposition of the "good news about Jesus" (Acts 8:35). This becomes a saving word for the eunuch, as his eagerness to be baptized confirms (Acts 8:36).

A TALE OF TWO CONVERSIONS

A critical moment in the gospel's initial movement from the domain of ethnic Judaism into the Gentile arena comes in the story of Cornelius and Peter (Acts

---

[30]Scholars are divided over whether Luke considers the eunuch to be a Jew or a Gentile. The main argument for viewing him as a Jew or a Jewish proselyte is that to introduce a Gentile at this point in the narrative would upstage the conversion of Cornelius in chapter 10, which Luke portrays as the start of the Gentile mission. The official's identification as an Ethiopian, however, who came from one of the remotest regions of the world, makes it unlikely he was a Jew, and eunuchs were prohibited by Jewish law from becoming proselytes (Deut 23:1). Apparently Luke intends this scene to be anticipatory. The conversion of a single Ethiopian Gentile who religiously is still attached to Israel foreshadows the church's *deliberate* Gentile mission initiated in chapters 10—15. See C. K. Barrett, *A Critical and Exegetical Commentary on the Acts of the Apostles* (Edinburgh: T & T Clark, 1994), 1:420-21.

[31]Homer *Odyssey* 1.22-24; Strabo *Geography* 17.2.1; Herodotus *History* 3.25.114; cf. Beverly R. Gaventa, *From Darkness to Light: Aspects of Conversion in the New Testament* (Philadelphia: Fortress, 1986), p. 103.

[32]F. S. Spencer, "Philip the Evangelist," in *Dictionary of the Later New Testament and Its Developments*, ed. Ralph P. Martin and Peter H. Davids (Downers Grove, Ill.: InterVarsity Press, 1997), p. 930.

10:1—11:18). The importance of this narrative for Luke can hardly be over-stated. Its sheer length, Luke's repeated telling of the story, and its numerous references to visions and miraculous elements all testify that, for Luke, it is a crucial test case for the acceptance of Gentiles as Gentiles into the people of God. Without this forward leap in the life of the church the translation of the gospel into new cultures and milieus would not be possible.

Acts 10—11 tell a story of *two* complementary conversions. One involves the Roman centurion Cornelius, who symbolically represents the inclusion of Gen-tiles into the Christian community (11:1, 18). Yet if Cornelius is a *representative* Gentile, he is hardly a *typical* Gentile. Luke goes to no small effort to paint him as a pious, God-fearing[33] adherent of the Jewish synagogue. The angel sent by God addresses him like a Jew (Acts 10:4), and his prayers, faith and alms reveal an openness to divine grace.[34] God's grace has been at work in the life of this sincere Gentile long before his encounter with Peter, preparing the centurion for acceptance of the gospel when he hears it. Cornelius is no pagan, but neither is he a proselyte, since he is not circumcised and does not keep Jewish food laws. Cornelius and his company thus function as a natural "bridge group" for the progress of the gospel into the Gentile arena.[35]

The second "conversion" is that of Peter, the spokesman and representative of the Jerusalem apostles and the Jewish Christian church. It is not a conversion to faith in Jesus Christ as it is for the Cornelius group, but rather a *theological* and *cultural* transformation. Peter must be converted to a new vision of what consti-tutes the people of God, one that includes uncircumcised and "unclean" Gentiles as well as Jews. This is perhaps the more difficult and dramatic change of the two, because it challenges deep-seated cultural values and Jewish ethnocentrism. Luke underscores this through his dual emphasis on God's persistent initiative in these events on the one hand and the repeated resistance of Jewish Christians to what God is doing on the other. It takes interlocking visions (Acts 10:3-16; 11:5-

---

[33]There has been considerable scholarly debate about whether or not there was an actual cat-egory of "God-fearers," i.e., Gentiles who worshiped the God of Israel and were attached to the synagogue but did not submit to circumcision or observe the Torah in its entirety. See the valuable discussions in Jack T. Sanders, "Who Is a Jew and Who Is a Gentile in the Book of Acts?" *NTS* 37 (1991): 439-43 and Witherington, *Acts of the Apostles*, pp. 341-44. The evidence points to the conclusion that even if "God-fearers" is something less than a technical term, there *were* non-Jewish synagogue adherents in antiquity like Cornelius.

[34]Fitzmyer, *Acts of the Apostles*, p. 448.

[35]Luke's characterization of Cornelius as a boundary-bridging figure is not only cultural and re-ligious, but geographical as well. He lives in a Roman, thoroughly Hellenized city, but one that is still within the territory of Palestine. Like the God-fearing Gentiles, bridge groups that participate in more than one culture (e.g., overseas students or multilingual city dwellers) are often highly instrumental in the advance of the church's mission yet today.

10), angels (Acts 10:3-8), trances (Acts 10:10), three distinct hearings of God's command (Acts 10:16; 11:10), and finally the unexpected outpouring of the Spirit, resulting in the conversion of the Cornelius household (Acts 10:44-48; 11:15-17), before Peter and his compatriots are convinced. Dollar captures this dynamic well: "Luke shows that the theological challenge of the Gentile mission is not the reluctance of the Gentiles to respond to the gospel but the reluctance of the Jews to preach to them." Consequently, "the 'conversion' of the messenger" must come before the conversion of those who need the message.[36]

Overcoming barriers of exclusion. The Cornelius story highlights two major obstacles that must be cleared away for the gospel to be liberated from an exclusive Jewish ethnic and cultural identity. The first is a *soteriological* barrier. Peter and his fellow Jewish Christians need to understand that God has granted salvation to Gentiles *as Gentiles.* This is the point of Peter's vision. God's command not to call profane what God has made clean applies to people as well as to food (Acts 10:15; 11:9; cf. 10:28).[37] Peter's perceptual breakthrough comes in Acts 10:34-35 as he interprets the events that have taken place: "I truly understand that God shows no partiality, but in every nation anyone who fears him and does what is right is acceptable to him." The notion of divine impartiality had Old Testament precedence (Deut 10:17; 2 Chron 19:7), but here the emphasis falls on the fresh realization that God's love and favor is independent of a person's nationality, culture or ethnic identity. God does not "play favorites" between Jews and Gentiles. What counts is whether they reverence him and practice righteousness.[38] Peter discovers that God accepts people as they are, within their concrete national and cultural homes, yet on a basis that transcends any single ethnic identity or practice. This is a foundational theological insight for a New Testament perspective on contextualization.

---

[36]Dollar, *Luke-Acts*, pp. 184-85.

[37]Gaventa, *From Darkness to Light*, pp. 114-15; Jerome H. Neyrey, "Ceremonies in Luke-Acts: The Case of Meals and Table Fellowship," in *The Social World of Luke-Acts: Models for Interpretation*, ed. Jerome H. Neyrey (Peabody, Mass.: Hendrickson, 1991), p. 381.

[38]This does not mean that God accepts all people as "believers" on the basis of their sincere righteous deeds. Cornelius is sometimes depicted as the leading New Testament example of a "non-Christian believer." E.g., John Sanders, *No Other Name: An Investigation into the Destiny of the Unevangelized* (Grand Rapids, Mich.: Eerdmans, 1992), pp. 64-67, 222-24; Clark H. Pinnock, *A Wideness in God's Mercy: The Finality of Jesus Christ in a World of Religious Pluralism* (Grand Rapids, Mich.: Zondervan, 1992), pp. 95-96, 165-66. On the contrary, Luke underscores that in spite of all of his preparation and piety, Cornelius still needs to hear the gospel and respond in faith. It is only upon hearing the message of Christ from Peter that Cornelius receives forgiveness (Acts 10:43), salvation (Acts 11:14) and life (Acts 11:18). See further, Dean Flemming, "Foundations for Responding to Religious Pluralism," *WesTJ* 31 (1996): 70-71.

Peter's preaching leads uncircumcised Cornelius and friends to experience forgiveness of their sins (Acts 10:43; cf. 11:14), which is divinely validated when the Gentiles receive the same gift of the Holy Spirit as the Jews did at Pentecost (Acts 10:45; 11:15-17). In the end, once-skeptical Jewish Christians come to the inescapable theological conclusion that God has graciously "given even to the Gentiles the repentance that leads to life" (Acts 11:18) without requiring them first to follow the prescriptions of the Jewish law.

But along with the soteriological hurdle, there was the equally significant *social* barricade of table fellowship. Food laws involved maintaining purity and functioned as distinctive boundary markers for the Jews, separating them from other peoples.[39] As long as Jewish dietary rules that blocked social interaction between Jews and Gentiles (cf. Acts 10:28) were in effect, the church could never become a multicultural community. For Jewish Christians like Peter, the problem focused on how they could maintain their purity and distinctiveness and at the same time eat with unclean Gentiles. Luke painstakingly describes each step in the process of breaking down social and ritual walls: Peter has a vision of a "nonkosher picnic"[40] that announces the divine decontaminating of unclean foods (Acts 10:9-16; 11:5-12); he decides to offer hospitality to Gentiles (Acts 10:23) and then to receive it from Cornelius (Acts 10:27-28, 48); Peter's Jerusalem critics level a charge that he had eaten with Gentiles (Acts 11:1-3); and finally, Peter offers the defense that he had received the Spirit's instruction to make no distinction between Jews and Gentiles in his behavior (Acts 11:12).

It is striking that at each stage of the story the primary adjustment needed for the gospel to bridge social and religious boundaries comes not from the Gentile "outsiders" but from Jewish "insiders," who must let go of their ethnocentric attitudes and practices. This demands acknowledging that the food laws they once considered nonnegotiable were in reality culturally specific impediments to God's plan for a unified church. The old exclusionary system of purity has to be dismantled and replaced by a new order of inclusion. In addition, since dietary laws that reinforced separateness were at the heart of Jewish self-identity, what is ultimately at stake is a reconfiguring of identity from an ethnic Jewish

---

[39]See Philip F. Esler, *Community and Gospel in Luke-Acts: The Social and Political Motivations of Lucan Theology*, Society for New Testament Studies Monograph Series 57 (Cambridge: Cambridge University Press, 1987), for a historical and sociological study of Jewish food regulations and table fellowship between Jews and Gentiles as these affect social relations in Luke-Acts.

[40]David A. deSilva, *Honor, Patronage, Kinship and Purity: Unlocking New Testament Culture* (Downers Grove, Ill.: InterVarsity Press, 2000), p. 285.

movement to a universal Christian community.[41] In the new "world" created by the death and resurrection of Christ, the gospel demands cultural transformation at a bedrock level. In the end, Peter's critics are silenced (Acts 11:17). Christian identity is redefined. Barriers to full intercultural fellowship come down.

With both the theological and sociological obstructions removed, the path is cleared for the gospel to be preached to the Gentiles as cultural Gentiles. Although foreshadowed in the conversion of a solitary Ethiopian Gentile in an isolated setting in chapter 8, for Luke the events in Caesarea constitute the decisive missional and cultural breakthrough for the church. This impression is heightened by the confirmation of both the Spirit and the community. The Holy Spirit's unforeseen descent upon a Gentile household in parallel fashion to the experience of Jewish believers in the upper room in Jerusalem signals God's acceptance of the Gentiles and changes their status. Significantly, Peter recontextualizes Jesus' promise of the baptism with the Spirit originally delivered to Jewish followers (Acts 1:5), applying it to the new work of the Spirit among non-Jews (Acts 11:16). Furthermore, Luke's retelling of the tale in Acts 11:1-18 allows the Jerusalem community to catch up with what God is doing. As a result, they embrace the unconditional inclusion of the Gentiles into the people of God. Peter's "conversion" becomes, in effect, the transformation of the church (cf. Acts 11:18).

Doing narrative theology in a "God-fearing" context. What, then, can we learn about the theological process by which Peter and the Jewish Christian church rethink their understanding of the faith in light of new circumstances? First, Luke stresses that the church's fresh grasp of its identity and mission comes about through *God's design and initiative.* The Spirit is the divine choreographer of the encounters and events that lead to Peter's theological conversion.[42] Second, narratives of the *experience* of the Spirit's working play a pivotal role in the church's theological reflection. Peter only comes to fully realize the meaning of his own vision regarding God's full acceptance of Gentiles after Cornelius relates his story of receiving God's direction (Acts 10:29-34). This insight into God's surprising grace is confirmed when Peter witnesses the Gentiles' experience of the gift of the Spirit in a similar way to his own (Acts 10:44-48). Later, when Peter is challenged by the Jerusalem believers, he narrates his own experience of God's action "step by step" (Acts 11:4; cf. 11:1-17), which persuades them to accept his new inclusive interpretation of God's offer of salvation (Acts

---

[41]Dunn, *Acts*, pp. 137-38; Luke Timothy Johnson, *The Acts of the Apostles* (Collegeville, Minn.: Michael Glazier/Liturgical Press, 1992), p. 200.

[42]Green, "Acts," pp. 17-18.

11:18). Third, the theological journey Luke describes has a notable *communal* character. When Peter goes to meet Cornelius, he is accompanied by fellow Jewish believers from Joppa, who recognize and interpret what God is doing among the Gentiles (Acts 10:38, 45-46); Cornelius gathers his friends and relatives to hear God's word, and the Holy Spirit descends on the whole company (Acts 10:24, 44, 48); Peter's home church in Jerusalem questions this theological innovation (Acts 11:2-3), but in the end they declare the saving implications of God's activity (Acts 11:18). The community is vital to each stage in the process of doing theology. Fourth, *intercultural encounter* contributes to new theological insight. On one hand, the witness of Jewish Christians enables Cornelius and the other Roman Gentiles to hear and embrace the saving word. On the other, through Peter's interaction with Gentile outsiders his own grasp of the gospel is stretched and enriched.

Fifth, Peter's proclamation of the good news to the Cornelius circle is the centerpiece of the story. This "narrative sermon"—the first speech to a group of Gentiles in Acts—functions in the story as a model of evangelistic contextualization:

> Then Peter began to speak to them: "I truly understand that God shows no partiality, but in every nation anyone who fears him and does what is right is acceptable to him. You know the message he sent to the people of Israel, preaching peace through Jesus Christ—he is Lord of all. That message spread throughout Judea, beginning in Galilee after the baptism that John announced: how God anointed Jesus of Nazareth with the Holy Spirit and with power; how he went about doing good and healing all who were oppressed by the devil, for God was with Him. We are witnesses to all that he did both in Judea and in Jerusalem. They put him to death by hanging him on a tree; but God raised him on the third day and allowed him to appear, not to all the people but to us who were chosen by God as witnesses, and who ate and drank with him after he rose from the dead. He commanded us to preach to the people and to testify that he is the one ordained by God as judge of the living and the dead. All the prophets testify about him that everyone who believes in him receives forgiveness of sins through his name." (Acts 10:34-43)

Despite Martin Dibelius's conclusion that Luke composed the speech on a stereotypical pattern that had little relevance to its narrative context,[43] I would argue that Peter's sermon is highly appropriate for an audience of Gentile God-fearers. Most commentators note that its narrative of what God has done in Christ has significant parallels with Peter's earlier missionary preaching to Jews

---

[43]Martin Dibelius, *Studies in the Acts of the Apostles*, ed. Heinrich Greeven (London: SCM Press, 1956), pp. 110-11.

(see especially Acts 2:17-36 and 3:12-26). Luke is keen to demonstrate throughout Acts that the apostolic gospel is rooted in the story of Jesus as the fulfillment of God's saving plan.[44] A number of aspects, however, speak either directly or indirectly to the context at hand: (1) the opening statement of God's impartiality toward all people (Acts 10:34-35; cf. v. 28) and the closing assurance of forgiveness of sins to "everyone who believes in him" (Acts 10:43) frame the speech with the keynote of God's acceptance of non-Jews for salvation; (2) Peter interjects into his narrative about Jesus Christ the affirmation that "he is Lord of all" (Acts 10:36), which speaks to the inclusion of the Gentiles;[45] (3) the command to preach and bear witness (Acts 10:42; cf. v. 41) links Jesus' commissioning of his disciples to begin a worldwide mission (Lk 24:47-48; cf. Acts 1:8) to Peter's preaching to Gentiles;[46] (4) the theme of Christ as "judge of the living and the dead" (Acts 10:42) is an extension of his universal lordship and is taken up again in Paul's address to Gentiles in Athens (Acts 17:31); (5) the more detailed narrative of Jesus' earthly life and ministry than we find in Peter's earlier Jerusalem sermons fits a non-Jewish audience, which presumably would not be as familiar with those events; (6) Luke recruits the language of benefaction in Acts 10:38 when Jesus is described as one who went about "doing good" *(euergetōn)*. This term, which was often applied to mighty rulers or emperors who conferred benefits on others, might speak with particular force to a Roman Gentile;[47] (7) Peter's unique reference to witnesses who "ate and drank" with Jesus "is especially appropriate for a story that concerns itself with hospitality for Gentiles"[48] (Acts 10:41; cf. 11:3); (8) in contrast to Peter's earlier sermons to Jews, there are no explicit quotations from the Old Testament, although a number of scriptural echoes are woven into the text (e.g., Ps 107:20 and Is 52:7 in Acts 10:36).

Considering this impressive evidence of contextualization for a Gentile audience, it might seem odd to find so much emphasis on the *Jewishness* of Jesus in the sermon. For example, Peter presses home that God sent his message "to the people of Israel," preaching peace through "Jesus Messiah" (Acts 10:36; cf. v.

---

[44]See Marion L. Soards, *The Speeches in Acts: Their Content, Context, and Concerns* (Louisville: Westminster John Knox, 1994), pp. 184-89; Hans F. Bayer, "The Preaching of Peter in Acts," in *Witness to the Gospel: The Theology of Acts*, ed. I. Howard Marshall and David Peterson (Grand Rapids, Mich.: Eerdmans, 1998), pp. 269-72.

[45]Robert C. Tannehill, "The Functions of Peter's Mission Speeches in the Narrative of Acts," *NTS* 37 (1991): 410-11. The phrase "Lord of all" is found in both Jewish and Greek writings, which makes it particularly appropriate to its context.

[46]Tannehill, "Mission Speeches," p. 412.

[47]Witherington, *Acts of the Apostles*, p. 358 n. 127.

[48]Gaventa, *From Darkness to Light*, p. 119.

42), and that "all the prophets" witness to him (Acts 10:43). Rather than missing the mark, however, the telling of the Jesus story in its Jewish context is appropriate for Peter's audience for two reasons. First, it underscores that the universal gospel for the Gentiles is rooted in concrete events that took place in space and time and within the framework of God's dealings with a particular nation, the people of Israel. For Luke, the heart of the gospel lies not in a series of christological propositions but in the story of Jesus of Nazareth. Robert Tannehill shows that Peter summarizes the Jesus narrative presented in Luke's gospel, from his birth announcement (Acts 10:36) to the commission of his followers as risen Lord (Acts 10:42): "By telling this story to Cornelius and his company and by placing it in a frame that affirms Jesus' universal significance, Peter is affirming that the story of the Jewish Messiah also has relevance for Gentiles."[49] Second, the presentation of the gospel as the fulfillment of God's promises to Israel that had now been offered to the Gentiles would be especially important for synagogue adherents like Cornelius, in a way that it would not to a purely pagan audience (cf. Acts 17:22-31). What we find, therefore, is a sermon that is carefully crafted to persuade an audience of Gentiles living on the fringes of Judaism to embrace the call to faith in Jesus Christ.

The conversion of the God-fearer Cornelius does not mean that the gospel has fully traveled from its strictly Jewish beginnings to the heartland of pagan culture and religion. That will come later. Nor are the issues it raises finally resolved, as the looming crisis of the Jerusalem Council makes all too clear. Nevertheless, Luke views the Cornelius story as a decisive catalyst that alters the identity and direction of the church and sounds the death knell to cultural exclusiveness. The Cornelius episode thus carries paradigmatic significance, both for Luke's readers and for the church today in its various cultural manifestations. Churches still struggle with ethnocentric perspectives, which resist acceptance of contextualized expressions of Christian theology and practice that are different from their own. Chan-Hie Kim, for example, finds arresting parallels between the attitude of the Jerusalem church toward the Gentiles in the Cornelius episode and that of the dominant church culture in North America regarding Asian immigrant Christians today.[50]

Peter's acceptance of Cornelius establishes a critical precedent for the inclusive character of the new Christian movement and the gospel's ability to tran-

---

[49]Tannehill, *Luke-Acts,* 2:140-42.
[50]Chan-Hie Kim, "Reading the Cornelius Story from an Asian Immigrant Perspective," in *Reading from This Place: Social Location and Biblical Interpretation in the United States,* ed. F. F. Segovia and M. A. Tolbert (Minneapolis: Fortress, 1995), 1:171-74.

scend humanly constructed barriers. But the contentious issue of the relationship of Gentiles to the Jewish heritage of that movement and to the law of Moses is yet to be resolved. Luke addresses that question in chapter 15.

THEOLOGIZING BY THE CHURCH: THE JERUSALEM COUNCIL

The Council of Jerusalem is the watershed event in Luke's narrative of the gospel's progress from a Jewish to a universal context. As Brian Rosner aptly pictures it, "The book of Acts without chapter 15 would be like a wedding ceremony without the crucial pronouncement. Everything that happens in chapter 1—14 leads up to this high point and what follows merely traces the implications of the decision."[51] Acts 15 is also vital to our study of patterns of contextualization in the New Testament church. In the first place, it describes a decisive moment in the encounter between faith in Christ and culture within the life of the early church, which helps to give the task of incarnating the gospel a historical and theological basis. Second, it offers perhaps the fullest and most significant narrative in the New Testament of the *process* of doing contextual theology by the church. This makes Acts 15 worthy of our careful attention.[52]

Resolving an intercultural conflict. The need for the Jerusalem Council is grounded in the progress of the Gentile mission. Having laid a theological foundation for the legitimacy of that mission in the story of Peter and Cornelius, Luke relates how a group of Jewish Hellenists evangelize Gentile "Greeks"[53] in Antioch and establish the first truly multicultural church (Acts 11:19-26). This "model" community in Luke's story reflects an ethos of innovation, evidenced by several notable characteristics. First, it shows a willingness to embrace uncircumcised non-Jewish converts and, apparently, partake in table fellowship (including the Lord's Supper) across cultural lines. The ability to transcend ethnic and social barriers is also evident in Antioch's "leadership team" (Acts 13:1), which probably includes two Africans, one of whom is black (Niger), and a well-placed person with close connections to Herod's court. Second, the Syrian community grows out of a mission that preached Jesus as Lord (Acts 11:20), "a

---

[51]Brian S. Rosner, "The Progress of the Word," in *Witness to the Gospel: The Theology of Acts,* ed. I. Howard Marshall and D. Peterson (Grand Rapids, Mich.: Eerdmans, 1998), p. 227.

[52]Acts 15 raises a number of historical questions, including the historical accuracy of the account, the relationship between Acts 15 and Galatians 2, and possible sources behind Luke's narrative. These are important issues, but they lie beyond the scope of this study. For a discussion of historical concerns related to Acts 15, see Martin Hengel, *Acts and the History of Earliest Christianity* (Philadelphia: Fortress, 1979), pp. 111-26.

[53]Whether the correct textual reading for Acts 11:20 is *Hellēnistas* ("Hellenists") or *Hellēnas* ("Greeks"), the context clearly indicates they are Gentiles (cf. "Jews," Acts 11:19). Luke does not identify these Gentiles more precisely.

message better suited to a Gentile audience than the proclamation of Jesus as the Christ or Son of Man."[54] Third, it is at Antioch that followers of the Way are first called "Christians" (Acts 11:26). This new name communicates a new status based not on ethnic or prior religious distinctions, but on faith in Christ.[55] Fourth, under the inspiration of the Spirit, the Antioch fellowship launches the first planned "overseas" mission to Gentiles as well as Jews (Acts 13:1-3). Finally, the Christians at Antioch maintain an ongoing link to the Jewish Christian mother church in Jerusalem (Acts 11:27-30; 15:1-35). This relationship, as Dean S. Gilliland points out, ensures "continuity with history and tradition while breaking new ground."[56] Luke further describes how on their missionary journey Paul and Barnabas respond to Jewish rejection by intentionally turning to the Gentiles (Acts 13:46-47). This strategic decision results in an influx of Gentile believers into the church (Acts 13:48; 14:1, 21). The two then report back to the home church in Antioch that God had "opened a door of faith for the Gentiles" (Acts 14:27). The situation has rapidly advanced from a test case involving the God-fearer Cornelius to the entry in mass of uncircumcised Gentiles into the community of faith.

Dissension (Acts 15:1-5). This sets the stage for a major test of the legitimacy of a culturally diverse fellowship. F. Scott Spencer helpfully observes that the dramatic narrative of the Jerusalem Council unfolds in four acts or stages: (1) Dissension (Acts 15:1-5); (2) Discussion (Acts 15:6-18); (3) Decision (Acts 15:19-29); (4) Dissemination (Acts 15:30-35).[57] Jewish Christians from Judea provoke a crisis in Antioch when they teach that circumcision is essential for salvation (Acts 15:1). When Paul and Barnabas arrive in Jerusalem to clarify the issue with the leadership there, certain believers who were still Pharisees demand that Gentile converts be circumcised and placed under obligation to keep the Jewish law (Acts 15:5). What precipitates the Jerusalem Council is not simply that Gentiles were being evangelized, but more importantly the *conditions* of their membership in the messianic community. Must Gentiles become "naturalized Jews," that is, Jewish proselytes, and live like Jews in order to have a place in the peo-

---

[54]Witherington, *Acts of the Apostles*, p. 369.

[55]Philip H. Towner, "Mission Practice and Theology Under Construction (Acts 18-20)," in *Witness to the Gospel*, ed. I. Howard Marshall and David Peterson (Grand Rapids, Mich.: Eerdmans, 1998), p. 422.

[56]Dean S. Gilliland, "New Testament Contextualization: Continuity and Particularity in Paul's Theology," in *The Word Among Us: Contextualizing Theology for Today*, ed. Dean S. Gilliland (Dallas: Word Books, 1989), p. 55.

[57]F. Scott Spencer, *Journeying Through Acts: A Literary-Cultural Reading* (Peabody, Mass.: Hendrickson, 2004), pp. 162-64. Although Spencer extends the last stage of dissemination through Acts 16:5, I have limited it to the account of the Jerusalem Council itself.

ple of God? Today we might put the question in terms of whether Gentile believers had to become culturally Jewish as a condition of their salvation and as
part of their obedience to Christ, or whether they could be accepted in all their
"Gentile-ness." Luke's narrative exposes genuine theological disagreement
within the young church, centered around two competing interpretations of the
gospel. The Pharisees could appeal to both Scripture (e.g., Gen 17:9-14) and a
long precedent of tradition in support of their theological position. For them,
circumcision was not simply an optional cultural form; it was a matter of religious life and death—the indispensable symbol of the covenant relationship. If
Jewish cultural distinctives, including law observance and the Jewish way of life,
were divinely sanctioned, how could they possibly be negotiable?

Discussion (Acts 15:6-18). The question becomes the subject of extensive
debate in Jerusalem (Acts 15:6-7). The stakes are high. If the Pharisaic position
prevails, not only would it place a massive stumbling block in the path of the
gospel's future progress to non-Jewish peoples, but it would effectively invali-
date the current Christian status of uncircumcised Gentile converts (Acts 15:1).[58]
Theologically, it would declare that God's grace and the gift of the Spirit were
not fully sufficient for salvation.

In Luke's narrative, the theological crisis is resolved by three speeches that
together present a unified case for God's purpose in accepting uncircumcised
Gentiles.[59] Peter's "farewell address" in Acts 15:7-11 begins by rehearsing once
again the precedent story ("in the early days," Acts 15:7) of Cornelius. But unlike
Acts 11:5-17, where Peter narrates the events in some detail, here he draws out
the theological implications of the experience in light of the problem at hand.
The speech is bristling with references to God's initiative and action. Peter has
now concluded that his vision about unclean foods means that God has purified
the hearts of Gentiles by faith, not through circumcision or law observance,
making no distinction between races (Acts 15:9). Acts 15:10-11 directly addresses the issues raised by the protestors—the Gentiles' obligation to the law
and what is necessary to be saved. The speech climaxes with the central theological insight that the sole basis of salvation for the Jews ("we"), as well as the
Gentiles ("they"), is "the grace of the Lord Jesus" (Acts 15:11). Peter's articulation
of the nature of the gospel effectively brands the culturally bound theology of
his opponents as a false message: they are guilty of "testing God" (Acts 15:10).

Next Paul and Barnabas talk about their experience of the miraculous evi-

---

[58]David Seccombe, "The New People of God," in *Witness to the Gospel: The Theology of Acts*,
    ed. I. Howard Marshall and David Peterson (Grand Rapids, Mich.: Eerdmans, 1998), p. 365.
[59]Tannehill, *Luke-Acts*, p. 184.

dences of God's working through them (Acts 15:12), providing further evidence for God's acceptance of the Gentiles. The turning point comes when James, the spokesperson for the mother church, gives the definitive response to the testimonies of the three previous witnesses (Acts 15:13-21). Recalling Peter's narrative, he interprets it to mean that God has acquired from the Gentiles "a people for his name" (Acts 15:14). This is remarkable, since previously in Acts (e.g., Acts 2:47; 3:23; 4:10) as well as in the Old Testament the term "people" *(laos)* refers to *Israel.* Here James redefines the notion of the "people of God" to include non-Jews. He then clinches the argument with an appeal to Scripture, a critical step for his Jewish Christian audience. He chooses Amos 9:11-12 because it supports Peter's testimony of what God is doing in the church ("the words of the prophets agree with this," Acts 15:14). Sharply put, God's present activity among the Gentiles becomes the hermeneutical key for understanding the biblical text.[60] James opts to follow the Greek translation (LXX), which announces the building of the eschatological Temple ("David's tent," Acts 15:16) and the conversion of the nations to the God of Israel in the messianic age. Amos's prophecy is read in light of the specific issue at hand to mean that "all the Gentiles" (Acts 15:17) will be incorporated into the eschatological temple of the new people of God (the Christian community) without having to surrender their Gentile identity.[61] Amos, rightly interpreted, gives Scripture's grounding for the theological principle of salvation for the Gentiles by faith apart from circumcision.

Decision (Acts 15:19-29) and dissemination (Acts 15:30-35). On the basis of both what God has done and the evidence of Scripture, James expresses the decision of the Council. First, Gentile converts should not be further "troubled" by requiring them to be circumcised and to keep the Mosaic law (Acts 15:19). Second, four concessions are made to Jewish believers. Gentiles should abstain from "things polluted by idols," sexual immorality, meat that has been strangled, and blood (Acts 15:20; cf. v. 29). The so-called decree seems to be based on the holiness code in Leviticus 17 and 18, where corresponding taboos are laid out for aliens living in the midst of Israel. Yet after stating the principle that Gentile Christians should not be burdened by keeping the Mosaic law, why immediately set forth specific aspects of the law that they must follow? Acts 15:28 tells the Gentiles that these regulations are "necessary" ("essentials," NRSV). But necessary for what? Has the Council confused "essentials" with "nonessentials," after all?

---

[60]Johnson, *Acts of the Apostles,* p. 271.

[61]Richard Bauckham, "James and the Gentiles (Acts 15:13-21)," in *History, Literature, and Society in the Book of Acts,* ed. Ben Witherington III (Cambridge: Cambridge University Press, 1996), pp. 165-69.

In a fascinating example of doing contextual theology, James is apparently drawing out the pragmatic *social* implications of the *soteriological* decision of the church. The inclusion of uncircumcised Gentiles meant that the church was faced with the challenge of maintaining fellowship within a culturally diverse community. As J. Julius Scott reflects, "A framework was needed to permit Jewish Christians to accept and associate with Gentile believers while, at the same time, maintaining the regulations which would make possible their continued participation in at least parts of Jewish culture and their association with non-Christian, practicing Jews."[62] The decree provides such a framework. Three of the four taboos deal with food laws, and the other, "sexual immorality" *(porneia)* was closely linked to the issue of full social association (cf. 1 Cor 5:9-11). In a reversal of the original function of Jewish purity rules to *separate* peoples, James appropriates these requirements precisely to provide a basis for table fellowship and a shared identity between two culturally distinct communities within the church.[63] Gentile believers "will do well" (Acts 15:29) to abstain from these practices, but not because they are under obligation to the law or because these pollution taboos are essential for salvation. Rather, they do so out of respect for the cultural sensitivities of others in the Christian fellowship. This would also allow Jewish Christians to associate across cultural lines without hindering the Jewish mission by making themselves impure and thereby unacceptable to their fellow Jews, who heard Moses read every sabbath (Acts 15:21).

Finally, the entire Jerusalem church sends a letter, along with a personal delegation, to communicate the Council's decision to the Gentiles in Antioch (Acts 15:22-23). This letter is more than an edict from above. It is an act of intercultural fellowship which exudes a spirit of warmth and mutual respect. The Jerusalem leaders address the letter to "the Gentile brothers" (Acts 15:23 my translation), highlighting both their acceptance by the mother church and their distinctive cultural identity. By the end of the narrative, the church has said "no" to cultural imperialism by Jewish Christians on one hand, and to "ecclesial apartheid" on

---

[62]J. Julius Scott Jr., "The Jerusalem Council: The Cross-Cultural Challenge in the First Century," unpublished paper presented to the National Meeting of the Evangelical Theological Society, San Francisco, November 20, 1992, pp. 12-13. The issues surrounding the precise background and function of the apostolic decree (Acts 15:20, 29) are complex and much-debated. See e.g., Fitzmyer, *Acts of the Apostles,* pp. 556-58.

[63]Jerome H. Neyrey, "Ceremonies in Luke-Acts: The Case of Meals and Table Fellowship," in *The Social World of Luke-Acts: Models for Interpretation,* ed. Jerome H. Neyrey (Peabody, Mass.: Hendrickson, 1991), p. 382. Luke Timothy Johnson is likely correct that the kinds of elemental purity taboos found in Leviticus 17 and 18 reflected in the decree would have been a particular stumbling block to fellowship between Jews and Gentiles, since they are associated with "defiling" the land and the people, and breaking them results in "being cut off from the people" (Lev 17:7, 9,10,14; 18:21, 24-25, 28-30; *Acts of the Apostles,* p. 273).

the other. The delegates return "in peace" (Acts 15:33).

A story of contextual theologizing. For Luke, the story of the Jerusalem Council is a paradigmatic narrative. In it we see a pattern of God's people articulating their faith within an intercultural context, which carries implications for the church in any generation.[64] Luke is interested not only in the theological outcomes of the Council, but especially the theological *process* within his story. A number of aspects of that process—some of which parallel what we discovered in the narrative of Cornelius and Peter—are important for understanding Luke's perspective on how the gospel can speak a fresh word to new and challenging circumstances within the life of the church.

1. *The work of the Spirit in the community as the context for creative theologizing.* The narrative teems with references to the action of God or the Holy Spirit. God's activity in the recent past in bringing the Gentiles into the messianic community guides the church in rethinking its theology and discerning God's will for the present circumstances. The basis of the church's decision is that "it has seemed good to the Holy Spirit and to us" (Acts 15:28). This conveys both divine and human participation in the theologizing process. However, the order in which the two are mentioned leaves no doubt that the church is subordinate to the will of the Spirit.[65] Because the community has been open to the Spirit's work, it is able to resolve its conflict and come to a new awareness of how to live out its identity as the people of God within a multicultural setting.

2. *The appeal to the church's experience of God's activity.* It is the experience of Gentile conversion that creates the need for the Council to settle the issue that liberates the church for a full-fledged mission to the Gentiles. In Antioch and Jerusalem alike, the experience of God's activity by God's people and the narrative of that experience become the catalyst for both theological crisis and for the theological reflection that follows (Acts 14:27—15:1; 15:4-5).[66] When the Council meets to decide the issue, it listens to the testimonies of the key players and weighs them in order to come to a responsible theological understanding. Peter retells the tale of the breakthrough in Caesarea and interprets it theologically (Acts 15:7-11). Paul and Barnabas rehearse the mighty acts of God and the assembly is silenced (Acts 15:12). James appeals to Peter's story and builds a

---

[64]See Luke Timothy Johnson, *Scripture and Discernment: Decision Making in the Church* (Nashville: Abingdon, 1983), pp. 78-79; cf. Hilary, *Inculturation Theology*, pp. 73-75.

[65]Brian Rapske, "Opposition to the Plan of God and Persecution," in *Witness to the Gospel: The Theology of Acts*, ed. I. Howard Marshall and David Peterson (Grand Rapids, Mich.: Eerdmans, 1998), p. 243.

[66]See Robert Wall, "Israel and the Gentile Mission in Acts and Paul: A Canonical Approach," in *Witness to the Gospel: The Theology of Acts*, ed. I. Howard Marshall and David Peterson (Grand Rapids, Mich.: Eerdmans, 1998), p. 449.

new understanding of the people of God (Acts 15:13-19). These individual stories eventually become the community's story. The church responds to its new intercultural challenge not simply on the basis of *a priori* theological principles or traditional practices, but by reflecting on their experience of God's work among them. Such an experiential component to doing theology might be particularly significant for today's churches ministering in postmodern contexts, where living narratives of faith and transformed lives tend to have far greater impact than tightly reasoned arguments.

3. The role of Scripture in guiding the community. Scripture plays a critical role in the process of the Council's theological reflection. Pivotal to James' argument is that the multicultural character of the new people of God was prophesied long ago (Acts 15:17). Yet the way James frames his appeal to Scripture is somewhat surprising. Instead of saying that the church's experience of God's inclusion of the Gentiles is confirmed by the words of Scripture, he maintains that the Scripture is confirmed by "this" action of God (Acts 15:15).[67] James comes to a deeper understanding of the meaning of Amos's prophecy as a result of what God is doing in the community. In turn, this fresh interpretation of Scripture helps him to make sense of what has taken place. It leads him to the conclusion that Gentiles should be free from the obligations of circumcision and Torah observance (Acts 15:19). In this case, the hermeneutical process moves from context to text and then back to context. Scripture also apparently provides the basis for the minimal requirements imposed on Gentile converts to ensure table fellowship with Jewish believers within a specific intercultural setting (Acts 15:20, 29). In Acts 15 the authoritative role of Scripture is intertwined with the experience and concrete needs of the community.

4. Contending for the truth of the gospel. Despite his interest in maintaining the unity of the church, Luke shows that the truth of the gospel cannot be compromised. He treats the Pharisaic group as false teachers whose improper contextualization of the gospel among the Gentiles threatens to undermine the entire Gentile mission and God's redemptive plan (cf. Acts 15:1, 5, 10, 24). Their interpretation of the basis for membership in the people of God may be sincere, but it exceeds the bounds of acceptable theological diversity in the church. Peter articulates the transcultural principle that salvation is by grace through faith for Jews and Gentiles alike (Acts 15:9, 11). Consequently, the church emphatically rejects the added requirements of circumcision and Torah keeping for Gentiles. The gospel affirms that all peoples and cultures come to God on an equal basis.

---

[67]Unfortunately, the NRSV completely reverses the Greek text of Acts 15:15: "This agrees with the words of the prophets."

Christian theology has no place for national, cultural or ethnic "add-ons." It is a striking feature of the narrative that Luke shows no embarrassment whatsoever in exposing sharp disagreement and open debate within the church's process of doing theology (Acts 15:2, 7). The gospel is worth contending for, and the false teaching and ensuing debate actually serve a positive role. They force the church to face issues that lead it to a clearer understanding of God's work and of its own inclusive identity.[68]

5. *Compromise on nonessential issues for the sake of unity and fellowship.* Bruce Chilton is right that the Jerusalem Council needed to address two distinct but related questions: (1) whether Gentiles could be baptized without being circumcised and (2) whether they could be included in a single fellowship with believing Jews.[69] On the first count, no compromise was possible. The second matter, however, required a different approach. The decrees of the Council (Acts 15:20, 29; 21:25) are evidence of the church's effort to creatively grapple with the challenge of a culturally mixed community. Although these prohibitions have scriptural precedent, it seems best to view them as temporary and context-specific measures designed to avoid unnecessarily offending the Jews, thereby opening the door to full fellowship between Jewish and Gentile Christians.[70] Paul's own missionary practice appears to bear this out. When he is mainly dealing with Gentile Christians who live in an intensely pagan environment in Corinth, he can take a more liberal position than the Jerusalem Council: under certain conditions he allows Christians to eat food that has been offered to idols (e.g., 1 Cor 10:25-27). In such a context, the Council's outright ban on eating food sacrificed to idols is apparently not binding on Gentile converts.

But if the Council's policy regarding food regulations is not universally valid, the unity of the church surely is. Consequently, the decree is a "necessary" (Acts 15:28) compromise on the part of Gentiles for their particular ethnically diverse setting. On the other side, Jewish Christians also had to compromise by being

---

[68]Johnson, *Acts of the Apostles,* p. 271.

[69]Bruce Chilton, "Purity and Impurity," in *Dictionary of the Later New Testament and Its Developments,* ed. Ralph P. Martin and Peter H. Davids (Downers Grove, Ill.: InterVarsity Press, 1997), p. 993.

[70]The one apparent exception to this is the prohibition of sexual immorality (*porneia*), which is consistently treated as a nonnegotiable ethical issue in Scripture. This purity taboo is often limited to the question of marriage within prohibited degrees of kinship, based on Leviticus 18:13 (Fitzmyer, *Acts of the Apostles,* p. 558). Although this is possible, it seems unlikely that Luke would restrict *porneia* in this way without any further explanation. More likely, because sexual immorality was a widespread practice in Greco-Roman culture and a particular stumbling block to association between Jews and Gentiles, the Council felt the need to single it out. See Ajith Fernando, *Acts,* NIV Application Commentary (Grand Rapids, Mich.: Zondervan, 1998), pp. 419, 421.

willing to relax the traditional interpretation of purity laws that would have ruled out table fellowship with non-Jews altogether. Believers of different backgrounds must exercise their Christian freedom in a spirit of love and of sensitivity to the traditions and scruples of others, for the greater good of full communion in Christ. Today such issues of contextualization surface again and again. For example, Christians in the Philippines might need to abstain from eating popular dishes made from pork blood when they live in close contact with Muslims or recent converts from Islam who have strong scruples against it.[71] Or consider the current "wars" over worship styles in the West—contemporary or traditional, praise choruses backed up by bands or hymns accompanied by organs. The spirit of the Jerusalem Council suggests that Christians in both camps need to be willing to surrender their personal freedom and preferences for the sake of unity in Christ.

6. The role of the community and its leadership. Both the leaders of the church and the community as a whole are key players in the process of theological reflection and discerning God's will for the situation. The full range of leadership from both mother and daughter churches is involved and comes to agreement. The "apostles and elders" in Jerusalem ultimately debate (Acts 15:7), decide (Acts 15:25), and dispatch representatives with an authoritative letter, to Antioch (Acts 15:22-23). James, who represents continuity with Jesus and the church's Jewish Christian roots, plays the lead part. At the same time, it is not simply an individual or a "top-down" decision. Luke goes out of his way to report the participation of the wider church in the whole process.[72] It is the community that first sends delegates from Antioch to resolve the theological crisis (Acts 15:3) and the community that gathers in Jerusalem to receive them (Acts 15:4). It is the community that listens to and evaluates the testimonies of God's activity in the lives of its members (Acts 15:12), and the community that confirms the decision of its leaders (Acts 15:22). Likewise, the gathered community in Antioch receives and endorses the exhortation of the Council (Acts 15:31) and affirms its unity with the mother church (Acts 15:33). The collective mind of the church recognizes the Spirit's leading into creative conflict resolution: "It seemed good to the Holy Spirit *and to us*" (Acts 15:28). The church as a whole is indispensable to the theological process.

7. The church's contextualizing of the gospel is missional, ecclesial and trans-

---

[71]David K. Strong, "The Jerusalem Council: Some Implications for Contextualization," in *Mission in Acts: Ancient Narratives in Contemporary Contextualization. Act 15:1-35*, ed. R. L. Gallagher and P. Hertig (Maryknoll, N.Y.: Orbis, 2004), p. 205.

[72]See John Christopher Thomas, "Women, Pentecostals and the Bible: An Experiment in Pentecostal Hermeneutics," *JPT* 5 (1994): 49.

formational. First, the theological reflection we find in Acts 15 has as its goal the advancement of the church's mission. The community's spokespeople argue that both experience (Acts 15:7) and Scripture (Acts 15:15-19) testify that God has already sanctioned a law-free Gentile mission. In Luke's story, the Jerusalem Council decisively settles the question for the church that Gentiles could be evangelized without prior conditions and within their own culture. What began with an Ethiopian eunuch, what was symbolized by the centurion Cornelius, is now formalized by the church. At the same time, the Jewish mission is not discarded and Jews can continue to be evangelized as Jews. The missional impact of the Council's interpretation of the gospel in Acts is unmistakable. Immediately, it spurs further proclamation of the word of God in Antioch (Acts 15:35). More importantly, Jerusalem's official stamp of approval clears the path for Paul's ever widening horizon of mission that becomes Luke's dominant focus in the second half of Acts. David Seccombe is quite right that "[o]ne of the great strengths of Christianity . . . in every age has been its adaptability to any culture, the basis of which was hammered out at the Jerusalem Council."[73]

Second, not only is the location of the church's theological reflection in Acts 15 the faith community, but the process of doing theology serves to shape and redefine that community. The Jerusalem Council refuses to see the church as an exclusive sect, nor even as an enlarged Israel. Instead, Acts 15 describes a church on a journey to a deeper understanding of its identity as the one people of God comprised of two distinct cultural groups who believe in Jesus. Neither group must surrender its cultural identity, and Jews may continue to observe their ancestral traditions. Unity does not mean uniformity. The resolution of the Council allows for theological diversity regarding the way of life and approach to missionary outreach of the two cultural groups. By the same token, not even the original, divinely sanctioned culture of God's elect nation has the right to universalize its particular expression of Christianity. Acts 15 promotes a vision of a new people of God potentially inclusive of all peoples, in which every nation and culture can stand on equal footing before the cross. Such a vision is no less a touchstone for the church's theological identity in our time.

Because it is *one* people of God and not two, the church cannot be allowed to split into ethnically and religiously separate factions. Emerging out of the theological process described in Luke's narrative is a beautiful picture of a unified body earmarked by mutual respect. The mother church in Jerusalem shows remarkable pastoral concern for the Gentile believers who have been offended (cf. Acts 15:24), and its representatives remain in Antioch to encourage and

---

[73]Seccombe, "New People," p. 366.

strengthen them (Acts 15:32). At the same time, the multicultural "mission church" in Antioch accepts the Council's decision and maintains continuity with its heritage in the Jewish Christian community. Jewish traditional ways and sensitivities are taken seriously. The fellowship that characterized the early days in Jerusalem (Acts 2:42-47; 4:32-35) is restored, at least for the time being, on an intercultural level (Acts 15:23-29, 32-33).[74] Likewise today, any contextualized theology that leads to the dividing of the church along cultural or ethnic lines is in tension with the gospel of Christ. It may be pragmatically the case that people prefer to worship and fellowship with others who are like them. But intentionally homogeneous churches, where everybody is basically of one culture, one race, or one socioeconomic background, must not be the dominant model for the people of God. We must learn, however painfully, to sing the gospel in all the rich harmonies that enhance the beauty of the song.

Third, the result of the church's adapting the gospel to new circumstances is the transformation of individuals and of the community. The stories of faith that provide the raw materials for the church's theologizing highlight God's transforming power at work among the Gentiles through the preaching of the word (Acts 15:7-9, 11, 12, 14, 19). The apostles' testimony confronts and capsizes the ethnocentric worldview of those who thought God's election had endowed them with a permanent "most-favored-nation" status. Luke's attention to the unanimity of the decision (Acts 15:22, 25) implies a change among the believing Pharisees. In the end, the Council's work brings joy (Acts 15:31) and a reconciled community (Acts 15:33).

CONCLUSION

The book of Acts presents the church in Luke's day and ours with significant resources for the task of contextualizing the gospel. On one hand, Luke's work is itself an example of articulating the Christian faith within the cultural landscape of the ancient Mediterranean world. He draws upon the literary forms, rhetorical conventions and stories of the setting he shares with his readers, targeting the gospel for an audience of Gentile Christians who need to know who they are and how to live out their calling within their life circumstances. Plainly put, Luke does narrative theology first-century style. He engages his world and beckons his readers to be transformed by the story of God's activity in the life of the church. This is the task of the church in every culture and age—to enable the gospel to address its world in transforming ways even as it utilizes the stories and cultural resources at hand.

---

[74]Hilary, *Inculturation Theology*, pp. 266-67.

At the same time, the individual stories within the larger narrative of God's purpose in the first half of Acts have an exemplary function for the church. In the first place, they provide theological foundations for the task of contextualization. They reveal a gospel that by its very nature crosses barriers, transcends any single, normative cultural expression, and accepts all peoples as they are, within their concrete circumstances. Beyond this, these events offer models of Spirit-guided theological reflection for new situations. Luke lets us discover step by step how the one apostolic gospel that centers on the saving events in Christ can be expressed in a variety of context-sensitive ways to different groups of people, whether to Jews in the beginning, to peoples on the periphery of Judaism like the Samaritans and the Ethiopian eunuch, to a bridge figure like the God-fearer Cornelius, or to the wider circle of Gentiles as in the decision of the Jerusalem Council. Each time the missional church crosses another cultural, social or religious barrier, the church's ministry of the word must be tailored to fit the new context.

The final two accounts of Cornelius and the Jerusalem Council in particular serve as case studies for doing contextual theology. In the Cornelius narrative, Peter is dragged "kicking and screaming" by the Spirit into a new understanding of the wideness of God's mercy. The messenger and his church must undergo a conversion every bit as profound as those who receive the message. Later in Acts 15 Luke lets us peer in on a multicultural church in conflict, a church that is struggling with the extent to which the old ways of perceiving and living out the faith need to be transformed in light of a new situation fashioned by the Spirit. These narratives carry powerful implications for churches and intercultural communicators of all generations. At times we must be willing to allow our own culture-bound theologies and practices to be confronted and renewed. Only then can the gospel hope to address new challenges and constituencies with Spirit-graced authenticity. Those of us who are a part of dominant cultures and "mother" churches especially need to confess that we, like the Jerusalem Jews, have too often tried to impose our "superior" interpretations and cultural expressions of the faith upon Christians in other settings.

The church's theological task that Acts portrays is far from simple. It is clearly a *process* in which a whole array of elements come into play: the leading of the Spirit, the witness of Scripture and the words of Jesus, the audience-sensitive proclamation of the word, the church's experience of God and the stories that testify to what God is doing, the corporate insight of the community and its leadership, respect for traditional ways and a willingness to compromise on nonessentials for the sake of Christian unity, and a firm commitment to the truth of the gospel. The result is a church that allows diversity in theological understanding and mission praxis yet is united in its enriched understanding of the gospel of Christ and in its commitment to a boundary-free mission. Acts invites us to inscribe ourselves into these paradigmatic stories. It bids us learn from the journey they describe. There are still barriers that must be hurdled—sociocultural, theological, linguistic, generational—as we attempt to articulate and embody the gospel within our various cultures and circumstances today. Yet we can draw hope from the knowledge that the same God who discloses himself in unexpected ways to Philip, Peter, James, and the Jerusalem church encounters us, as well, in the midst of our diverse contexts. Luke's narrative of God's plan to bring salvation to the world through the church's witness to the gospel is an unfinished story, one that is still being lived out in London and Lagos and Lima and a myriad of other concrete settings that extend "to the ends of the earth."

2. CONTEXTUALIZATION IN ACTS
The Preaching of Paul

What therefore you worship as unknown, this I proclaim to you.

ACTS 17:23

Martin Hengel is right. For Luke, Paul is the model missionary.[1] Virtually the entire second half of Acts is dedicated to Paul's catalytic role in the advance of the gospel throughout the Roman Empire. Luke portrays Paul of Tarsus as a missionary of extraordinary flexibility and cultural sensitivity. On the one hand, he regularly associates with Gentiles, shares meals with them, even stays in Gentile homes, all without deference to boundary-marking Jewish food laws (cf. Acts 11:26; 16:15, 34, 40; 17:4-7). On the other hand, for the sake of his missionary work among Jews, Paul has his coworker Timothy circumcised (Acts 16:3), and later he consents to undergo the Jewish rite of purification in the temple at Jerusalem (Acts 21:23-24, 26; cf. 18:18). For our immediate purpose, however, it is Paul's missionary preaching that is most significant. Unlike Paul's letters, which are documents exclusively targeted to Christians, Acts introduces Paul the evangelist who proclaims the Word of God in various settings to diverse groups of unbelievers.[2] In this chapter we will examine the three missionary speeches

---

[1]Martin Hengel, *Acts and the History of Early Christianity* (Philadelphia: Fortress, 1979), p. 125.
[2]Any study of Paul's missionary preaching in Acts raises the complex question of whether it is really the historical Paul speaking or Luke presenting his own ideas through Paul's mouth. Recent examination of the function of speech recording in ancient historiography has shown that serious Greek historians such as Thucydides and Polybius were in fact concerned about *both* historical *and* literary appropriateness. See Conrad Gempf, "Public Speaking and Published Accounts," in *The Book of Acts in Its Ancient Literary Setting*, ed. Bruce W. Winter and Andrew D. Clarke (Grand Rapids, Mich.: Eerdmans, 1993), pp. 259-303. Consequently, although we should not expect Paul's sermons in Acts to be verbatim transcripts of what was said—this is clear from their brevity alone—we can expect them to be faithful representations of how Paul addressed particular audiences on specific occasions. I will therefore refer to "Paul" as the preacher of the gospel, with the understanding that what Paul says in Acts 17 also reflects Luke's own literary and rhetorical concerns. In any case, in the "world" of Luke's

of Paul in Acts (Acts 13:16-41, 46-47; 14:15-17; 17:22-31) as compelling examples of evangelistic contextualization.

A SERMON FOR THE SYNAGOGUE: ACTS 13:13-52

The synagogue speech at Pisidian Antioch (Acts 13:13-52) is the first of Paul's evangelistic sermons recorded in Acts, and the only one to a predominantly Jewish audience. Like Jesus' first sermon in Nazareth (Lk 4:18-21) and Peter's preaching at Pentecost (Acts 2:14-40), Paul's initial address in Acts 13 has a programmatic character.[3] It comes at a crucial juncture in Luke's story that is signaled by two important developments: the beginning of Paul's ministry, which dominates the rest of Acts, and an emerging pattern of Jewish rejection of the gospel that leads to a growing focus on the Gentile mission (cf. Acts 13:45-51). Considering that it is Paul's custom in Acts to preach in the synagogue and explain the Messiah's death and resurrection from the Scriptures (Acts 17:2-3), Luke no doubt views this as a representative sermon for a synagogue crowd. Throughout the book of Acts, Luke takes pains to demonstrate how the gospel was proclaimed in various key contexts and to different kinds of people.[4] Paul's unfolding of the gospel in Antioch thus represents not only a targeted message for a particular occasion. It also functions for Luke's readers as a model sermon for an audience of Diaspora Jews.

Audience and setting. When Paul arrives in the cosmopolitan Roman colony of Antioch, he finds a vital and well-established Jewish community. It is impossible to know the extent to which these Antiochene Jews had been "Hellenized" in practice, since patterns of assimilation to Greco-Roman culture varied greatly in Diaspora Judaism. However, their interaction with non-Jews (Acts 13:16, 26) and their ties with people of influence in local civic life (Acts 13:50) suggest at least some measure of integration into the surrounding culture. In addition to the Jews, Luke identifies two other groups, "devout proselytes" (Acts 13:43) and "God-fearers" (Acts 13:16, 26), the latter term apparently referring to Gentile worshipers who are not full converts (cf. Acts 10:2). Although the speech seems to be primarily targeted to Jews (see Acts 13:17, 32-33), Paul singles out these non-Jewish sympathizers as part of the listening audience (Acts

---

narrative, Paul is assumed to be the one communicating on the occasion described. For a careful defense of the essential coherence between the Paul of Acts and the Paul of the letters, see Stanley E. Porter, *The Paul of Acts: Essays in Literary Criticism, Rhetoric, and Theology* (Tübingen: Mohr/Siebeck, 1999).

[3]Robert C. Tannehill, *The Narrative Unity of Luke-Acts* (Philadelphia: Fortress, 1990), 2:160.

[4]Ben Witherington III, *The Acts of the Apostles: A Social-Rhetorical Commentary* (Grand Rapids, Mich.: Eerdmans, 1998), p. 119 n. 18.

13:16, 26). The synagogue community also seems to have included people of considerable social standing, since the Jews were able to incite devout women of high status—probably at the very least synagogue adherents—who in turn influence "the leading men of the city" (Acts 13:50).

Appropriately, the setting for Paul's address is the synagogue, the center of religious and community life and a focus of shared identity for Diaspora Jews. It is common ground for Paul and his audience. His listeners are prepared for his message by their gathering for Sabbath worship and by the reading of the Law and the Prophets (Acts 13:14-15). Paul receives an invitation to speak from the proper source, the synagogue officials. Evidently, there is at least an initial openness to what he has to say. Paul speaks to his hearers as fellow Israelites and children of Abraham, along with those God-fearers who have aligned themselves with Abraham's family (Acts 13:16, 26). The audience, the setting, the address and the content of Paul's sermon affirm with one voice that this is *not* a case of crosscultural communication of the gospel. Paul speaks as a Diaspora Jew to fellow Diaspora Jews within the framework of the Jewish Scriptures and the worship of the God of Israel.

Persuasive features. Ancient rhetoric stressed the importance of tailoring an oral speech to the specific audience and occasion.[5] In keeping with this aim, Paul's "word of exhortation" (Acts 13:15)—presumably delivered in Greek —is carefully crafted to persuade an audience of intelligent, Greek-speaking Jews. For example, Paul establishes rapport with his listeners by the way that he directly addresses them. He begins with the formal "Men, Israelites" (Acts 13:16), using the sacred covenant name of "Israel" (cf. Gen 32:28-29). As the speech continues, however, he addresses them less formally as "men brothers" and as "children of the family of Abraham" (Acts 13:26, 38). This succession of addresses not only functions to apply Paul's message to those who are listening, but suggests as well a progressive winning over of his audience.[6] Paul connects with his hearers in other ways. Throughout the speech, he identifies himself with his audience as an insider, one of the Jewish family (cf. "our," "us," Acts 13:16, 27). In addition, the speech is brimming with language, themes and quotations from the Greek Old Testament. It seems that Luke consciously adapts his style of writing to the Septuagint, the Bible of the Diaspora. By imitating the familiar patterns of the Greek Bible, Luke contextualizes the

---

[5]E.g., Quintilian *Inst. or.* 11.1.43-56. See Whitney Shiner, *Proclaiming the Gospel: First-Century Performance of Mark* (Harrisburg, Penn.: Trinity Press International, 2003), pp. 26-30.

[6]See Witherington, *Acts of the Apostles*, p. 139. A similar pattern of salutations occurs in Peter's Pentecost speech (Acts 2:14, 22, 29, 37).

form of the speech to its Jewish subject matter and setting.[7]

At the same time, the speech's structure fits conventional patterns of Greco-Roman rhetoric. We can observe the following elements: (1) a brief introduction (called the *exordium,* Acts 13:16b); (2) a narration (Acts 13:17-25); (3) a proposition, or thesis statement (Acts 13:26); (4) a proof (called the *probatio,* Acts 13:27-37), which demonstrates the proposition through an appeal to both the saving story (Acts 13:27-31) and Scripture (Acts 13:32-37); and (5) a concluding exhortation (called the *peroratio,* Acts 13:38-41).[8] This suggests that Luke wants to show that Paul is a speaker who is rhetorically persuasive, not only to educated diaspora Jews (who no doubt would have at least some familiarity with the oratory that was "in the air" in the Greco-Roman world), but also to Theophilus and the audience of Acts. As Ben Witherington has suggested, Paul's discourse takes on the character of a piece of *deliberative* rhetoric, the kind of ancient rhetoric that aims for a change in the belief and behavior of its listeners (cf. Acts 13:40-43).[9]

Paul's targeted evangelistic message. The content of Paul's Antioch address reveals a masterfully contextualized presentation of the gospel for its target audience. I will highlight several features of how the Christian message is adapted to a synagogue congregation.

Common ground: A shared story. The speech begins with a rehearsal of God's mighty acts in the history of Israel. At the outset, Paul establishes common ground with his Jewish hearers by reminding them of the familiar story of salvation they and he share. The lead actor in this story is "the God of this people Israel" (Acts 13:17). The sacred narrative opens with God's choice of the patriarchs, progresses through Israel's deliverance from Egypt, God's gift of the land of inheritance and the judges, and the establishing of the kingdom, then climaxes with God's raising up of David (Acts 13:17-22). That this is *selective* history becomes plain when we compare this sermon with Stephen's defense speech before the Jewish Council in Jerusalem in chapter 7, the only other extended survey of salvation history in Acts. Whereas Stephen focuses on Moses and Israel's repeated rebellion, Paul, in contrast, spotlights David and God's ongoing faithfulness toward his people. And while Stephen's account hones in on

---

[7]On the Hellenistic practice of imitating literary models *(imitatio)* in Acts, see Bill Arnold, "Luke's Characterizing Use of the Old Testament in the Book of Acts," in *History, Literature, and Society in the Book of Acts,* ed. Ben Witherington III (Cambridge: Cambridge University Press, 1996), pp. 301-02.

[8]Witherington, *Acts of the Apostle: A Socio-Rhetorical Commentary* (Grand Rapids, Mich.: Eerdmans, 1998), p. 407.

[9]Ibid., pp. 406-7.

the Jerusalem temple in order to confront the corrupt temple council (Acts 7:46-
50), Paul's stress on the *pre*-temple period reigns of kings Saul and David (13:21-
22) better suits a diasporal crowd. Paul's audience and evangelistic purpose require a fresh way of telling the story.

Underlying Paul's review of Old Testament history are a number of shared
presuppositions. These function not only to bind the speaker and audience
together but also to lay a foundation for Paul's unfolding argument in the
speech. In particular, Paul and his listeners can agree that (1) God has chosen
Israel and has acted sovereignly and graciously on its behalf; and (2) God has
chosen David, who was pleasing to God and carried out the divine plan (Acts
13:22).[10] This allows Paul to come to the real point of reciting Israel's past in
Acts 13:23: God's promise to bring Israel a Savior has been fulfilled in David's
seed, Jesus of Nazareth. Israel's theocentric story has a christological goal. Immediately, Paul calls John the Baptist as a witness to verify this new and surprising development (Acts 13:24-25; cf. Lk 3:15-17).[11] The early part of the sermon thus places the proclamation of the gospel to the Antioch synagogue
crowd in a narrative framework. Paul sees the coming of Jesus the Davidic
Messiah as the crucial moment in the entire history of redemption. The sermon
emphasizes the continuity between the story of Israel and the stories of John
and Jesus. Yet, the saving meaning of Israel's past is not self-evident for Paul's
hearers. The story must be interpreted from the perspective of God's new
work in Jesus and the church, an interpretation that Paul sets forth in the remainder of the speech.[12]

The kerygma: God's action in Christ. Paul articulates the content of the gospel, the "word of salvation" (Acts 13:26), for his audience of Jews and sympathizers in Acts 13:26-41. That proclamation centers on a christological narrative
(Acts 13:27-31) which is supported by Scripture (Acts 13:32-37) and brings saving effects (Acts 13:38-39).

Paul does not express the message of Christ in a series of theological prop-

---

[10]Tannehill, *Luke-Acts*, 2:166.

[11]See Marion Soards, *The Speeches in Acts: Their Content, Context, and Concerns* (Louisville:
Westminster John Knox, 1994), pp. 83-84. It is also possible that the reference to John the
Baptist was included because of the presence of disciples of John the Baptist in the cities of
Asia Minor (cf. Acts 19:3-4). It may have been important in the Antioch setting to clarify the
Baptist's role in the history of salvation and underscore his subordinate relationship to Jesus.
See C. A. J. Pillai, *Early Missionary Preaching: A Study of Luke's Report in Acts 13* (Hicksville,
N.Y.: Exposition Press, 1979), pp. 94-95.

[12]Joel B. Green, "Acts of the Apostles," in *Dictionary of the Later New Testament and Its Developments*, ed. Ralph P. Martin and Peter H. Davids (Downers Grove, Ill.: InterVarsity Press,
1997), pp. 11-12.

ositions; instead he narrates the story of God's saving intervention in Jesus. The Christ kerygma (preached message) announces the death, burial, and especially the resurrection of Jesus, as well as confirming testimony from eyewitnesses (Acts 13:27-31; cf. 1 Cor 15:3-7). Paul's telling of the story of Jesus and its scriptural support in chapter 13 have much in common with Peter's earlier preaching to Jewish audiences in Acts (Acts 2:14-36; 3:12-26; 5:29-32), particularly the Pentecost sermon in chapter 2.[13] Luke apparently wants his readers to see that the gospel Paul preaches is not unique or idiosyncratic; it is the one apostolic gospel proclaimed by all of God's true witnesses. At the same time, Paul's particular expression of that common gospel in a Diaspora setting shows some distinctive features. Paul, for instance, singles out the responsibility of "the residents of Jerusalem and their leaders" for the crucifixion of Jesus (Acts 13:27). This serves as a calculated warning to his Diaspora audience not to follow in the footsteps of their Jerusalem counterparts. Furthermore, Paul's reference to "the words of the prophets that are read every Sabbath" (Acts 13:27) recalls the reading of the Law and the Prophets in Acts 13:15 and is particularly appropriate for a synagogue gathering.

The theme of fulfillment. A key element of Paul's contextualized gospel message in Acts 13 is the fulfillment motif, mentioned three times in the sermon. First, we have seen that Acts 13:23 announces a Savior from David's line who fulfills God's promise to Israel, apparently echoing 2 Samuel 7:12. Second, the fulfillment theme is linked to Jesus' crucifixion. Although the people of Jerusalem were ignorant of the true meaning of the words of the prophets, they ironically fulfilled them by condemning Jesus to death (Acts 13:27). In crucifying Jesus, they "carried out everything that was written about him" (Acts 13:29). The notion of Jesus' suffering and death as the fulfillment of God's plan revealed in Scripture is a common refrain when the gospel is announced to Jewish or synagogue congregations (cf. Acts 2:23; 3:18; 17:2-3), but it is conspicuously absent from Paul's later preaching to pagans. Third, Paul identifies the content of the gospel he proclaims with the idea that God has fulfilled the promise of a Davidic Messiah to Israel by "raising Jesus" (Acts 13:32-34). Paul stresses that this promise to the Jewish ancestors is now fulfilled "for us, their children," among whom he numbers himself (Acts 13:33). The idea of the fulfillment of God's messianic promise in Jesus becomes a keynote in Paul's proclamation for his Diaspora audience.

Use of Scripture. Appropriately, Paul's speech to a Sabbath gathering is thick with scriptural allusions and quotations. The telling of Israel's story in Acts

---

[13]For common features, see Soards, *Speeches in Acts*, pp. 84-87.

13:17-22 loudly echoes the language of the Greek Bible, and the divine "testimony" about David (Acts 13:22) is dependent on several Old Testament texts (Ps 89:20; 1 Sam 13:14; Is 44:28). The main concentration of Scripture citations, however, comes in support of Paul's reflection in Acts 13:32-37 on the story of Jesus, particularly the resurrection, as the fulfilling of God's promise:

> And we bring you the good news that what God promised to our ancestors he has fulfilled for us, their children, by raising Jesus; as also it is written in the second psalm, "You are my Son; today I have begotten you." As to his raising him from the dead, no more to return to corruption, he has spoken in this way, "I will give you the holy promises made to David." Therefore he has also said in another psalm, "You will not let your Holy One experience corruption." For David, after he had served the purpose of God in his own generation, died, was laid beside his ancestors, and experienced corruption; but he whom God raised up experienced no corruption.

Here several Old Testament texts are strung together in succession. First, Acts 13:33 cites Psalm 2:7 in relation to Jesus' resurrection, which demonstrates that he is the Son of God described in the psalm.[14] The second and third quotations, drawn from Isaiah 55:3 and Psalm 16:10 (Acts 13:34-35), are linked by their common verb ("I will give"/"You will not give") and especially by the term "holy," which they share ("the holy things of David"/"your Holy one"). Here Paul adapts his christological argument to the audience, not only by citing Scripture, but also in the way those passages are interpreted. As Luke Timothy Johnson observes, verses 34-35 reflect a type of midrashic exposition used by the rabbis, later known as *gezerah shawa* (verbal analogy), which involves "comparing the use of the same word in different passages in order to discover their full or precise meaning."[15] By quoting the two "holy" passages in tandem, Paul is able to interpret Isaiah's prophecy (Acts 13:34b) in light of Psalm 16:10. Because the Psalmist's ancient promise of incorruptibility ("You will not let your Holy One experience corruption") is fulfilled, not in David, but in Jesus, whom God raised from the dead, God's covenant blessings originally promised to David have now been extended to Christians, including Paul's listeners (Acts 13:34; cf. Is 55:3).[16]

---

[14]G. Walter Hansen, "The Preaching and Defense of Paul," in *Witness to the Gospel: The Theology of Acts*, ed. I. Howard Marshall and David Peterson (Grand Rapids, Mich.: Eerdmans, 1998), p. 303.

[15]Luke Timothy Johnson, *The Acts of the Apostles* (Collegeville, Minn.: Michael Glazier/Liturgical Press, 1992), p. 238.

[16]See Darrell L. Bock, *Proclamation from Prophecy and Pattern: Lucan Old Testament Christology*, JSNTSup 12 (Sheffield: Sheffield Academic Press, 1987), pp. 249-54; David A. deSilva, "Paul's Sermon in Antioch of Pisidia," *BSac* 151 (1994): 43-44.

Here Paul's speech takes up familiar methods of interpretation from Jewish culture—midrashic techniques such as using strings of Scripture citations, and verbal analogies that allow passages to illuminate one another—in order to build a persuasive argument for a synagogue audience about the meaning of the Christ event.[17]

Paul appeals to Scripture on two more occasions in the passage, once to warn his hearers of the danger of end-time judgment (Acts 13:41; cf. Hab 1:5), and again to explain and justify his mission to the Gentiles (Acts 13:47; cf. Is 49:6). The speech as a whole assumes that Paul and his listeners share a common regard for the authority of the Scriptures, and Paul finds testimony in the Old Testament as to the significance of the saving events he proclaims.[18] At the same time, Joel B. Green is right that from the perspective of Acts, "it is not the Scriptures per se that speak authoritatively but the Scriptures as they bear witness to God's purpose, an interpretation accessible only in light of the mission, death and exaltation of Jesus of Nazareth."[19] This means that Paul's sermon confronts its Diaspora hearers not only with an evangelistic decision but also a *hermeneutical* one: Who interprets the Bible faithfully—the Jerusalem Jews and their leaders, who repeatedly read the prophets without understanding (Acts 13:27), or God's true witnesses who declare the good news of messianic fulfillment in Jesus' resurrection from the dead (Acts 13:31-33)?[20] It is striking that this practice of citing the Old Testament does not spill over into Paul's missionary preaching to pagans. In Acts, it is only Jewish audiences that hear direct appeals to Scripture in order to explain God's new work in Christ.

Evangelistic appeal. The sermon reaches its climax in verses 38-41. Only now does Paul confront his synagogue audience with the transforming meaning of God's action in Christ. Because God sent the promised Messiah to Israel; because Jesus has fulfilled God's purpose, hanging on a tree, being raised and exalted incorruptible, the saving message of forgiveness and justification is proclaimed *to you* (Acts 13:38-39). The gospel brings "forgiveness of sins" through Jesus (Acts 13:38), a notion we hear repeatedly in sermons to Jews or God-fearers (see Acts 2:38; 5:31; 10:43), but not in Paul's preaching to pagans. Furthermore, the offer of justification by faith and not by the law

---

[17]See the discussion of the use of midrashic methods of exegesis in this speech in E. E. Ellis, "Midrashic Features in the Speeches of Acts," in *Prophecy and Hermeneutic in Early Christianity* (Grand Rapids, Mich.: Baker, 1993), pp. 198-208.

[18]See Arnold, "Luke's Characterizing Use," p. 321.

[19]Green, "Acts," p. 18.

[20]See ibid., pp. 18-19.

of Moses (Acts 13:39)—language that echoes familiar themes in Paul's letters—is highly appropriate for a synagogue congregation.[21] At the same time,
forgiveness and justification are for "everyone who believes" (Acts 13:39; cf.
10:43; Rom 1:16). This universal offer expands the horizon of messianic salvation beyond the boundaries of Israel and anticipates Paul's turning to the
Gentiles (Acts 13:46-47).

Balancing the announcement of salvation blessings in Christ, the speech fin-
ishes with a high-volume note of warning to the audience (Acts 13:40-41). Once
again Paul invokes Israel's past. The prophet Habakkuk's appeal to the danger
of not recognizing the Chaldean invasion as divine judgment (Hab 1:5 LXX) is
applied to the present peril of failing to discern God's activity in sending a Savior.[22] This assumes a parallel between the ancient story of Israel's unbelief and
the rejection of the gospel by the Jews of Paul's day. The synagogue crowd's
ability to appropriate the blessings of forgiveness and justification depends on
their embracing the interpretation of God's saving work as proclaimed by Paul.[23]
Otherwise, they are in jeopardy of revisiting the mistakes of their Jewish predecessors and of reaping the same dismal consequences. This powerful warning
signal forebodes the reaction to come.

The response: Rejection and embrace. In the narrative that follows, Paul's
message gets mixed reviews from the audience. Initially, many Jews and proselytes show an openness to the grace of God (Acts 13:43), but later, jealousy
over the success of Paul and Barnabas among the Gentile population of Antioch
breeds rejection and hostility (Acts 13:44-45, 50). This Jewish spurning of the
word of God leads the missionaries to solemnly announce their resolve to turn
to the Gentiles. It is clear from the context, however, that while provoked by
immediate circumstances, this is no "spur-of-the-moment" decision. God's plan
all along has been that the gospel would be preached first to the Jews, but that
the Gentiles would be offered the same gift of eternal life (Acts 13:46, 48). Still
addressing the Jews in the crowd, Paul appeals to Isaiah 49:6 as a rationale for

---

[21]Because of the parallels with terminology in Paul's letters, Acts 13:38-39 have often been
viewed simply as Luke's attempt to inject some Pauline flavor into the speech. See e.g., Phil-
ipp Vielhauer, "On the 'Paulinism' of Acts," in *Studies in Luke-Acts*, ed. L. E. Keck and J. L.
Martyn (Philadelphia: Fortress, 1980), esp. pp. 41-42. However, the differences between these
verses and Paul's theology are not as great as is sometimes supposed. G. Walter Hansen's
conclusion that "Luke has provided a fairly accurate summary of Pauline soteriology at this
point" seems reasonable ("Preaching," p. 305).

[22]I. Howard Marshall, *The Acts of the Apostles* (Grand Rapids, Mich.: Eerdmans, 1983), p. 229.

[23]See Joel B. Green, "'Salvation to the End of the Earth' (Acts 13:47): God as Saviour in the Acts
of the Apostles," in *Witness to the Gospel: The Theology of Acts*, ed. I. Howard Marshall and
David Peterson (Grand Rapids, Mich.: Eerdmans, 1998), p. 103.

his Gentile mission (Acts 13:47). The task of being "a light for the Gentiles," originally given to the Lord's Servant, who was identified with Israel herself, and elsewhere related by Luke to the ministry of Jesus (Lk 2:32; Acts 26:23), now belongs to the risen Lord's messengers who continue his mission. Once again God's Word and God's work challenge Jewish particularism. In contrast to the hostile Jewish response, the Gentiles of Antioch enthusiastically embrace the word of the Lord (Acts 13:48; cf. 13:49) and give evidence of genuine conversion (Acts 13:52).

Luke's narrative in chapter 13 makes it clear that even though Paul shares the same basic culture and much of the same worldview as his audience, and although he communicates the gospel in language that is targeted to the Jews, the barriers to faith in Jesus are still substantial. Indeed, the very worldview and cultural assumptions of the synagogue community become a stumbling block to their receiving the good news. Now, as well as then, a shared cultural experience is no guarantee that our efforts at contextualizing the gospel will meet with a positive response.

Conclusion. What does Paul's evangelistic encounter at Pisidian Antioch show us about the process of contextualizing the gospel in Acts? First, the fundamental content of Paul's preaching is the apostolic gospel, the "word of salvation" (Acts 13:26; cf. 13:44, 48, 49), which centers on the death and resurrection of Christ as the fulfillment of God's redemptive plan for humanity. The gospel that Paul proclaims shares many common elements with Peter's earlier sermons in Acts. These include the witness of the Scriptures and their fulfillment in Christ, the telling of the story of Jesus, which climaxes in the resurrection, the appeal to personal witnesses, the offer of forgiveness of sins through faith, and the universal promise of salvation. There is unity in both method and message when the gospel is addressed to a primarily Jewish setting, although no two evangelistic messages are identical.

Second, Paul's missionary sermon in Acts 13 is a masterpiece of contextualization for a synagogue gathering. When preaching to Jews, Paul incorporates his audience's history, its expectations, its Scriptures and its culturally accepted methods of interpretation in order to persuasively proclaim the good news. Even the climactic announcement of Jesus' resurrection is put forward as the realization of the Davidic promise to Israel. There is continuity in the narrative thread that moves from God's saving activity in the story of Israel to the story of John and Jesus to the ongoing story of Paul's mission to Jews and Gentiles, all of which are related to Scripture and to God's promise.[24] As Mary E. Hinkle

---

[24]See Green, "Acts," pp. 11-12.

suggests, Paul does not tell a brand new story, but rather proclaims a new, defining chapter in a story his hearers already know and participate in.[25] Paul's Jewish listeners hear the good news within a familiar cultural and religious framework. It is a language that strikes home.

Third, Paul's gospel message is not simply contextually appropriate. It also challenges its Jewish hearers' entire way of seeing the world. It seeks to reshape their understanding of their national history and their Scriptures in light of the new story of the resurrected Jesus of Nazareth. It calls them to reject the perspective of their Judean coreligionists on the events that took place in Jerusalem and embrace Paul's revealed interpretation. It summons them to abandon their religious exclusivism and to lay hold of God's offer of forgiveness of sins and eternal life by faith. In short, the gospel confronts its Jewish audience with a new Christian vision and the need for profound change.

PREACHING TO PAGANS AT LYSTRA: ACTS 14:8-20

In Luke's accounts of Paul's preaching in Lystra (Acts 14) and Athens (Acts 17), the gospel enters a brave new cultural and religious world. Here we encounter the only speeches in Acts directed to pagan Gentiles. Consequently, these two sermons are critical to understanding how the word of salvation bridged cultural barriers within the early Christian mission. Luke is unequivocal that the Christian message is not captive to the original language and culture of Judaism. It addresses people at the point of their understanding and life circumstances.

Paul's speech at Lystra in Acts 14:15-17 is actually a "minisermon" cut short by circumstances before reaching its proper conclusion.[26] These hurried remarks contrast with Paul's more reasoned Areopagus address in Acts 17, which it foreshadows. Yet, despite its brevity (the sermon itself covers only three verses), Paul's Lystra message carries no small significance in Acts. It is the first speech to a purely Gentile audience, as well as the sole representative example of communicating the good news to unsophisticated pagans.

Audience and setting. The Gentiles Paul and Barnabas encounter in Lystra are altogether different from pious God-fearers like Cornelius or those of the synagogue in Pisidian Antioch. These people present a new challenge to the communication of the word of God. Although Lystra had been a Roman colony since 6 B.C., the crowds who listened to Paul's preaching were probably com-

---

[25]Mary E. Hinkle, "Preaching for Mission: Ancient Speeches and Postmodern Sermons: Acts 7:2-53; 13:16-41; 14:15-17," in *Mission in Acts: Ancient Narratives in Contemporary Context*, ed. R. L. Gallagher and P. Hertig (Maryknoll, N.Y.: Orbis, 2004), p. 94.

[26]According to Acts 14:14 both Paul and Barnabas spoke, but the speech is probably intended to be a summary of what Paul said.

mon people, the indigenous Lycaonian population. Unlike the educated and landowning Roman colonists who spoke Latin, these are simple upcountry folk who converse in the local dialect (Acts 14:11). There is no reason to think they had been significantly influenced by either the Jewish Scriptures or the Greek philosophical schools.[27] At the time, the Lycaonians were well-renowned as primitive rustics, living in the cultural backwaters of Greco-Roman civilization.[28] Luke portrays them as unsophisticated but sincere believers in the traditional pantheon of Greek popular religion. Their worship centers around the local civic cult with its temple outside of the city (Acts 14:13). It is entirely possible that they had syncretized their native deities with the Greek gods and given them names like Zeus and Hermes (Acts 14:12-13).[29] Clearly they do not share either the biblical story or the monotheistic worldview that could be assumed in earlier evangelistic preaching in Acts.

The setting for the speech is not the synagogue, as was Paul's usual custom. Instead he addresses the crowds on the street like an itinerant philosopher.[30] His message is prompted by the healing of a man who was lame from birth and the subsequent misunderstanding of its meaning. Luke, it seems, does not view these pagans in a wholly negative light. The crippled man has faith to be made whole (*sōzō,* Acts 14:9). The crowd immediately recognizes divine power at work. In Luke's narrative the manifestation of God's miracle-working power and the proclamation of the good news of salvation go hand in hand. Not surprisingly, however, the Lycaonians erroneously interpret this healing event against their polytheistic religious template. A collision of worldviews is unavoidable. Their behavior in excitedly welcoming Paul and Barnabas as epiphanies of Greek deities (Acts 14:11-12) is probably conditioned by a folk legend about a visitation of the gods Zeus and Hermes to the Phrygian region.[31] According to the tale, when the two Olympians arrived in human form, a thousand homes refused them hospitality and were destroyed. Only an elderly couple, Baucis and Philemon, took them in and were spared. Apparently, the inhabitants of

---

[27]Richard N. Longenecker, "Acts of the Apostles," in *Expository Bible Commentary*, ed. Frank E. Gaebelein (Grand Rapids, Mich.: Zondervan, 1981), 9:436.

[28]See Dean P. Bechard, "Paul among the Rustics: The Lystran Episode (Acts 14:8-20) and Lucan Apologetic," *CBQ* 63 (2001): 84-101.

[29]Marshall, *Acts of the Apostles*, p. 237.

[30]Craig S. Keener, *The IVP Bible Background Commentary: New Testament* (Downers Grove, Ill.: InterVarsity Press, 1993), p. 362.

[31]Ovid *Metamorphoses* 8:617-725 preserves the legend. For archaeological evidence for the worship of Zeus and Hermes in the region of Lystra, see Colin J. Hemer, *The Book of Acts in the Setting of Hellenistic History,* ed. Conrad H. Gempf, Wissenschaftliche Untersuchungen zum Neuen Testament (Tübingen: J. C. B. Mohr/Paul Siebeck, 1989), p. 111.

Lystra do not want to make the same mistake as their predecessors, so they prepare to honor Barnabas and Paul with a great sacrifice, according to the tradition of their local cult. Furthermore, the missionaries face a barrier of language as well as religion. Although the crowd presumably understands enough Greek to know the gist of what is being said to them, their use of their Lycaonian mother tongue (Acts 14:11) may explain why Paul and Barnabas are so slow to catch on and put a halt to what was happening.

Persuasive features. Discovery of the mistaken identity triggers a swift and strong reaction from the missionaries (Acts 14:14), leading to Paul's impassioned message. As Mariane Fournier has shown, even this brief speech summary seems to feature elements of ancient deliberative rhetoric that seeks to persuade the audience toward future action: an introduction (*exordium*), designed to establish rapport with the audience (Acts 14:15); a narration, which recounts what God has done in the past (Acts 14:16); and a proof *(probatio)* that appeals to the audience's own present experience of God (Acts 14:17). This is appropriate to the occasion, since "Paul would have been expected to use a Greek style when speaking to people of Greek culture."[32]

Good news for the Lycaonians. For the first time in Acts, the gospel addresses a religiously plural environment. Paul's offer of "good news" (Acts 14:15) to the Lystrans demonstrates a willingness to interact with the worldview, beliefs and practices of his audience.

Initial point of contact: A shared humanity. Paul begins by engaging the Lycaonians where they are (Acts 14:15, "why are you doing this?"). He then responds to their specific misunderstanding, particularly the claim, "The gods have come down to us in human form" (Acts 14:11). Addressing them appropriately as "men" (not "brothers," as with Jewish or Christian audiences, cf. Acts 13:26, 38), Paul seizes the opportunity to correct the theological distortions that were conditioned by their polytheistic worldview. Yet, he does so by finding a point of identification with his audience: "we are human beings like you" (Acts 14:15). Rather than starting with a shared *history*, as in the sermon at Antioch (Acts 13:17-22), Paul appeals to a shared *humanity*. Establishing that he and Barnabas are only mortals, too, enables Paul to challenge the idolatry implicit in the Gentiles' misguided worship of the missionaries (Acts 14:15), while pointing them to the true source of the power to heal. At the same time, it places Paul and Barnabas on common ground with the Lycaonians as people created in the image of the true and living God. Paul approaches this crowd of pagans with respect.

---

[32]Marianne Fournier, *The Episode at Lystra: A Rhetorical and Semiotic Analysis of Acts 14:7-20a* (New York: Peter Lang, 1997), pp. 185-94, here p. 193.

A Theo-logical kerygma? Paul announces in verse 15 that he and Barnabas have come to bring the gospel to the Lystran pagans. The shape that good news takes, however, is conspicuously different from Paul's synagogue preaching in the previous chapter. Paul cannot begin to evangelize raw pagans by rehearsing the story of God's past dealings with Israel or by presenting Jesus as the Davidic Messiah who fulfills Old Testament prophecy. These Gentiles simply do not have the background to appreciate such an argument. Instead, he begins at their most basic point of need—to acknowledge the one true Creator God.

Paul's theological kerygma introduces his audience to five fundamental truths about the character and activity of God. First, he is the one, living God (Acts 14:15). The belief in one God, which could be presupposed when preaching to Jews and God-fearers, becomes an essential starting point for addressing people in a context of idolatry and religious pluralism. Second, this living God is the Creator of all things (Acts 14:15). The creation language of verse 15 clearly echoes the Old Testament (Ex 20:11; Ps 146:6). Paul does not shy away from scriptural language simply because his hearers are unfamiliar with it. In this case, however, there is no attempt to identify his words as a biblical citation, presumably since it would neither be recognized as such by the audience, nor its authority accepted.[33] Third, the one whom Paul proclaims is God of the nations. God is not simply a tribal or national deity; in the past "he allowed *all the nations* to follow their own ways" (Acts 14:16). Fourth, God has revealed himself to all peoples, leaving in every human culture a silent witness of the Creator's goodness through nature (Acts 14:17; cf. Rom 1:19-20). Fifth, God is the provider and sustainer of human life (Acts 14:17). The language of God's loving care for human needs by supplying seasonal rains and bountiful harvests once again recalls Old Testament themes (see Ps 145:15-16; 147:8-9; Jer 5:24). God's gracious activity in creation and nature furnishes a point of contact between the biblical story and the story of the Gentiles.

The specific allusions to God's providing rain from heaven and crops in season, the basic needs of life, are well suited to the Lycaonian peasant crowd. Although they have not received a special revelation from God or been a part of Israel's story, the living God is *their* creator and sustainer as well.[34] At the same time, there is evidence that the heavenly god Zeus was worshiped in southern Asia minor as the god of weather and of vegetation, functions which are specif-

---

[33]C. K. Barrett, *A Critical and Exegetical Commentary on the Acts of the Apostles* (Edinburgh: T & T Clark, 1994), 1:680.
[34]Tannehill, *Luke-Acts,* 2:179.

ically mentioned in verse 17.[35] Paul's appeal to general revelation and God's providential care of all peoples enables him to introduce pagans to the true Creator God while touching on themes that resonate with their religious background and life experience.

There are limits, however, to how far Paul is willing to adapt to his audience. For example, he steers clear of any attempt to identify the living God with Zeus—a move that could have opened the door to syncretism.[36] While the Lycaonians recognize divine activity in the supplying of rain and abundant harvests, it is the transcendent Creator God, not Zeus, who has graciously cared for them. Zeus and Hermes are idols, and there is only one Lord in heaven (Acts 14:15). The gospel's truth claims about the one true God must ultimately confront the pluralistic worldview of the pagans.

Evangelistic appeal. The purpose of Paul's bringing the good news to the Lycaonians is that they should "turn from these worthless things to the living God" (Acts 14:15; cf. 1 Thess 1:9). These Gentiles must leave behind their lives of idolatry and be converted to the one true God. This implies the need for repentance, even if the reason for repenting is stated differently than in sermons to Jews (cf. Acts 2:38; 5:31). David Lim rightly points out that in an environment where religion was viewed in inclusive, not exclusive terms, "this demand to change one's faith, ethic and cult entirely was totally new to the peoples in the Greco-Roman world."[37]

Yet why does Paul appeal to his audience to turn to God the Creator alone, and not to the risen Christ, as in other sermons in Acts? I. Howard Marshall thinks that the absence of any reference to the story of Christ in this truncated speech does not mean that Paul said nothing about it in Lystra. Rather, Luke's purpose is to reveal what was distinctive in Paul's preaching to pagans.[38] We know from Paul's address to Gentiles in Athens (Acts 17:31), as well as the close parallel to Acts 14:15 in 1 Thessalonians 1:9-10, that the message to turn from idols to the living God led ultimately to the proclaiming of Jesus, whom God raised from the dead. There is also a hint in chapter 14 that a turning point in the history of God's dealings with the nations has arrived—God will no longer

---

[35]See Cilliers Breytenbach, "Zeus und der lebendige Gott: Ammerkungen zu Apostelgeschichte 14.11-17," *NTS* 39 (1993): 396-413.

[36]See Clinton E. Arnold, "Syncretism," in *Dictionary of the Later New Testament and Its Developments*, ed. Ralph P. Martin and Peter H. Davids (Downers Grove, Ill.: InterVarsity Press, 1997), p. 1148.

[37]David Lim, "Evangelism in the Early Church," in *Dictionary of the Later New Testament and Its Developments*, ed. Ralph P. Martin and Peter H. Davids (Downers Grove, Ill.: InterVarsity Press, 1997), p. 354.

[38]Marshall, *Acts of the Apostles*, pp. 238-39.

let them go their own way (Acts 14:16). Consequently, "it is hard to believe that [the sermon] was not meant to point to Jesus Christ and his work as the divine climax of history."[39] In any case, both the speech's function as an attempt to bridle the Lycaonians' misplaced worship and the crowd's sudden interruption that keeps the address from reaching its conclusion signal that we should not expect a full explanation of the gospel on this occasion. What Luke records is the story of the one true God—an indispensable preparation for preaching Christ in a pluralistic context.

The response. As with the synagogue audience at Pisidian Antioch, the response of the Lystran pagans to Paul's appeal is divided. There are some converts to the Way (Acts 14:20; 16:2), evidence that the Lord has "opened a door of faith for the Gentiles" (Acts 14:27). But the majority apparently persist in their misreading of the healing miracle. They are only barely restrained from completing their veneration of God's messengers (Acts 14:18). Later, when Jewish opponents arrive from neighboring cities, they persuade the fickle Lystrans to turn an "about face" and support the stoning of Paul (Acts 14:19). Luke does not paint a naive picture of pagans eagerly embracing the good news when first they hear it. In fact, his account highlights the difficulties in communicating the gospel to peoples who do not believe in the one God revealed in the Scriptures. Paul and Barnabas encounter some of the same challenges as Christian communicators do today when facing barriers of language, culture and religious pluralism.

Conclusion. In the brief speech summary in Acts 14 we discover a groundbreaking "translation" of the Christian message for a radically new cultural and religious environment. In this world of popular pagan piety, the Jewish-oriented arguments used in Antioch would have been both ineffective and incomprehensible. Paul must tailor both the emphasis and the expression of his evangelistic preaching to fit a crowd of rustic Gentile polytheists. Starting at the point of their immediate confusion, he directs them to the true source of miraculous power. He engages their presuppositions and belief system at the level of foundational *theo*-logy. Points of contact are uncovered in their shared humanity and in the Creator's loving witness in the creation. Paul weaves his listeners' life experiences into the larger story of God revealed in the Scriptures.[40] Yet, in the process he refuses to dilute the substance of the gospel and its call for repentance and transformation. The "good news" of the one living God subverts the Lystrans' pluralistic worldview. The speech thus models a context-sensitive approach to

---

[39]Longenecker, "Acts," p. 436.
[40]Hinkle, "Preaching for Mission," p. 96.

unsophisticated pagans and lays the vital groundwork for a fuller proclamation of the Word.

THE GOSPEL IN ATHENS: ACTS 17:16-34

Paul's address to the Athenians in Acts 17 is perhaps the outstanding example of intercultural evangelistic witness in the New Testament. This makes it a pivotal text for our study of New Testament patterns of contextualization. As with the two previous sermons, Luke does not want his audience to hear this speech simply as a record of Paul's preaching on an isolated occasion. This sermon synopsis offers a paradigmatic case of Paul's approach to an educated pagan audience. At the same time, the speech's content is enmeshed with the concrete setting and occasion described in the narrative. In Acts 17, Luke gives us a snapshot of Paul at the height of his powers as a missionary communicator, transposing the gospel for the Greeks with both firmness and flexibility. I will therefore explore not only the content and method of doing missionary theology that this passage brings to light, but also its potential to serve as a model for the encounter between God's Word and God's world today.[41]

Audience and setting. Although by the first century the university city of Athens had already lost much of its former glory, for Luke it still symbolizes the cultural, intellectual and religious nerve center of the Greco-Roman world. When the gospel comes to Athens, it penetrates the very heartland of urban pagan culture. Athens is therefore the ideal setting for Paul's major missionary speech to the Greeks. Luke describes the context for Paul's sermon with meticulous detail. In particular, verse 16 sets the tone for what follows. Rather than being impressed by Athenian architecture and learning, Paul is "deeply distressed" over the pervasive idolatry and religious pluralism he observes there.

---

[41]The literature on Acts 17 is immense. In addition to the major commentaries, see Martin Dibelius, *Studies in the Acts of the Apostles*, ed. Heinrich Greeven (London: SCM Press, 1956), pp. 26-83; B. Gärtner, *The Areopagus Speech and Natural Revelation* (Uppsala: C. W. K. Gleerup, 1955); Hans Conzelmann, "The Address of Paul on the Areopagus," in *Studies in Luke-Acts*, ed. L. E. Keck and J. L. Martyn (Philadelphia: Fortress, 1966), pp. 217-30; G. L. Bahnsen, "The Encounter of Jerusalem with Athens," *Ashland Theological Bulletin* 31 (1980): 4-40; Dean Zweck, "The *Exordium* of the Areopagus Speech, Acts 17.22,23," *NTS* 35 (1989): 94-103; C. J. Hemer, "The Speeches of Acts II. The Areopagus Address," *TynBul* 40 (1989): 239-59; J. D. Charles, "Engaging the (Neo) Pagan Mind: Paul's Encounter with Athenian Culture as a Model for Cultural Apologetics (Acts 17:16-34)," *TJ* 16 (1995): 47-62; Yeo Khiok-khng, *What Has Jerusalem to Do with Beijing: Biblical Interpretation from a Chinese Perspective* (Harrisburg, Penn.: Trinity Press International, 1998), pp. 165-97; L. A. Losie, "Paul's Speech on the Areopagus: A Model of Cross-cultural Evangelism: Acts 17:16-34," in *Mission in Acts: Ancient Narratives in Contemporary Context*, ed. R. L. Callagher and P. Hertig (Maryknoll: N.Y.: Orbis, 2004), pp. 220-38.

A city rife with pagan images, temples, sanctuaries and altars provides the back-drop to the whole narrative.[42] Luke almost completely ignores Paul's synagogue ministry in Athens, choosing instead to focus on his encounter with the pagan inhabitants of the city. Paul adapts his evangelistic approach to the populace. Like a Greek philosopher, he goes to the marketplace (agora) and publicly de-bates the intellectuals of Athens on their own turf (Acts 17:17).[43]

In verse 18, Luke introduces us to two groups of philosophers, the Epicure-ans and the Stoics, who initially spar with Paul in the agora and later become the primary audience for his address. The identification of these two Athenian philosophical schools is critical to the narrative, since Paul interacts with their beliefs—especially those of the Stoics—in his sermon. The reaction of the edu-cated sophisticates to Paul's market preaching is a mixture of outright contempt, large-scale confusion and faddish curiosity (Acts 17:18, 21). Without a doubt this is a difficult crowd. The accusation that Paul was introducing foreign deities into the Greek pantheon is probably based on the false assumption that he was en-dorsing multiple gods; "Jesus" and his feminine counterpart, "Anastasia" (Resur-rection).[44] This misunderstanding simply underscores that the Athenians' poly-theistic perspective creates a serious hurdle to their hearing the gospel rightly. As in chapter 14, Luke's narrative exposes a fundamental clash of worldviews between Paul and his audience.

The Stoic and Epicurean philosophers are not Paul's only hearers. The im-mediate setting for the sermon is the meeting of the Areopagus, the supreme governing council of Athens, which had responsibility for deciding religious questions.[45] Paul is asked to explain his novel and exotic teaching to this pow-erful body of leading citizens (Acts 17:19-20). In addition, Luke's description of the response to Paul's address implies a wider listening audience, including a woman named Damaris who became a convert (Acts 17:33-34). That Paul ad-

---

[42]Zweck, "*Exordium*," p. 103.

[43]Apparently Luke wants his audience to draw a parallel between the experience of Paul and that of the great Athenian philosopher Socrates, who also engaged in dialogues in the agora and who was put on trial for the introduction of other new divinities (Plato *Apologia* 24B; cf. Acts 17:18). This association of Paul and Socrates would provide a point of contact for Luke's Hellenistic readers and encourage a favorable disposition toward Paul's Areopagus address. See Hansen, "Preaching," p. 310.

[44]The Greek term *anastasia* is feminine and may have been taken as the name of the female consort for the male god "Jesus." This interpretation goes back to John Chrysostom (*Hom. Act.* 38.1).

[45]There has been extensive discussion over whether the term *Areopagus* refers to the judicial and administrative council or the hill near the Acropolis from which it derives its name. Al-though there are good arguments on both sides, in light of the reference to Dionysius the Areopagite in Acts 17:34, the former meaning is more likely.

dresses not simply the philosophers, but also the council and perhaps other curious citizens of Athens (cf. Acts 17:22, "men of Athens"), is important for understanding the critique of popular Athenian religion in his speech, especially
since the Areopagus is the very group that is responsible for religious matters.[46]
Paul turns the occasion of a complete misunderstanding of his preaching and
the ensuing demand for an explanation into an opportunity to proclaim the gospel afresh in the very epicenter of Greek thought and culture.

Persuasive features. The form and style of the Areopagus speech are ex-
quisitely adapted to a sophisticated Gentile audience. In contrast with the frequent use of language and quotations from the Greek Bible that we find in sermons preached to Jews in Acts, this discourse reflects a more Hellenized style,
which is suited to the occasion and hearers.[47] Luke shows Paul addressing the
council with rhetorical skill and sensitivity. He stands in their midst like a Greek
orator and opens with a conventional form of address for a speech in Athens
("Men, Athenians," Acts 17:22),[48] enabling his audience right away to feel at
home. The sermon itself is highly rhetorical in its structure. We can observe the
following elements: (1) an opening *exordium*, designed to gain a hearing from
his listeners (Acts 17:22-23a); (2) a thesis (Acts 17:23b), stating the desired goal
of the speech—to make the unknown God known to the Athenians; (3) the
main proof (*probatio,* Acts 17:24-29), in which he argues his case; and (4) a concluding exhortation (*peroratio,* Acts 17:30-31), which attempts to persuade the
audience to take the right course of action, namely, to repent (Acts 17:30).[49]
Once again, the purpose of the speech is deliberative; Paul wants to convince
his audience to change their ways of thinking and living.[50] The speech "proclaims" to the Athenians (Acts 17:23; cf. 4:2; 13:5, 38) a message they need to
hear and embrace. In addition, Witherington observes that the speech seems to
follow the common pattern in ancient rhetoric of first establishing the speaker's
ethos, or character, then offering *logos* in the form of persuasive arguments, and
finally using *pathos* in verses 30-31 in order to generate an emotional response
from the audience.[51]

Paul's sermon features various rhetorical techniques that would have been
familiar to educated Greeks, notably the delaying tactic of "insinuation" *(insin-*

---

[46]Tannehill, *Luke-Acts,* 2:216-17.
[47]Witherington, *Acts of the Apostles,* p. 44 n. 156.
[48]Zweck, *"Exordium,"* p. 101.
[49]This follows the basic outline of Witherington, *Acts of the Apostles,* p. 518. With minor differences, see Zweck, *"Exordium,"* p. 97; Yeo, *Jerusalem,* pp. 169-70.
[50]Zweck, *"Exordium,"* p. 95; Yeo, *Jerusalem,* p. 168.
[51]Witherington, *Acts of the Apostles,* p. 518.

uatio). Paul postpones the difficult subject of the resurrection of Jesus to the very end (Acts 17:31), after first establishing rapport and building a foundation for understanding.[52] The speech is also laced with irony. The recurring theme of human *ignorance* (Acts 17:23, 30), for example, would not have been missed in this center of learning and before a body composed of the intelligentsia of Athens.[53] In addition, Paul's message draws upon the language and ideas of his Greek contemporaries, particularly the Stoic philosophers, in order to establish points of contact with his hearers. He even quotes pagan poets—authorities recognized by his audience—in support of his argument about the relationship of humanity to the living God (Acts 17:28). This does not mean that such pagan sources carry the same weight of authority for Paul as do citations from Scripture in sermons to the Jews. Paul, however, can recognize the common ground with the writings of the pagans. He uses them as bridges to his audience without sanctioning the belief system to which they originally belong. In short, we see Paul at his rhetorical best, drawing upon whatever persuasive tools are in his kit in order to engage the Athenian worldview and culture.

Preaching to the Athenian intellectuals.

Initial point of contact. Like their provincial counterparts in Lystra, the sophisticated Athenians have no understanding of Christ, or for that matter, the Scriptures, upon which to build. Taking them on a tour through Hebrew history or talking about Jesus as the promised Jewish Messiah would no doubt have made as little sense to Greek philosophers as to rustic religionists. Instead, the Areopagus address unfolds a classic example of what today we might call "pre-evangelism."

Paul begins his sermon with an introduction that establishes rapport and credibility with his listeners. It was customary for Greek orators to gain the good will of their audience by opening their remarks with a *captatio benevolentiae* ("currying of favor"), as Paul does in verses 22 and 23. Here the point of contact is the religiosity of the Athenians themselves: "I see how extremely religious you are in every way" (Acts 17:22b). Although the term *religious* can at times mean "very superstitious," it is likely that here Paul uses it in a neutral and nonjudgmental sense.[54] Initially, Paul takes a respectful and somewhat conciliatory approach to his hearers' pagan religious life. He further engages his audience by

---

[52]Ibid. For examples of other rhetorical techniques in the speech, see Yeo, *Jerusalem*, p. 173.

[53]Charles, "Engaging the (Neo) Pagan Mind," p. 54.

[54]Dean Zweck is probably correct to see an ironical twist to the statement for Luke's Christian readers ("*Exordium*," p. 102). Paul's distressed reaction to Athenian idolatry in Acts 17:16 makes it clear that his audience's religiosity is not entirely favorable (cf. Acts 25:19).

highlighting a concrete example of their worship that he has observed, an altar to an unknown god (Acts 17:23a). Such altars were probably intended as safety precautions, motivated by the fear of offending and incurring the wrath of an anonymous deity. According to a local legend, during a plague in which no sacrifices had successfully pleased the gods, Epimenides of Crete counseled the Athenians to release a flock of sheep on top of the Areopagus. Wherever the sheep stopped, altars were erected to unnamed gods, and the city was spared.[55] Although we cannot be sure to what extent Paul was aware of this local tradition, it illustrates a common fear of unknown powers among the Greeks. Paul's mention of the altar to the unknown God therefore identifies an underlying religious need of his audience. At the same time, it picks up on the theme of knowledge, which is highly valued by the Greeks. The Athenians' worship of the *unknown* serves as a springboard for Paul to launch into his evangelistic message about the one true God who is *known* because this God has revealed himself. Additionally, the reference to the altar inscription allows Paul to build credibility with his audience by removing the suspicion that he is trying to introduce foreign deities to Athens (cf. Acts 17:18): the God he proclaims is not *entirely* unknown to them.[56]

Paul thus begins where his audience is and builds on as much common territory as possible. Rather than demeaning their belief system or condemning their religiosity, he recognizes there is something genuine in their religious aspirations and felt needs, and he uses them as steppingstones for communicating the gospel.[57] There are definite boundaries, however, to the plot of common ground. When Paul says he is about to proclaim to them what they were worshiping as unknown, he is not simply identifying for them the God they had been honoring all along without realizing it, as some have claimed.[58] The Athenians are hardly "anonymous Christians." The wording of Acts 17:23 makes it clear that they have been worshiping a "what" *(ho),* not a "whom"; an object, not a personal God (cf. Acts 17:29). Paul is keenly aware that their present state of ignorance must be corrected by a *true* knowledge of God through the proclamation of the gospel.

Constructive and corrective engagement. Paul states his basic thesis about the

---

[55]Diogenes Laertius *Lives* 1.110. Cf. Hemer, "Speeches of Acts," pp. 245-46.

[56]Zweck, "*Exordium,*" pp. 102-3.

[57]See Fernando, *Acts,* pp. 479-81.

[58]So, e.g., Raimundon Pannikar, *The Unknown Christ of Hinduism: Towards an Ecumenical Christophany,* rev. ed. (Maryknoll, N.Y.: Orbis, 1981), p. 168. Cf. John Sanders, who insists that "in some clearly imperfect but nonetheless genuine sense, the Athenians did worship the true God. . . . His preaching was a success in that those who were believers became Christians" (*No Other Name: An Investigation into the Destiny of the Unevangelized* [Grand Rapids, Mich.: Eerdmans, 1992], pp. 246-47).

"unknown God" in Acts 17:23, then develops it through various apologetic arguments in verses 24-29.[59] Similar to chapter 14, his message is primarily theocentric. It focuses on God's character, revelation in nature and relationship to humanity. This seems to be Paul's basic approach to people without a biblical heritage. Specifically, he is making the unknown God, the God of the Scriptures, *known* to his audience. Paul, then, does not respond immediately to the Athenians' specific questions about "Jesus and the resurrection." First he must address them at the level of their basic worldview assumptions, creating a necessary context and foundation for proclaiming the risen Christ. In Athens, Christology is grounded in theology.

The extent to which Paul accommodates his message to the philosophical ideas of his pagan audience has sparked considerable debate. Martin Dibelius argues that this is a Hellenistic speech about the true knowledge of God that everyone possesses by nature, a line of thought that is "foreign to the entire New Testament."[60] Viewed from this perspective, Acts 17 becomes an example of "*over*contextualizing," where Luke's Paul sacrifices the Jewish Christian gospel at the altar of Greek philosophy in order to win favor with the Athenians. On the other hand, there are those who think that Paul's categories come solely out of the Old Testament and Judaism, and that he finds no points of agreement whatever with his hearers, only contrasts.[61]

Neither of these views fully grasps Paul's contextual approach. While it is true that the speech's theology is firmly rooted in the Old Testament and Judaism, Paul is able to convey biblical revelation in the language and categories of his Greek listeners—without, as N. T. Wright puts it, traveling "down the slippery slope towards syncretism."[62] Paul takes advantage of similarities between the Jewish Scriptures and Hellenistic thought in order to construct apologetic bridges to his listeners. Greek philosophy becomes "a legitimate conversation partner"[63] in Paul's attempt to contextualize the Jewish Christian gospel for his educated contemporaries.

Paul's strategy involves both constructive and corrective engagement of his hearers' beliefs and worldviews. He finds his primary touch points in the Stoic

---

[59]I borrow the subhead phrase from William Larkin, "The Contribution of the Gospels and Acts to a Biblical Theology of Religions," in *Christianity and the Religions: A Biblical Theology of World Religions*, ed. E. Rommen and H. Netland (Pasadena, Calif.: William Carey, 1995), p. 85.

[60]See Dibelius, *Studies in the Acts*, pp. 26-77, here, p. 71.

[61]E.g., Bahnsen, "Encounter," pp. 33-34; cf. B. Gärtner, who stresses similarities between Paul's Areopagus speech and Hellenistic-Jewish apologetic writings *(Areopagus Speech)*.

[62]N. T. Wright, *What Saint Paul Really Said: Was Paul of Tarsus the Real Founder of Christianity?* (Grand Rapids, Mich.: Eerdmans, 1997), p. 81.

[63]Johnson, *Acts of the Apostles*, p. 319.

teaching that is familiar to his audience. In fact, Bruce Winter argues that Paul may have consciously followed a conventional outline for a Stoic presentation on the nature of divinity.[64] Not surprisingly, Paul paints the true God in universal strokes as the God of the whole world who has graciously revealed himself to all of humankind through creation. Paul expounds this general revelation in three basic proofs, or arguments, which proclaim (1) God's role as maker and maintainer of the cosmos (Acts 17:24-25); (2) God's providential care of all nations (Acts 17:26-27a); and (3) God's immanent relationship to humankind (Acts 17:27b-29). Although these arguments reflect an Old Testament background, all three touch upon familiar Stoic themes and terms as well. Stoics could agree that God is the source of all life (Acts 17:25) and that the world is ruled by divine providence.[65] Other points of contact include the Stoic ideas that the human race is one (Acts 17:26), that God is near (Acts 17:27), and that humankind is in kinship with God (Acts 17:28). Paul buttresses this final point with a direct quotation from the Stoic philosopher/poet Aratus ("one of your poets") originally written in praise to *Zeus*. Paul seems willing to travel a sizeable distance in order to identify with his audience and find common ground. In addition, terms like "world" (Acts 17:24), "his offspring" (Acts 17:28) and "the divine" (Acts 17:29) are characteristic of Hellenistic philosophers, including the Stoics.[66] Paul's appropriation of indigenous language, concepts and literary traditions would surely resonate with the Mars Hill crowd.

Although Paul's discourse has less in common with the Epicureans, Winter notes that they, too, could find several points of agreement: that God is living and can be known, that God is self-sufficient and needs nothing from human beings, and that God does not live in human-built temples.[67] But despite Paul's efforts to be sensitive to the contextual needs of his audience, an identificational approach can only go so far. His deeper purpose is to confront and correct their understanding of God at a fundamental level. He accomplishes this not by overtly attacking pagan doctrines, but rather by positively confessing the God of the Scriptures. Against the Epicurean vision of the gods as material in essence and blissfully detached from humanity, Paul proclaims a God who is actively and intimately involved in the world. This God reveals himself as Creator and

---

[64]Bruce W. Winter, "In Public and in Private: Early Christians and Religious Pluralism," in *One God, One Lord*, ed. Andrew D. Clarke and Bruce W. Winter (Grand Rapids, Mich.: Baker, 1992), pp. 131, 136.

[65]See ibid., pp. 131-35.

[66]E.g., Epictetus *Discourses* 4.7.6 ("world," *kosmos*); Aratus *Phaenomena* 5; cf. Cleanthes *Hymn to Zeus* 4 ("offspring," *genos*); Epictetus *Discourses* 2.20.22 ("the divine," *to theion*).

[67]Winter, "In Public and in Private," pp. 136-37.

Lord of the universe (Acts 17:24), as providential Ruler (Acts 17:26) and Judge (Acts 17:31). He is a God who is near, who desires that all should seek him and enter into a personal relationship of accountability.[68]

Paul likewise challenges the Stoic idea of God as the all-pervasive and impersonal *logos*, the cosmic principle of reason. In its place, he announces a personal God, the Creator who is transcendent and distinct from his creation, the Lord and Judge who stands over the world instead of being fully expressed within it. And in contrast to the Athenians' claim to racial superiority, fostered by the belief that they had sprung from Attic soil, Paul asserts that all human beings descended from the one man, Adam, who was created by God (Acts 17:26). Finally, with a series of three negative statements that lay bare the misconception of confining God to something humans create (whether a temple, an offering, or an image; Acts 17:24, 25, 29), the speech builds a crushing case against Athenian idolatry.[69] Throughout the sermon, Paul uses convergences between Jewish, Christian and Greek ideas in order to challenge pagan polytheism. This indictment is not simply aimed at the general culture of religious pluralism in Athens; it boomerangs on the philosophers as well, since they too tended to adopt a pragmatic policy of accommodating their beliefs and practices with popular religion.[70]

The genius of Paul's context-sensitive preaching in Acts 17 is that he intentionally uses the philosophical language of his audience, not simply to stake out common ground, but in order to transform their worldview. Behind this strategy stands a deep conviction that the pagan world was capable of being redeemed. Familiar terminology is, therefore, co-opted and infused with new meaning in light of biblical revelation and the Christ event. For example, Paul reinterprets the words of the pagan poet (Acts 17:28). We are God's "offspring," not in a Stoic pantheistic sense, but rather in a biblical sense of being created in the image of God. The quotation then becomes the platform for Paul's critique of pagan idolatry: if the living God has made us in his image, we surely cannot create "gods" out of lifeless objects (Acts 17:29). Likewise, in Acts 17:27, "seeking God" is not a philosophical quest through which God could be easily known from examining nature, as the Stoics believed. Rather, Paul perceives the religious seeking of the Greeks as a groping search, a fumbling in the darkness, which

---

[68]See Larkin, "Contribution," p. 86.

[69]On the significance of the negative statements, see Tannehill, *Luke-Acts*, pp. 215-16.

[70]Winter, "In Public and in Private," pp. 139-40. No doubt Paul's rejection of religious pluralism would have been all the more offensive in the context, since, as Eckhard Schnabel observes, "the cultic veneration of deceased emperors was an essential and increasingly important element of Roman culture in the larger cities" (Eckhard J. Schnabel, *Early Christian Mission, Vol. 2: Paul and the Early Church* [Downers Grove, Ill.: InterVarsity Press, 2004], p. 1400).

awaits fulfillment in the gospel of the risen One.[71] With laser-like focus, he moves them on to the defining revelation of God in Christ.

Evangelistic appeal. The summit of the speech comes in Acts 17:30-31. Rhetorically, Paul's conclusion achieves two things. First, it directs his audience to the focal point toward which the entire speech has been building—the announcement that Jesus, whom God has raised from the dead, will be Judge of the world.[72] This fulfills the stated goal of the speech (Acts 17:23b) by making the unknown God known, now in a more specific way in the person of Jesus. Second, it calls to his listeners to take the right course of action. They must repent of their idolatry and be rightly related to God through Christ. To this point in the speech, Paul has taken great care to identify with his audience, highlighting a number of points of agreement. Only now does he bring the Athenians eye to eye with the crux of the gospel, God's saving action in the risen Christ, as he takes up familiar themes that appear in other evangelistic sermons in Acts (e.g., Acts 2:38; 3:19-20; 10:42). God's new and decisive work in Jesus means that the time for Gentile ignorance is over; "all people everywhere" need to repent (Acts 17:30), including enlightened philosophers as well as pagan idolaters. Paul's speech, as Robert Tannehill rightly insists, "is basically a call to repentance, a call for the Greco-Roman world to break decisively with its religious past in response to the one God who now invites all to be part of the renewed world."[73] As a result, the understanding of salvation at work here is not simply a matter of purifying and redirecting the pagans' natural knowledge of God.[74] What they need is not education, but *transformation.*

The themes given in Acts 17:31 as the reason the Athenians need to repent are end-time judgment and the resurrection of Christ, both of which pose a firm challenge to Greek thought. The concept of a divine judgment at the end of history subverts the Stoic picture of the cosmos moving perpetually in cycles. As J. Daryl Charles puts the matter, "The Judeo-Christian understanding of history, which begins and ends with divine fiat, marks a radical discontinuity with the world view of Paul's audience."[75] In addition, the notion of judgment in righteousness implies that Paul's hearers are morally accountable before God. Their "ignorance" (Acts 17:30) is clearly not bliss. They must respond to the knowledge of the Creator they have received with repentance and conversion.[76]

The address concludes with the assurance that God will righteously judge the

---

[71]See Witherington, *Acts of the Apostles,* p. 528.
[72]Hansen, "Preaching and Defense of Paul," p. 317.
[73]Tannehill, *Luke-Acts,* 2:218.
[74]Against Paul Vielhauer, "On the 'Paulinism' of Acts," p. 36.
[75]Charles, "Engaging the (Neo) Pagan Mind," p. 59.
[76]Ibid., pp. 59, 61.

world by "a man" whom he has appointed and raised from the dead (Acts 17:31). Paul waits until the very end of the speech—after he has taken great pains to lay the proper groundwork—to return to the controversial and easily misunderstood subject of "Jesus and the Resurrection" (cf. Acts 17:18). The rhetorical "proof" *(pistis)* that God has revealed himself in the One who will judge the world is Jesus' resurrection from the dead. That Paul's proclamation of the Christian story in Acts 17 highlights the resurrection and not the cross is entirely appropriate in the context, since it is the former that the Athenians questioned him about specifically (Acts 17:18-20). The notion of "resurrection from the dead," which implies a bodily resurrection, was alien to Greek thought. The Greeks generally assumed a dichotomy between spirit and matter (including the body), and for many the body was a prison from which to escape at the time of death. Epicureans, for their part, denied the reality of an afterlife altogether, and Stoics had a vague concept of the future that involved the soul's mystical absorption into the cosmos. To make matters worse, within their worldview, "resurrection" would have meant the disgusting reanimation of a dead corpse.[77] Nevertheless, Paul does not water down the gospel in order to make it taste better to the Greeks. Despite his painstaking efforts to contextualize his message for a Greek audience, the gospel's inevitable offense must stand. Paul's apologetic approach in Athens is to interest, to engage and to confront.

The response. Following the common pattern in Acts, Paul's sermon gets a mixed response (Acts 17:32-34). Both in the marketplace and before the Areopagus, the dissonance between the worldview of the Athenians and that of the gospel is so great that it provokes puzzlement and scorn. Luke underscores (Acts 17:32) that the central truth of a resurrected Savior was the stone over which these Greek intellectuals stumbled. On the other hand, Luke is careful to point out that the speech was not without positive results. Some were prepared to hear more, and others embraced the message and became believers.

Implications for contextual evangelism today. Although some have judged Paul's attempt to adapt his message to the philosophically minded Athenians as a sell out of the simple gospel of "Christ crucified"—a mistake which he later corrected in Corinth (cf. 1 Cor 2:1-2)—there is simply nothing in the text to support this view.[78] All indications are that Luke regards the Areopagus speech, not as a misguided failure, or as some kind of temporary experiment,

---

[77]Porter, *Paul of Acts*, pp. 124, 149; Yeo, *Jerusalem*, p. 186.

[78]Most modern commentators have rejected this once popular interpretation. Paul's statement that he decided to know nothing among the Corinthians but the crucified Christ (1 Cor 2:2) reflects an entirely different background. There Paul is not reacting to his poor results in Athens, but rather drawing a contrast between his gospel and the worldly wisdom of the Corinthians.

but as a model of missionary preaching to educated pagans. Can Paul's approach instruct Christians in the twenty-first century, as well? I believe it can. Acts 17 has been rightly characterized as "a classic of intercultural communication applicable to our own increasingly pluralistic world."[79] Luke's account gives us an instructive example of proclaiming the gospel to people for whom the biblical tradition is unfamiliar. This applies not only to traditional missionary communication to those of different cultural and religious backgrounds but also to the church's witness in today's postmodern contexts, where pluralism and biblical illiteracy are increasingly the norm. The story of the apostle and the Athenians carries some profound implications for the church's mission in our agora settings today.

First, Paul's ministry in Athens is a model of cultural sensitivity and adjustment to his audience. Paul demonstrates an awareness of Athenian culture that gains credibility and earns him the right to be heard.[80] He keenly observes their religious beliefs and shows familiarity with their ancient literary and philosophical traditions. He uses this insight to respectfully engage their worldview, drawing upon indigenous language, images and concepts to communicate the gospel in culturally relevant forms. As N. T. Wright notes, the Areopagus address exemplifies Paul's own principle of "taking every thought captive to obey Christ" (2 Cor 10:5).[81] In Athens, Paul sings the gospel story in a new Achaian key. The church must always sensitively listen to the culture in which it ministers and draw upon that culture's internal resources if it hopes to proclaim the gospel in a credible and convincing way. This is especially crucial when that communication must span significant cultural and worldview barriers, as Paul's did.

At the same time, Paul refuses to syncretize his message or to compromise its truth claims; we must do likewise. Paul engages Athenian culture with the goal of its transformation. There are nonnegotiables to Paul's message that confront the prevailing assumptions of his audience: the sovereign lordship of the Creator and Ruler of the nations (which means there are no other gods), the universal need for repentance (which presupposes sin and guilt), and the reality of a future judgment (which implies moral accountability). Above all, Paul announces the supreme revelation of God in Christ, validated by Jesus' resurrection from the dead (which flies in the face of Greek notions of death and im-

---

[79]Hemer, "Speeches of Acts," p. 255. See also Lars Dahle, "Acts 17:16-34: An Apologetic Model Then and Now?" *TynBul* 53 (2002): 313-16 and Yeo Khiok-khng's stimulating attempt to apply Paul's rhetorical approach in Acts 17 to a contemporary Taoist context in China (*Jerusalem*, pp. 190-97).

[80]See Charles, "Engaging the (Neo) Pagan Mind," p. 60.

[81]Wright, *Saint Paul*, pp. 80-81.

mortality).[82] Ultimately, both the Athenians and their worldview need to be converted. Taking our lead from Paul, we must sensitively and critically engage a pluralistic world, while offering that world an alternative vision of reality. The gospel, in some ways, is countercultural to *every* culture.

Finally, Paul's encounter at Athens gives us a perspective for contextualizing the gospel among people of different religious traditions and spiritualities. Three aspects of Paul's ministry are relevant here. First, Paul's *attitude*. Although distressed about the idolatry he finds in Athens, Paul refuses to flatly condemn the pagans or their religious and philosophical systems. Instead, he recognizes that the Athenians, their past, and even their religious yearnings, have been touched by the grace of God. The speech affirms that all human beings are made in the divine image and that God has created them for the purpose of seeking him. This groping search, prompted by God's seeking grace, may reflect humanity's sincere response to God and desire to know him. Consequently, Paul does not hesitate to look for points of intersection with Christian truth in the Athenians' religion and philosophy. Realizing that God's prevenient grace is at work among people of other faiths and worldviews, drawing them to himself, will keep us from seeing them as adversaries to be "conquered." It will also encourage us to look for where God is already at work; to recognize signs of grace wherever they are found.

Second, Paul's *approach*. In presenting the good news to people who are biblically illiterate, Paul is careful to prepare the ground. He spends time personally dialoguing with the Athenians in the agora. His speech begins by affirming that which is universal and is shared human experience—God's creation and general revelation. Only after laying out a basic biblical worldview about God the Creator of the whole world, the Ruler of nature and history, and the universal Judge, does Paul raise the issue of God's particular revelation in Jesus Christ. Likewise today, the questions of who God is and how God has revealed himself, as well as our shared creaturehood as people made in the image of God may be appropriate starting points for approaching non-Christian people within a pluralistic world.

Third, Paul's *answer*. Nothing in the passage gives any assurance that the Athenians' religious searchings will result in their finding the true God by themselves. In fact, their very religiosity has led them to worship out of fear and to create gods of their own. But the Athenians no longer need to grope blindly in the dark. At the end of the speech, Paul points them to the definitive answer to their fear, religious ignorance and absence of future hope—the gospel of the

---

[82]See Charles, "Engaging the (Neo) Pagan Mind," pp. 60-61.

resurrected Christ. Ultimately, the religious longings of human beings can only be fulfilled in the transforming word of the gospel. Authentic evangelistic contextualization, even at the risk of rejection, must ultimately bring people face to face with Christ crucified and risen.

COMPARING THE THREE SERMONS

A comparison of the three missionary speeches of Paul in Acts reveals the extent to which the proclamation of the gospel is tailored to each audience and context (see the chart at the end of this chapter).[83] Not surprisingly, the greatest differences arise between Paul's sermon to the synagogue crowd in Pisidian Antioch and his mission to pagan Gentiles in Lystra and Athens. Paul's approach to peoples with such dissimilar cultural and religious backgrounds requires quite different starting points. When Paul is speaking to Jews and God-fearers, he can assume from his audience a commitment to monotheism, an acceptance of the authority of Scripture, and an understanding of the biblical story. As a result, he can begin by simply appealing to the sacred history he and his listeners share, and then proceed to reinterpret that story by showing how God's new work in Jesus fulfills the ancient promise to their ancestors. He speaks as a cultural insider to his diaspora compatriots.

When Paul communicates the gospel across cultural and religious barriers, we find a strikingly different pattern. He addresses Gentile pagans in a way that does not require a knowledge of the Scriptures to understand. He still tells the biblical story—it is the only one he knows—but he tells it in fresh ways. Carefully preparing the soil, he begins with universal themes with which his audiences can identify: God's creation and care for the world, God's nearness to humanity, and peoples' aspirations to seek and to know God. Instead of directly citing Scripture, he finds points of contact in their philosophy and literary traditions and in their experience of the Creator's silent witness in nature. He connects with *their* story, which is a different story than that of the synagogue crowd. Whether addressing Jews or Gentiles, Paul begins where his audience is, builds on it, and draws them into a respectful and noncoercive encounter with the gospel.

Although the variations between Paul's sermons to the rustic polytheists in Lystra and the intellectual elite in Athens are not as striking, those groups still require a different hearing of the gospel. For example, in chapter 14, the speech concentrates on themes that would relate well to a crowd of townspeople and

---

[83]Cf. the analysis of the three sermons by Roy Joslin, *Urban Harvest* (Welwyn, U.K.: Evangelical Press, 1982), pp. 160-61. Cited in John R. Davis, "Biblical Precedents for Contextualization," *ATA Journal* 2 (1994): 30-31.

peasants—God's provision of rain, crops and food—the basic needs of life (Acts 14:17). In chapter 17, the speech also appeals to God's activity in nature, but this time in the framework of a more sophisticated argument that finds various touch points with Greek philosophy and poetry. In Lystra, Paul challenges the blatant polytheism of his audience by simply exhorting them to turn from worthless idols to the living God. In Athens, he takes a more rhetorically subtle approach, portraying the gospel as in some sense the fulfillment of their religious searchings (Acts 17:23). In each case, Paul's preaching ministry exudes a dynamic, audience-oriented flexibility. "Luke," concludes Beverly Roberts Gaventa, "describes a mission that is willing and able to speak in a language that can be heard. The message does not exist in one language or in a single cultural system."[84]

At the same time, basic commonalities run through all three sermons. Each of the speeches is structured in order to be rhetorically persuasive, both to the audience in the narrative and to the readers of Acts. All of them herald the saving content of the "good news" (Acts 13:32; 14:15; 17:18), even if that message is communicated with distinct emphases and in different ways. All three present the gospel primarily in the form of what could be called narrative theology. Paul consistently proclaims the grand old story of the true God and his past actions on behalf of people (either Israel or humankind as a whole) in a way that intersects with the story of his audience. In two of the sermons, the narrative reaches its goal and focal point in the story of Jesus, whom God has miraculously raised from the dead. Each address engages and confronts the cherished beliefs and the competing stories of its audience. It calls them to repent of their sins and embrace an entirely new vision of the world. The aim of Paul's targeted preaching is not simply intellectual assent, but salvation, resulting in changed lives. Yet, contextualizing the gospel does not guarantee evangelistic success. In each case a decidedly mixed reaction follows Paul's evangelistic appeal. Luke is far too realistic to portray a uniformly favorable response to the preaching of the Word.

CONCLUSION

In what sense are Paul's missionary sermons patterns for modern Christians to follow? We have seen that Luke probably intends Paul's evangelistic speeches in Acts to provide a model for how the gospel approaches various groups of people, which his readers can appropriate in their own witness to the world. Likewise, the church today has much to learn from these first-century narratives. For us, the value of Paul's preaching in Acts is not in slavishly imitating either

---

[84]Beverly Roberts Gaventa, "'You Will Be My Witnesses': Aspects of Mission in the Acts of the Apostles," *Missiology* 10 (1982): 423.

its specific content or method. To do so would contradict the whole character of evangelistic flexibility that Paul's communication embodies. Rather, these speeches model for us a magnificent balance between, on the one hand, an *identificational* approach that proclaims the gospel in ways the audience can understand and, on the other, a *transformational* approach that resists compromising the gospel's integrity in a pluralistic world. This is a challenge that every preacher or communicator of the Word must face. Whether in a familiar setting or within cultures or contexts significantly different from our own, we must learn to enunciate the good news with that same passion for both local relevance and courageous fidelity to the transforming word of salvation.

Comparison of Paul's Missionary Sermons in Acts

	Acts 13:13-52	Acts 14:8-20	Acts 17:16-34
The Context			
Geographical location	Pisidian Antioch	Lystra	Athens
Audience: cultural and religious background	Diaspora Jews and God-fearing Gentiles	Pagan Gentiles, indigenous Lycaonians	Pagan Greek Gentiles
Audience: education and socioeconomic background	Probably educated, including some people with social status (v. 50)	Unsophisticated townspeople and peasants	Educated, cultural elite, including Stoic and Epicurean philosophers and members of the Areopagus (vv. 18, 22, 34)
Setting	Diaspora synagogue	Public forum	Meeting of the Areopagus council
Preparation for the sermon	Synagogue worship, reading of Scripture (vv. 14-15)	Healing of a lame man (vv. 8-10)	Paul is distressed over idolatry (v. 16); days of dialogue in the synagogue and marketplace (v. 17)
Occasion for the sermon	Synagogue worship, Paul invited to speak	Misinterpretation of the healing by Lystrans, attempt to offer sacrifices to the missionaries (vv. 11-13)	Misunderstanding of Paul's preaching; Paul brought before the ruling council to explain (vv. 18-19)

	Acts 13:13-52	**Acts 14:8-20**	**Acts 17:16-34**
	The Contextualized Message		
How the message is characterized	"Word of salvation" (v. 26; cf. vv. 44, 48, 49); "good news"—that the promise to our fathers has been fulfilled (vv. 32-33)	"Good news" of turning from idols to the one true God (v. 15)	"Good news about Jesus and the resurrection" (v. 18)
Address	"Men, Israelites, and God-fearers" (v. 16); "Brothers" (vv. 26, 38)	"Men, why are you doing this?" (v. 15)	"Men, Athenians" (v. 22)
Initial point of contact	A shared history; the story of God's election and faithfulness toward Israel (vv. 17-22)	A shared humanity (v. 15)	The Athenians' religiosity; worship of the unknown God (vv. 22-23)
Rhetorical style	Deliberative rhetoric; imitation of the Septuagint	Deliberative rhetoric (interrupted before completion)	Deliberative rhetoric; use of rhetorical techniques (insinuation, irony, etc.)
Preparation for the gospel	Recital of Israel's history, God's promise of a Davidic messiah (vv. 17-22)	General revelation, God's gracious witness through nature (vv. 15-17)	General revelation, God made humans to seek him (v. 27)
Description of God	"God of this people Israel" (v. 17); active in Israel's history	"The living God," Creator of all things (v. 15), gracious Provider and Sustainer of human life	"The God who made the world and everything in it" (v. 24); Ruler of nature and history, universal Judge. Not confined to human temples or made by human hands; self-sufficient
God's dealings with people in the past	God's faithfulness throughout Israel's history, focusing on David (vv. 17-22)	God graciously allowed all the nations to follow their own ways (v. 16)	God allotted the (historical) times of all nations' existence (v. 26); God graciously overlooked their former ignorance (v. 30)

	Acts 13:13-52	Acts 14:8-20	Acts 17:16-34
Themes tailored to the audience	Fulfillment of God's messianic promise to the Israel; Scripture testifies to Jesus' resurrection	God's provision of rain, fruitful crops, and food (v. 17)—basic needs of life	Various points of contact with Stoic and Epicurean philosophy; e.g., God's providential care (vv. 26-27), unity of the human race (v. 26), God is near (v. 27), we are his offspring (v. 28)
Cultural resources used	Citations from the Hebrew Scriptures; Jewish methods of interpretation	Local religious background; Zeus seen as god of weather and vegetation (v. 17)	Language and traditions from Greek philosophy quotations from their poets (v. 28)
The kerygma	The story of Jesus' crucifixion at the hand of the Jews, burial, and resurrection as the fulfillment of prophecy (vv. 27-33)	*Theological* kerygma (incomplete?); the story of the Creator God (vv. 15-17)	God has appointed the "man" Jesus, whom he raised from the dead, to judge the whole world (v. 31)
Challenge to the audience's worldview	Call to reshape Israel's interpretation of its history and Scriptures in light of the resurrection; Jews must abandon religious exclusivism	Challenges pagan polytheism and idolatry	Confronts the fundamental worldview of Stoicism, Epicureanism and popular religious pluralism; Greek notions of history and the afterlife
Evangelistic appeal	They must believe in Jesus for forgiveness of sins and justification (vv. 38-39); warning of judgment for following the pattern of Israel's unbelief (vv. 40-41)	Turn from idols to the living God (v. 15)	All people must repent, on account of God's coming judgment through the resurrected Jesus (vv. 30-31)
The Response			
Response to Paul's preaching	Initial openness to the grace of God, then rejection and persecution from the Jews; the gospel is offered to the Gentiles, who receive it (vv. 42-52)	Some "disciples" (v. 20), but most Gentiles continue in their misunderstanding (v. 18). Jews from neighboring towns win over the crowds, stone Paul and leave him for dead (vv. 19-20)	Some scoff at the resurrection, others want to hear more, some believe (vv. 32-33)

3. PAUL'S LETTERS

Doing Theology in Context

*From Jerusalem and as far around as Illyricum I have
fully proclaimed the good news of Christ.*

ROM 15:19

If Acts tells us stories of contextualizing the gospel in evangelistic settings,
then Paul's letters are unrivaled in offering examples of doing contextual theology for diverse Christian communities.[1] To be sure, Paul's epistles have not always been read in this way. Earlier generations of scholars tended to think of
Paul chiefly as a dogmatic theologian, the originator of a grand system of belief.
If, however, there is agreement on anything about Paul today, it is that the man
from Tarsus was not a systematic theologian, at least not in the modern sense
of someone who wrote treatments of different theological topics. Recent interpreters of Paul have viewed him as a pastoral theologian, a task theologian, a
missionary theologian, a hermeneutical theologian, and the like. These different
portraits all support the understanding that Paul is a *contextual theologian*—his
letters, case studies in the contextualizing of the gospel in ways that intersect
the concrete lives and cultures of his hearers. My concern in this chapter, then,

---

[1]Regarding which letters should be included in Paul's authentic writings, see the brief but in-
cisive discussion of Luke Timothy Johnson (*The Writings of the New Testament: An Interpretation*, rev. ed. [Minneapolis: Fortress, 1999], pp. 271-73). Johnson questions the methodolog-
ical assumptions behind the widespread view that Colossians, Ephesians, 2 Thessalonians, and
the Pastoral Letters (1-2 Timothy, Titus) are non-Pauline. I agree with Johnson that, in particular, criteria which evaluate the style and content of these disputed letters against some perceived norm of consistency in the seven unquestioned epistles tend to be highly subjective.
Such measures of which letters could or could not have been written by Paul fail to reckon
with the great variety in style and theme within *all* of Paul's letters, including the seven normally taken to be Pauline. As a matter of practical method, I will base my conclusions about
Paul's theological contextualization primarily on the generally accepted letters and Colossians,
which is considered to be authentic by many interpreters of Paul. I believe that these findings,
however, can find support in the entire Pauline corpus.

is not simply in the *what*—the theological content we find in Paul's letters—but especially in *how* they model for us the theological process of drawing out the implications of the gospel for new circumstances.

What motivated Paul's audience-sensitive approach to doing theology? More than bald pragmatism. Surely it was propelled by his sense of mission as one compelled by Christ's love (2 Cor 5:14). Paul was first and foremost a missionary-pastor who planted churches and wrote pastoral communications in order to build up his converts in their newfound faith in the crucified and risen Jesus. As one recent interpreter explains, "Paul's theological activity in writing letters to churches was an extension of his missionary activity, which he understood as an apostolic commission."[2] The dichotomy between evangelism and theology that is present in much contemporary theological education would have seemed quite strange to Paul. He did not consider his missionary work to be confined to his initial preaching of the gospel. Paul was profoundly concerned that believers would persevere in the faith and that his apostolic work would not be in vain (1 Thess 3:1-5; cf. 1 Cor 15:2). As a result, his Spirit-guided theological reflection focused on those issues that would sustain his missionary purpose for the churches. Paul's theology was a living, breathing theology of the mission field, capable of being enfleshed in a whole variety of human contexts.

The Center of It All

Before we take a closer look at Paul's missional approach to doing theology, there is a prior question that needs to be addressed: what is Paul actually contextualizing in his letters? If Paul's theology takes many shapes due to his mission concerns and the specific needs he encounters, what keeps it from becoming a "chameleon-theology," where the content itself is constantly morphing to fit the circumstances? Is there a nonnegotiable message that remains stable throughout all of its multiple manifestations? That Paul can speak of the "truth of the gospel" (Gal 2:14) in a setting in which he believes the gospel is under threat implies that he understands something normative, something *trans*contextual about the faith he conveys. Here is where the sea starts to get rough, however. Uncovering the constant center of Paul's thought has proved to be one of the most complicated and intriguing problems in all Pauline interpretation. Older scholarship searched for some controlling *idea* or core doctrine that could capture the true essence of Paul's theology—like "justification by faith" or "participation in Christ" or "salva-

---

[2]Mark A. Seifrid, *Justification by Faith: The Origin and Development of a Central Pauline Theme* (Leiden: E. J. Brill, 1992), p. 261-62. See also Thomas R. Schreiner, *Paul, Apostle of God's Glory in Christ: A Pauline Theology* (Downers Grove, Ill.: InterVarsity Press, 2001), pp. 38-39, 60-68.

tion."[3] But that approach fails to capture the contextual nature of Paul's theological reflection. Paul is more than a talking head—someone who simply thinks in terms of theological concepts that are of greater or lesser importance. If we abstract Paul's theology from its specific mission context and from its connection to the life experience of God's people—including Paul's own—we risk cutting the vital artery between Paul the theologian and Paul the missionary-pastor.

More recently, interpreters of Paul have begun to think about the normative element in Paul's thought in more dynamic ways—as a foundational narrative or story about God and Christ that underlies Paul's concrete theological arguments in his letters,[4] or as an abiding coherence within Paul's thought that is constantly interacting with the contingent circumstances of the mission field.[5] Such approaches point us in the right direction, not least because they recognize that to understand Paul's contextual way of doing theology, we cannot shortchange either the stable dimension of his thought or the specificity in which it comes to speech and engages Christians in the Roman Empire. "Coherence" and "contingency," as J. Christiaan Beker notably puts it, are inseparable.[6]

THE GOSPEL AS THE HEART OF PAUL'S THOUGHT

If there is something abiding in Paul's thought that transcends its many contextual expressions, can we be more specific about its actual content? What

---

[3]On the various attempts to identify the center of Paul's thought, see Joseph Plevnik, "The Center of Pauline Theology," *CBQ* 51 (1989): 461-78, esp. pp. 469-76; Dean Flemming, "Essence and Adaption: Contextualization and the Heart of Paul's Gospel" (Ph.D. diss., University of Aberdeen, 1987), pp. 52-84.

[4]The recognition of a narrative substructure to Paul's thought has gained considerable momentum in recent years. See, e.g., Richard B. Hays, *The Faith of Jesus Christ: An Investigation of the Narrative Substructure of Galatians 3:1-4:11*, rev. ed. (Grand Rapids, Mich.: Eerdmans, 2002); Richard B. Hays, "Crucified with Christ," in *Pauline Theology, Volume 1: Thessalonians, Philippians, Galatians, Philemon*, ed. J. M. Bassler (Minneapolis: Fortress, 1991), pp. 227-46; N. T. Wright, *The New Testament and the People of God* (Minneapolis: Fortress, 1992), esp. pp. 403-9; Ben Witherington III, *Paul's Narrative Thought World: The Tapestry of Tragedy and Triumph* (Louisville: Westminster John Knox, 1994); Norman R. Peterson, *Rediscovering Paul: Philemon and the Sociology of Paul's Narrative World* (Philadelphia: Fortress, 1985); Michael J. Gorman, *Cruciformity: Paul's Narrative Spirituality of the Cross* (Grand Rapids, Mich.: Eerdmans, 2001). See also the important analysis and critique of the narrative approach to Paul in B. W. Longenecker, ed., *Narrative Dynamics in Paul: A Critical Assessment* (Louisville: Westminster John Knox, 2002).

[5]The "coherence-contingency" approach was articulated by J. Christiaan Beker. See *Paul the Apostle: The Triumph of God in Life and Thought* (Philadelphia: Fortress, 1980); idem, "Recasting Pauline Theology: The Coherence-Contingency-Scheme as Interpretive Method," in *Pauline Theology, Volume 1: Thessalonians, Philippians, Galatians, Philemon*, ed. J. M. Bassler (Minneapolis: Fortress, 1991), pp. 15-24.

[6]See Beker, *Paul the Apostle*.

makes the task so challenging is that we have no access to Paul's thinking (or that of any other New Testament writer) in a "noncontextualized" form. Much of what he writes is intended to mold moral behavior and change thoughts and attitudes in order to establish young Christians in their faith. Rather than simply stating his core beliefs themselves, Paul's letters largely consist of specific applications and interpretations of those beliefs within the course of his pastoral communication. Furthermore, his theological convictions are often embedded in rhetorical arguments that are designed to persuade a particular audience. To put it plainly, when Paul writes letters, *all* of his theology is contextual theology.

We need to look beyond Paul's targeted theological statements alone to determine the heart of his thought. Paul's primary calling as a missionary-pastor was not to formulate a theology but to proclaim the one gospel in order to "save some" (1 Cor 9:22) and to shape the lives of his converts in light of that gospel (e.g., Phil 1:27). Paul leaves little doubt that "the gospel" was the singular passion of his life and apostolic ministry (1 Cor 9:23). Paul J. Achtemeier is quite right that "what one confronts in Paul's letters are reflections on how the gospel intersects with the world in which his readers live and how they are to think and act in that world."[7] I would argue, then, that if we want to discover the coherent element of Paul's thought, the matrix that gives shape to everything else, we must find it in "the gospel."[8]

If the gospel is at the heart of Paul's message, then what did he mean by it? By its very nature, *gospel (euangelion)* is a rather imprecise term. It has roots in the Old Testament announcement of the good news of God's coming salvation (e.g., Is 40:9; 52:7=Rom 10:15), and its Christian usage may go back to both Jesus himself (Mt 11:5; Lk 4:16-21) and the church before Paul (e.g., Acts 10:36-38).[9] But *gospel* was also used to refer to the good news about the birth, accession, or victory of a king or emperor in the Greco-Roman world. As a result, the term *gospel* would no doubt have triggered political and religious associations related to the rule of the imperial "savior" in the minds of Paul's Gentile read-

---

[7]Paul J. Achtemeier, "Finding the Way to Paul's Theology: A Response to J. Christiaan Beker and J. Paul Sampley," in *Pauline Theology, Volume 1: Thessalonians, Philippians, Galatians, Philemon*, ed. J. M. Bassler (Minneapolis: Fortress, 1991), p. 25.

[8]The noun *gospel (euangelion)* appears sixty times in the Pauline corpus, forty-eight of them in the so-called undisputed letters. In addition, Paul often substitutes nearly equivalent terms such as "proclamation" *(kērygma)*, or "word" *(logos*, e.g., "word of the cross," 1 Cor 1:18; "word of Christ," Col 3:16; "word of reconciliation," 2 Cor 5:19; "word of truth, the gospel," Col 1:5; Eph 1:13).

[9]See Peter Stuhlmacher, "The Pauline Gospel," in *The Gospel and the Gospels*, ed. Peter Stuhlmacher (Grand Rapids, Mich.: Eerdmans, 1991), pp. 156-66.

ers.[10] Not unusually, Paul seizes a term that has both a Jewish and a pagan past, and gives it a distinctively Christian meaning.

First and foremost, the gospel stands for the powerful proclamation of Christ so that people will believe in him and receive salvation (Rom 1:16; 1 Cor 9:16-18; 1 Thess 1:5; Col 1:5-6). This gospel proclamation, however, is not limited to what Paul preached in missionary settings to non-Christian audiences. When Paul expresses his eager desire "to proclaim the gospel *(euangelisasthai)* to *you* also who are in Rome" (Rom 1:15), he is speaking not to unbelievers, but to Roman *Christians.* Peter T. O'Brien crafts a compelling case that Paul uses "gospel" language to include the full exposition of the gospel that is designed to edify believers and ground them in the faith.[11]

Although the gospel is "the power of God for salvation" (Rom 1:16), it also has a coherent and stable content. This is clear from passages such as Galatians 1:6-9 and 2:5, 14 ("the truth of the gospel"), where "the gospel" stands for the nonnegotiable message Paul preaches and to which he expects obedience. The gospel is normative for both Christian belief and behavior (e.g., Rom 1:1-4; 10:16; 1 Cor 15:1-2; 2 Cor 9:13; 11:4; Phil 1:27; Col 1:5; Eph 1:13; 2 Thess 1:8; 1 Tim 1:11). Yet, in his letters the substance of Paul's gospel is generally assumed rather than spelled out. Paul only discusses those aspects of it that are relevant to the situation at hand. He could grant that his converts had already received instruction in the basic understanding of the faith, and in general Paul does not need to repeat this unless there is some misunderstanding of the gospel that needs to be corrected. Just as a sermon may not continually retell the story of the text on which it is based, but presuppose it throughout, so Paul's letters constantly assume and interpret the gospel story of God's redeeming action in Christ.[12]

When Paul does offer foundational theological statements or quote Christian confessions that are obviously close to the heart of his gospel (e.g., 1 Cor 15:1-5; Rom 1:3-4; Gal 4:4-7; 1 Thess 1:9-10), he always does so in the course of a contextual argument. In no case does he try to give the gospel a comprehensive or definitive expression. For example, Romans 1:3-4 defines the gospel christologically ("the gospel concerning his Son"), while later in the same chapter Paul articulates the gospel in terms of its saving purpose ("the power of God for salvation," 1:16-17). Even a basic affirmation like 1 Corinthians 15:3-5, which Paul

---

[10]See e.g., R. A. Horsley, "Rhetoric and Empire—and 1 Corinthians," in *Paul and Politics: Ekklesia, Israel, Imperium, Interpretation: Essays in Honor of Krister Stendahl,* ed. R. A. Horsley (Harrisburg, Penn.: Trinity Press International, 2000), pp. 91-92.

[11]Peter T. O'Brien, *Gospel and Mission in the Writings of Paul: An Exegetical and Theological Analysis* (Grand Rapids, Mich.: Baker, 1993), pp. 61-65.

[12]Hays, *Faith of Jesus Christ,* p. 227.

explicitly states is the gospel he preached to the Corinthians (1 Cor 15:1) is a minimal definition, chosen for its relevance to Paul's immediate argument concerning the Corinthians' misunderstanding of the future resurrection.

The gospel, then, has a coherent content, but determining its scope and limits is far from easy. Nonetheless, Paul's theological reflections on the gospel and his occasional restatements of it point to a number of features that seem to be indispensable to its meaning.[13]

1. The focus. Like the sun in our solar system, Paul's gospel has a radiating center—the Christ event. In simplest terms, the content of the message Paul preaches is "Christ" (Rom 16:25; 1 Cor 1:24; 15:12; Phil 1:15-18) or the "Son of God" (Rom 1:9; 2 Cor 1:19; Gal 1:16) or "Jesus Christ as Lord" (2 Cor 4:5), all of which can stand as shorthand terms for his gospel. It is above all the "gospel of Christ" (Rom 15:19; 2 Cor 9:13; Gal 1:7; Phil 1:27), a message about Jesus, God's beloved Son. Yet, it is also *God's* gospel (Rom 1:1; 15:16; 2 Cor 11:7; 1 Thess 2:2, 8). Paul's interest is not in Christology as such, but rather in the "good news" of God's loving and saving intervention in Jesus Christ "for us" (Rom 8:31-32). As Paul puts it to the Corinthians, "We proclaim *Christ crucified*" (1 Cor 1:23). This redemptive work focuses on Christ's death and resurrection as the saving events (1 Cor 15:3-4; Rom 4:24-25; 2 Cor 4:14; 1 Thess 4:14), but also includes his present lordship (2 Cor 4:5; Phil 2:9-11) and future return (1 Thess 1:10; 4:13—5:11; 1 Cor 1:7-8; 15:23; Phil 3:20-21). Furthermore, God's intervention in history in Christ is a political as well as a religious event. When Paul announces that Jesus, the cursed and crucified criminal, is Lord (Rom 10:9; 1 Cor 12:3; Phil 2:11), he rules out giving ultimate allegiance to all other so-called gods and lords, including the emperor himself.[14]

Consequently, Paul's whole understanding of the Christian faith and life fixes its gaze, not on some timeless theological truth or "supracultural" principle, but on a contingent, historical happening: the event of the crucifixion and resurrection of Jesus of Nazareth. Indeed, it is the scandalous particularity of the gospel that perhaps makes it so compelling for Paul, as well as for us today. Yet, it is also an event that transcends the particularities of history and culture, because through the crucified and risen Messiah, God has revealed his saving power and love to all of humankind. All of Paul's theological reflection, then, centers on

---

[13]After writing this section, I became aware that Gordon Fee has structured Paul's *theology* under categories that overlap with my own. See *God's Empowering Presence* (Peabody, Mass.: Hendrickson, 1994), p. 12. Of course, all such attempts at categorizing no doubt reflect more of our own efforts to understand Paul's thought than how he himself would have described it.

[14]See Michael J. Gorman, *Apostle of the Crucified Lord: A Theological Introduction to Paul and His Letters* (Grand Rapids, Mich.: Eerdmans, 2004), pp, 102, 107-9.

the one gospel of what God has done in and through Jesus Christ.

2. The framework. Is there a framework or underlying structure that holds this gospel together? Although there have been a number of suggestions—apocalyptic, eschatology, salvation history, the covenant, the Jewish Scriptures, among them—I believe that when we recognize that Paul's gospel has a *narrative* framework, we best capture the heart of his thought.

Although Paul nowhere narrates the story in detail, his writings provide considerable evidence that he conceived of God's saving work within the framework of an overarching metanarrative of God's dealings with humankind, a story that spans from creation to the consummation of history. Ben Witherington is no doubt close to the mark when he claims that this comprehensive story of redemption is actually made up of several tightly interwoven stories:[15] first, the story of God, the Maker, Sustainer and Redeemer of the universe (Rom 8:18-25; 1 Cor 8:6); second, the story of humankind, which includes the story of Adam, the head of the old humanity, and his sin (Rom 5:12-21); and third, the story of Israel, within which we find the stories of Abraham and his faith (Romans 4, Galatians 3) and of Moses and the law (Galatians, Romans, 2 Corinthians 3). The sacred narrative comes to a focal point in the defining story of Christ, who through his death and resurrection delivers humanity from Adam's sin and the law and who is the head of the church, the community of those who are redeemed through faith in him. Yet it is an unfinished story awaiting a sequel, because the church's hope lies in the future, in the return of Christ (1 Thess 4—5) and God's final triumph (1 Cor 15). Within this grand narrative of redemption, the story of Christians, including Paul's own story, is intertwined with the story of Christ; they initially participate in his death and resurrection (Romans 6), they pattern themselves after him and are transformed into his image through the power of the Spirit in the present (Phil 2:5-11; 3:10), and they will be fully conformed to the likeness of Christ in the future when they are raised from the dead. The "master story" of Christ crucified and risen is a paradigmatic narrative for those who are "in" him. Paul reads all other subplots, whether the earlier narratives of God and Israel, or the stories of Paul and his churches that are still being written, through the lens of the story of Christ.[16]

This storied structure overlaps with the familiar notion of salvation history, which especially highlights the *continuity* of Paul's gospel with God's past deal-

---

[15]Ben Witherington III, *The Paul Quest: The Renewed Search for the Jew of Tarsus* (Downers Grove, Ill.: InterVarsity Press, 1998), pp. 237-53.

[16]David G. Horrell, "Paul's Narratives or Narrative Substructure? The Significance of 'Paul's Story,' " in *Narrative Dynamics in Paul: A Critical Assessment*, ed. B. W. Longenecker (Louisville: Westminster John Knox, 2002), p. 168.

ings with Israel and the gospel's fulfillment of Scripture (Rom 1:1; 3:21; Gal 3:8). God's eternal plan of salvation has now been revealed in the fullness of time when "God sent his Son . . . to redeem those who were under the law" (Gal 4:4-5), fulfilling the ancient promise to Abraham (Gal 3:6-9, 15-18). Given this emphasis on continuity in the sacred story, we might be tempted to frame Paul's gospel like successive acts in a well-plotted drama—a story that passes from creation through God's dealings with Israel to the return of Christ, with the climax coming in the events of the cross and the resurrection.

Paul's gospel, however, also has what is commonly called an *apocalyptic* dimension, which highlights a surprising *discontinuity* between the story of Christ and what has gone before. For Paul, Jesus' death and resurrection bring an end to the world as it was and usher in the age to come. The "new creation" has dawned (Gal 6:14-15; 2 Cor 5:17). Through faith in Christ and in union with him, people can transfer from the old aeon of Adam, sin, death, and the law to the new time of salvation. Believers are called to embody the new creation through the gift and empowering of the Spirit. Still, the new era has not yet fully replaced the old. The church lives in the "eschatological twilight zone" at the turn of the ages, enduring the weaknesses and sufferings of the old order even as it awaits the full and final redemption of creation and the future resurrection (Rom 8:18-27).

How then do we reconcile the continuity and the discontinuity of Paul's gospel, the salvation-historical perspective and the apocalyptic one? Rather than pitting one against the other, it is better to hold them in tension. Both are integral to the narrative framework of Paul's thought.[17] The Pauline metanarrative is not a single unbroken line, but rather a multilayered story in which the decisive story of the Christ event and its saving meaning is superimposed, so to speak, upon the story of God's gracious dealings with Israel. It is the fulfillment of the former story, but at the same time it is something revolutionary which mandates a rereading of Scripture as a witness to the gospel (e.g., Gal 3:8; 1 Cor 10:11). The sacred story is comprehensive enough to embrace both of these elements. This grand "theodrama," which views the entire history of God's saving activity for humanity from the perspective of its eschatological climax in Christ, is the underlying framework of Paul's thought. Like the girders of a great building, it is seldom in plain view, but without it, Paul's gospel could not stand.

   3. Formative elements. In addition to a narrative framework, we can dis-

---

[17]See James D. G. Dunn, "How New Was Paul's Gospel? The Problem of Continuity and Discontinuity," in *Gospel in Paul: Studies on Corinthians, Galatians and Romans for Richard N. Longenecker,* ed. L. A. Jervis and P. Richardson (Sheffield: Sheffield Academic Press, 1994), pp. 382-88.

cover three foundational elements or building blocks that helped to shape the gospel message that Paul came to believe and preach: the Scriptures, the early church tradition, and Paul's own experience of Christ on the Damascus road. Each of these participates in the coherence of his thought.

The Jewish Scriptures. Paul's gospel is rooted in the symbolic world of Pharisaic Judaism and of the Scriptures of Israel. It is true that Paul's experience of Christ dramatically altered his perspective on his Jewish past (see Phil 3:4-11) and that this new standpoint influences how he reads Scripture. All the same, the grand story that provides the framework of Paul's thought is anchored in the Old Testament. Paul claims that the gospel he preached was "promised beforehand through his prophets in the holy scriptures" (Rom 1:1-2; cf. 3:21; 1 Cor 15:3-4). Paul can even make the bold assertion that "the scripture . . . declared the gospel beforehand to Abraham" (Gal 3:8). It is to Israel's Scripture that he continually appeals to explain and interpret God's present redeeming actions in Christ (e.g., Rom 10:5-21; Gal 3:16); his letters are teeming with quotations from it and allusions to it. The Scriptures are an indispensable building block for Paul's understanding of the gospel, as well as a continual reference point for his reflections *on* the gospel in the course of his letters.

The Christian tradition. In a striking statement, Paul reminds the Corinthians that the gospel he preached to them was precisely what he had "received" in the form of tradition from other Christians and "handed on" to his converts (1 Cor 15:1-3; cf. 15:11). On occasion, Paul can call upon creed-like statements he inherited from the church and shared with the other apostles to express the heart of the gospel (Rom 1:3-4; 1 Cor 15:3b-5; 1 Thess 1:9-10). This gospel tradition, not surprisingly, centers on the narrative of the death and resurrection of Christ and its saving significance for people. Moreover, Paul's theological and ethical arguments are peppered with allusions to what are probably early confessional statements that help to express the central truths of the gospel.[18] In addition, Paul occasionally vocalizes the gospel story with what appear to be early Christian hymns that were used in the worship of the Greek-speaking community (Phil 2:6-11; Col 1:15-20). The content of Paul's gospel is built not only on the foundation of the Scriptures but also the faith affirmations he held in common with those who had believed and preached the word before him.

In addition to the apostolic confessions, Paul was also aware of the story and

---

[18]These may include (1) "sending" statements—"God sent his Son" (Gal 4:4; Rom 8:3); (2) "giving up" statements—"he was given up (or gave himself up) for us" (e.g., Rom 4:25; 8:32; Gal 2:20; Eph 5:2); (3) resurrection statements—"God raised him from the dead" (e.g., Rom 4:24-25; 10:9; 1 Thess 1:10); and (4) confessional statements—"Jesus is Lord" (e.g., Rom. 10:9; 1 Cor. 12:3). Scholars still debate whether some of these are traditional or not.

teachings of Jesus that he received from the church. The degree to which Paul knew and was influenced by the Jesus tradition has long been a matter of debate. A number of recent studies, however, have put together a persuasive case that the Jesus traditions were more significant for Paul's understanding of the gospel than is often recognized.[19] While explicit references to sayings of Jesus are relatively sparse (e.g., 1 Cor 7:10; 9:14; 11:23-26; cf. 1 Thess 4:15), allusions and echoes of Jesus' life and teaching occur throughout Paul's letters with enough frequency that "this material [cannot] be dismissed as inconsequential in quantity or quality."[20]

Yet, did these remembrances of Jesus help to shape Paul's *gospel?* This is not the place for an in-depth exploration of this complex question. Nevertheless, there are enough points of contact between the gospel Paul announces and the Jesus tradition that we must be open to the possibility. It is likely, for example, that Paul's use of the term *gospel* itself reflects the church's collective memory of Jesus as the one "who was sent to bring good news to the poor" (Is 61:1; Lk 4:17-19; Acts 10:38).[21] Further, we find connections with Jesus in Paul's Christology (e.g., his allusion to Jesus' use of *Abba* in relation to Christ's sonship [Rom 8:15; Gal 4:4; cf. Mk 14:36]), his understanding of salvation (e.g., the parallels between Jesus' kingdom parables [Mt 20:1-16; Lk 18:14] and Paul's notion of justification by grace through faith), and his eschatological teaching (1 Thess 4:15-17; 5:1-7; cf. 2 Thess 2:1-12).[22] Indeed, there is a real theological continuity between Jesus' preaching of the kingdom and Paul's notion of God's eschatological rule that is both manifested in the present through the Spirit and "inherited" in the future (e.g., Rom 14:17; Col 1:13; 1 Cor 6:9; 15:50; Gal 5:21). If we only occasionally hear the specific language of Jesus' kingdom preaching in Paul's letters, it is probably, as Seyoon Kim proposes, because Paul has recontextualized that language in light of Jesus' death and resurrection and the new situation of his largely Gentile churches.[23]

Although allusions to the Jesus tradition are not always clear cut and differ-

---

[19]See especially David Wenham, *Paul: Follower of Jesus or Founder of Christianity?* (Grand Rapids, Mich.: Eerdmans, 1995); Seyoon Kim, "Jesus, Sayings of," in *Dictionary of Paul and His Letters*, ed. Gerald F. Hawthorne, Ralph P. Martin and Daniel G. Reid (Downers Grove, Ill.: InterVarsity Press, 1993), pp. 474-92; Seyoon Kim, *Paul and the New Perspective: Second Thoughts on the Origin of Paul's Gospel* (Grand Rapids, Mich.: Eerdmans, 2002), esp. pp. 259-92.

[20]Witherington, *Paul's Narrative Thought World,* p. 153. Seyoon Kim cites over twenty-five instances where he finds "certain or probable" references to the Jesus tradition, as well as over forty "possible echoes" of it in Paul ("Jesus, Sayings of," pp. 475-82, 490).

[21]Stuhlmacher, "Pauline Gospel," pp. 162-63.

[22]See Kim, "Jesus, Sayings of," pp. 475-77; Wenham, *Paul: Follower of Jesus,* pp. 305-19.

[23]Kim, *Paul and the New Perspective,* pp. 275-81.

ences remain, the cumulative evidence suggests that Paul was not only significantly aware of the story and sayings of the historical Jesus, but that the church's memories of Jesus significantly informed his understanding of the Christian message. Paul would surely have been perplexed by the wedge often driven between his gospel and the message of Jesus by modern interpreters. If our conclusion is right, it links Paul's gospel through the tradition not only with the other apostles but, even more importantly, with Jesus himself (1 Cor 11:23). Furthermore, it suggests that, for Paul, the gospel story embraces not just Jesus' death, resurrection and return, but his earthly life and ministry as well.[24]

This all points to the conclusion that there is strong continuity between early Christian tradition and Paul's coherent gospel. This does not mean that the traditions themselves constitute Paul's gospel—he is still their interpreter throughout. Nevertheless, the church's creeds, confessions and hymns, as well as its memories of Jesus' life and teaching, served to shape his understanding of the message he taught and preached.

The Damascus road revelation. Most importantly of all, Paul's perception of what is constant and nonnegotiable about the Christian message is grounded in his own conversion and call. In Galatians, he defends his gospel and his apostleship against the charges of his critics with the claim that he received this gospel, not from any human source, but "by a revelation of Jesus Christ" (Gal 1:11-12). It is this revelational origin of the gospel that allows Paul to distinguish its content from the alternative interpretation of his Judaizing opponents (Gal 1:6-7) and to defend the "truth of the gospel" against those who would distort it (Gal 2:5; cf. 2:11-14).

When Paul speaks of receiving a "revelation of Jesus Christ" and of God revealing his Son in him (Gal 1:16), he is recalling his vision of the risen and exalted Christ on the Damascus road. Much of the heart of Paul's gospel and theology is a natural outworking of his reflection on this initial encounter with the Lord.[25] In the first place, Paul's conversion meant a "Copernican revolution" for his evaluation of Jesus (cf. 2 Cor 5:16). Instead of seeing a messianic pretender

---

[24]This raises the question of why Paul did not refer to Jesus material more openly and more often. No doubt Paul could assume knowledge and acceptance of shared traditions about the life and teachings of Jesus among his converts, much of which he likely passed on himself in his missionary preaching. Paul had no reason to restate stories and sayings of Jesus to Christians who were already familiar with them, since the contingent needs of his hearers did not require it.

[25]See, e.g., Seyoon Kim, *The Origin of Paul's Gospel* (Grand Rapids, Mich.: Eerdmans, 1982); Kim, *Paul and the New Perspective*; and the various essays in R. N. Longenecker, ed., *The Road from Damascus: The Impact of Paul's Conversion on His Life, Thought, and Ministry* (Grand Rapids, Mich.: Eerdmans, 1997).

who was cursed by God because of his crucifixion on a Roman cross (Deut 21:22; Gal 3:13), Paul recognized that Jesus was alive and had been vindicated by God. Paul's experience of Christ convinced him that Jesus was indeed Israel's Messiah, the Christ (cf. Rom 9:5), God's long-awaited agent of salvation. The connection of the cross to messianic identity would have been revolutionary for Paul, but later the notion of "Christ crucified" became a cornerstone of his message (1 Cor 1:23; 2:2). Furthermore, Jesus appeared to Paul as the living, risen and exalted Lord (1 Cor 9:1; cf. Acts 9:5), in whom the very glory and image of God were manifested (2 Cor 4:4-6). Paul also recalls that Christ was revealed to, or perhaps *in,* him on the Damascus road as the Son of God (Gal 1:16). This name comes to represent for Paul the one who stands in closest relationship to God and who has been lovingly sent by the Father as bearer of his promised salvation (Rom 1:2-4; 8:3, 32; 2 Cor 1:18-20; Gal 4:5-7).[26] In short, Paul's world-flipping encounter on the Damascus road provided him with the basic narrative structure of his gospel—that the crucified Jesus, whom God the Father has sent into the world as Messiah, is risen and has been exalted as Lord (cf. Acts 9:20-22, 28).

Second, Paul sees the purpose of his Damascus revelation to be his call and commission as apostle to the Gentiles (Gal 1:16; cf. 1 Cor 9:1; 15:8-9; Acts 9:15). This sense of missionary calling became foundational to Paul's life and thought; apart from it, the gospel he preached makes little sense.

Third, Paul's own experience of God's transforming love and grace undoubtedly played a critical role in the formation of these insights. Raymond Brown rightly perceives that it is Paul's personal encounter with God's overwhelming love in Christ that enabled love to be a primary motivation for Paul's mission to the Gentiles and a hallmark of his message:

> In the [Damascus] revelation Paul . . . discovered a love that went beyond his previous imagination. He felt "taken over" by Christ Jesus (Phil 3:12). With awe Paul exclaims: "The Son of God loved me and gave himself for me" (Gal 2:20). . . . This love became the driving factor of Paul's life when he came to understand how encompassing it was: "The love of Christ impels us once we come to the conviction that one died for all" (2 Cor 5:14).[27]

---

[26]Martin Hengel observes that although Paul speaks of Jesus as God's Son less often than as Christ or Lord, the title frequently appears in highly theological statements that describe the heart of his gospel (e.g., Rom 1:3-4, 9; 8:3, 32; 2 Cor 1:18-20; Gal 1:15-16; 4:4-5; Col 1:13-14; 1 Thess 1:10). See *The Son of God: The Origin of Christology and the History of Jewish-Hellenistic Religion* (Philadelphia: Fortress, 1976), pp. 8-14.

[27]Raymond E. Brown, *An Introduction to the New Testament* (New York: Doubleday, 1997), p. 449.

For Paul, cruciform love, God's love manifested in the cross of Christ, was central to his gospel and provided the pattern that shaped his own life and that of the Christian community (Rom 5:5, 8; 8:35-39; 1 Cor 13; 2 Cor 5:14; Eph 5:2; Col 3:12; 2 Thess 2:16).[28] Moreover, Paul repeatedly testifies that it was by God's surprising grace that he, a violent persecutor of the church of God, was justified and called to be an apostle on the Damascus road (Gal 1:13-15; cf. 1 Cor 15:9-10; 1 Tim 1:12-16). James Dunn underscores the connection between Paul's initial experience of God's grace and his gospel:

> It was the experience of seeing Jesus risen and exalted on the road to Damascus which stopped him dead in his tracks and turned his whole life into a new channel. . . . To put it another way, it was his own experience of grace which made 'grace' a central and distinctive feature of his gospel—grace as not merely a way of understanding God as generous and forgiving, but grace as the experience of that unmerited and free acceptance embracing him, transforming him, enriching him, commissioning him.[29]

Fourth, such a world-altering encounter no doubt contributed to Paul's radically new evaluation of the Jewish law and righteousness. This former Pharisee who had singularly devoted his life to upholding the law came to the stunning awareness that all his zeal for the Torah had only led him to the heinous sin of opposing God's will as expressed in his own Son.[30] God's vindication of the law-cursed Jesus signaled that Christ, not the law, must become the new fulcrum on which all things turn, the one valid passport for entering the people of God. In Philippians 3:4-11, Paul testifies that his whole system of values underwent a 180-degree turnaround as a result of his conversion. He has judged his former confidence in his Jewish identity and the law to be rubbish; now his life is shaped wholly by his experiential knowledge of Christ and the sharing in his death and resurrection (Phil 3:10). Righteousness by the law and righteousness by faith in Christ have become mutually exclusive alternatives (Phil 3:9). The core values and experience that Paul sets forth in this passage are surely close to the heart of his gospel.[31]

Other elements of Paul's gospel have been linked to his Damascus road encounter, including his "already/not yet" eschatological perspective, the Spirit, new creation, reconciliation, and transformation into God's image, which we do

---

[28]On the centrality of love for Paul's life and thought, see esp. Gorman, *Cruciformity*, pp. 155-267.

[29]James D. G. Dunn, *Unity and Diversity in the New Testament: An Inquiry into the Character of Earliest Christianity,* 2nd ed. (London: SCM Press, 1990), p. 190.

[30]Kim, *Origin*, pp. 280-81.

[31]Paul J. Achtemeier, "Finding the Way," p. 30.

not have time to explore. Suffice it to say that if we want to know what is formative and constant about Paul's thought, we cannot bypass the Damascus road. This has important implications for our study. It means that Paul's theology does not arise out of his ad hoc responses to specific problems or circumstances in the course of his missionary work. It is grounded in a much deeper well: his "revelation of Christ" and his conversion on the road to Damascus. Paul's contextual theological activity in his letters flows out of a coherent and enduring gospel that is anchored, not only in Scripture and Christian tradition, but in his own transforming experience of a divine revelation and calling.[32] Paul's *gospel* of Christ and his *experience* of Christ go hand in glove.

These three foundational building blocks for Paul's gospel—Scripture, tradition, and revelation—reinforce our conclusions about the narrative framework for his understanding of the Christian message. The Old Testament places the gospel in the context of Israel's story, Christian tradition proclaims the story of Jesus, and in Paul's Damascus encounter the story of the risen and universal Lord becomes his own story. It is also true that the elements of Scripture, the church's collective memories, and Christian experience continue to serve as primary resources and reference points for Christian communities as they ponder the meaning of the gospel for their life circumstances today.

Fundamental convictions. Paul's reflection on Scripture, tradition and revelation, as well as his own and other Christians' experience of Christ and the Spirit, generated a coherent set of theological convictions, a tapestry of interrelated elements that participate in the heart of Paul's thought. These include the various images and beliefs that are vital to Paul's understanding of the gospel (e.g., being "in Christ," dying and rising with Christ, faith, righteousness, election, sanctification, reconciliation, the body of Christ, the gift of the Spirit, the end-time resurrection). For Paul, the gospel not only reveals what God has done in Christ, but also how what God has done is good news *for us*. Because Paul normally articulates these crucial convictions in response to the specific concerns of his communities, it would be difficult to come up with any comprehensive list.[33] It is therefore better to think of what is abiding in Paul's thought as an organic "heart," not a fixed "core." As J. C. Beker reminds us, the lines be-

---

[32]We have no way of knowing, of course, how many of the implications of his gospel and its theological outworkings Paul grasped at or around the time of his Damascus revelation. He would surely have reflected extensively on that experience in light of the Christian proclamation and Scripture, as well as the contextual demands of his own missionary work. Refining and development would inevitably follow.

[33]For one recent attempt to summarize twelve "fundamental convictions" of Paul, see Gorman, *Apostle of the Crucified Lord*, pp. 131-44.

tween coherence and contingency cannot be firmly drawn.[34]

On the one hand, these abiding symbols and beliefs are anchored in the defining story of God's saving activity in Jesus, and they interpret its meaning for Paul and his readers. On the other hand, these motifs and images facilitate the dynamic interaction between Paul's gospel and the missional contexts in which he does theology. Paul can articulate specific elements of these convictions when he argues theologically, enabling him to contextualize the gospel in a way that is appropriate for each situation. This is why, for instance, the notion of righteousness looms large in Paul's exposition of the meaning of the Christ story for God's people in Galatians, but in 2 Corinthians he turns to the symbol of reconciliation (2 Cor 5:18-20). In one sense, these big ideas lie behind Paul's concrete theological arguments in his letters. They are sometimes assumed rather than stated.[35] Yet our only access to Paul's coherent gospel is through what he actually *says* when these core convictions come to living expression in language. As a result, when Paul talks about sanctification or the Lord's Supper or Christ's victory over the powers in the course of his letters, these "surface-level" communications are not just relativized pastoral arguments that are peripheral to his thought. Rather, they interpret the normative meaning of the Christ event for his readers in a way that each community of faith needs to hear it. Paul's theological reflection flows out of a deep spring, the abiding gospel, whose various elements cohere together and support one another.

The fruit. Since the gospel is in the first place the proclamation of good news that has the power to transform people by the Spirit (Rom 1:16; 1 Thess 1:5), it always has a goal. Paul does not think of the gospel as a body of propositional truth or as simply a matter of correct belief. Its purpose is to elicit saving faith and to create a redeemed community that is being reshaped in the image of the Lord (2 Cor 3:18). This perspective springs naturally out of Paul's own experience when his life was turned upside down through his encounter with the risen Lord on the road to Damascus. The gospel story has meaning for Paul and his communities because it is their story as well. Through the Spirit, God's saving action in the death and resurrection of Christ becomes an experienced reality (Gal 4:4-7). The gospel transforms the world of Paul and his readers; it brings about a new creation, which demands a new way of living.

The gospel's ability to redeem and renew governs all of Paul's interactions with the churches under his care. He announces both at the beginning and the

---

[34]Beker, "Recasting Pauline Theology," p. 19.

[35]J. C. Beker speaks of the "subtextual location of 'the coherent' " in Paul's thought (*The Triumph of God: The Essence of Paul's Thought* [Minneapolis: Fortress, 1990], p. 125).

end of Romans that the goal of his gospel and apostleship is to bring about the "obedience of faith" among the Gentiles (Rom 1:5; 16:26). This means not only their conversion, but also a *life* of obedience that flows from their faith in Jesus Christ. Paul ministers the gospel in order that the Gentiles might be an offering that is acceptable and "sanctified by the Holy Spirit" (Rom 15:16). His fervent desire is that Christ might be formed in them (Gal 4:19) and that he might present them mature in Christ (Col 1:28). Conformity to Christ means living out the cross-shaped life of self-giving love (Gal 2:20; Phil 2:1-5). Richard B. Hays states it well: "There is no meaningful distinction between theology and ethics in Paul's thought, because Paul's theology is fundamentally an account of God's work of transforming his people into the image of Christ."[36]

Ultimately, the goal of the gospel is to lead Christians to experience God's re-forming work in a full and final sense (Rom 8:29-30; 1 Cor 15:49; Phil 3:21). Thus, the gospel's redeeming, transforming character is part of what is nonnegotiable in Paul's thought. Whenever Paul reflects theologically on the gospel in his letters it is with this end in view.

CONTEXTUALIZING THE GOSPEL IN PAUL'S LETTERS

The matrix of Paul's thought, then, is the gospel, God's good news about Christ, which Paul announced and which defined his life and missionary work. Paul's letters, however, are not the gospel as such; rather, they bear witness to the gospel and reflect upon it in light of the contingent circumstances of the mission field.[37] When Paul writes to the Thessalonians or the Corinthians, he *interprets* the gospel and draws out its ramifications in ways that are relevant and meaningful to his audience. As Beker describes it, this interpretation embodies the movement of the incarnation, "so that the eternal Word of the gospel is able to become ever anew a word on target for the people to whom the gospel is addressed."[38] Put differently, the gospel serves as a kind of lens through which Paul views the various pastoral, moral and doctrinal issues that he confronts in the course of his ministry as an apostle.[39]

But if Paul's letters are not *the* gospel, neither are they deposits for prepackaged doctrines. Paul's "theology" never stands on its own, independent of his

---

[36]Richard B. Hays, *The Moral Vision of the New Testament: Community, Cross, New Creation: A Contemporary Introduction to New Testament Ethics* (San Francisco: Harper Collins, 1996), p. 46.

[37]See Joel B. Green, "Scripture and Theology: Uniting the Two So Long Divided," in *Between Two Horizons: Spanning New Testament Studies and Systematic Theology*, ed. Joel B. Green and M. Turner (Grand Rapids, Mich.: Eerdmans, 2000), p. 40.

[38]Beker, *Triumph of God*, p. x.

[39]Charles B. Cousar, *The Letters of Paul* (Nashville: Abingdon, 1996), p. 92.

communications to real people within their real lives.[40] Instead, we encounter a theology in action—Paul's theological reflections on the gospel in light of the different pastoral situations he faced. Paul's writings are less a collection of doctrinal studies than a series of theological conversations between the apostle and his diverse audiences within their life circumstances.

One consequence of this is that none of Paul's individual letters, not even Romans, can serve as a ready-made summary of his *theology*. I therefore take issue with James D. G. Dunn's proposal that Romans—seen as a letter that is relatively unaffected by contingent circumstances and written by a mature Paul to a church he did not found—sets out "in complete terms the theology of the gospel."[41] In the first place, Romans is by no means a comprehensive statement of Paul's gospel or his theology. Issues that receive extensive treatment in Romans (e.g., the role and future of Israel in God's plan in chapters 9—11) do not get much attention elsewhere in Paul, while other key elements of Paul's thought (the Lord's Supper, the resurrection, the second coming) are largely missing from his longest letter. If we take Romans as the defining expression of Paul's theology, we might conclude that such matters were not after all very important to the man from Tarsus. Second, even if we recognize the relatively well-ordered and reflective character of Romans, Paul's theological arguments there are no less contextual than in his other letters. Although Paul's specific combination of reasons for writing Romans has been a matter of lively debate, there is a wide consensus that the letter is hardly a context-neutral rehearsing of the gospel.[42] Like all of Paul's letters, Paul's exposition of the gospel in Romans is linked to concrete historical and missiological circumstances. To ignore this orientation is to misunderstand the entire thrust of the letter.

It is therefore Paul's interactive *theologizing*—theology as a verb—that is of particular interest for our understanding of New Testament patterns of contextualization. Paul's ongoing theological and ethical reflection on the gospel enables the eternal word to be fleshed out in particular forms of language and

---

[40]This does not mean that the effort to discover a Pauline theology, in the sense of a synthesis of the results of Paul's theological activity in his letters, is misguided. This is a valuable and necessary task. However, it goes beyond the scope of this study, which focuses on Paul's *theologizing*—his method of theological reflection on the gospel. For instructive efforts to articulate a Pauline theology, see James D. G. Dunn, *The Theology of Paul the Apostle* (Grand Rapids, Mich.: Eerdmans, 1998) and Schreiner, *Paul: Apostle of God's Glory*.

[41]James D. G. Dunn, "Romans," in *Dictionary of Paul and His Letters*, ed. Gerald F. Hawthorne et al. (Downers Grove, Ill.: InterVarsity Press, 1993), p. 840; see also idem, *Theology of Paul*, p. 25. Dunn generally recognizes the contextual nature of Paul's theologizing but thinks that Romans is a relative exception to this pattern.

[42]For an excellent introduction to this discussion, see *The Romans Debate*, ed. K. P. Donfried, rev. ed. (Peabody, Mass.: Hendrickson, 1991).

modes of persuasion, and applied to a whole range of pastoral problems. Whether the issue at hand happens to be eating food offered to idols, the basis of Gentiles' acceptance into the people of God, the collection of an offering, or confusion over the Lord's return, Paul believes that the gospel story of what God has done in Christ speaks a specific and transforming word. Although Paul's stated evangelistic principle of being "all things to all people" (1 Cor 9:19-23) relates in the first place to his apostolic conduct, it would hardly be surprising if his way of doing theology shows that he can adapt to various human needs and circumstances as well.

Contextualizing theological language. Paul's ability to contextualize the heart of the gospel becomes clear in his flexible use of theological language. This creative adaptability takes several forms:

1. *Paul's letters display a richness and variety of vocabulary.* This diversity allows him to interpret the Christ event for multiple contexts. For example, Paul has no single, stock way of expressing the meaning of the death of Christ, which we have seen lies at the heart of his gospel. Instead, he draws upon a kaleidoscope of metaphors and symbols to communicate its meaning: reconciliation (2 Cor 5:18-20; Rom 5:10-11; Eph 2:16; Col 1:20-22), sacrifice (Rom 3:25; 8:3, 1 Cor 5:7), representation (1 Cor 15:14-15), redemption (Rom 3:24; 1 Cor 7:21-23; Gal 4:5), righteousness (Rom 3:21-26; 5:9; 2 Cor 5:21), curse (Gal 3:13), self-giving/emptying (Rom 8:32; Gal 1:4; 2:20; Phil 2:7), victory over the powers (Col 2:15), paradoxical power and wisdom (1 Cor 1:24-25; 2 Cor 13:4), to name only some.[43] This plurality of images not only testifies to the breadth of meaning of the death of Christ for Paul, but it also enables him to tailor his interpretation of that atoning death to fit the needs and circumstances of his audience. Thus, Paul turns to the metaphor of redemption in Galatians, where he must counter opponents who are trying to enslave Gentile believers by adding to faith in Christ the yoke of circumcision and law obedience. Redemption language not only evokes Israel's ransom from bondage in Egypt, giving it a grounding in Scripture and tradition; it would also have been familiar to Gentile readers from the secular practice of buying back slaves in the Greco-Roman world. The power of the metaphor for the Galatians is obvious. Christ's death means ransom and release for those who have been slaves under the law and its curse (Gal 3:13; 4:1-5). Yet, Paul is free to adapt the image for his purposes as well. I. Howard Marshall keenly observes that "[a] preacher would surely have delighted . . . to con-

---

[43]These varied metaphors frequently overlap in their usage and meaning, as pregnant passages such as Romans 3:21-26, Galatians 3:10-14, 2 Corinthians 5:14—6:2 and Colossians 2:11-15 demonstrate.

trast the price paid by the slave in the secular world with the free gift of God in Christ."[44]

The diversity of metaphors and symbols expressing the meaning of Christ's death is perhaps excelled only when Paul comes to describe the believer's experience of the new life in Christ. Paul's salvation language draws upon a wealth of images from both Scripture and secular culture, including those from everyday life experience (inheritance, putting on or off clothes, salvation/rescue, putting on armor), commerce (redemption, "seal" of ownership), agriculture (grafting, first fruits), the customs and practices of society (justification, reconciliation, freedom/liberation, citizenship), religious practice (sanctification, washing, cleansing, anointing), major life events (birth, adoption, marriage, death and life), as well as various others (new creation, transformation, union with Christ).[45] Rather than consistently talking about the meaning of salvation in Christ in a few standard terms, he deploys whatever language will bring out the particular dimension of salvation a given church needs to hear. This observation has implications for our efforts to describe the experience of God's saving work to contemporary people. It surely ought to caution us against exalting any single metaphor or theme—whether "justification by faith" or being "born again" or "Spirit baptism"—to a dominant position. If we follow Paul's lead, we will recognize both the richness of language available to us to describe the church's multidimensional experience of salvation and the variety of situations to which that language must be applied.

2. *Paul can use the same image in multiple ways or with different emphases as the context demands.* Thus the symbol of the cross—a scandalous stigma in the first century world—becomes an emblem of God's "foolishness" that contradicts worldly wisdom and boasting in 1 Corinthians (1 Cor 1:18-2:8), a means of liberation from the law and its curse in Galatians (Gal 2:19-20; 3:13; cf. 6:14), a model for Christian humility and obedience in Philippians (Phil 2:5-8), a wrecking bar to demolish the wall separating Jew and Gentile in Ephesians (Eph 2:14-16), or a venue of victory over the hostile powers in Colossians (Col 2:15). Paul likewise uses the metaphor of reconciliation, which interprets Christ's death in terms of bringing together two parties at enmity, for a variety of pastoral purposes. Reconciliation language allows him to target the restoring of his ruptured relationship with Christians at Corinth, as he appeals for them to "be reconciled

---

[44]I. Howard Marshall, "The Development of the Concept of Redemption in the New Testament," in *Jesus the Savior: Studies in New Testament Theology* (Downers Grove, Ill.: InterVarsity Press, 1990), p. 242.

[45]See Dunn, *Theology of Paul*, pp. 328-33.

to God" (2 Cor 5:20), and later affirms his openness and affection for his Corinthian "children" (2 Cor 6:11-13).[46] In Romans 5 such language is closely linked to the theme of justification that is so prominent in chapters 1—4, helping to describe the blessings of justification for the believer (Rom 5:1; 9-10). Colossians 1:20 speaks of God's reconciling himself to the entire cosmos, while in Ephesians 2:16 the focus is the reconciliation of Jews and Gentiles both to God and to one another. Each of these applications of the image fits the particular context that Paul addresses.

3. *The contextual dimension of Paul's theologizing helps to explain why one symbol or theme appears predominantly in certain letters and not in others.* This sheds light on the uneven distribution of the language of justification or righteousness by faith, which has been a flashpoint for the debate about what is the kernel of Paul's theology. Paul's interpreters have tended either to heap too much weight on the notion—making it the controlling principle of Paul's entire gospel, as in the case of Luther and much of Reformed Protestant theology—or too little, viewing it merely as a byproduct of Paul's battles with Jewish Christian opponents. In reality, Paul unpacks the theme theologically in just three letters—Galatians, Romans, and, to a lesser extent, Philippians. In each case, there is a question over the significance of the Jewish law and the conditions for Gentiles' membership in the people of God. Since justification is only one among many metaphors for expressing what God has done for believers through Christ, when those issues are not at stake, Paul generally turns to other ways of articulating the gospel. In 1 and 2 Corinthians, for example, justification language appears as just one of a number of images (see especially 1 Cor 1:30; 6:11; 2 Cor 5:21). It is an indispensable, but hardly a comprehensive or controlling, image of God's saving work.[47] The Reformers discovered a contextualized message for their own time in the doctrine of justification by faith, but in their reading of Paul, it seems they overplayed their hand.

Paul is free to draw upon whatever theological themes or images enable the gospel to be incarnated into the life worlds of the communities to which he writes. Beker uses the analogy of a military field command center that is able to dispatch the required material according to the needs of the various field outposts.[48] For the Romans and the Galatians, the theme of "righteousness" is crucial to Paul's exposition of the gospel. In 1 Corinthians he turns to other sym-

[46]Joel B. Green, "Death of Christ," in *Dictionary of Paul and His Letters*, ed. Gerald F. Hawthorne, Ralph P. Martin and Daniel G. Reid (Downers Grove, Ill.: InterVarsity Press, 1993), p. 204.

[47]See the studies of Seifrid, *Justification*, and Colin G. Kruse, *Paul, the Law, and Justification* (Peabody, Mass.: Hendrickson, 1996) for detailed support for this conclusion.

[48]Beker, *Triumph of God*, p. 131.

bols, such as the cross, wisdom, and the body of Christ. He develops the motif of the weakness of the cross in 2 Corinthians in response to the triumphalist theology of his rivals. Contextual needs in Thessalonica prompt him to focus on the second coming and sanctification. In Philippians Paul draws upon political language that befits a Roman colony (Phil 1:27; 3:20) and exhorts Christians over and over to have joy in the face of suffering. In Ephesians and Colossians the language of power and of reconciliation come into focus. In each case, Paul crafts a targeted response to the concrete issues he faces. The result is a distinctive exposition of the abiding gospel that addresses the needs of the audience.

In this regard, the Pastoral Letters of 1-2 Timothy and Titus present us with a particularly intriguing case. It has long been recognized that the vocabulary and theological emphases of these letters differ from the rest of the Pauline writings in significant ways. There is little doubt that the gospel is still at the very heart of the Pastorals (1 Tim 1:11-16; 2 Tim 1:9-10; 2:8; Tit 2:11-14; 3:4-7). But we hear that gospel voiced in new language—language that has more of a "Greek" accent than what we encounter elsewhere in Paul. The Christian message is described as a "deposit" to be guarded and as "sound" or "healthy" teaching. Both God and Jesus are repeatedly called "Savior" (cf. Phil 3:20; Eph 5:23), a title that was commonly used of various Hellenistic deities and the divine emperor. The striking terminology of "epiphany" is applied not only to Jesus' second coming (1 Tim 6:14; 2 Tim 4:1, 8; Tit 2:13, instead of *parousia*), but to his *first* advent, as well (2 Tim 1:10; Tit 2:11; 3:4). The Christian life is depicted in the language of popular Greco-Roman moral teaching, above all as "godliness" *(eusebeia)*, which never shows up in Paul's other letters. All of this vocabulary seems to be drawn from a Hellenistic or Hellenistic Jewish well.

How do we account for this new "translation" of the gospel? Many assume that the Pastoral Letters were written at some point after Paul's death in order to speak to an altered set of circumstances and needs in the church. In the words of one recent commentator, these letters "represent a creative attempt to re-express Pauline theology in new ways for a new situation and to use fresh terminology to do so."[49] I agree with the basic thrust of this statement. Yet, if what we have seen about Paul's versatile use of theological language and emphases is true elsewhere in his writings, could not this "creative theologian" of the Pastoral Epistles have been Paul himself? The issues that surround the answer to this question are many and complex. Nevertheless, I would suggest that a number of factors at least make this a plausible option.

---

[49]I. Howard Marshall, *A Critical and Exegetical Commentary on the Pastoral Epistles* (Edinburgh: T & T Clark, 1999), p. 78.

Terms like "sound teaching" and "godliness" that are singular to the Pastoral Letters are probably borrowed from the false teaching that the author is trying to counteract. Paul commonly seizes language from his opponents—such as "wisdom" in 1 Corinthians or "weakness" in 2 Corinthians—and redefines it in light of the gospel, and that seems to be the case in the Pastorals as well. Likewise, the frequency of the term "Savior" could be connected to Paul's desire to correct the false teachers' limited and exclusive view of salvation. Salvation is for "all" people, and God in Christ is Savior of all (1 Tim 2:3-4). The need to confront theological error results in fresh ways of articulating the gospel. Furthermore, Philip Towner makes the credible suggestion that Paul's heavy use of Hellenistic ethical terms was related to his concern that the behavior of Christians in Ephesus and Crete was bringing disrepute to the gospel (1 Tim 3:7; 6:1; Tit 2:10; 3:2) and thereby damaging the church's mission in the world. Consequently, "for him to encourage the churches to live a life that would measure up even to the pagans' critical estimate was sound evangelistic technique" (cf. Phil 4:8).[50]

I would suggest, then, that even in the Pastoral Letters, the distinctive theological language we encounter probably has more to do with form of expression than with widely different content. Nothing is incompatible with Paul's gospel as it is found elsewhere. If we allow for factors such as (1) the possibility of some development in Paul's thought; (2) the role of a secretary in perhaps helping to shape the letters' style and theological language; and (3) the recognition that Paul's addressees are close associates with at least moderately Hellenistic backgrounds, it seems quite conceivable that the Pastoral Epistles offer a prime example of Paul's creative contextualizing of the gospel for new circumstances.[51] In any case, whether one accepts Paul as the author of these letters or not, the contextualization principle holds true. The Pastoral Epistles give striking testimony that new challenges and situations require a fresh minting of the gospel into language that speaks to the context.

4. *Paul's flexibility enabled him to appropriate traditional language and images and recontextualize them under the guidance of the Spirit.* This occurs regularly with Jewish cultic terms. Paul can, for example, appeal to the religious

---

[50]Philip H. Towner, *1-2 Timothy and Titus* (Downers Grove, Ill.: InterVarsity Press, 1994), p. 30.

[51]When we talk about "new circumstances," we cannot forget that each of the three Pastoral Letters has a somewhat different concern and situation that Paul is addressing. Consequently, his responses to those concerns vary from letter to letter, as well. See the recent defenses of the position that Paul himself is the creative theological force behind the Pastoral Letters by William W. Mounce, *The Pastoral Letters* (Nashville: Thomas Nelson, 2000), pp. xlvi-cxxxv, and Luke Timothy Johnson, *The First and Second Letters to Timothy: A New Translation with Introduction and Commentary* (New York: Doubleday, 2001), pp. 55-99.

language of sanctification taken from the Old Testament purity code that particularly focused on separation from ceremonial defilements. He transposes that language, consistently applying it to the ethical character and behavior that was the responsibility of every believer (Rom 6:19; 12:1; 1 Thess 3:13; 4:3-7; 5:23; Eph 1:4; 5:26-27). Again, Paul draws upon the notion of "sacrifice" from Israel's worship (language that would also have carried religious significance for first century Gentile audiences) and uses it to speak of the atoning death of Christ (Rom 3:25; 5:21; 8:3; 1 Cor 5:7; Eph 5:2), as well as the moral response of God's people (Rom 12:1). Surprisingly, he can even adopt "circumcision"—in spite of his robust opposition to requiring Gentile converts to be circumcised—as a metaphor for the death of Christ and its saving significance for believers (Col 2:11). True circumcision is no longer an outward Jewish rite, but an inward work of God and a matter of the heart (Rom 2:28-29; Phil 3:3).

Paul's recontextualizing of traditional language is not limited to cultic terms. Consider the "kingdom of God" language that was so characteristic of Jewish thought and Jesus' own teaching. Paul can invoke it to help resolve divisions over food and drink in Rome (Rom 14:17), or to warn the boastful Corinthians that they may face the "rod" of apostolic discipline (1 Cor 4:20-21). In Galatians the traditional theme of inheriting God's kingdom is combined with Paul's crucifixion language (Gal 5:21, 24).

We find in Paul's letters, then, a delightful creativity in the use of theological language and imagery that allows him to express the meaning of the gospel with both flexibility and precision. Contemporary interpreters of the gospel would do well not only to learn from the end product of Paul's theologizing but also from his way of doing the theological task. Paul's pattern of creatively engaging his world and using familiar images to draw out the implications of the gospel speaks to the ongoing challenge of reimagining our expression of the gospel for our changing social and cultural worlds.

Does the content change with the context? Paul has been compared to a jazz musician, someone who "improvises" theologically as he innovatively adapts his message and methods to changing circumstances.[52] There is much truth in this. Paul was certainly capable of exercising theological imagination when the Corinthians were confused about marriage obligations (1 Corinthians 7) or the Galatians were in danger of surrendering their Christian freedom. But this also raises an important question. How fluid *was* Paul's thought? Was it being generated ad hoc as he wrote his letters, so that his coherent message was

---

[52]Mark Strom, *Reframing Paul: Conversations in Grace and Community* (Downers Grove, Ill.: InterVarsity Press, 2000), p. 182.

continually being shaped and altered by the new circumstances he addressed? Did Paul's core assumptions about the gospel itself only progressively emerge in the process of his contextual theologizing, as many interpreters of Paul now hold?[53] If this were true, it would fly in the face of much of what we have seen earlier in this chapter regarding the stable and transcontextual dimension of Paul's thought.

I would argue that the contexts Paul addresses do not create or reinvent his understanding of the coherent gospel. Leander Keck's conclusion about the theology of Romans can be applied to Paul's letters as a whole: "Romans ticks because Paul did not allow his immediate situation to govern completely what he had to say, but allowed the inner logic of his gospel to assert itself."[54] Ultimately, it is *the gospel* that directs the process of Paul's theological reflection, not the audience or the issues he addresses. Paul's thought transcends the shifting tides of contingent circumstances precisely because it is anchored in the abiding truth of the gospel. This means that Paul's contextualization does not take place at the level of the basic content of the gospel itself, which focuses on God's saving activity in Christ. It happens when Paul articulates, interprets and applies that gospel in light of real human needs. The context, in turn, helps to determine what aspects of his thought Paul appropriates in a given situation and how they come to expression in language that will be persuasive to his hearers.

Second Corinthians might illustrate this process. Behind the letter is a bubbling conflict, as a group of opponents try to discredit Paul's ministry among the Corinthians, apparently claiming that his personal weakness, lack of status and suffering nullify his gospel and apostleship. In response, Paul re-presents the gospel for the Corinthians through a series of striking paradoxes—suffering/comfort (2 Cor 1:3-11; cf. 4:8-9; 6:3-10), death/life (2 Cor 4:10-12; 5:14-15), slavery/triumph (2 Cor 2:14), poverty/wealth (2 Cor 4:7; 6:10; 8:9)—which above all come to expression in chapters 10—13 in the notion of "power in weakness." Engaging in a daring act of countercultural rhetoric, he actually parades his own social humiliations and physical sufferings as evidence of his experience of God's power that is manifested in weakness (2 Cor 11:16—12:10). "If I am accused of *weakness*," Paul seems to say, "I plead 'guilty as charged.'" Paul

---

[53]This is the position of, e.g., Strom (*Reframing Paul*, pp. 182-83) and of Paul W. Meyer, who claims that the "coherence" of Pauline theology is itself the product of historical process, i.e., it is itself "contingent" ("Pauline Theology: A Proposal for a Pause in Its Pursuit," in *Pauline Theology, Vol. 4: Looking Back, Pressing On*, ed. E. E. Johnson and D. M. Hay [Atlanta: Scholars, 1997], p. 150).

[54]Leander Keck, "What Makes Romans Tick?" in *Pauline Theology, Volume 3: Romans*, ed. D. M. Hay and E. E. Johnson (Minneapolis: Fortress, 1995), p. 29.

grounds this reframing of the gospel in the Christ event itself. The one who was "crucified out of weakness" yet who "lives by the power of God" (2 Cor 13:4) becomes the paradigm for Paul's own apostleship and for the Corinthians' discipleship. The gospel story, articulated in this way, turns the triumphalism and self-promotion of the apostle's opponents upside down. The humiliation and weakness of the messenger, far from subverting Paul's apostleship, enables him to embody the heart of the gospel itself—the "weakness" of the crucified One. Both the message he proclaims and the manner of life he lives bear the marks of the cross.

Other theological images emerge in the course of Paul's conversation with the Corinthians, such as "reconciliation" in chapter 5. This metaphor, as well, is tailored to a context of conflict and mistrust. On the basis of God's already accomplished reconciling work in Christ (2 Cor 5:18-19), Paul entreats the disaffected and alienated Corinthians to "be reconciled to God" (2 Cor 5:20). His appeal encompasses their need to be restored to both the gospel and to God's messenger. The life situation in Corinth thus draws out particular theological images and ideas that are a part of Paul's understanding of the gospel, enabling this letter to become a well-aimed message for his audience. At the same time, because Paul's theological reflection has its mooring in the story of Christ crucified, he is able to reframe the gospel in fresh terms without syncretizing or distorting the message. This is the fundamental difference between Paul and his ancient critics, who have taken their cues from Greco-Roman cultural models of self-praise and the flaunting of personal power rather than the pattern of Jesus' self-giving love. The rivals' triumphalistic interpretation of the Christian story is outside the pale of the gospel (2 Cor 11:4) precisely because it tries to bypass the cross on the road to resurrection power and glory.

If, then, Paul reappropriates the story of Christ in light of the realities in Corinth, is the relationship between gospel and context simply a one-way street running from Paul's core convictions to his readers' life circumstances? This seems unlikely. No doubt the adversarial environment in Corinth led him into a deeper reflection on the meaning of the Christ event as the "gospel of weakness," but one that was in continuity with his understanding of the story of Christ from the beginning. Likewise, the distinctively Pauline image of reconciliation, which is probably rooted in Paul's experience of God's reconciling him, a former persecutor, on the Damascus road,[55] no doubt came into sharper focus as a metaphor of God's saving work in Christ as a result of Paul's clash with the Corinthians. This dynamic interplay between substance and situation

---

[55]See Kim, *Paul and the New Perspective*, pp. 214-38.

is characteristic of Paul's way of doing theology. On the one hand, the eternal purpose of God in Christ is contextualized in light of ever-new horizons and challenges. On the other, that very theological task brings fresh insight into the meaning of the gospel for the interpreter. We can therefore be open to the possibility of growth in Paul's theological understanding under the guidance of the Spirit (cf. 1 Cor 13:8-12; Phil 3:12-16) without having to assume that Paul continually changed his mind about his fundamental convictions as he faced new problems.[56] This also suggests that our efforts to sing the gospel in new keys today may well gift us with a fresh and fuller grasp of the old, old story of God in Christ.

Inconsistency or flexibility? Context-sensitive theology will no doubt produce some logical and rhetorical tensions. Paul's interpreters have long struggled with how to handle the diversity of his thought, particularly when individual theological arguments, either in different writings or within a single letter, seem to be in conflict. Rather than viewing those statements as purely situational arguments that lack internal consistency,[57] we need to see them as part of a larger coherent whole, one that transcends a strict side-by-side comparison of individual assertions. At times, the particular needs of the communities to which Paul writes may require him to emphasize different aspects of an issue, which might stand in logical tension with one another.

How Paul deals with the similar themes of justification and the law in both Galatians and Romans presents a case in point. In Galatia, Paul responds to a state of emergency in which Gentile believers have come under the influence of "Judaizing" intruders. In light of Paul's concern to rescue the Galatians from impending disaster, it is hardly surprising that we do not find a carefully balanced and comprehensive theological discourse.[58] Instead, Paul launches into a highly polemical and passionate defense of the gospel, enlisting a whole series

---

[56]I agree with Eduard Lohse that theories of major development in Paul's thought do not best account for theological differences among his letters. See E. Lohse, "Changes of Thought in Pauline Theology? Some Reflections on Paul's Ethical Teaching in the Context of His Theology," in *Theology and Ethics in Paul and His Interpreters: Essays in Honor of Victor Paul Furnish*, ed. E. H. Lovering Jr. and J. L. Sumney (Nashville: Abingdon, 1996), pp. 146-60. Lohse points out that Paul was already a mature Christian teacher, with many years behind him to reflect on the gospel, by the time he wrote his first letter. Any major development in Paul's thought likely took place prior to that time, not after.

[57]Finnish scholar Heikki Räisänen has in particular claimed that circumstances such as the conflict with Jewish Christian opponents in Galatia forced Paul into offering a whole array of circumstantial and self-contradictory arguments as he tried to explain the relationship between faith in Christ and the law (*Paul and the Law* [Philadelphia: Fortress, 1983]). Few scholars, however, have been willing to endorse Räisänen's portrait of a muddle-headed Paul.

[58]See Cousar, *Letters of Paul*, p. 80.

of rhetorical and polemical arguments to demonstrate that the law cannot justify. In contrast, when Paul writes to the Romans, he communicates with a church he has never visited and that does not seem to be in crisis. The different circumstances of both Paul and his audience require a less combative treatment of the themes of righteousness and the law, along with more carefully constructed arguments. Whereas in Galatians Paul emphasizes the law's temporary validity and its primarily negative function in relation to righteousness (Gal 3:19—4:7),[59] Romans reveals a more balanced perspective and, overall, a more positive assessment of the role of the law. Although believers have died to the law (Rom 7:4) and the law functions to increase transgression (Rom 5:20; cf. 3:20; 4:15; 7:13), the law still remains holy, righteous and good (Rom 7:12). The gospel of Christ, far from invalidating the Torah, offers its true fulfillment (Rom 3:31; 8:4). In each case, Paul draws upon the language of righteousness by faith for all apart from the law, which represents something fundamental to his understanding of the gospel. The "facts on the ground," however, call for different yet complementary theological approaches.

Paul's eschatological teaching in 1 Thessalonians and Galatians gives us a second example of diversity within theological unity. In 1 Thessalonians, Paul stresses the future dimension of God's saving work, when Jesus returns in glory. Galatians, however, concentrates on the present liberating effects of the cross of Christ for believers. Explicit references to the "not yet" side of salvation are noticeably absent from this letter (but see Gal 5:5). This apparent theological disparity is no doubt due to the way that Paul interprets the one gospel story for two different contexts, not to any major shift in his eschatological understanding.[60] The Thessalonians needed to hear the consummation of the Christ story applied to their specific misunderstandings about the Day of the Lord (1 Thess 4:13—5:11), while the pressing issue in Galatia was to grasp how the death of Jesus had already guaranteed freedom from a yoke of slavery to circumcision and the law (Gal 5:1-13; 6:12-15). Paul brings out the particular dimension of God's saving work in Christ that was appropriate for the circumstances of his hearers.

These two brief examples suggest that apparent discrepancies in specific theological statements or perspectives may signal Paul's concern to emphasize one side of the equation or the other because of the contextual needs of the audiences

---

[59]But cf. Galatians 6:2, where Paul speaks positively of Christians fulfilling the "law of Christ" (cf. Gal 5:14). For a valuable summary of Paul's contextual argument in Galatians, see Frank Thielman, *Paul and the Law: A Contextual Approach* (Downers Grove, Ill.: InterVarsity Press, 1994), pp. 119-44.

[60]See Hays, "Crucified with Christ," pp. 234-35.

he is addressing. Since Paul is often responding to imbalances and misunderstandings on the part of his churches, it is important that we try to grasp his specific persuasive strategies when he does theology.[61] Charles B. Cousar suggests the analogy that "parents, acting out of a consistent love, know that each child warrants a particular treatment, often differing from that appropriate for his or her sibling."[62] Yet behind all of Paul's varied, "parental" responses to specific pastoral needs stands the one gospel story of God's loving intervention in Christ.

Any adequate account of Paul's contextualizing activity in his letters, then, must recognize a coherent unity within a flexible diversity. It was part of Paul's genius that his thought could be contextual without becoming changeable, that his theological activity could be audience-sensitive without being audience-driven. Paul walks the via media, which avoids abstract formulas and generic theological solutions on the one hand and fickle pragmatism on the other. Inevitably, a tension emerges between the one gospel that cannot be compromised and demands obedience (Gal 1:6-9) and the versatility that enables the gospel to be interpreted in ways that address people on many levels within their life situations. Failure to do justice to one side of this tension or the other invariably leads to a misunderstanding of both Paul's gospel and his contextual way of doing theology.

CONCLUSION

Paul's letters reveal a complex conversation between the Christ-centered gospel and the diverse mission communities of the Mediterranean world to which it speaks. His writings bear witness to a process of creative and flexible theologizing that enables the abiding message of God's redeeming work in Christ to be contextualized in a variety of ways for ever-new settings. The conversation is guided by the constant gospel, not by ever-changing circumstances. Yet Paul's understanding of the coherence of the gospel was capable of expanding and deepening in light of the new challenges he faced. The goal of this process is not simply intellectual assent to a creed, but rather the total transformation of people within their circumstances, as they allow the story of Christ to rewrite their own scripts.

Today's missional church has the opportunity to embrace the same theological task of incarnating the gospel within the life worlds of contemporary people

---

[61]See J. Paul Sampley, "From Text to Thought World: The Route to Paul's Ways," in *Pauline Theology, Volume 1: Thessalonians, Philippians, Galatians, Philemon*, ed. J. M. Bassler (Minneapolis: Fortress, 1991), pp. 6-7.
[62]Cousar, *Letters of Paul*, p. 80.

in transforming ways. We must partner with Paul in the theological dance between fidelity and innovation. Following Paul's lead, we must have a clear vision of the normative truth of the gospel, or else we take the risk that our theology will drift from its moorings. This has been a particular danger for many of the so-called contextual theologies that have emerged in recent decades from various global settings. There is much confusion about what constitutes the common faith and even if there is such a thing as a universally valid Christian message. Paul's confidence in the abiding "truth of the gospel" speaks with a clarion voice to such a state of affairs. And in a time when postmodern sensibilities in the West bristle at the very thought of an overarching metanarrative, we have no other course than to ground our theologizing in the one sacred story of what God has done "for us" in Christ.

At the same time, as Paul sensitively and respectfully engaged his world in all of its particularity, we must engage ours. Although Paul's ways of articulating the message, as Scripture, continue to carry foundational significance for God's people, we cannot be content merely to imitate his terminology or use identical images when we address our world. A contextualized gospel cannot be exclusively bound to the Greek vocabulary and thought forms that were meaningful to people in the first-century Greco-Roman world. If we would learn from Paul, we must seek forms of expressing the gospel, guided by the Spirit, that draw upon our own stories and cultural resources while remaining faithful to the witness of Scripture. Thus, Croatian theologian Miroslav Volf, doing theology out of the bitter ethnic conflict in the Balkan Peninsula, draws upon the powerful imagery of *exclusion* and *embrace*. These metaphors facilitate a fresh encounter between God's word and a fractured world. They point to the healing embrace of the crucified Christ, which enables us to open ourselves to enfold the other.[63] Or in settings where the community's relationship to ancestors is fundamental to peoples' worldviews, Christians might consider enlisting this discourse in order to clarify the role of Christ. Yet traditional beliefs must be challenged and language infused with new content, lest Jesus be reduced to one ancestor among many. Churches in affluent societies might co-opt images from the financial world in order to expose their cultures' worship of Mammon. The Pauline paradigm challenges every church in every place to enable the one gospel of Christ crucified to address and transform people within their life circumstances. Only then will we have a truly missional theology—one that motivates and sustains the church in its witness and service to the world.

---

[63]Miroslav Volf, *Exclusion and Embrace: A Theological Exploration of Identity, Otherness, and Reconciliation* (Nashville: Abingdon, 1996).

4. PAUL AND CULTURE
Engaging the Greco-Roman World

To the Jews I became as a Jew . . . to those
under the law I became as one under the law. . . . I have become
all things to all people, that I might by all means save some.

1 COR 9:20, 22

ulture is the fertile soil of contextualization. If we want to understand how Paul contextualized the gospel within his setting, we cannot avoid the fascinating question of the interface between the gospel and culture. In the last chapter, we considered how Paul's theological activity in his letters enabled the Christ-centered gospel to become a word on target for particular audiences and circumstances. Now we turn to a second and equally important dimension of the contextualizing task, which we could call "inculturation"—understanding how the gospel engages the cultural and social worlds in which it comes to life.

OF CULTURES AND WORLDVIEWS

Culture has always been a difficult notion to pin down, and there is no shortage of ways to define it. For our purposes, however, a reasonable working definition is that culture stands for "the more or less integrated systems of ideas, feelings, and values and their associated patterns of behavior and products shared by a group of people."[1] This understanding brings out culture's cognitive, affective and evaluative dimensions. When the gospel intersects culture, it does not operate on the level of theological ideas and information alone; it does so holistically. Likewise, culture embraces both our beliefs and our social practices, that is, the ways people live out their everyday lives in society.

At their deepest level, all cultures and subcultures have a shared set of as-

---

[1]Paul Hiebert, *Anthropological Insights for Missionaries* (Grand Rapids, Mich.: Baker, 1985), p. 30.

sumptions about the way things are—a worldview.[2] Like a pair of glasses, it goes largely unnoticed. Nevertheless, it provides the lens through which people see and make sense of their world. Worldviews tend to integrate culture by providing stories that tell us who we are and why we are here (e.g., "the American Dream" or God's rescue of his people from slavery in Egypt), as well as "maps" that organize perceptions of reality and of the way people should live within their context. But that integration is far from total. In complex societies, such as India, the United States or the first-century Greco-Roman world, it is impossible to speak of a single worldview, just as we cannot talk about a single unified culture. While there are shared assumptions and dominant scripts (e.g., concern for individual freedom and rights in America or group-oriented identity in the ancient Mediterranean world), worldviews may vary considerably depending on peoples' age group, socioeconomic status, ethnic identity, religion, education, or family background.

In addition, worldviews and basic cultural assumptions can be challenged and changed by both external and internal factors. At times, people experience profound shifts in personal or collective worldviews, as in the case of conversion, whether we think of a Saul journeying to Damascus or a tribe of animists who decide that Christianity provides a better explanation of the way things are than do their former beliefs.[3] A consistent feature of cultures as a whole is that they are not static, but rather ever-changing realities, particularly in response to outside influences and relationships. This applies both to underlying worldviews as well as to specific cultural practices. For example, Western societies are now apparently in the midst of a profound shift from a modern to a postmodern worldview. This dynamic quality allows the gospel to be good news within cultures and to address them in transforming ways.

When Paul articulated the gospel and its implications to believing communities of the first-century Mediterranean world, he had no neutral place to stand *outside* of culture. The theology and ethical teaching we encounter in his letters are rooted in the particular worldview and symbolic world[4] that Paul shares. At the same time, he had to express his message in ideas and concrete symbols

---

[2]On worldviews, see Charles H. Kraft, *Anthropology for Christian Witness* (Maryknoll, N.Y.: Orbis, 1996), pp. 51-68; Brian J. Walsh and J. Richard Middleton *The Transforming Vision: Shaping a Christian Worldview* (Downers Grove, Ill.: InterVarsity Press, 1984).

[3]See Hiebert, *Anthropological Insights*, p. 49; N. T. Wright, *The New Testament and the People of God* (Minneapolis: Fortress, 1992), p. 125.

[4]By "symbolic world," I mean the system of symbols that embody the patterns of meanings, feelings and values that Paul shared and that give his worldview cultural expression. Anthropologists have recognized that cultures are made up of many *symbol systems*—language, rituals, gestures, customs, games, lifestyles, technology, and so forth—which embody and

that could make sense to his readers within their cultural homes. In this chapter we will consider first Paul's own worldview and cultural location and then try to understand the role that culture plays in Paul's contextualizing of the good news for people who came largely out of a different background than his own.

PAUL'S WORLDVIEW: HEBREW, HELLENIST, CHRISTIAN?

"I am a Jew, born in Tarsus in Cilicia, but brought up in this city [Jerusalem] at the feet of Gamaliel" (Acts 22:3). Interpreters of Paul have long debated whether we should understand the apostle's identity and thought primarily against the backdrop of "Tarsus" or "Jerusalem." Even today, one stream of scholarship tends to read Paul's letters as witnesses to his Jewishness[5] while another tries just as energetically to demonstrate the influence of Greco-Roman philosophy, rhetoric and social practice on Paul.[6] Is he "Paul the Hebrew" or "Paul the Hellenist"? How we answer this question will have a clear impact on our perception of the way Paul interacted with the Jewish and Greco-Roman cultural and social worlds of his day.

Unfortunately, there is no simple solution, and the issue needs to be addressed on more than one plane. Consider Paul's "worldview," the core assumptions through which he interprets his experience in the world. In spite of attempts by history-of-religion scholarship to paint Paul as a Hellenistic Jew of the Diaspora who thoroughly accommodated his thought to Greco-Roman religion, his worldview remained firmly rooted in Jewish soil. We saw earlier that the framework for Paul's core commitments was a story of God's dealings with humanity that is anchored in the Old Testament and in first-century apocalyptic Judaism. This Jewish story, and his participation in it, is foundational for Paul's way of seeing the world. Consequently, an argument like that of W. L. Knox,

---

interpret the specific patterns of meanings and values of a given group. On the symbolic dimension of culture, see Clifford Geertz, *The Interpretation of Cultures* (New York: Basic Books, 1973), pp. 3-141. Robert J. Schreiter, *Constructing Local Theologies* (Maryknoll, N.Y.: Orbis, 1985), pp. 49-73.

[5]This has especially been the case since the publication of E. P. Sanders's *Paul and Palestinian Judaism* (Philadelphia: Fortress, 1977) triggered a "new perspective" on Paul, which has diligently sought to understand his thought against its (reinterpreted) Palestinian Jewish context. See, e.g., E. P. Sanders, *Paul, the Law, and the Jewish People* (Philadelphia: Fortress, 1983); James D. G. Dunn, *The Theology of Paul the Apostle* (Grand Rapids, Mich.: Eerdmans, 1998); N. T. Wright, *The Climax of the Covenant: Christ and the Law in Pauline Theology* (Minneapolis: Fortress, 1991).

[6]E.g., Troels Engberg-Pedersen, *Paul and the Stoics* (Louisville: Westminster John Knox, 2000); Abraham J. Malherbe, *Paul and the Popular Philosophers* (Minneapolis: Fortress, 1989); F. Gerald Downing, *Cynics, Paul and the Pauline Churches* (Edinburgh: T & T Clark, 1994). See also the collection of articles in *Paul and His Hellenistic Context*, ed. T. Engberg-Pedersen (Edinburgh: T & T Clark, 1994).

which concludes that Paul deliberately abandoned his native Jewish apocalyptic worldview in favor of Greek categories of thought in order to make the Christian message more attractive to educated Gentiles, misreads both Paul's thought and his missionary strategy.[7] Paul can no more "de-contextualize" his thought from its underlying biblical and apocalyptic worldview than, as Jeremiah says it, a leopard can change its spots (Jer 13:23).[8] Emerging from a Chinese or Indian or Greco-Roman matrix, the gospel would be a decidedly different message.

But what impact did Paul's Christian conversion have on his worldview? Couldn't it be argued that this devout Pharisee, this zealot for the law, gained a new, distinctively "Christian" worldview, one that replaced his entire pre-Christian way of looking at things, as a result of his being confronted by Christ on the Damascus Road? Yes and no. It is true that Paul could talk about his "former life in Judaism" (Gal 1:13) and testify that the glittering trophies of his old symbolic world, including circumcision and law obedience, had unexpectedly become "loss" because of Christ (Phil 3:4-10). His Jewish worldview and beliefs were profoundly, permanently transformed by his experience of the risen Lord. Nevertheless, they were not totally displaced. Paul retained his fundamental Jewish assumptions about the one true God of Israel, God's election of and covenant faithfulness toward his people, the apocalyptic framework of this age and the age to come, and the hope of a future resurrection, throughout his life. Although he speaks of a radical reshaping of each of these convictions in light of God's surprising intervention in Jesus Christ, he did not simply bury them under the dust of the Damascus road. Whenever people embrace the truth of the gospel, they must do so in relation to their preexisting worldviews and patterns of relationships if it is going to carry any meaning for them.[9] Given that Paul's Jewish heritage was a vehicle of God's revelation, more continuity with the new Christian perspective was possible than would be true of his pagan converts in Thessalonica or Corinth—people whose dominant worldviews were to a large degree incompatible with the gospel.

---

[7]W. L. Knox, *St. Paul and the Church of the Gentiles* (reprint; Cambridge: Cambridge University Press, 1961); cf. idem, *St. Paul and the Church of Jerusalem* (Cambridge: Cambridge University Press, 1925), pp. 126-49.

[8]The well-known "demythologizing" program of Rudolf Bultmann also stumbled at this point. Bultmann argued that the New Testament message, or "kerygma," needed to be stripped of its mythical language that was bound up with a primitive, pre-scientific worldview, so that it could be reexpressed within a worldview more relevant to modern people. E.g., Rudolf Bultmann, *Kerygma and Myth*, vol. 1, ed. H. W. Bartsch, ET, 2nd ed. (London: SPCK, 1964), pp. 1-16. Unfortunately, when Paul's gospel was dehusked of what Bultmann considered to be mythological, little of what could meaningfully be called the gospel survived.

[9]See Sherwood Lingenfelter, *Transforming Culture* (Grand Rapids, Mich.: Baker, 1992), p. 210.

In addition, the gospel that was handed on to Paul from the Jewish Christian community was already framed within particular cultural forms. Richard B. Hays demonstrates that even the most basic theological affirmations of the New Testament are only intelligible within the symbolic world of first century Judaism. Take 1 Corinthians 15:3-5:

> For I handed on to you as of first importance what I in turn had received: that Christ died for our sins in accordance with the scriptures, and that he was buried, and that he was raised on the third day in accordance with the scriptures, and that he appeared to Cephas, then to the twelve.

Hays asserts that "every element of this early Christian confessional statement derives its sense from its participation in the particular symbolic universe of Jewish apocalyptic thought: Christ (i.e., "Messiah"), sins, scriptures, resurrection, the twelve (corresponding to the twelve tribes of Israel)."[10] In other words, the gospel that Paul received was already inculturated into a Jewish worldview and thought structure.

If, then, Paul's controlling beliefs are grounded in a Jewish story that has been radically reconfigured by Jesus Christ, does this mean that he approaches his Gentile converts as a cultural outsider, as someone who shares little in common with their cultural heritage? The matter is not that simple. In the first place, we know that the Judaism of Paul's day, not just in the diaspora but in Palestine as well, was highly diversified and already significantly influenced by Hellenism.[11] To hold that Paul's gospel and ethics were shaped exclusively by Jewish rather than Greco-Roman cultural influences would be to perpetuate a false dichotomy. In the contexts in which Paul lived, thought and ministered, there was a constant overlapping and intermingling of the two. Second, recent cultural analysis of the New Testament has shown that some of the fundamental values and elements of Paul's symbolic world were shared throughout many of the cultures and subcultures of his Mediterranean environment. The values of honor and shame, for example, the concern for kinship and group identity, the belief in good and evil supernatural powers, all of which run through Paul's letters, are widely attested in both Jewish and Greco-Roman sources.[12] Consequently, although Paul's deep-level worldview assumptions were primarily shaped by

---

[10]Richard B. Hays, *The Moral Vision of the New Testament: Community, Cross, New Creation: A Contemporary Introduction to New Testament Ethics* (San Francisco: Harper Collins, 1996), p. 299.

[11]This was decisively demonstrated by Martin Hengel, *Judaism and Hellenism*, 2 vols. (Philadelphia: Fortress, 1977).

[12]See David A. deSilva, *Honor, Patronage, Kinship and Purity: Unlocking New Testament Culture* (Downers Grove, Ill.: InterVarsity Press, 2000), esp. pp. 19-20 n. 4.

his Jewish heritage and his revelation of Christ, this in no way excludes his participation in the Hellenistic cultural world, nor its influence on his thinking, values and behavior.

PAUL'S INTERCULTURAL SETTING

If, then, we want to talk about Paul's cultural background, we need to move beyond the old dichotomy of Jewish *or* Hellenist and recognize that he was a part of a complex cultural, religious and social environment. Paul was directly influenced by three converging cultural worlds: Jewish, Greek and Roman. Without question, the most important of the three was his identity within Judaism—one of the minority subcultures of the Greco-Roman world. Paul himself testifies that, although born outside of Palestine, he was a "Hebrew of Hebrews" (Phil 3:6; 2 Cor 11:22). This not only means he considered himself a "Jew among Jews," but probably also that he was taught to speak Hebrew or Aramaic in his home.[13] His parents were likely orthodox Jews who brought him as a youth to Jerusalem to receive his formal education "at the feet of Gamaliel" (Acts 22:3), one of the leading Jewish teachers of the day. Paul's principle socialization in the Jerusalem Pharisaic circles would have enabled him to identify culturally with Palestinian Judaism. Evidence of his Jewish cultural heritage, such as the concern for ordering his world to maintain purity and avoid defilement, surfaces regularly in his letters (e.g., 2 Cor 6:14—7:1).

At the same time, Paul spent his early years in Tarsus of Asia Minor, one of the great Hellenistic centers of philosophy and learning of the ancient world (Acts 21:39). There he learned Greek, probably as his mother tongue,[14] and he was exposed to Gentiles and Gentile culture. He likely participated in a Diaspora Jewish community that was steeped in the Septuagint, as evidenced by his masterful command of the text of the Greek Bible. Although we do not know how much of a formal Greek education Paul would have had, or even precisely where he received it, his writings reveal a familiarity with Greek philosophy (especially popular Stoicism) and a fairly extensive use of Greco-Roman rhetoric.[15]

---

[13]Martin Hengel, *The Pre-Christian Paul* (Philadelphia: Trinity Press International, 1991), pp. 25-26.

[14]Ibid., pp. 35, 38.

[15]Hengel rightly questions W. C. Van Unnik's contention that Paul must have been brought to Jerusalem by his parents in his earliest childhood (*Pre-Christian Paul*, pp. 34-35). Acts 22:3, which states that Paul was "brought up" in Jerusalem, does not require it, and the likelihood that Greek was Paul's first language argues against it. It is therefore possible that Paul received at least some of his early schooling in Tarsus. Even if he did not, Paul would have had the opportunity for a Jewish-Greek education in Jerusalem that included instruction in Greco-Roman rhetoric (pp. 38-39; 57-61).

Certainly prior to the time of his major missionary work, this Jew from Tarsus had become fluent in Hellenistic culture—its cosmology and religious life, its political and social institutions, its ethical teachings and athletic pursuits. Paul was no alien to the cultures of either Diaspora Judaism or the wider urban Hellenistic world.

Finally, Paul was a Roman citizen, a privilege he inherited from his family (Acts 22:25-28). Although his Roman connection was the least influential for his cultural identity, it did provide him with clear advantages as an itinerant evangelist, including unusual access to the entire Mediterranean world. Roman citizenship meant that Paul was a person of considerable social status, as Luke's account of the respectful treatment he received during his Roman imprisonment (Acts 28:16) suggests.[16] Paul was at home in the presence of Roman magistrates; he appears to have had a generally positive attitude toward the ruling authorities and the Roman system of justice (cf. Rom 13:1-7; 1 Tim 2:1-2). And although we have no firm evidence of it, it is possible that Paul, as a Roman citizen, also knew at least a bit of Latin.[17]

Paul's cultural background, then, involved a rich interplay of Palestinian and Diaspora Jewish, Greek and Roman, as well as more pervasive "Mediterranean," elements. In a sense, he was a product of the complex cultural bazaar that was the first-century Mediterranean world. Recognizing that Paul was a multilingual person who participated in more than one cultural world is crucial for understanding his activity in contextualizing the gospel. Not only did Paul's multilingual abilities equip him with the flexibility to become "as a Jew to the Jews and as a Greek to the Greeks" (1 Cor 9:19-23); it also meant that when he targeted the gospel to his Gentile converts, he did so, not as a cultural outsider, but as one who could appreciate how the good news could be incarnated from within their own life situation. Lucien Legrand observes that "unlike Philo and the other Alexandrian Jewish writers, Paul did not attempt systematically to bridge his way to the surrounding Greco-Roman world. He spoke and wrote as a citizen of that world."[18] Paul was able to quite naturally make use of the rhetorical and ideological resources of his Hellenistic environment in order to articulate the gospel in ways that resonated with Gentiles.

Consequently, Paul's role as "apostle to the Gentiles" is not a precise paradigm for that of a crosscultural missionary, if by that term we mean someone

---

[16]Ben Witherington III, *The Paul Quest: The Renewed Search for the Jew of Tarsus* (Downers Grove, Ill.: InterVarsity Press, 1998), p. 27.

[17]Ibid., p. 89.

[18]Lucien Legrand, *The Bible on Culture: Belonging or Dissenting?* (Maryknoll, N.Y.: Orbis, 2000), p. 146.

who moves from one culture into another and learns its language and ways in order to bring the gospel to it. Although Paul's primary cultural identity was ever as a Jew in both worldview and practice, his immersion in Hellenistic culture and city life was too extensive for it to be simply a question of external cross-cultural adjustment.[19] From the beginning, he was a "wanderer between two worlds."[20] He communicated the Word of God to *both* Jewish and Gentile hearers from an insider's perspective. At the same time, he was able to distance himself enough from both cultures to understand where they needed to be judged by the gospel. It is little wonder, then, that this Jew from Tarsus was uniquely suited to become a bridge between the original Palestinian Jewish context of the gospel and its penetration into the wider Roman world.

Neither were Paul's churches monocultural communities. They featured considerable diversity—ethnical, cultural, social—which mirrored the urban Greco-Roman world from which they emerged. The majority of Christians were Gentile converts from paganism (1 Cor 12:2; 1 Thess 1:9), but there were also Jews and former God-fearing Gentiles with synagogue connections. Paul's letters give evidence of an increasingly Gentile Christian movement that was struggling to define its relationship to Judaism on the one hand and its pluralistic pagan environment on the other. Furthermore, the first-century urban Gentile world embraced a medley of cultural influences—Greek, Roman, Syrian, Egyptian, Anatolian and others. Both Paul and his readers operated out of a complex, intercultural mosaic, which has much in common with some of the many-faceted settings in which the gospel must be contextualized today.

PAUL'S ATTITUDE TOWARD CULTURE

How would Paul view the relationship between the gospel and culture? Would he regard human cultures as a help or a hindrance to the Christian message? What role did culture play in Paul's contextualizing of the gospel? Since Paul obviously never addresses the modern notion of culture as such, we must try to uncover implications and insights from his writings than can shed light on these questions. Given what we have observed about the multi-layered character of Paul's own cultural situation and that of his readers, it should not surprise us that Paul's attitude toward culture is complex as well. For Paul, incarnating the gospel within the dominant Greco-Roman culture of his world involved more than simply exchanging Jewish Christian categories and expressions for Greek ones without any loss of meaning. We can find at least four processes at work

---

[19]Ibid., p. 139.
[20]Hengel, *Pre-Christian Paul*, pp. 4, 37.

as the gospel interacts with Paul's cultural world: affirming, relativizing, confronting and transforming culture.[21]

Affirming culture. Culture has a theological dimension that is rooted in God's creation and ongoing commitment to the world.[22] Paul assumes God's active presence in the created order, which includes human cultures. Early in Romans, we hear of God's gracious activity outside of specific revelation to Israel or the gospel proclamation. It comes in two arenas: creation and conscience. Co-opting the language of Hellenistic religious philosophy (especially from Stoicism) that would resonate with Gentile readers, Paul declares that God's "eternal power" and "divine nature" are visible to all people through God's creation, giving them a genuine knowledge of the Creator (Rom 1:19-20). As a result, pagan peoples stand without excuse before God, accountable for their sins. Furthermore, Gentiles, apart from the law, have the witness of their conscience, which provides them with an inner knowledge of right and wrong (Rom 2:14-15). This moral consciousness is not some innate human capacity, but rather the result of the Holy Spirit's ministry of grace. Presumably, this takes place not only through peoples' individual consciences, but also collectively, in human cultures and religions. Whenever cultures and their ethical and religious values reflect God's truth and right action, it is evidence that grace is at work.[23]

Far from rejecting human cultures as merely the product of the fall, Paul affirms cultural particularity and uses it to bring the message of Christ to the world. In his celebrated statement of flexibility for the sake of mission in 1 Corinthians 9:19-23, Paul declares that he is willing to adapt his social behavior

---

[21]The reader may recognize some overlap between the following approaches to culture and the classic analysis of the relationship between "Christ and culture" by H. Richard Niebuhr in *Christ and Culture* (New York: Harper and Row, 1951). Niebuhr explored five answers to the question of Christ and culture that have emerged throughout Christian history: (1) Christ against culture (rejection); (2) the Christ of culture (accommodation); (3) Christ above culture (synthesis); (4) Christ and culture in paradox; and (5) Christ the transformer of culture (conversion), with his own sympathies clearly falling with the last strategy. Despite its widespread influence, John Howard Yoder has shown that Niebuhr's way of framing the issue is problematic. See John Howard Yoder, "How H. Richard Niebuhr Reasoned: A Critique of *Christ and Culture*," in G. H. Stassen, D. M. Yeager and John Howard Yoder, *Authentic Transformation: A New Vision of Christ and Culture* (Nashville: Abingdon, 1996), esp. pp. 54-61. For instance, Niebuhr treats culture as a monolithic whole, so that each of his categories describes a particular stance toward every aspect of culture. As I will argue, this fails to appreciate that cultures are complex realities, and that different approaches are required for various elements within a given culture.

[22]William A. Dyrness, *The Earth Is God's: A Theology of American Culture* (Maryknoll, N.Y.: Orbis, 1995), p. 58.

[23]Dean Flemming, "Foundations for Responding to Religious Pluralism," *WesTJ* 31 (spring 1997): 66-67.

to either a Jewish or a Gentile ("those outside the law," 1 Cor 9:21) cultural setting in order to win both Jews and Gentiles to Christ. This is no less than an
application of the incarnation principle; people only have access to the eternal
God and the gospel of the crucified Christ through the particularity of culture.
By voluntarily identifying with Jews and Gentiles, Paul validates their distinctive
cultural commitments. He concludes his extended discussion of the appropriateness of eating meat offered to idols (1 Corinthians 8—10) by urging the
Corinthians to follow his own example, as he imitates Christ: "Give no offense
to Jews or to Greeks or to the church of God" (1 Cor 10:32). Believers must
show respect for cultural and ethnic distinctions and erect no unnecessary barriers to the gospel.

Elsewhere, Paul exhorts Roman Christians whose divisions between the
"weak" and the "strong" seem to split largely along Jewish and Gentile lines:

> Welcome one another, therefore, just as Christ has welcomed you, for the glory of
> God. For I tell you that Christ has become a servant of the circumcised on behalf
> of the truth of God in order that he might confirm the promises given to the patri-
> archs, and in order that the Gentiles might glorify God for his mercy. (Rom 15:7-9)

The basis for the command to "welcome one another" is Christ's having become
"servant of the circumcised" (the Jews), an act which leads to the inclusion of
the Gentiles among the people of God. Charles B. Cousar discerns that the verb
"welcome" here "connotes more than merely tolerating or indulging the other
person with his or her ethnic and cultural features; it entails accepting, giving
space for, respecting the distinctiveness of the other."[24] What this means practically is that Gentile Christians should allow their "weak" Jewish sisters and
brothers to practice abstaining from certain foods and observing special days as
expressions of their ongoing loyalty to the Jewish law. At the same time, Jewish
Christians must refrain from judging Gentile believers who do not follow such
Jewish cultural practices (Rom 14:1-13). It was Paul's desire "to safeguard the
cultural particularity of Jew as Jew and Gentile as Gentile, though challenging
both Jews and Gentiles to find in Jesus Christ their true affirmation."[25]

Paul did not lay aside his cultural identity as a "Hebrew of Hebrews" (Phil
3:6; cf. 2 Cor 11:22; 1 Cor 16:8) when he was called to proclaim the gospel to
the Gentiles. Nor did he try to make Jewish Christians into Greeks and force

---

[24]Charles Cousar, "Paul and Multiculturalism," in *Many Voices, One God: Being Faithful in a
Pluralistic World*, ed. Walter Brueggemann and G. W. Stroup (Louisville: Westminster John
Knox, 1998), p. 56.
[25]Lamin Sanneh, *Translating the Message: The Missionary Impact on Culture* (Maryknoll, N.Y.:
Orbis, 1989), p. 47.

them to give up their cultural symbols, such as circumcision and kosher food laws. He continued to radically identify with his "own people," his "kindred according to the flesh," and agonized over their unbelief (Rom 9:2-3). Paul never lost his conviction that God had a plan for the Jewish people precisely *as Jews* (Rom 1:16; 11:26-29). For Paul, Jesus remained the Messiah of the Jews and the gospel continued to make a home within their Scriptures and cultural traditions.

At the same time, Paul is a debtor "to Greeks and to barbarians" (Rom 1:14). His missionary calling to the Gentiles unveiled the insight that the gospel had to come to live within the language and culture of the Hellenistic world. Urban Greco-Roman culture became the new destination of God's saving promise. This is what West African missiologist Lamin Sanneh refers to as the "translatability" of the gospel.[26] In contrast to Islam, which views the Arabic of the Qur'an as a sacred revealed language, from the beginning the Christian message had the capacity to be translated from Aramaic and Hebrew into new linguistic and cultural forms. For this to happen, Gentile culture had to be destigmatized so that it could become a natural extension of the life of the Christian movement.[27] Paul plays a vital role in that process. In what ways, we must ask, did Paul affirm and utilize Greco-Roman culture as a legitimate context for a fresh translation of the good news?

Cultural language and images. For the gospel to be intelligible in a new situation, Paul could not be content simply to repeat the teaching of Jesus. The translation of the Christian message from Aramaic, the language of Jesus' preaching ministry, into Greek, the primary mode of religious discourse for the Hellenistic world, was crucial in allowing Christianity to transcend its Palestinian cultural roots. Language and culture are closely wedded. A people's particular way of perceiving and interpreting reality (its worldview) is to a large extent built into its language.[28] African theologian John Mbiti, for example, insists that the Swahili words for time, *sasa* and *zamani*, cannot be pressed into the Western temporal categories of past, present and future. *Sasa* time, in which people currently participate, embraces the recent past, the present and the immediate future. Yet, for many Africans, time is not pictured as a movement forward into an eternal future, as in the West; instead, events move backwards and *sasa* disappears into an ever increasing *past* (*zamani*).[29] Language, then, "provides the

---

[26]Ibid., pp. 1, 51 and passim.

[27]Ibid., p. 1.

[28]Kraft, *Anthropology for Christian Witness*, p. 247.

[29]John S. Mbiti, *African Religions and Theology*, 2nd ed. (London: Oxford, 1990); idem, "The Bible in African Culture," in *Paths of African Theology*, ed. R. Gibellini (Maryknoll, N.Y.: Orbis, 1994), pp. 34-35.

symbolic world of a linguistic community by which that community orders and maintains its 'world' as well as confirms and communicates it."[30] The Greek language enabled Paul to share much of the symbolic world of his Greek-speaking audience, thereby expressing the gospel with a new vocabulary and set of images that would communicate to urban Gentiles.

Paul's letters are brimming with theological language appropriated from the life world of his readers. He regularly draws upon words that were current in Greco-Roman philosophical and religious circles in order to express Christian meaning. Many of these terms, such as "wisdom" *(sophia)* or "knowledge" *(gnōsis)*, already had a history in the Greek Bible that informed how Paul understood them. Yet he can also adopt a word like "conscience" (e.g., Rom 2:15; 1 Cor 8:7-12; 10:25-29; 2 Cor 4:2; 5:11), which is virtually absent from Jewish writings but commonly occurs in popular Greek sources such as the writings of the Stoic philosophers. On occasion, Paul also articulates the gospel in language taken from a secular, rather than a religious, context. A good example of this is *reconciliation*, a notion that appears almost exclusively in secular Greek literature or in materials heavily influenced by Hellenism.[31] It is language that Greco-Roman people used to speak of restoring peace between enemies and exchanging friendship (a notion with far-reaching social implications) for hostility. For Paul, this secular image becomes a key way of picturing God's reconciling work on behalf of humankind in the death of Christ.

Paul can likewise co-opt the language of Hellenistic moralism in his ethical teaching. Philippians 4:8 provides a striking example. Here Paul lists a series of virtues that would no doubt have sounded quite familiar to his audience: "whatever is true, whatever is honorable, whatever is just, whatever is pure, whatever is pleasing, whatever is commendable, if there is any excellence and if there is anything worthy of praise, think about these things." These are qualities that come out of the common stock of moral teaching from his readers' Greco-Roman culture. Paul seems to be urging Gentile Christians to adhere to the best in their own cultural heritage—as long as it is consistent with the gospel of Christ. Gordon D. Fee rightly notes that the exhortation that immediately follows in verse 9 places these cultural virtues in the context of the Philippians' "imitation" of Paul in his cruciform lifestyle.[32] This passage thus suggests something of

---

[30]M. Robert Mulholland Jr., "Sociological Criticism," in *New Testament Criticism and Interpretation*, ed. D. A. Black and D. S. Dockery (Grand Rapids, Mich.: Zondervan, 1991), p. 302.

[31]S. E. Porter, "Peace, Reconciliation," in *Dictionary of Paul and His Letters*, ed. Gerald F. Hawthorne, Ralph P. Martin and Daniel G. Reid (Downers Grove, Ill.: InterVarsity Press, 1993), p. 695.

[32]Gordon D. Fee, *Paul's Letter to the Philippians* (Grand Rapids, Mich.: Eerdmans, 1995), pp. 416-17, 419-20.

Paul's understanding of the relationship of Christians to their surrounding cultural environment: they can embrace the good wherever it is found, provided it is viewed in the light of the story of Christ. At the same time, whatever we are and do, whether sacred or secular, that is pleasing and commendable and excellent is sanctified by life "in Christ."[33]

All cultures have virtues and values that can be affirmed and drawn into the service of the gospel. During my time of teaching in the Philippines, I was struck by the way that Filipinos named their characteristic cultural values. If Paul were writing a letter to the Philippines, instead of to the Philippians, I suspect he would affirm such core values as *pakikipagkapwa-tao* (literally, being a fellow to others). This cultural virtue that involves sharing, treating others with respect and equality, and extending help to those in need, would cohere well with Paul's notion of *koinōnia* ("sharing," "fellowship"). Such language and the values they stand for can be embraced and sanctified by the gospel of Christ.[34]

In addition, Paul taps into a deep pool of images and symbols from the cultural setting of his churches in order to communicate the Christian message in a way his readers could grasp. Earlier we noted that Paul uses a wide assortment of metaphors to drive home the meaning of theological concepts such as the atonement or the believer's salvation. Here I want to stress that the greater part of those images is drawn from the culture and the symbolic world Paul shares with his converts. Whereas Jesus had spoken to Galilean villagers using pictures of fields and fig trees, foxes and fishermen, Paul had to adopt a whole new set of symbols for the city dwellers of the Roman Empire.[35] As a result, he invokes metaphors from the sporting world that was highly significant to urban Gentile culture, such as the track and boxing images we find in 1 Corinthians 9:24-27 (cf. Gal 2:2; 5:7; Phil 3:13-14; 1 Tim 4:7-8; 2 Tim 2:5; 4:7). From education he borrows the figure of the pedagogue, the family slave in Hellenistic society who functioned as guardian, teacher and disciplinarian of children until they reached adulthood, in order to spotlight the temporary role of the law (Gal 3:23-25).

Paul can also deploy military images like that of the triumphal procession, in which a victorious general led his conquered captives through the streets of Rome. This vivid picture is flexible enough to represent both the "weak" character of Paul's apostolic ministry (Paul is the defeated slave; 1 Cor 4:9; 2 Cor

---

[33]Ibid., pp. 417 n. 17, 421.

[34]For a helpful treatment of the relationship between Filipino values and biblical faith, see Evelyn Miranda-Feliciano, *Filipino Values and Our Christian Faith* (Manila: OMF Literature, 1990).

[35]Legrand, *Bible on Culture*, p. 131.

2:14-16) and Christ's decisive victory on the cross over the powers (Col 2:15). From commerce, the "seal" (2 Cor 1:22; Eph 1:13; 4:30) signifies a visible mark of ownership, while the "guarantee" *(arrabōn)*, which Paul applies to the Holy Spirit, is a down payment of what was yet to come (2 Cor 1:22; 5:5; Eph 1:14). The figure "gentle . . . as a nurse" (1 Thess 2:7), used by Cynic philosophers, portrays Paul's tender care for his readers and their responsibility to one another.[36] The world of images he evokes is a world of builders and peddlers, mirrors and musical instruments, slave markets and letters of recommendation. In each case, Paul appropriates images from daily life in urban Hellenistic society that provide a lens through which people can gain a fresh vision of God's saving work and their response to it. His willingness to mine new forms of imagining the gospel from his cultural world not only facilitated communication with Gentiles, but it surely enriched and deepened his understanding of the Christian message itself.

Even religious metaphors that come out of a Jewish heritage, like the church as God's temple (1 Cor 3:16-17; Eph 2:21), Paul's ministry as a priestly service (Rom 1:9; 15:16; Phil 2:17), or Christians presenting their bodies as a "living sacrifice, holy and acceptable to God" (Rom 12:1), hold an intercultural significance, since the language of sacrifice was virtually universal in the ancient Mediterranean world. At the same time, Paul does not shy away from using distinctively Jewish images when doing theology for largely Gentile communities. The allusion to the Jewish Passover feast and the picture of Christ as the "paschal lamb" (1 Cor 5:6-8), for instance, does not hail from the familiar cultural territory of the Corinthian Gentiles. But because the biblical story is foundational for the church, scriptural images join contemporary ones in the service of communicating the good news. Paul's willingness to adopt new ways of expressing the saving word does not mean a wholesale abandoning of the old. His communications to the churches show continuity with biblical and traditional language as well as innovation. Paul gladly embraces whatever linguistic and cultural resources are available to him in order to convey the significance of Jesus Christ to his readers.

Greco-Roman rhetoric. Paul wrote letters within a largely oral culture. In the Greco-Roman world, rhetoric as a means of communication was both pervasive and highly esteemed. Despite Paul's insistence that his preaching did not imitate the kind of ornamental rhetoric practiced by the Sophists of the Hellenistic world (1 Cor 2:1-5; cf. 2 Cor 11:6), he makes extensive use of the cultural forms of ancient rhetoric with a view to influencing the thinking and behavior

---

[36]See Malherbe, *Paul and the Popular Philosophers*, pp. 35-48.

of his audiences.[37] It is only natural that he would do so, since Paul's letters are stand-ins for his own face-to-face communication, intended to be "read publicly to a corporate audience who use their ears rather than their eyes."[38]

Although there has been a flurry of attempts in recent years to classify Paul's letters according to the types of rhetoric described in the classical handbooks,[39] we must be careful not to force Paul into rhetorical pigeonholes. His creativity as a contextual theologian would certainly have enabled him to flexibly adapt existing rhetorical types and layouts to his own ends, and he appears to have done just that. Paul's use of rhetoric is affected not only by conventional forms but also especially by the specific rhetorical situation of the audience he was addressing.[40] More important than how closely he adhered to classical models is the realization that Paul used the conventions of rhetoric in order to effect change in his audience, as well as to aid their retaining what they heard. For instance, Gordon Fee proposes that Paul deliberately left his "thanksgiving" for the gift he received from the Philippians until the end of the letter (Phil 4:10-20) for rhetorical purposes: "These are intentionally the last words left ringing in their ears as the letter concludes, words of gratitude, theology, and doxology that simply soar."[41] In contrast, 2 Corinthians 10—13 resounds with a powerful pattern of forensic rhetoric, the rhetoric of attack and defense. Responding to a charge that his speech is "contemptible" (2 Cor 10:10) and freely admitting he is "untrained in speech" (2 Cor 11:6), Paul launches a stinging counterassault at his opponents. In a rhetorical tour de force, he turns some of their own verbal weapons against them, wielding devices such as irony, sarcasm, mock boasting and self-parody in order to undermine their attacks.[42]

In addition, Paul enlists the modes of proof identified by Aristotle as essential

---

[37]On Paul's use of rhetoric, see Witherington, *Paul Quest*, pp. 115-29; G. W. Hansen, "Rhetorical Criticism," in *Dictionary of Paul and His Letters*, ed. Gerald F. Hawthorne, Ralph P. Martin and Daniel G. Reid (Downers Grove, Ill.: InterVarsity Press, 1993), pp. 822-26, and Hansen's bibliography.

[38]Anthony C. Thiselton, *The First Epistle to the Corinthians* (Grand Rapids, Mich.: Eerdmans, 2000), p. 49. This is a point that Stanley E. Porter, who questions the usefulness of applying ancient rhetorical categories to epistolary writings like Paul's letters, fails to adequately appreciate. See Stanley E. Porter, *The Paul of Acts: Essays in Literary Criticism, Rhetoric, and Theology* (Tübingen: Mohr/Siebeck, 1999), pp. 101-9.

[39]The three basic categories of ancient rhetoric were *forensic* (defending or accusing so that the audience will make a judgment regarding past events or actions), *deliberative* (persuading the listeners to take some future action); and *epideictic* (praising or blaming in order to move the audience to a particular attitude or action in the present). Efforts to classify entire letters as one of these types have achieved less than full success.

[40]Richard A. Horsley, "Rhetoric and Empire—and 1 Corinthians," in *Paul and Politics: Ekklesia, Israel, Imperium, Interpretation*, ed. R. A. Horsley (Harrisburg, Penn.: Trinity Press International, 2000), pp. 82-84.

[41]Fee, *Philippians*, p. 17.

[42]Cousar, *Letters of Paul*, p. 37.

to persuasive communication. *Ethos*, the character and credibility of the speaker, was inseparable from the message and helped to secure the goodwill of the audience. Thus, in 1 Thessalonians 2:1-2, Paul appeals to *ethos* when he reminds the Thessalonians of his own integrity and his care for them. An example of *pathos*, the appeal to the listeners' emotions, is found in 2 Corinthians 11:23-29, when he defends himself with a profoundly moving list of his own trials (cf. Gal 4:12-20). *Logos*, or logical arguments, feature prominently in all of Paul's letters. Paul adapts his tone of address to the audience as well, as would have been expected of ancient rhetoricians. A crisis situation like Paul faces in Galatia calls for a direct, confrontational strategy ("You foolish Galatians!" Gal 3:1), whereas Paul communicates his message to the Philippians with the warmth that befits their relationship to the apostle. What is more, the oral performance of a letter by a trusted messenger who embodied Paul's own presence could heighten the rhetorical impact. Michael B. Thompson is quite right that "written messages to a Christian community were delivered with a power and immediacy that was far more gripping than text on a printed page or a computer monitor's screen."[43]

Paul, then, finds value in the rhetoric that was "in the air" in Greco-Roman culture and uses it as part of his strategy to "by all means" win people to Christ. Just as Luke pictures Paul in Acts as an effective preacher who adopts familiar rhetorical strategies in order to persuade Gentile audiences, so in Paul's letters rhetoric becomes a tool for Paul's "preaching for a decision." In an oral culture in which rhetorical effectiveness was prized, Paul makes use of a form of communicating that will help the gospel to have maximum impact in transforming the lives of his Gentile converts. He speaks their language.[44] Given the rapid change in popular culture today from literary to more aural-visual forms of communication, there may be much we can learn from Paul's use of rhetoric in the service of the gospel.

Cultural institutions and conventions. Finally, Paul can enlist, in a qualified way, conventions and institutions of Greco-Roman society in the service of the gospel. The basic building block of social life in the Hellenistic world was the household, which could encompass not only the extended family, but also slaves, hired workers and sometimes even tenants and business associates. Beyond providing the setting for the gathering of the Pauline communities (Rom 16:5; 1 Cor 16:19; Col 4:15; Philem 2), Paul makes extensive use of the household concept to describe the church (Gal 6:10; Eph 2:19; 1 Tim 3:15; 2 Tim 2:20-

---

[43]Michael B. Thompson, "The Holy Internet: Communication Between Churches in the First Christian Generation," in *The Gospel for All Christians: Rethinking the Gospel Audiences*, ed. Richard Bauckham (Grand Rapids, Mich.: Eerdmans, 1998), p. 66.

[44]Witherington, *Paul Quest*, pp. 126-27.

21) as well as his own ministry (1 Cor 4:1-2; 9:17; Col 1:25).

Paul does not envision the church as a sectarian enclave, like the Jewish separatists at Qumran or modern day Amish communities. His theology of creation and his confidence in the activity of God's prevenient grace in the world are far too robust for that. For Paul, believers' interaction with "the immoral of this world" (1 Cor 5:9-10) is not something to be feared or forbidden. He apparently draws upon the Hellenistic ethical tradition in order to urge Christians' continued participation in society (1 Thess 4:11-12; 2 Thess 3:6-13).[45] He exhorts them in Romans 13:1-7 to acknowledge the authority of the Roman "powers that be" as having been instituted by God. In this passage, Paul reinforces the values of an "honor/shame" culture by encouraging Christians to give the submission and honor that was appropriate to those authorities to whom it was due.[46] They are to "do good" (Rom 13:3) in a public setting as part of their witness and service as God's people in the world (cf. 1 Thess 3:12; 5:15).[47]

We see, therefore, that Paul does not stigmatize the dominant Greco-Roman culture as inherently sinful or something from which Christians should withdraw outright. On the contrary, he seems to recognize the breath of God's grace in human culture, and as apostle to the Gentiles, he himself becomes a catalyst for the gospel's inculturation within it. Paul demonstrates enormous flexibility in making use of the cultural materials that were available to him—whether from language, religion, philosophy, ethics, rhetoric, literature, politics, social institutions, family and community life—as long as they did not conflict with the gospel. We can only speculate as to how much of this was a conscious decision. Paul was an intercultural person at home in the urban Greco-Roman world he shared with his readers. It is only natural that his dynamic theologizing would tap into the language and life of that environment as the gospel interacted with the cultural and religious contexts of the Mediterranean world. Surely his ultimate concern was not whether a particular expression or idea was Jewish or Greek in its origin, but whether it could be used in service of the gospel and the mission of Jesus Christ.[48]

---

[45]See A. J. Malherbe, "Exhortation in First Thessalonians," *NovT* 25 (1983): 251-52.

[46]See Halvor Moxnes, "Honor, Shame, and the Outside World in Paul's Letter to the Romans," in *The Social World of Formative Christianity and Judaism*, ed. J. Neusner et al. (Philadelphia: Fortress, 1988), pp. 210-12.

[47]Philip H. Towner, "Romans 13:1-7 and Paul's Missiological Perspective: A Call to Political Quietism or Transformation?" in *Romans and the People of God: Essays in Honor of Gordon D. Fee on the Occasion of His 65th Birthday*, ed. S. K. Soderlund and N. T. Wright (Grand Rapids, Mich.: Eerdmans, 1999), pp. 166-69. On the implications of Romans 13:1-7 for the transformation of the Roman cultural convention of benefaction, see esp. pp. 160-69.

[48]R. David Kaylor, *Paul's Covenant Community: Jew and Gentile in Romans* (Atlanta: John Knox, 1988), p. 13.

RELATIVIZING CULTURE

If Paul had simply affirmed cultural distinctives and viewed them as points of contact for inculturating the gospel, his approach to culture would be quite straightforward. Alongside this perspective, however, we discover another stream in Paul's thought—that cultural distinctions are relativized in light of the gospel. Paul believes that God has done something radically new in Christ that signals an end to the old order of things. In what is probably an early baptismal formula, he calls the Galatians to perceive the world in a radically different way from the default setting of their culture: "There is no longer Jew or Greek, there is no longer slave or free, there is no longer male and female; for all of you are one in Christ Jesus" (Gal 3:28; cf. Col 3:11). In the new creation, the former barriers that divided people collapse in a heap. Being "in Christ" effects a new set of relationships for believers that largely relativizes the major distinctions of human society, whether ethnic, cultural, socioeconomic or gender.

This "new creation" perspective comes into high definition in Galatians, which at least in part responds to a problem of Jewish cultural imperialism.[49] Jewish Christian missionaries apparently were trying to force Gentile converts to observe the law of Moses as a requirement for being full members of the people of God. The issue focused especially on customs and rites such as circumcision (Gal 6:12-13), food laws (Gal 2:11-14), and observance of Jewish holy days (Gal 4:10)—key cultural symbols that were recognized by Jews and non-Jews alike to stand for Jewish distinctiveness. In short, the agitators were absolutizing Jewish culture and imposing it on Gentiles by mandating that they become Jewish proselytes in order to be acceptable to God. Paul will have none of it. He summarizes his position with a stunning antithesis at the letter's climax: "For neither circumcision nor uncircumcision is anything; but a new creation is everything!" (Gal 6:15; cf. 5:6). God's new creative work makes every external cultural symbol *spiritually* unnecessary. Earlier in the letter, Paul denounces Peter's refusal to maintain table fellowship with Gentiles as a denial of the "truth of the gospel" itself, since it draws cultural boundaries for the Christian community other than faith in Christ (Gal 2:11-14); it forces Gentiles "to live like Jews" (Gal 2:14). In the new creation, cultural "border-crossings" that split the Christian fellowship into pure and impure, first- and second-class citizens, no longer apply. For a Jew like Paul, this was no less than a cultural revolution.[50] Paul must depose the normative status of his Jewish cultural and religious heritage, including the role of the law itself. It must have appeared to many of his Jewish con-

---

[49]Hays, *Moral Vision*, p. 33.
[50]Legrand, *Bible on Culture*, pp. 122-23.

temporaries as a shocking betrayal of his own culture.

In the Roman church Paul finds the opposite problem—the notion that *Gentiles* are now in a preferred cultural and religious position. Apparently the Gentile majority in Rome assumed they had replaced the Jews in God's favored nation status and wanted to sever themselves from their Jewish roots. Paul warns them about the costly consequences of such presumption (Rom 11:17-24). In modern language, ethnocentrism cannot be tolerated from *any* cultural group.

More evidence of the relativizing of Gentile cultural distinctions comes in Colossians 3:11, where Paul affirms that in the new humanity "there is no longer . . . barbarian, Sythian." In contrast to the verse's earlier antitheses (Jew/Greek, circumcised/uncircumcised) that are viewed primarily from a Jewish perspective, these terms directly address the cultural superiority of the Greeks. "Barbarian" was a cultural, not an ethnic term, commonly used to disparage the "uncivilized" and culturally inferior status of non-Greeks. Every culture becomes provisional in light of the cross.

Several passages in 1 Corinthians reinforce Paul's culturally plural stance. We return first to Paul's remarkable claim in 1 Corinthians 9:20, "To the Jews I became as a Jew, in order to win Jews." How is it possible for a Jew to intentionally decide to *become as a Jew*? The answer seems to be that Paul no longer understands what it means to be a Jew in the same sense as he did before he trusted in Christ. As Richard B. Hays explains, "Since Paul was in fact a Jew, this formulation shows how radically he conceives the claim that in Christ he is . . . in a position transcending all cultural allegiances."[51] Later he admonishes the Corinthians not to become a stumbling block to Jews and to Greeks *and to the church of God* (1 Cor 10:32). The old duality of Jews and Gentiles (Greeks) has given way to a new contrast: Jews/Gentiles on the one hand, and the church of God on the other.[52] The former definitions of kinship based on ethnicity and genealogy have been superseded by Christians' adoption into a single family of believers under one Father (Rom 8:14-17; 9:6-8; Gal 3:26-29; 4:5-7). In terms of identity, they are not in the first place Christian *Jews* or Christian *Greeks*, but rather Jewish or Greek *Christians*. By analogy, in the faith community in which I currently minister, our primary identity is not as Christian *Germans* or Christian *Croatians* or Christian *Americans*, but as German, Croatian or American *Christians*. Each group must be willing to lay down their cultural rights in order to

---

[51]Richard B. Hays, *First Corinthians* (Louisville: Westminster John Knox, 1997), p. 151.

[52]Oda Wischmeyer, "Paul's Religion: A Review of the Problem," in *Paul, Luke and the Graeco-Roman World: Essays in Honour of Alexander J. M. Wedderburn*, ed. A. Christophersen et al. (Sheffield: Sheffield Academic Press, 2002), p. 93.

participate in a community that finds its transcending allegiance in Jesus Christ.

A final relevant passage is 1 Corinthians 7:14-24, where in the midst of dealing with questions about marriage and sexuality, Paul states the principle, "Let each of you remain in the condition in which you were called" (1 Cor 7:20; cf. 7:17). Neither ethnic identity (circumcision or uncircumcision) nor any social status (slavery or freedom) constitutes a privileged position in the eyes of God or within the Christian fellowship. In fact, within Christ's household there is a *reversal* of relative status: the slave is a "freed person belonging to the Lord," while the one who was free becomes a "slave of Christ" (1 Cor 7:22), the *lower* social position of the two.[53] Furthermore, the issues of circumcision and slavery illustrate Paul's wider concern in the chapter, that the institution of marriage itself is relativized. Whether a person is married or single is not of ultimate significance; Christians should serve God as they are (1 Cor 7:8, 10-16, 26-35, 40). Paul responds to the status-obsessed Corinthians by relativizing *all* social institutions and affiliations in light of the believer's primary relationship to Christ. "What is really important," concludes Ben Witherington, "is not one's social position but one's soteriological condition."[54] Once again, Paul's new-creation perspective beams through. Christ's death and resurrection mean that believers are already living in the eschatological age; the time has been "shortened" (1 Cor 7:29). Because this world even now is in the process of passing away, they must take a wholly new attitude toward its cultural institutions and values. If all social relationships have only relative significance, Christians are free to live out their calling and bear witness to the gospel in whatever cultural situation they are found.

Relativizing, not removal. How, then, can we square this radical relativizing of culture with what we observed in the last section, that Paul affirms cultural particularity and co-opts it in the service of the gospel? If there is no longer any "Greek and Jew, circumcised and uncircumcised, slave and free" (Col 3:11), does Paul anticipate the blending of all Christians into a bland sameness that expunges cultural and social distinctions? In a provocative study, Jewish scholar Daniel Boyarin argues this is precisely Paul's intention. Reading Paul through the interpretive lens of Galatians 3:28, Boyarin insists that "what drove Paul was a passionate desire for human unification, for the erasure of differences and hierarchies between human beings."[55] Boyarin believes that although Paul's im-

---

[53]Hays, *First Corinthians*, p. 125. See also the illuminating discussion of 1 Cor 7:22 in Dale B. Martin, *Slavery as Salvation* (New Haven, Conn.: Yale University Press, 1990), pp. 63-68.

[54]Ben Witherington III, *Conflict and Community in Corinth: A Socio-Rhetorical Commentary on 1 and 2 Corinthians* (Grand Rapids, Mich.: Eerdmans, 1995), p. 179.

[55]Daniel Boyarin, *A Radical Jew: Paul and the Politics of Identity* (Berkeley: University of California Press, 1994), p. 106.

pulse toward establishing a nondifferentiated humanity was admirable, its results were not; it required the forced eradication of all human cultural differences, particularly those of the Jews, and ultimately a merging of all people into a single, dominant culture.[56]

Surely this is a misreading of Paul. For the apostle, the cross of Christ *relativizes* cultural and social distinctions; it doesn't remove them. The principle "there is no Jew or Greek" does not mean that believers must shed their cultural identities when they walk through the door of faith. Earlier we saw that Paul refuses to compel Jews to give up their Jewish lifestyle, and he holds a continuing place for the Jews in God's salvation plan (Rom 9:4-6; 11:26). He likewise campaigns for the right of Gentiles to be accepted into the people of God as Gentiles, not as Jewish proselytes. They are branches from the *wild* olive tree, different in character from the cultivated tree into which they are grafted (Rom 11:17-24).[57]

Boyarin's argument does, however, spotlight a genuine and necessary tension in Paul's thought. On the one hand, Paul recognizes ethnic and cultural diversity; on the other, he posits a new humanity in Christ in which those differences are transcended. He affirms cultural particularity but rejects cultural privilege. Which side of the tension Paul stresses depends largely on the pastoral and theological needs of the context he is addressing. When facing agitators who are attempting to absolutize the Jewish law and culture, he insists that religious and cultural identity badges mean nothing. In other contexts he follows a more balanced approach. Categories such as Jew and Greek, circumcised and uncircumcised, continue to have ethnic and social significance within the church, but soteriologically "there is no distinction" in the sight of God (Rom 10:12). As Miroslav Volf notes, "Paul deprived each culture of ultimacy in order to give them all legitimacy in the family of cultures."[58]

Paul's delicate dance between cultural particularity and cultural relativity bears implications for the task of contextualizing the gospel. Because no single cultural expression is ultimate, the gospel is free to come to life in a plurality of cultures and circumstances. Yet because God values all cultures and because the gospel cannot be heard in the abstract apart from a cultural home, God must speak to the Jew as a Jew, to the Greek as a Greek, to the Filipino as a Filipino; to the Gen-X'er as a Gen-X'er. We must hold on to both sides of the tension. Our articulation of the gospel must be culture-specific, but not culture-bound.

---

[56]Ibid., p. 8.
[57]Andrew Walls, "The Gospel as the Prisoner and the Liberator of Culture," *EvRT* 7 (1983): 231.
[58]Miroslav Volf, *Exclusion and Embrace: A Theological Exploration of Identity, Otherness, and Reconciliation* (Nashville: Abingdon, 1996), p. 49.

CONFRONTING CULTURE

Another dimension to Paul's attitude toward what we think of as human culture has direct relevance for contextualizing the gospel. Culture not only provides the locus for God's gracious activity through his Spirit, it is also the theater of human sinfulness. In Romans 1, Paul paints the sinful predicament of humankind in pitch dark colors. He demonstrates the universal need for God's righteousness by exposing the global *unrighteousness* of fallen humanity, against which the wrath of God is revealed (Rom 1:18—3:20). The root of human alienation is idolatry and rebellion against God (Rom 1:25). The result is that God gave humankind up to all kinds of ungodly behaviors, relationships and attitudes (Rom 1:24-32). The disease that afflicts all of humanity, whether Jew or Gentile, is that they have turned their backs on God and come under the enslaving power of sin (Rom 3:9; Rom 6:17).[59] Paul's sober analysis of the fallen human condition applies not only to the plight of individual sinners but also to human cultures and societies in a collective sense. Cultures, along with their worldviews and social behaviors, are not simply neutral conduits for the gospel. They are riddled with the cancer of sin.

Moreover, the world *(kosmos)* in which culture operates is enemy-occupied territory. Paul assumes the Jewish contrast between the present age, which is comparable to "this world" (1 Cor 3:19; 5:10; cf. Eph 2:2), and the age to come. Although God's creation is good (1 Tim 4:4; cf. 1 Cor 1:26) and humankind still bears the image of God (1 Cor 11:7), the present age, this world, is evil and opposed to God (Gal 1:4). It is ruled by "the god of this age" (2 Cor 4:4), the "elemental spirits of the world" (Gal 4:3, 9; Col 2:8, 20) and the pernicious powers of darkness (Col 1:13; Eph 2:2; 6:11-12). Societies embody institutions, structures and power relationships that are threatened by the gospel and oppose its advance (cf. 1 Cor 2:6-8; 1 Thess 2:14-16). Because the power brokers of this world resisted the saving purposes of God they "crucified the Lord of glory" (1 Cor 2:8). It is important to see that we cannot simply equate culture with what Paul means by "the world."[60] Culture, as what humans have made of God's good creation, continues to be the arena of God's gracious activity and is capable of being transformed. Nevertheless, inasmuch as all cultures reflect "the spirit of the world" (1 Cor 2:12) and embody human rebellion against God's creative and redemptive purpose, they must be challenged and confronted.

---

[59]Hays, *Moral Vision*, p. 388.
[60]This seems to be the case with H. Richard Niebuhr, who identifies "the world" in the New Testament, particularly the Johannine writings, with the modern notion of culture (*Christ and Culture*, pp. 32, 45-49).

Consequently, the gospel speaks to human culture with a clarion "no" as well as a "yes." The gospel cannot be good news without prophetically judging the sinful elements of culture and the "works of darkness" (Rom 13:12) in human society. "The claims of God," argues Sanneh, "however successfully mediated and embodied in earthly structures, must ultimately be seen to be in radical tension with them, for obedience to God overthrows other rival sovereignties that make their home in culture."[61]

In Paul's thinking, this prophetic principle manifests itself by judging both his native Jewish culture and the pagan culture of his Gentile mission. Boyarin is on the mark that Paul was "an internal critic of Jewish culture."[62] Paul's discovery that salvation was the birthright of both Jew and Greek apart from the Torah and his experience of God's gracious activity within the Gentile mission forced him to come face to face with the ethnocentrism of his own Jewish tradition. Like few of his contemporaries, Paul was able to critique the place of the law and Jewish culture as an insider (Phil 3:3-9; Gal 5:6; Rom 2:1—3:20). He managed to distance himself enough from his own culture to perceive elements in it that were incompatible with the gospel. This is no easy task. It has been said that "trying to criticize one's own culture is like trying to push a bus while you're still sitting in it."[63] Yet it was essential that Paul "push the bus" if he were to offer a gospel to the Gentiles that was rooted in the Jewish Scriptures but freed from Jewish ethnocentrism.

This speaks to the challenge of inculturating the gospel today. Too often in the story of Christian missions, the "gospel" that has been introduced into a society has been indistinguishable from the missionary's own culture. As a result, missionaries have sometimes been too quick to judge the notions and practices of the new culture and too eager to replace them with familiar elements from their own. The gospel, however, must challenge the presuppositions of the missionary's culture if it has any hope of speaking prophetically to the new culture in which it is being contextualized. On more than one occasion I have discovered that in the process of engaging another culture and witnessing God's working within it, I have come to see the weaknesses of my own culture more clearly. But this is more than a missionary problem. Each Christian community must grapple with the gospel's critique of its own, often rapidly changing culture, particularly when that culture claims in some sense to be "Christian." It is vastly easier to recognize the cul-

---

[61]Sanneh, *Translating the Message*, pp. 32-33.
[62]Boyarin, *Radical Jew*, p. 12. Vernon K. Robbins calls Paul's relationship with Jewish culture "*contra*cultural"—"deeply embedded in it, but inverting key aspects of it" (*The Tapestry of Early Christian Discourse: Rhetoric, Society and Ideology* [New York: Routledge, 1996], p. 187).
[63]Lesslie Newbigin, *The Gospel in a Pluralist Society* (Grand Rapids, Mich.: Eerdmans, 1989), p. 95.

tural speck in another's eye than to come to terms with the log in my own. The gospel is not only a searchlight that I allow to uncover the sinful in the cultures of others; it is also a mirror that I must hold up to my own face.[64]

In addition to critiquing his own Jewish heritage, Paul's gospel confronts the worldviews (see, e.g., 1 Cor 15), values and practices of the Greco-Roman society into which it was inculturated. Consider how Paul's preaching "the word of the *cross*" (1 Cor 1:18) directly challenges the culture of status, power and self-promotion that characterized Roman Corinth. In the Roman world, the cross of Christ was an inherently offensive, countercultural symbol. Victor Paul Furnish observes that during their pagan past, most of Paul's converts would have belonged to religious groups that adopted culturally pleasing symbols of life, power and fertility—perhaps a basket of fruit or a stalk of grain.[65] In contrast, Paul could hardly have found an image that would seem more inappropriate or repugnant to Greco-Roman sensibilities than the cross. Crucifixion was the ultimate instrument of Roman torture, used as a political tool to subjugate the provinces of the Empire. It was reserved for those with no status, like despised slaves, hardened criminals and rebellious peasants. The message of a crucified Savior would have been unspeakably shameful and humiliating within the Greco-Roman context. No wonder the Greeks thought it was "folly" (1 Cor 1:23). We might imagine that if Paul wanted to gain acceptance for his gospel within the ordered and status-obsessed Roman world, he would play down so contemptuous and vulgar an image. But Paul does not shrink in the least from embracing the cross as the central symbol of the gospel he proclaims to the Corinthians. Instead, he unleashes the powerful message of Christ *crucified* to subvert what was "normal" in the Roman world, to turn the cultural value system upside down.

The gospel's judging function likewise extends to commonly held ethical mores. Paul, for instance, in line with Jewish tradition, rules out homosexual relations among both men and women (Rom 1:26-27; 1 Cor 6:9-11; 1 Tim 1:10). This is a countercultural move within Greco-Roman society, where the practice of homosexuality was not only widely accepted, but in some circles highly admired.[66] In Romans 1, Paul portrays homosexual activity as a distortion of God's created order

---

[64]Dyrness, *The Earth Is God's*, pp. 66-67.

[65]Victor Paul Furnish, *The Theology of the First Letter to the Corinthians* (Cambridge: Cambridge University Press, 1999), p. 39.

[66]Dunn, *Theology of Paul*, p. 122. For examples of a positive contemporary assessment of homosexual practice, see esp. Plato's *Symposium* and Plutarch's *Lycurgus*; cited in James D. G. Dunn, *Romans 1-8* (Dallas: Word Books, 1988), p. 65. Greco-Roman attitudes were not uniform in their approval of homosexuality, however. Homosexual prostitution, for example, was generally denounced. See Robin Scroggs, *The New Testament and Homosexuality: Contextual Background for Contemporary Debate* (Philadelphia: Fortress, 1983), pp. 17-62.

(Rom 1:24-25), one which breaks down divinely established boundaries of sexual relations between male and female.[67] Using categories familiar to both Stoicism and Hellenistic Judaism, he characterizes homosexual behavior as being "contrary to nature." Here "nature" describes not simply the way things are, but rather the way things *ought to be* according to God's creative intention for human life.[68] Because homosexual practice embodies the theological reality that humanity has rebelled against the Creator and "exchanged the truth . . . for a lie" (Rom 1:25), Paul believes it cannot be sanctioned, regardless of prevailing cultural attitudes or behaviors.

The gospel for Paul is in many respects countercultural and counterethical. It has a prophetic role that says "no" to such elements of culture as its world-views, its religious institutions and its ways of behaving, whenever they clash with the creative and redemptive purposes of God. In a time when efforts to "contextualize" are often more successful at accommodating to culture than pro-phetically judging it, Paul's witness needs to be heard. Each culture, without ex-ception, has dimensions that must be confronted. Yet, it is the sinful in culture, culture as a land occupied by an alien power, that Paul's gospel resists, not cul-ture itself. One more crucial attitude remains.

TRANSFORMING CULTURE

The gospel's judgment on culture is never the last word. Paul's optimism of grace opens up the potential for cultures to be re-formed *from within*. Just as sin had a negative impact on culture, so the new creation in Christ that the gos-pel proclaims will affect culture, with its values and practices.[69] Ultimately, that will mean the renewal of the whole of creation (Rom 8:19-23). In the meantime, however, God's reconciling purposes focus on the church as the transformed and transforming community.

---

[67]Hays, *Moral Vision*, p. 396; William J. Webb, *Slaves, Women, and Homosexuals* (Downers Grove, Ill.: InterVarsity Press, 2001), pp. 250-51. Robin Scroggs argues that Paul's critique of homosexual behavior is limited to the practice of pederasty (homosexual relations between a male adult and a boy or younger youth), primarily in its more exploitive and dehumanizing forms (*New Testament*, pp. 99-122, 126). This interpretation stumbles on Romans 1:26-27, where Paul condemns female, as well as male, homosexual activity. William J. Webb seems to be right that although recent studies of homosexual practice in the ancient world have been illuminating for understanding the biblical texts, for Paul the central issue is not particular ex-ploitive forms of homosexual activity, but rather same-gender sexual acts themselves (*Slaves, Women, and Homosexuals*, pp. 250-51).

[68]Hays, *Moral Vision*, p. 387; Moo, *The Epistle to the Romans* (Grand Rapids, Mich.: Eerdmans, 1996), pp. 114-15. See Hays, pp. 379-406, for a sensitive and informed treatment of the issues of homosexuality in light of the New Testament witness and the contemporary debate.

[69]William A. Dyrness, *How Does America Hear the Gospel?* (Grand Rapids, Mich.: Eerdmans, 1989), p. 8.

For Paul, cultural transformation starts with individual Christians and Christian communities themselves experiencing the renewal of God's grace. The church is not to be "conformed to this world"—accommodating to its worldviews or practices—but inwardly transformed, with a renewed mind (Rom 12:2). New persons in Christ are in the process of being reshaped in the image of their Creator through the work of the life-giving Spirit, resulting in an entirely new set of understandings, values and social relationships (Col 3:10-11; 2 Cor 3:18). How then does this redeemed and transformed community relate to the surrounding culture?

The letter to the Philippians is important here. Borrowing the language of politics from the pagan Roman empire, Paul assures the Philippians that their "citizenship" *(politeuma)* is in heaven and they await a Savior from there (Phil 3:20; cf. 1:27). This statement plays on Philippi's standing as a Roman colony populated by many Roman citizens, no doubt including at least some of the Philippian converts. The city prided itself in its colonial status and the benefaction of Caesar. But the apostle redirects the Philippian believers to a higher, more compelling loyalty. By virtue of their faith in Christ, they are citizens of a "heavenly commonwealth." Their first allegiance is no longer to Caesar, but to Christ. When Paul calls Jesus "Savior" and "Lord" (cf. Phil 2:11), he enlists terms that imperial subjects commonly applied to their "divine" emperor. Considering the burgeoning influence of the imperial cult in the Greek cities, particularly a Roman colony like Philippi, the Philippians could scarcely miss the point. N. T. Wright lays out the alternatives: "Jesus is Lord, and Caesar isn't. Caesar's empire, of which Philippi is a colonial outpost, is the parody; Jesus' empire, of which the Philippian church is a colonial outpost, is the reality."[70] The Philippians must reconstruct their cultural and political identity in light of their loyalty to Jesus, the true Lord and Savior, who reigns over a counterempire to that of Caesar.

Does Paul then think of this Christian commonwealth as an island in a sea of wickedness, a world-renouncing colony in a foreign country that is simply biding its time until the Savior returns to rescue it? On the contrary, the church's existence "in Christ" is not something totally outside of their life "in Philippi" (Phil 1:1).[71] In a sense the Philippians hold dual citizenship. There is in fact considerable overlap between the empire of Caesar and the kingdom of Christ. Yet

---

[70]N. T. Wright, "Paul's Gospel and Caesar's Empire," in *Paul and Politics: Ekklesia, Israel, Imperium, Interpretation,* ed. R. A. Horsley (Harrisburg, Penn.: Trinity Press International, 2000), p. 173.

[71]See Miroslav Volf, "When Gospel and Culture Intersect: Notes on the Nature of Christian Difference," in *Pentecostalism in Context: Essays in Honor of William W. Menzies,* ed. William M. and Robert Menzies (Sheffield: Sheffield University Press, 1997), pp. 229-30.

their life in the earthly Roman colony of Philippi is now governed by their heavenly commonwealth (cf. Phil 1:27).[72] The church is to function here and now, in its culturally embedded existence, according to the character, the values and the conduct of the heavenly life to come. Using the same political language, Paul urges the Philippians to live out their citizenship *(politeuesthe)* in Philippi "in a manner worthy of the gospel of Christ" (Phil 1:27). This is more than a call to fulfill their civic duty.[73] Their change in allegiance demands a change in lifestyle. In contrast to their pagan neighbors, they are to conduct themselves as God's children, "without blemish in the midst of a crooked and perverse generation" (Phil 2:15).

For Paul as for the Philippians, embodying the gospel in the midst of a hostile society entails suffering and persecution (Phil 1:29-30; cf. 3:10). Their example is Christ, whose self-emptying love took him to a criminal's death (Phil 2:1-8). Paul is convinced that the gospel can only engage the world from the vulnerable position of the cross. There is no question of Christians capturing their culture by force or trying to impose a Christian worldview or lifestyle upon it from the outside. The history of Christianity is replete with unsuccessful attempts to do so.[74] The gospel paradigm is not possession by force, but transformation from within.

Paul, therefore, does not envision Christians retreating from their earthly cultural existence to form some kind of new "Christian culture" that is outside of their own. They stand, as Volf puts it, "with one foot outside their own culture while with the other remaining firmly planted in it."[75] They function within their society as a prophetic subculture, whose cross-shaped living offers a visible alternative to the ethos of the dominant culture.

Transforming cultural language. One means of engaging culture in order to transform it is through resignifying its language. We have seen that Paul com-

---

[72]Neil Elliot, *Liberating Paul: The Justice of God and the Politics of the Apostle* (Sheffield: Sheffield Academic Press, 1994), p. 197.

[73]Ben Witherington III, *Friendship and Finances in Philippi: The Letter of Paul to the Philippians* (Valley Forge, Penn.: Trinity Press International, 1994), p. 51.

[74]Alan Neely cites the example of the "Christianization" of tiny Pitcairn Island in the South Pacific by American Seventh Day Adventist missionaries. As a condition of their conversion, the islanders drove their herds of pigs, which were considered by the missionaries to be spiritually unclean, into the sea, and gave up eating crawfish. The traditional Polynesian feast, at which suckling pig was the favorite meal, was banned. On the sabbath (observed on Saturday), the Pitcairners are still prohibited from fishing, swimming, cooking and watching videotaped movies (*Christian Mission: A Case Study Approach*, [Maryknoll, N.Y.: Orbis, 1997], p. 7). For the islanders, Christianity meant forced adoption of the culture of American Adventism.

[75]Volf, *Exclusion and Embrace*, p. 49.

municates Christ to his largely Gentile audiences using terms and ideas that were already a part of their cultural and religious experience. The point here is that on occasion Paul is not afraid to "convert" language from pagan belief systems that were incompatible with the Christian message. The once popular view that Paul's use of such language shows that he blended Christian truth with pagan beliefs has been rightly debunked. As Wright insists, "whatever faults Paul may have had, syncretism was not one of them. . . . [W]hen he took on an idea from pagan culture he made sure it was well and truly baptized before it could join the family."[76] The notion of "transformation" *(metamorphōsis)*, for instance, was a part of the specialized language of the Greek mystery religions and apparently has no Old Testament or Jewish pedigree. Paul, as it were, wrests the *form* from its Hellenistic thought world only to inject it with a new Christian meaning that could represent the inner renewal of the believer in conformity with Christ (Rom 12:2; 2 Cor 3:18). More often he conscripts vocabulary that operated in both Jewish and Greek thought worlds. Words like "mystery" (Rom 16:25-26; 1 Cor 2:7; Eph 1:9; 3:3, 5; Col 1:26-27), "libation" (Phil 2:17), even "gospel" itself, would no doubt have triggered associations with pagan religious practice or the Caesar cult for Paul's Gentile audiences, even though these words had impressive Old Testament and Jewish credentials. Paul seems quite willing to risk misunderstanding by co-opting language from the religious culture of his readers and infusing these forms with new meaning that in part alters and in part replaces the old.

The language of Greco-Roman philosophy, particularly from the Stoic tradition, also becomes eligible for adoption and reinterpretation. It is likely that in Philippians 4:11, Paul consciously reworks the concept of "self-sufficiency" *(autarkeia;* cf. 2 Cor 9:8; 1 Tim 6:6), which for Stoics and Cynics meant independence from external circumstances and pressures. Fee considers Philippians 4:11-13 to be one of Paul's more remarkable moments: "he uses the language—and outwardly assumes the stance—of Stoic 'self-sufficiency,' but radically transforms it into Christ-sufficiency. The net result is that Paul and Seneca, while appearing to be close, are a thousand leagues apart."[77] Paul apparently chose this term in order to suggest and then subvert its popular Stoic understanding in light of his Christian perspective that true contentment is rooted in the grace of God and comes only through the enabling power of Christ (Phil 4:13). Paul's use and redefinition of Stoic themes is less like a friendly merger than it is a hostile takeover—or, as Paul himself puts it, taking "every thought captive to obey Christ" (2 Cor 10:5).

---

[76]N. T. Wright, *What Saint Paul Really Said* (Grand Rapids, Mich.: Eerdmans, 1997), p. 81.
[77]Fee, *Philippians*, p. 427.

We have already seen how Paul enlists and transforms the language and ideology of the Roman Empire in the service of the gospel in Philippians. Something similar happens in 1 Thessalonians 4 and 5. Paul's readers would have recognized the term *parousia* (1 Thess 4:15; 5:23) in relation to an imperial "arrival" at a city, in which emperors were honored as gods. Such visits were accompanied by a festive "meeting" (1 Thess 4:17) of the sovereign by the townspeople outside of the city. Later, Paul introduces the slogan "peace and security" (1 Thess 5:3), which is precisely what Roman propaganda claimed that Rome had brought to the cities of the Empire. It is hard to avoid the conclusion that Paul employs language that deliberately subverts the imperial ideology. The parousia Christians eagerly await is not that of Caesar, but rather of the one divine Lord from heaven, an event that will shatter the counterfeit "peace and security" of Rome.[78] Paul's rearticulation of the language of his culture bears witness that Christian communities do not invent their own special language. Instead, they use existing language from their social worlds in different and transforming ways.[79]

Transforming moral behavior. Unfolding the implications of the Christ event also transforms the values, ethical teaching and conventions that shape behavior in Greco-Roman society. The notion of "humility" (Phil 2:3; Eph 4:2; Col 3:12; cf. Col 2:23) is a case in point. It would not have been lost on either Paul or his readers that the call to follow Jesus' downwardly mobile path of humbling himself (Phil 2:5-8) was a countercultural message. In the Greco-Roman world, "humility" meant servility and having the mentality of a slave—obviously not a trait to be admired or imitated. Dominant cultural values promoted a lifestyle of competition for honor, praise and higher status; Paul tells his converts that they should "in humility" consider others as *better* than themselves (Phil 2:3).

The so-called household codes of Ephesians and Colossians (cf. 1 Tim 2:1-15; 5:1-2; 6:1-2, 17-19; Tit 2:1—3:8) that foster appropriate behavior for various members of the Christian household present us with an especially intriguing case of cultural engagement.[80] It is hardly surprising that Paul would be interested in how Christians should live out their faith in the context of the basic re-

---

[78]See Helmut Koester, "Imperial Ideology and Paul's Eschatology in 1 Thessalonians," in *Paul and Empire: Religion and power in Roman Imperial Society*, ed. R. A. Horsley (Harrisburg, Penn.: Trinity Press International, 1997), pp. 158-66.

[79]Volf, "Gospel and Culture," pp. 228, 232.

[80]The literature on the "household codes" is vast. See the bibliography in David Balch, "Household Codes," in *Anchor Bible Dictionary*, ed. D. N. Freedman (New York: Doubleday, 1992), 3:319-20.

lationships of their cultural world—as husbands and wives, parents and children, masters and slaves. Concerns for the well-ordering of the household were not unique to Christians. Paul's advice has numerous parallels in contemporary Stoic and Hellenistic Jewish moral teaching, and it particularly reflects discussions of "household management" by Aristotle and others.[81]

Paul, then, uses a form of instruction that would have sounded quite familiar to his Greek readers in order to advance an ethic that shares much in common with the standards of contemporary social behavior. It is clear that Paul wants his converts neither to disregard the social structures of their culture nor to try to radically overturn them. The household codes presuppose that Christian mission can best be carried on through engagement with the culture and its institutions. So far, this sounds more conventional than transformational. Has Paul simply put a stamp of approval on the status quo by giving it a Christian rationalization? Do the household codes capitulate to a sub-Christian cultural ethic that sanctions slavery and encourages the domination of women?

Such conclusions fail to recognize that, although there is overlap between the household codes and conventional Greco-Roman morality, there is also an internal difference. Three features of the table in Colossians (3:18—4:1) bring this transforming difference to light. First, its function within its letter context gives it a distinctive orientation. In Colossians 3, Paul describes the "new self" that is being renewed according to the image of the Creator (Col 3:10). That renewal relativizes existing social relationships (Col 3:11) and makes love the binding cord of all human interactions (Col 3:14). In particular, 3:18—4:1, with its piling up of "Lord" language develops the meaning of the plea to "do everything in the name of the Lord Jesus" (Col 3:17). Relationships within the household thus become a concrete expression of what it means to live under the lordship of Christ. Second, the list stands out within its cultural setting for its reciprocity, where wives, children and even slaves are addressed equally with husbands, parents and masters—the household power brokers—and are treated as ethically responsible persons.[82] What is more, even when the more powerful member of the relationship is addressed, it is not in terms of rule and authority, as might have been expected, but rather love for wives (Col 3:19), and justice and fair treatment for slaves (Col 4:1), which were hardly the norm. Third, when

---

[81]See especially Aristotle *Politica* 1.1253b.1-14; for references to various ancient parallels to the New Testament codes, see James D. G. Dunn, *The Epistles to the Colossians and to Philemon: A Commentary on the Greek Text* (Grand Rapids, Mich.: Eerdmans, 1996), pp. 243-44. Dunn rightly cautions against assuming there was a standard form of "household rules" in the ancient world from which Colossians 3:18—4:1 is derived.

[82]See Peter T. O'Brien, *Colossians, Philemon* (Waco, Tex.: Word, 1982), p. 218.

Paul adds a phrase such as "in the Lord" (Col 3:18, 20) to his instructions to wives or children, or when he tells slaves that by their working for their earthly masters they are in reality serving their heavenly Lord (Col 3:23), this is no mere attempt to coat a pagan institution with a Christian veneer. It gives mundane household relationships an entirely new focus and motivation; the way Christians behave toward others is an outworking of Christ's lordship over the community (Col 3:17). When masters are urged to treat slaves justly because "you know that you also have a Master *(kyrios)* in heaven" (Col 4:1), this poses a direct challenge to dominant Roman models for relationships between masters and slaves.

The contextualizing and christological grounding of the code cuts an even sharper edge in Ephesians (5:22—6:9). Here the entire table is subsumed under an introductory headline, "Be subject to *one another* out of reverence for Christ" (Eph 5:21), which is in turn dependent on the command to "be filled with the Spirit" (Eph 5:18). The attitude of mutual submission that transforms traditional hierarchies, along with the infilling presence of the Spirit in the community, become the context for all household interactions. Furthermore, Paul appeals to the gospel's counternarrative itself as the pattern for those relationships. Marriage for believers is no longer simply a patriarchal institution but is redefined by Christ's sacrificial love for the church (Eph 5:25-33). The socially superior member of the household becomes the *servant* of the lesser. Not only are slaves to serve their masters "as to the Lord," but, in a stunning reversal of expectations, masters are to "*do the same* to them" (Eph 6:5-9). In short, "the conventional authority structures of the ancient household are . . . subverted even while they are left in place."[83]

We might ask why, if the gospel had transforming implications for Greco-Roman culture, Paul did not challenge social institutions such as slavery and the patriarchal treatment of wives and children more directly. If Paul could call for the immediate dismantling of the barriers that prevented social interaction between Jews and Gentiles, why does he take such a "conservative" stance in relation to women and slaves? To understand this, we need to see the place of the household codes within the broader mission of the church. Within the first century Roman world, sweeping changes in society were simply not an option. As a minority and a marginalized community in the midst of a dominant culture, the church had no platform from which to try to restructure society as a whole. Any attempt to do so might have jeopardized not only its evangelistic mission, but even its very existence within the Roman world. Rather, Christians were to

---

[83]Hays, *Moral Vision*, p. 64.

live out their calling within the existing structures of Greco-Roman society while displaying a visible internal difference. As a result, Paul calls believers to an attitude of "transforming engagement" with their culture that will sometimes put them in tension with that culture. As Philip Towner puts it,

> The theological grounding in the codes reveals a belief in a God who has opened up the whole world to his program. God's *oikonomia* [household] envelops the whole of life, and corresponding to this, Christian living will need to be done within culture. . . . But God's presence in this world aims at reformation and transformation of its structures, never uncritical acceptance of them.[84]

Cultural institutions and patterns are not rejected but rather granted a higher calling. The marriages of Paul's readers may visibly resemble those of the wider culture in their outward roles and responsibilities, but the attitude of mutual submission and the pattern of Christ's love for the church transforms them from within.[85] Paul does not push for the immediate dismantling of the institution of slavery, but he urges Christian masters and slaves to live within the community with a cross-shaped difference. Witherington seems close to the mark in concluding that Paul's main strategy for social and cultural transformation is to place the yeast of the gospel within the Christian community and household and allow it to do its work over time.[86] Ultimately, the kind of modified vision of the community we find in the household codes that treats slaves as valued persons and as full and equal members of the people of God would undermine the existence of the institution itself.[87] The gospel has a leavening influence from within.

How does Paul's treatment of first century social conventions in the household tables speak to the church's engagement with its culture today? Craig Keener rightly points out that Paul is addressing the authority structures of the Greco-Roman world in which he lived; he is not mandating those same structures relating to women and slaves for all periods and for every culture.[88] We cannot expect Paul's specific household rules that were contextualized to the social and interpersonal realities of his time to correspond in full to societal con-

---

[84]Towner, "Romans 13:1-7," p. 159.

[85]A. J. M. Wedderburn and A. T. Lincoln, *The Theology of the Later Pauline Letters* (Cambridge: Cambridge University Press, 1993), pp. 123-24.

[86]Witherington, *Paul Quest*, p. 202.

[87]William J. Webb suggests that a number of statements in Paul's letters provide "seed ideas" that encourage further movement toward the undermining of the oppressive institution of slavery (see 1 Cor 7:21; 12:13; Gal 3:28; Col 3:11, Philem 15-16) (*Slaves, Women, and Homosexuals*, p. 84).

[88]Craig S. Keener, *Paul, Women, and Wives: Marriage and Women's Ministries in the Letters of Paul* (Peabody, Mass.: Hendrickson, 1992), p. 211.

ventions that may be quite different in our world. Instead, we must reenact Paul's pattern of transforming contextualization from within our own circumstances. For example, even as the gospel considerably improved the situation of women within the social context of the ancient world, so we must allow the gospel leaven to continue to move us toward a more just, equitable and loving treatment of women today. This is true whether we live in cultures where male-female relationships are highly patriarchal or where they are relatively egalitarian. Christ's example of self-sacrificing love makes a positive difference in existing structures in every setting.

For Paul, as well as for us, the gospel engages all dimensions of culture: worldview, language, symbols, religion, politics, social practices, ethics. Yet, this does not happen on a macro level. Volf is right that "Christians have no place from which to transform the whole culture they inhabit."[89] Instead, this happens as transformed communities live out the gospel in the culture they share with the unbelieving world. They will both reflect their culture and at the same time disrupt it. Such holy subversion can only take place from within, using the cultural materials that are available to us. We must resist captivity to the culture, even as we follow Paul in taking "every thought captive" for the sake of Christ.

CONCLUSION

Both Paul's own cultural identity and his attitude toward culture resist any simplistic appraisal. Although he never abandons his primary Jewish heritage, he is able to stand simultaneously in several of the crisscrossing currents that make up his cultural world. His "at-homeness" within overlapping Jewish, Greek and Roman environments put him in a singular position to contextualize the gospel for both Jews and Gentiles, not as a foreigner, but as a cultural insider. At the same time, his identity as a person "in Christ" is more compelling than any cherished cultural identity, and he envisions believing communities in which both Jews and former pagans lay all claims to cultural advantage at the foot of the cross. The Pauline paradigm carries growing significance for the complex global village that comprises much of the mission field of the church today. To articulate and embody the gospel in multilayered and fast-changing intercultural settings requires flexibility, creativity, humility, and a willingness, like Paul, to become "as a Jew to the Jews and as a Greek to the Greeks." Increasingly, the church needs modern-day "Pauls"—servant leaders who can become living bridges between different cultures, socioeconomic groups and generations.

There was also an inherent tension in Paul's attitude toward the world in

---

[89]Volf, "Gospel and Culture," p. 233.

which God's mission was carried out. Paul could affirm human culture as an expression of the Creator's gracious working in the world and draw upon its ways of speaking and living in order to contextualize the gospel for particular Christian communities. At the same time, there were dimensions of culture that had to be relativized in light of "new creation" realities and others which, as expressions of the sinful in culture, could only be rejected or replaced. Yet the goal of the gospel's engaging its world is to bring about the re-formation and transformation of culture in its various dimensions from within, enabling it to increasingly reflect the image of Christ. These four attitudes—affirming, relativizing, confronting and transforming culture—are by no means isolated processes. There is often considerable overlap and flexibility in how Paul addresses his world in a given setting. Different elements of culture call for varying responses. No one way of dealing with Greco-Roman society would suffice.

The same is true for the church's interaction with culture today. Contextualizing the gospel within a particular human arena can take any of these forms and probably will involve all of them. Cultures are complex organisms and cannot be treated as monolithic wholes. The church has no uniform strategy for engaging its world. Our great challenge is to be able to discern, under the guidance of the Spirit, when to affirm culture and when to undermine it, when to *in*-culturate the gospel and when to *de*-culturate it in order to liberate it from being captive to the spirit of the age.[90] This is what Robert Wuthnow refers to as the problem of articulation—how to let our message and practice remain enough a part of our cultural environment that it will not come across as being irrelevant, while at the same time maintaining enough distance from the culture so that we are in the position to shape and maybe even subvert it from within.[91] Like Paul, we must critique our own culture without rejecting it, and transcend our culture even while remaining in it. Likewise, we must be willing to identify with another's culture without uncritically accommodating to it; we must let the gospel speak transformingly to that culture without imposing a foreign culture upon it. This is the calling of the missional church in every place and every generation.

---

[90]See ibid., p. 235.

[91]Robert Wuthnow, *Communities of Discourse: Ideology and Social Structure in the Reformation, the Enlightenment, and European Socialism* (Cambridge, Mass.: Harvard University Press, 1989), pp. 3-5.

5. PAUL AS INTERPRETER
Contextualizing Scripture and Tradition

For whatever was written in former days was written for our
instruction, so that by steadfastness and by the encouragement
of the scriptures we might have hope.

ROM 15:4

The passage under consideration in a class on the Pastoral Letters was 1 Timothy 4:1-5, which in part reads, "For everything created by God is good, and nothing is to be rejected, provided it is received with thanksgiving; for it is sanctified by God's word and by prayer" (1 Tim 4:4-5). In the midst of our discussion, I spotted a ray of illumination suddenly break out on the face of one of my Asian students. His hand shot up and he announced, "I just realized what this text *means*. I am free to eat dog meat!" Admittedly, since I had not come from a culture where the issue of whether or not to eat dog meat was a raging ecclesiastical controversy, I had some trouble sharing both his enthusiasm and his hermeneutical insight. His response does illustrate, however, that our cultural, sociological and church contexts profoundly influence what we *hear* the text saying to us.

From one perspective, contextualization is largely a hermeneutical issue. The question is this: how do we articulate the meaning of the gospel or of Scripture, which came to expression in one cultural, social and historical setting, for people who are living in quite another? Paul grappled with this problem within his own world. He was not simply a missionary and a theologian. He was also an interpreter of traditions, namely, the Hebrew Scriptures—the great written text of the Jews and first Christians—and the oral Christian tradition that he inherited and passed on. How Paul interpreted and applied Scripture and the early Christian confessions to his diverse audiences, then, is an important piece of the mosaic for our understanding of contextualization in the New Testament. In this chapter, we will investigate Paul's hermeneutical approach to the Old Testament as well as his use of Christian tradition for specific contexts.

PAUL AS INTERPRETER OF SCRIPTURE

Paul's thought world is steeped in the Scriptures and the stories of Israel. Not only does he formally quote Scripture[1] but, as Richard B. Hays has shown, his letters resonate with Old Testament allusions and indirect echoes of scriptural texts as well.[2] This is hardly surprising. Paul in his upbringing had been formed to a large measure by his peoples' Scripture and traditions, and Israel's sacred texts continued to profoundly shape him as a Christian. What is more, we saw in chapter three that underlying Paul's letters is a grand saving story that incorporates the foundational stories from the Old Testament about Adam, Abraham and Moses. Few would question that Scripture, whether explicitly cited or echoed from backstage, plays a vital role in Paul's theological reflection. What has not always been recognized, however, is the degree to which Paul's use and interpretation of the Old Testament are contextually oriented. I will first examine Paul's use of interpretive practices that were a part of his world, and then I will consider how and why he reappropriates the Scriptures of Israel for the audiences he addresses.

Paul's use of scripture citations. When Paul quotes Scripture, he does so primarily from the Greek translation of the Old Testament, the Septuagint.[3] Just as a modern pastor who knows Greek would cite Scripture from a translation familiar to his audience, Paul, who probably knew both Hebrew and Aramaic, chooses in most cases to quote the version that would have been familiar to his Greek-speaking converts.[4] When Paul uses the Greek Bible, this is already a form of interpretation. The very act of translation means that the original Hebrew terms and ideas frequently take on new connotations when

---

[1] D. Moody Smith lists approximately 100 explicit Scripture quotations in the Pauline corpus. See "The Pauline Literature," in *It Is Written: Scripture Citing Scripture*, ed. D. A. Carson and H. G. M. Williamson (Cambridge: Cambridge University Press, 1988), pp. 268-72.

[2] Richard B. Hays, *Echoes of Scripture in the Letters of Paul* (New Haven, Conn.: Yale University Press), 1989. Hays has popularized the study of *intertextuality*, which concerns how the New Testament writer, in this case Paul, draws upon and alludes to Old Testament texts and themes.

[3] For statistics, see E. Earle Ellis, *Paul's Use of the Old Testament* (Edinburgh: Oliver and Boyd, 1957), pp. 12, 150-52. According to Ellis's assessment, of the approximately one hundred Scripture quotations in the Pauline corpus, over half are in full or virtual agreement with the Septuagint (LXX), while four agree with the Hebrew Masoretic Text over the LXX, and approximately 40 vary from either the Hebrew or any known Greek text form.

[4] Darrell Bock, "Use of the Old Testament in the New," in *Foundations for Biblical Interpretation*, ed. D. S. Dockery, K. A. Matthews and R. B. Sloan (Nashville: Broadman & Holman, 1994), pp. 99-100.

they are expressed in Greek language and terminology.[5]

How closely Paul follows textual traditions that are known to us in his Scripture quotations varies. At times, he can focus on the exact wording of Scripture when it illuminates the point he wants to make. A well-known example is Paul's reference to the singular form of the word *seed* in Galatians 3:16, which enables him to identify Abraham's seed with Christ. On other occasions, however, he can show considerable freedom in citing Scripture. In some cases he apparently selects from the variety of Greek versions of the text available to him. In others, where the text does not agree with any known version, he may be quoting Scripture roughly from memory. In still other instances, he seems to adapt the language of the Old Testament in order to highlight the particular nuance he wants his audience to hear. Christopher Stanley, in an extensive study of Paul's practice of quoting Scripture, concludes that Paul's Scripture citations often show some form of textual adaptation, and that many of these alterations appear to be motivated by Paul's rhetorical or pastoral concerns.[6] In Romans 10:11, for example, Paul inserts the word *all* into the text of Isaiah 28:16 in order to accent the universal offer of salvation ("*all* who believe in him will not be put to shame," my translation) for which he is arguing in Romans 10:9-13. This sharpening of the meaning of Isaiah's words is all the more noteworthy because he cites the same text in a different form just twelve verses earlier (Rom 9:33, "*whoever* believes in him").

Paul's willingness to flexibly handle the wording of Scripture allows him, in some cases, to target the quotation more specifically to the needs of the church. Clearly, when Paul quoted from the Old Testament, he was more concerned about the meaning of the text than its precise form. This is not altogether unlike preachers today who choose a rendering from the various translations available to them or refer to a passage without quoting it precisely in order to bring out a specific emphasis for their listeners. For Paul, the authority of Scripture derives not primarily from the precise words of the text or translation, but from the God

---

[5]David deSilva, "Writing and Literature: Jewish," in *Dictionary of New Testament Background*, ed. Craig A. Evans and Stanley E. Porter (Downers Grove, Ill.: InterVarsity Press, 2000), p. 1292. A classic example of this occurs when the Septuagint translates the Hebrew "young woman" more precisely as "virgin" *(parthenos)* in Isaiah 7:14 (cf. Mt 1:23).

[6]Christopher D. Stanley, *Paul and the Language of Scripture: Citation Technique in the Pauline Epistles and Contemporary Literature*, Society for New Testament Studies Monograph Series 69 (Cambridge: Cambridge University Press, 1992), pp. 259-64. For a more cautious assessment of Paul's adaptation of scriptural texts, see Timothy Lim, *Holy Scripture in the Qumran Commentaries and Pauline Letters* (Oxford: Clarendon, 1997), esp. pp. 140-43. Lim rightly insists that due to the diversity of textual versions that would have been available to Paul, it is sometimes difficult to determine when he is adapting a text and when he is citing a variant text form.

behind them who continues to speak his word to his people.

Paul's use of Scripture is context-oriented not only in *how* he cites the Old Testament, but also in *when* he quotes the Bible. Explicit quotations are largely confined to the four major letters (Romans, 1 and 2 Corinthians, Galatians), with over half in Romans alone.[7] Not surprisingly, appeals to the Old Testament are most integral to Paul's theological arguments in Romans and Galatians, where he extensively addresses the relationship of the gospel to Israel and the law. More than Paul's other letters, these two have a distinctly "biblical" feel.[8] But what of 1 and 2 Corinthians, where Jewish-related issues are not a dominant concern? In these letters, Paul faces significant challenges to his apostleship or to his vision of the gospel and the Christian lifestyle. It seems he naturally turns to the Scriptures in order to provide special authority for his arguments. This pattern is consistent with his training as a Pharisee, but it was also common for Hellenistic writers and rhetors to cite the sayings of recognized authorities in the course of their rhetorical arguments to make them more convincing.[9] In the Corinthian correspondence a number of Paul's appeals to the Old Testament are for the purpose of ethical instruction or exhortation, giving authoritative guidance for Christian conduct (e.g., 1 Cor 5:13; 6:16; 9:9; 10:7; 10:26; 14:21; 2 Cor 6:16-18; 8:15; 9:9; 13:1). That Paul quotes biblical texts repeatedly when writing to a church made up largely of converts from paganism (1 Cor 12:2) shows that he considers the Scriptures of Israel to be foundational for the spiritual formation of Gentile Christians. The Old Testament has become their heritage, as well.

On the other hand, specific biblical citations are completely absent from 1 and 2 Thessalonians, Philippians, Colossians and Philemon. This does not mean, however, that Scripture plays no role in these letters, since Paul often depends on the Old Testament even when he does not quote it directly.[10] Perhaps the subject matter of these shorter communications to young Gentile congregations, or in the case of Philemon, an individual, makes direct authoritative appeals to Scripture less imperative.[11] The Thessalonian letters deal with specific misunderstandings and practical concerns, while Philippians has a strongly personal orientation. Yet we might well expect Paul to appeal to scriptural authority in Co-

---

[7]In addition to the four major letters, there are explicit Old Testament quotations only in Ephesians, 1 Timothy and 2 Timothy.

[8]See Luke Timothy Johnson, *Letters to Paul's Delegates* (Harrisburg, Penn.: Trinity Press International, 1996), p. 18.

[9]Jerome Collins, *First Corinthians* (Collegeville, Minn.: Glazier/Liturgical Press, 1999), p. 94.

[10]See e.g., the list of Old Testament allusions in Philippians in M. Silva, "Old Testament in Paul," *Dictionary of Paul and His Letters*, ed. Gerald F. Hawthorne, Ralph P. Martin and Daniel G. Reid (Downers Grove, Ill.: InterVarsity Press, 1993), pp. 634-35 (e.g., Phil 2:10-11/Is 45:23).

[11]See Smith, "Pauline Literature," p. 276.

lossians, especially since the error he is combating includes a Jewish influence (Col 2:16). Apparently, the particular nature of the syncretistic teaching that threatens the church in Colossae leads him to follow a different strategy, one in which he seizes the language of his opponents and infuses it with Christian meaning. In short, the extent to which Paul feels the need to appeal to the explicit authority of Scripture varies according to his particular subject matter, rhetorical strategy and the circumstances to which he is speaking, even if that authority is assumed throughout.[12]

Paul's use of contemporary interpretive methods: Midrash and pesher. For our study of New Testament patterns of contextualization, even more important than the way that Paul quotes the text of Scripture is how he *interprets* it for his varied audiences. It has long been recognized that Paul uses methods of interpreting the Bible that reflect his cultural and religious world. Trained as a Pharisee, he stands in the exegetical tradition of Judaism. It would be curious indeed if his writings did not in some way reflect the influence of contemporary ways of reading and interpreting Scripture. Much ink has been spilled over Paul's use of Jewish methods such as midrash and pesher when he interprets sacred texts.[13] Unfortunately, both of these terms are notoriously hard to pin down, and scholars use them in a bewildering variety of ways. Our purpose here is not to provide a detailed discussion of Jewish hermeneutical methods but simply to show that when Paul reads Scripture, he draws upon practices that were familiar to his time and culture.

Midrash as an interpretive activity[14] rests on the premise that Scripture was a record of God's revelation in which every word and letter had a purpose. It therefore seeks to explain the ambiguities of the text and to bring out its every nuance and implication. This allows the sacred text to speak directly to a new situation.[15] The emphasis falls on the recontextualizing of Scripture in relation

---

[12]Christopher Stanley concludes that such a variation in the use of outside sources from one treatise to the next is not unusual among contemporary Jewish and Greco-Roman writings (Stanley, *Paul and the Language,* p. 339).

[13]See, e.g., Ellis, *Paul's Use;* Richard N. Longenecker, *Biblical Exegesis in the Apostolic Period,* 2nd ed. (Grand Rapids, Mich.: Eerdmans, 1999), pp. 88-116.

[14]The Hebrew term *midrash* simply means "interpretation" or "commentary" and is by nature imprecise. We must therefore distinguish between midrash as an activity and midrash as a literary genre, which, according to E. Earle Ellis, "has traditionally been identified with certain rabbinic commentaries on the OT" ("Biblical Interpretation in the New Testament Church," in *Mikra: Text, Translation, Reading and Interpretation of the Hebrew Bible in Ancient Judaism and Early Christianity,* ed. Martin Jan Mulder [Philadelphia: Fortress, 1988], p. 703); cf. A. G. Wright, "The Literary Genre Midrash," *CBQ* 28 (1966): 105-38, 417-57.

[15]For helpful discussions of midrashic interpretation, see Ellis, "Biblical Interpretation," pp. 702-9; Jacob Neusner, *What Is Midrash?* (Philadelphia: Fortress, 1987).

to the life of God's people rather than on the meaning of the text itself.

Various exegetical principles *(middoth)* were developed by the rabbis in order to facilitate this contemporizing of Scripture, some of which have parallels
in Paul's writings. Paul seems to follow the principle of *qal wahomer* (what is
true in a less important case is surely true in a more important case) in a passage
such as 2 Corinthians 3:7-11. Here he argues that if the old covenant ministry of
Moses was glorious, *how much more* glorious is the new covenant ministry of
the Spirit (cf. Rom 5:10, 15-21). Likewise, Romans 4:3-8 reflects the principle of
gezerah shawa (combining different passages that have common terms for the
sake of interpretation), where the key verb *to reckon* enables the bonding of
Psalm 32:1-2 ("blessed is the one against whom the LORD will not *reckon* sin")
to Genesis 15:6 ("it was *reckoned* to him [Abraham] as righteousness"; cf. Rom
9:32-33). Others have detected a midrashic kind of argument in an extended
passage such as Romans 9:6-29. Here Paul chains a series of quotations together
from different parts of the Bible and deploys other exegetical strategies that are
similar to those of later rabbinic works.[16]

The rabbinic *middoth*, however, were not confined to Jewish exegesis in the
ancient world and may even have originated in part out of Hellenistic rhetoric.[17]
The "from the lesser to the greater" type of argument, for instance, was not un-
common in Greco-Roman rhetoric and philosophical writings. It is therefore
likely that at least some of Paul's "Jewish" interpretive methods would have
been familiar to his Gentile readers, and that Paul dipped from the well of both
Jewish and Hellenistic interpretive cultures. As Ben Witherington reasons, "If
Paul was an effective communicator with his largely Gentile audience we would
expect some effort on his part to use some more universal forms of argument."[18]

We can discover further analogies between Paul and the exegetical tradition of
the community at Qumran, which was also interpreting Scripture during the first
century. The Qumran sectarians used a variety of exegetical methods, many of
which overlap with those of the rabbis. Nonetheless, their distinctive hermeneu-

---

[16]See William R. Stegner, "Romans 9.6-29—A Midrash,"*JSNT* 22 (1984): 37-52. It is important to
exercise caution in any comparison of rabbinic midrash to Paul's writings, since the rabbinic
works that are available postdate Paul by several centuries. Nevertheless, E. Earle Ellis makes
a good case that since it is unlikely the rabbis borrowed their methods of interpretation from
Christians, and given that similar first-century patterns can be found in Philo, the presence of
midrashic forms in the New Testament "reflects a common, rather widespread Jewish usage"
("Biblical Interpretation," p. 706).

[17]See David Daube, "Rabbinic Methods of Interpretation and Hellenistic Rhetoric," *HUCA* 22
(1949): 239-64.

[18]Ben Witherington III, *Grace in Galatia: A Commentary on Paul's Letter to the Galatians*
(Grand Rapids, Mich.: Eerdmans, 1998), p. 222.

tical pattern goes on display in the so-called pesher literature, which provided a kind of running commentary on Old Testament books, especially prophetic writings such as Habbakuk (1QpHab). Characteristic of pesher interpretation was the use of an explanatory formula like "the interpretation (pesher) is" or "this is," when commenting on a portion of Scripture. In addition, the Dead Sea community interpreted Scripture from a privileged eschatological perspective. They read biblical texts in light of present and near future events relating to their own community and its enemies, events which were seen as part of the unfolding of the last days. The prophets, they believed, did not know the significance of the mysteries they spoke; only the Qumran interpreters held the hermeneutical keys to unlock the true meaning encrypted in the text. Through this eschatological lens, they contemporized the ancient prophecies for the times at hand.[19]

Paul does not undertake the sustained verse-by-verse interpretation of the Old Testament found at Qumran, nor does he accept all of the hermeneutical presuppositions of the sectarians, which at times led to fanciful interpretations of the text. Nevertheless, similar to the Qumran interpreters, he could read Old Testament prophecies as witnesses to God's current activity in the eschatological community. Thus in 2 Corinthians 6:1-2, the words of Isaiah that originally referred to the return of Israel from exile are contemporized to speak of Paul's apostolic ministry among the Corinthians, which announces that the end-time "day of salvation" has now arrived.[20]

Another fascinating parallel to Qumran interpretation appears in Romans 10:6-9:

> But the righteousness that comes from faith says, "Do not say in your heart, 'Who will ascend into heaven?' " (that is, to bring Christ down), "or 'Who will descend into the abyss?' " (that is, to bring Christ up from the dead). But what does it say? "The word is near you, on your lips and in your heart" (that is, the word of faith that we proclaim); because if you confess with your lips Jesus is Lord, and believe in your heart that God raised Him from the dead, you will be saved.

Formally, Paul seems to follow a pesherlike method of interpreting Deuteronomy 30:12-14.[21] In Qumran fashion, three times the formula "that is" intro-

---

[19]On Qumran interpretation, see Michael Fishbane, "Use, Authority and Interpretation of Mikra at Qumran," in *Mikra: Text, Translation, Reading and Interpretation of the Hebrew Bible in Ancient Judaism and Early Christianity*, ed. Martin Jan Mulder (Philadelphia: Fortress, 1988), pp. 339-77; Maurya P. Horgan, *Pesharim: Qumran Interpretations of Biblical Books* (Washington, D. C.: Catholic Biblical Association of America, 1979).

[20]Joseph A. Fitzmyer, "The Use of Explicit Old Testament Quotations in Qumran Literature and in the New Testament," *NTS* 7 (1961): 316.

[21]Hays, *Echoes of Scripture*, p. 79.

duces his application of the words of Scripture to contemporary events. In addition, the Old Testament text is given an unexpected eschatological interpretation. The word that is "near you" refers, not to the law of Moses, as in Deuteronomy, but to the Christian gospel, "the word of faith" that Paul preaches to Jews and Gentiles (Rom 10:8). What is more, in Paul's interpretive comments on the text, the assurance to Israel that there was no need to ascend into heaven to find God's *commandment* is recontextualized into a reference to the incarnation of *Christ* (Rom 10:6). Although Paul's handling of Deuteronomy 30 does not seem to follow the Qumran exegetes in seeking to decode the concealed meaning of the text, he shares with pesher interpretation the concern to contemporize Israel's Scripture and directly apply it to the present context. Viewed through the lens of God's end-time revelation in Christ, the old text which spoke in the past to Israel takes on a fresh significance for the church. Thus, both Paul and Qumran find an actualization of Scripture for the eschatological community that goes beyond the text's original sense.

Paul's use of contemporary interpretive methods: Allegory. The hermeneutical strategy of allegory is one to which Paul rarely turns (but see 1 Cor 9:8-10). In one case, however, he makes the explicit claim that he is interpreting the Hagar-Sarah story from Genesis "allegorically" (Gal 4:24).[22] In Paul's world, allegorical interpretation was well known both as a convention of Hellenistic rhetoric and as a Jewish method of handling texts. Quintilian identifies allegory as "a manner of speech denoting one thing by the letter of the words, but another by their meaning" (*Inst. or.* 8.6.44), and he attests that it was frequently used by Greco-Roman orators (*Inst. or.* 8.6.47). Witherington may well be right that Paul could assume familiarity with allegory as a literary device among the Galatian Gentiles through their hearing rhetorical speeches or through training in rhetoric, and that Paul would have had reason to make use of such a method as one means of persuading his audience.[23]

On the Jewish side, the leading first century allegorist was the Hellenized Jew Philo of Alexandria. Philo attempted to "contextualize" the Scriptures of Israel for an Alexandrian audience by wedding them to the categories of Stoic and Platonic philosophy. It is enlightening to compare Philo's own allegorical treatment of the story of Hagar and Sarah with that of Paul in Galatians 4:21-31. For Philo, Hagar

---

[22]The verb *allēgoreō* in Galatians 4:21-31 should probably be seen as referring not to an allegory as such, but rather to an allegorizing interpretation of a text that is not in itself an allegory. In other words, Paul likely did not view the story of Hagar and Sarah as originally given as an allegory, but as a biblical narrative, certain elements of which are now being treated in an allegorical fashion. See Richard N. Longenecker, *Galatians* (Dallas: Word, 1990), pp. 209-10.

[23]Witherington, *Grace in Galatia*, p. 322.

symbolizes preliminary learning, which gives birth to sophistry (Ishmael), while Sarah represents virtue and her offspring true wisdom (Isaac). As Sarah cast out Hagar and Ishmael, so "it is necessary to move beyond mere sophistry and mundane learning if one wishes to attain wisdom and virtue."[24] In some ways, Paul and Philo are poles apart: Paul does not share Philo's Hellenistic philosophical assumptions, nor does he dehistoricize the figures of Hagar and Sarah into human symbols for timeless moral truths, as Philo does.[25] Nevertheless, Richard N. Longenecker suggests that "Philo's Hagar-Sarah allegory bears several striking surface similarities to Paul's. . . . Both depend on similar elements in the story: the contrast between slave and free; the two sons; the banishment of Hagar and Ishmael in favor of Sarah and Isaac. In both, Hagar and Ishmael represent a preliminary and preparatory stage that is superseded by something greater."[26]

Although not as common as in Hellenistic Judaism, allegorical interpretation played a role in Palestinian Judasim as well. Parallels to Paul's allegorical contemporizing of Scripture in Galatians 4 can be found in the Qumran writings. In one treatment of Numbers 21:18 ("the Song of the Well" CD 6:3-11), for example, the well represents the Law, those who dig it the members of the community, and the stave with which it is dug "the Interpreter of the Law." Here contemporary events outside of the story, viewed from an eschatological perspective, determine how the story is allegorically interpreted and applied.[27] This is also the case in Galatians 4:21-31, where Paul allegorically reinterprets the Genesis narrative in light of the presence of Jewish Christian troublemakers in the church. Although the passage raises many interpretive questions, the present point is not that Paul is dependent on any contemporary method of allegorizing or any particular interpretation of the Hagar-Sarah story, but rather that when Paul claims he is reading the Scripture "allegorically," he is drawing upon a widely recognized rhetorical and hermeneutical strategy in order to reappropriate a text for his audience.

We can draw the following conclusions from this brief observation of Paul's use of contemporary hermeneutical methods: (1) When Paul comes to interpret Scripture, he frequently makes use of exegetical traditions and practices that are

---

[24]Longenecker, *Galatians*, p. 204.

[25]J. Louis Martyn, *Galatians* (New York: Doubleday, 1997), p. 436. For this reason, some interpreters think that Galatians 4:21-31 is an example of typology rather than allegory. Typology, however, assumes a genuine historical correspondence between the Old Testament and New Testament person or event (e.g., 1 Cor 10:1-11). The connections Paul draws between Hagar and both Mount Sinai and the present Jerusalem seem to go well beyond the kind of historically grounded type-antitype relationship that is characteristic of typology.

[26]Longenecker, *Galatians*, p. 205.

[27]Witherington, *Grace in Galatia*, p. 223.

no doubt rooted in his Pharisaic education and are wholly appropriate to his time and culture. To this extent, he participates in a tradition of Jewish interpretation. At the same time, he handles such traditions and cultural tools with considerable restraint and avoids the kinds of fanciful exegesis often found in Jewish midrash, pesher or allegorical readings of Scripture. (2) Paul does not consistently follow any single hermeneutical method, such as midrash or pesher, but rather he selectively adopts and adapts current practices when they serve his rhetorical or pastoral purpose. (3) Deserving more recognition than is normally given is the possibility that Greco-Roman rhetoric plays a significant role in Paul's methods of interpreting and citing Scripture. This is true not only because principles of Hellenistic rhetoric apparently lay behind many Jewish hermeneutical strategies, but also because Paul would likely draw upon methods of communicating that would be plausible and persuasive for his mainly Gentile readers. (4) All three of the hermeneutical strategies we have examined have a similar aim of contemporizing and contextualizing biblical texts for a community of readers in the present, although they take quite different paths toward that goal. Paul, too, has a "contextualizing hermeneutic," which becomes a key to his use of such methods when he unfolds the meaning of Scripture for his readers.

Can we follow Paul's methods of interpretation? Is there any sense, then, in which Paul's use of contemporary Jewish exegetical methods such as midrash or pesher could serve as a model for communities of believers as they interpret Scripture today? In other words, should we contextualize not only the *content* of our readings (our theology), but also the specific *methods* we use to read Scripture? This question becomes especially relevant in light of the recent proliferation of "cultural" readings of the Bible throughout the world. Such efforts often trade in modern historical-critical models of interpretation for hermeneutical strategies that claim to be more suited to the particular cultures and life experiences of the readers.

Richard N. Longenecker has argued on more than one occasion that because apostolic interpretive methods such as midrash, pesher and allegory were culturally specific and based on a unique revelatory stance, they are *not* normative for today. "Ours," he reasons, "is to reproduce the faith and doctrine of the New Testament in ways appropriate to the apprehension of people today, not to attempt to reproduce . . . the specific exegetical procedures contained therein."[28]

---

[28]Richard N. Longenecker, "Who is the Prophet Talking About? Some Reflections on the New Testament's Use of the Old," in *The Right Doctrine from the Wrong Texts? Essays on the Use of the Old Testament in the New*, ed. G. K. Beale (Grand Rapids, Mich.: Baker, 1994), p. 385; see also idem, *Biblical Exegesis*, pp. xxxiv-xxxix.

If the question is one of simply aping particular interpretive techniques from ancient Jewish culture, such as pesher and midrash, then I fully agree. But can we not learn from Paul's example that there is no single legitimate strategy for interpreting Scripture, and that our hermeneutical *methods*, as well as our message, ought to be appropriate to the context?

Missiologist Larry W. Caldwell thus appeals to Paul's and other New Testament writers' use of "receptor-oriented" interpretive methods as a model for what he calls *ethnohermeneutics*. By this he means using context-appropriate hermeneutical methods for communicating the biblical message in various cultures—methods which sometimes resemble those employed by the New Testament writers.[29] Non-Western theologians and intercultural communicators, he argues, need to be free to discover and practice the hermeneutical methodologies that are already being used to interpret oral traditions or sacred writings within a given culture. Caldwell gives an example from the Cotabato Manobo tribe of the Philippines, where the hermeneutical method of *peligad*—figurative speech that is interpreted according to what it symbolizes—is used to bring out the meaning of oral literature. Such a method, he suggests, might be used to interpret the parables of Jesus, where for instance the figurative language of the mustard seed symbolizes the kingdom of God and its growth.[30]

I appreciate Caldwell's concern to explore culturally appropriate resources for contextualizing the message of Scripture that go beyond the critical methodologies developed in the West. After all, the historical-critical method that has been so dominant in the modern history of biblical interpretation arose itself out of a particular context and time; it is also a form of "contextual hermeneutics." But Caldwell's plea for "ethnohermeneutics" also raises cautions. One problem is that methods of interpretation existing within a given culture often reflect worldviews, values and religious beliefs operating within that culture, some of which may not be compatible with reading Scripture as the Word of God. David J. Hesselgrave and Edward Rommen, for example, point out the risks of reading the Bible according to the ahistorical categories of myth that are normally used to interpret and contextualize Japanese Shinto writings.[31] Regardless of how contextually relevant a given hermeneutical method may be, if it does not allow

---

[29]Larry W. Caldwell, "Third Horizon Ethnohermeneutics: Re-Evaluating New Testament Hermeneutical Models for Intercultural Bible Interpreters Today," *AJT* 1 (1987): 314-33; idem, "Cross-Cultural Bible Interpretation: A View from the Field," *Phronesis* 3 (1996): 24-30.

[30]Caldwell, "Cross-Cultural Bible Interpretation," pp. 29-30.

[31]David J. Hesselgrave and Edward Rommen, *Contextualization: Meanings, Methods, and Models* (Grand Rapids, Mich.: Baker, 1989), pp. 129-32, 140. Of course, the historical-critical methods that are dominant in the West often operate with rationalistic, skeptical and antisupernatural underpinnings that do not allow the Bible to function as the church's Scripture.

the Bible to speak as the authentic Word of God that is rooted in God's revelation in history, it is less than adequate.[32] Kevin Vanhoozer is quite right that "while there may be no single correct interpretive scheme, it does not follow that any scheme is as good as another."[33] "Ethnohermeneutics" may have potential for promoting culturally appropriate ways of reading Scripture in the global context, but it needs further reflection and development to determine its usefulness. In the final analysis, if we want to see Paul as a paradigm for context-sensitive interpretation, we need to focus not on specific exegetical methods, but rather his distinctive hermeneutical perspective.

Paul's hermeneutical perspective. Although there were precedents in the Jewish interpretive traditions for contemporizing Scripture for new realities, it is not the strategies Paul learned from his hermeneutical heritage that ultimately determine *how* or *why* he reappropriates the Old Testament for his readers. Above all, Paul's fundamental theological convictions, anchored in his experience of Christ, shape his hermeneutical approach. Like interpreters of all generations, Paul comes to Scripture from a particular vantage point. As J. Louis Martyn recognizes, "On the road to Damascus a true 'hermeneutical conversion' took place, producing an authentic revolution in Paul's understanding of the ancient Scriptures."[34] As a result, the gospel of God's saving intervention in Jesus Christ functions as a kind of interpretive matrix providing the fundamental assumptions and perspectives out of which Paul understands Scripture and applies it to the life circumstances of the Mediterranean mission field.[35]

In the first place, Paul reads the Old Testament through christological and eschatological lenses. Because he is convinced that Christians live in the end times, when God's purposes for the ages are being fulfilled in the crucified and risen Messiah, he can view all of Scripture as a witness to the gospel of Christ (Rom 1:2). Paul "sees in the coming of Jesus Christ not only the turning point of the ages but the turning point for understanding Scripture."[36] Only in Christ is the veil that has covered the Jews' reading of the old covenant taken away (2 Cor 3:14-15). Morna D. Hooker explains:

> The significant difference between Paul and his contemporaries is not . . . a question of method, since he uses techniques which would have been familiar to them,

---

[32]Caldwell acknowledges this point ("Cross-Cultural Bible Interpretation," p. 28).

[33]Vanhoozer, *Is There Meaning in This Text? The Bible, the Reader, and the Morality of Literary Knowledge* (Grand Rapids, Mich.: Zondervan, 1998), p. 322.

[34]Martyn, *Theological Issues*, p. 67.

[35]See James V. Brownson, *Speaking the Truth in Love: New Testament Resources for a Missional Hermeneutic* (Harrisburg, Penn.: Trinity Press International, 1998), pp. 39-43.

[36]Smith, "Pauline Literature," p. 282.

even though they are strange to us. Rather it is seen in his underlying assumption that Christ himself is the key to the meaning of scripture. It is not that Christ expounds the scriptures—as did the Teacher of Righteousness at Qumran, and as was perhaps expected of the Messiah—but that he is himself the one about whom all scripture spoke.[37]

There is no clearer evidence for this than Paul's regular practice of rereading Old Testament texts that name Yahweh as "Lord" (kyrios), so that now "the Lord" signifies Christ (e.g., Rom 10:13 [Joel 2:32]; 1 Cor 1:31 [Jer 9:23-24]; 2 Cor 10:17 [Jer 9:23-24]). Here Paul stands in an emerging tradition of Christian interpretation which, from the earliest days of the church, read Scripture at a witness to Jesus Christ (e.g., Acts 2:21, 25, 31, 34-35; 4:11; cf. Phil 2:9-11).

At the same time, it is striking that relatively few of Paul's Old Testament quotations or allusions explicitly talk about Jesus as the fulfillment of the Scriptures.[38] On the whole, Paul does not appeal to Scripture in order to demonstrate his understanding of Christ, as we might expect. The reason for this is no doubt tethered to Paul's contextual purpose in writing letters to largely Gentile Christian communities. In contrast to Luke's record of Paul's missionary preaching to Jews in Acts (see Acts 13:16-41; 17:3), in letters to Christians, there is simply no need to prove the identity or messiahship of Jesus. Christology functions more as an underlying assumption that governs Paul's reading of the Old Testament than as its specific focus.[39]

What Paul finds in the Scriptures of Israel and how he applies it relates to the needs of the churches to which he is writing and the particular vision of the gospel he wants to communicate to them. The emphases that emerge as the focus of Paul's contextual use of the Old Testament are twofold: the promised salvation, and the church as the eschatological community. J. W. Aegeson reckons that nearly four in ten of Paul's Scripture citations support his claim that God's saving righteousness is by faith and not the law for Jews and Gentiles.[40] It is hardly surprising that most of these occur in Romans and Galatians, where the issue is close to the heart of Paul's theological concerns. Furthermore, Richard B. Hays has demonstrated convincingly that Paul characteristically finds in Scripture "a prefiguration of the church as the people of God" (e.g., Rom 9—11;

---

[37]Morna D. Hooker, "Beyond the Things That Are Written? St Paul's Use of Scripture," in From Adam to Christ: Essays on Paul (Cambridge: Cambridge University Press, 1990), pp. 152-53.
[38]But see, e.g., Rom 9:33; 10:6-8; 11:26; 15:3, 12; 1 Cor 10:4; 15:24-27; Gal 3:13, 16; cf. Rom 1:1-2; 1 Cor 15:3-4.
[39]J. W. Aegeson, Written for Our Sake: Paul and the Art of Biblical Interpretation (Louisville: John Knox, 1993), pp. 34, 38. Contrast this with the Gospels of Matthew or John, for example.
[40]Aegeson, Written for Our Sake, p. 38.

1 Cor 10:1-22; Gal 4:21-31).[41] For Paul, the Old Testament witness to Israel is fulfilled in the end-time community made up of Jews and Gentiles. In Romans 15:7-13, for example, Paul draws upon passages from Israel's entire canon—the Law (Deut 32:43), the Writings (Ps 117:1) and the Prophets (Is 11:10)—to announce his vision of new covenant communities in which Gentiles join with Jews in glorifying God. This interpretive strategy is entirely appropriate for Christians who needed to know in what sense they were people of God and what their relationship was to Israel and to God's workings in the past.

Underpinning Paul's hermeneutical approach is his unshakable conviction that the Scriptures are written for the church (Rom 4:23-24; 15:4; 1 Cor 10:6, 11; 2 Tim 3:16). "For whatever was written in former days," he assures the Romans, "was written for our instruction, so that by steadfastness and by the encouragement of the scriptures we might have hope" (Rom 15:4). When Paul interprets the Old Testament, he never does so in an abstract, detached way. He reads the sacred texts in the context of his Gentile mission and for the sake of living mission communities in Rome, Galatia, Philippi or Corinth. Scripture, rightly understood, is intended to instruct, edify and transform the people of God.

The various dimensions of Paul's interpretive stance come into sharp relief in a passage such as 1 Corinthians 10:1-12. Here, in a midrashic type of argument, Paul appeals to the Old Testament narrative of Israel's Exodus experience as a negative example, warning the Corinthians of the deadly dividends of flirting with idolatry. On the one hand, he interprets the Old Testament christologically in some rather surprising ways. The Israelites, we are told, "drank from the spiritual rock that followed them, and the rock was *Christ*" (1 Cor 10:4). Whatever earlier Jewish traditions Paul may evoke in identifying the traveling rock with Christ, he seems to be saying that it was Christ himself who was actually present with Israel, nourishing them in the wilderness, in a way that is analogous to how Christ provides benefits to Christians now.[42] Again, it was *Christ* whom the Israelites put to the test in the desert (1 Cor 10:9), just as the Corinthians are now testing Christ through their association with idols. From his new hermeneutical horizon, Paul discovers Christ in the story of Israel.

It is not Christology, however, that is the focus of Paul's use of Scripture in the passage. Rather, it is the significance of the Exodus story for the present situation of the Corinthians. Paul reads the wilderness account in light of the experience of the church in Corinth. He begins by speaking of the Israelites as

---

[41]Hays, *Echoes of Scripture*, p. 86.
[42]Ben Witherington III, *Conflict and Community: A Socio-Rhetorical Commentary on 1 and 2 Corinthians* (Grand Rapids, Mich.: Eerdmans, 1995), pp. 218-19.

"*our* ancestors" (1 Cor 10:1), then proceeds to interpret the Old Testament wilderness narrative as a typological prefigurement of what is happening in Corinth: "these things occurred as examples *(typoi)* for us" (1 Cor 10:6; cf. 10:11). Because God has not changed, Paul can build a hermeneutical bridge by drawing a direct analogy between the experience of Israel in the desert and the present experience of the church. Paul summons the Corinthian Gentiles to find themselves in the Old Testament story—for it is *their* story, as well—and to allow it to reshape their current thinking and behavior. The Pentateuchal narratives should serve as a warning to the Corinthians, who are in danger of reenacting the perilous precedent of their ancestors. This is not simply a matter of right conduct. The analogies Paul uses of the Israelites being "struck down" (1 Cor 10:5) and "destroyed" (1 Cor 10:9, 10) suggest that the Corinthians' very salvation is at stake. Paul drives home the wilderness lesson: "if you think you are standing, watch out that you do not fall" (1 Cor 10:12). Here Paul's handling of Scripture is a two-way process; he reads Scripture in light of the church's experience and at the same time uses Scripture to interpret contemporary events and to transform the community.[43] A dialogue unfolds between the sacred text and the community's current experience of the Spirit.

Paul is able to discern this pattern of correspondence between the history of Israel and the church of his day in part because he interprets the Old Testament from an eschatological vantage point. The ancient events happened and were written down "to instruct us, *on whom the ends of the ages have come*" (1 Cor 10:11). He is convinced that the church stands at a watershed moment in which God's designs for his people in the past are being realized through God's climactic action in Christ and the church. Elsewhere, Paul can even inform the Galatians that Scripture "preached the gospel in advance" to Abraham that the Gentiles would be justified by faith and included in the people of God (Gal 3:8). The larger significance of Israel's story could only now become plain for the eschatological community.

In sum, Paul's interpretation of Scripture is determined by the gospel of Christ and directed to the church, the end-time community, with the goal of transforming the people of God. Yet, while the gospel serves as the matrix from which Paul contextualizes Scripture for the church, the integrity of Scripture is not undermined through a one-sided christological or eschatological reading. Because the Old Testament is the Word of God and therefore fully authoritative for Paul, it is essential that God's action in Christ also be read and interpreted

---

[43]Ben Witherington III, *The Paul Quest: The Renewed Search for the Jew of Tarsus* (Downers Grove, Ill.: InterVarsity Press, 1998), p. 256.

in light of Scripture (Rom 1:2; 3:21; 1 Cor 15:3-4). Hays is right that Paul brings Scripture into a kind of dialectical engagement with the gospel. Scripture and gospel interpret one another.[44]

Context-oriented interpretation. Paul's hermeneutical activity reveals a dynamic interplay between three elements: Israel's Scriptures, the gospel as an interpretive matrix, and the life situation of the mission churches. This interaction enables him to recontextualize the ancient text so that it speaks a direct "gospelized" word to his first century Jewish and Gentile readers. In many cases, Paul's interpretations follow the original sense of the passage. As one illustration, Romans 11:3-5 draws attention to the narrative setting of 1 Kings 19, recalling Elijah's complaint about Israel's apparent total defection and God's assurance that a faithful remnant of 7000 had refused to worship Baal (1 Kings 19:10, 14, 18). By retelling the story, Paul can read a direct analogy between Elijah's day and "the present time" (Rom 11:5), when once again a faithful God had preserved a righteous remnant out of an unfaithful Israel.

In some cases, Paul draws from the wider Old Testament context of a Scripture passage in order to apply it to his audience. In 1 Corinthians 3:20, he quotes from Psalm 94 to bolster his point that the Corinthians' human wisdom is foolishness in the eyes of God: "The Lord knows the thoughts of the wise, that they are futile" (Ps 94:11). Notably, the key term "wise" does not appear in the text of Psalm 94:11 (93:11 LXX), which speaks of "the thoughts *of humans*" *(anthrōpōn)*. Rather, Paul imports it from Job 5:13, which he has just quoted in the previous verse, using the principle of *gezerah shawa,* in which biblical passages that share common vocabulary can interpret one another. This move is fully consistent with the original meaning of Psalm 94, however, since verse 8 of the Psalm reads, "Understand, O dullest of the people; you fools, when will you become *wise?*" Paul's understanding of the larger Old Testament context allows the psalm, which originally petitioned the Lord to judge the "foolish" oppressors of God's people, to powerfully indict the "foolish" Corinthians who think they are wise.[45]

At times, however, Paul reappropriates the Old Testament for his audience in more creative, even surprising ways. This happens in a passage like Romans 9:25-26, where he draws upon two texts from Hosea (Hos 2:23 and 1:10) that originally spoke of the restoration of the northern tribes of Israel:

---

[44]Hays, *Echoes of Scripture,* pp. 176-77; cf. Francis Watson, "Is There a Story in These Texts?" in *Narrative Dynamics in Paul: A Critical Assessment,* ed. B. W. Longenecker (Louisville: Westminster John Knox, 2002), pp. 234, 238.

[45]See Hays, *First Corinthians,* p. 60.

Those who were not my people I will call "my people," and her who was not beloved I will call "beloved." And in the very place where it was said to them, "You
are not my people," there they shall be called the children of the living God.

In Romans, Paul applies these words directly to God's calling of the *Gentiles*.
The situation behind this fresh reading of Scripture is the ongoing debate in the
early church about the role of the Gentiles in God's saving plan and their relationship to Israel. Because he believes that the Old Testament prophecies of a
renewed Israel find their fulfillment in the end-time community, Paul hears a
new song break forth from the ancient voice of the prophet. Douglas Moo is
right in saying that what is happening is not so much that the original sense of
the text has totally vanished, but that "God's final revelation in Christ gives to
[Paul] a new hermeneutical key by which to interpret and apply the [Old Testa-
ment]."[46] The historical particularity of the Old Testament context does not keep
Paul from recognizing an appropriate contemporary meaning for his readers.

Paul can even resignify a command from the ceremonial law ("You shall not
muzzle an ox while it is treading out the grain," Deut 25:4) in 1 Corinthians 9:8-
10 to support his argument that he and his coworkers have a right to enjoy the
material benefits of their labor. While this allegorical reading might seem like an
astonishing stretch of the text to many modern readers, again Paul's immediate
concern is not with the meaning of the text in its Old Testament setting, but
rather with its application in the present. From Paul's eschatological perspective,
such laws were ultimately "written for our sake" (1 Cor 9:10); that is, for the sake
of God's people on whom the end of the ages had come. Paul is not doing historical exegesis—seeking to uncover the meaning of the text in its original context—but rather offering a pastoral contextualization of Scripture for a new situation. The Jewish law, transposed into a new key, has specific lessons for the
church.

A comparison of how Paul reappropriates the Genesis narratives about Abraham in Galatians and Romans spotlights his context-oriented approach to the
Old Testament. In Galatians, Paul unexpectedly interprets the "seed" of Abraham (Gal 3:16; cf. Gen 12:7; 13:15; 17:7; etc.) to refer to a single individual,
Christ.[47] In doing so, Paul may be providing a counterreading of the Abraham
story to that of the Jewish Christian troublemakers. They would have identified

---

[46]Douglas Moo, *The Epistle to the Romans* (Grand Rapids, Mich.: Eerdmans, 1996), p. 613 n. 13;
     cf. N. T. Wright, *The Climax of the Covenant: Christ and the Law in Pauline Theology* (Minne-
     apolis: Fortress, 1991), pp. 264-65.
[47]David Daube has shown that there are parallels for the technique of interpreting a generic
     singular in an individual sense in later Jewish rabbinic literature, *The New Testament and Rab-
     binic Judaism* (London: University of London, Athlone Press, 1956), pp. 438-44.

the "seed" with Abraham's plural, ethnically distinct descendants and those who are related to them through observing the law.[48] But Paul's christological rereading of history enables him to divorce the promise to Abraham from the kind of Torah obedience promoted by the agitators. The Galatian Gentiles become Abraham's offspring, not by joining ethnic Israel—an interpretation that is excluded by the gospel—but by being united with Christ (Gal 3:29), the one true heir of God's promised blessing (Gal 3:19b). This hermeneutical coup comes not from direct exegesis of the Old Testament text, but as a result of recontextualizing the Genesis narrative in light of the Christ event. Such a christological interpretation of Abraham's seed plays no role in Romans 4, however. Here Paul refers to the "seed" in its traditional collective sense (Rom 4:13, 16, 18). The accent is on Abraham as a representative character who prefigures all those who are justified by faith, without respect to ethnic identity. He is the "the father of many nations" (Rom 4:17, 18), whose "seed" is the unified *people* of God, the church comprised of Jews and Gentiles (Rom 4:16-18). This ecclesiological interpretation of Abraham's seed, however, is not incompatible with Paul's christological treatment in Galatians, as the reference to the whole community of those who belong to Christ as the "seed" in Galatians 3:29 makes clear. Nevertheless, the different settings of the two churches require two distinct but legitimate ways of contemporizing the story.

Paul's handling of Scripture is thus largely a matter of contextualization. Again and again we see Paul reappropriating ancient stories and texts so that they become a living word for the new circumstances of his Christian audiences. Unlike much of our exegetical interest today, Paul is not primarily concerned with determining what the passage was intended by its author to mean in its original time and setting, but rather with how Scripture speaks to the present community of faith. In his use of the Old Testament, Paul functions more like a preacher than an exegete whose focus is on historical meaning. He brings to Scripture concrete concerns out of a particular context and allows the sacred text to address them. In Paul's contextualizing hermeneutic, the relationship between understanding and application becomes almost seamless.

Does this mean that when Paul contemporizes the Old Testament he is being cavalier in his handling of Scripture? Do his creative contextualizations run roughshod over the Bible's original meaning? We have no indication that Paul considers the text's historical meaning to be wrong or irrelevant. He does not deny Isaiah's or Deuteronomy's sense for their own situation. For Paul, however, the meaning of Scripture is not something frozen in a "once upon a time"

---

[48]So Martyn, *Galatians*, pp. 340, 346; Longenecker, *Galatians*, pp. 126, 131-32.

past. Sylvia Keesmaat, speaking of Paul's use of Old Testament narratives in Galatians, observes that "Paul, as he wrote to those communities, told the story anew so that the circumstances of the Galatian Christians were intricately identified with the tale he was telling."[49] With the eyes of a missionary-pastor, Paul extends and rereads old meanings for new circumstances in light of the eschatological realities of his own time.[50] At the same time, Paul's interpretations are constrained and given coherence by two guiding pillars of fire: the gospel story of what God has done in Jesus Christ, as the fulfillment of what God has been doing in human history all along; and Paul's conviction that the "mystery" of God's divine plan for the ages had been revealed to him, not by human wisdom, but by the Holy Spirit (1 Cor 2:6-16; cf. Rom 16:25-26; Eph 3:3-6). Although seldom explicitly stated, Paul's consciousness of the Spirit's vital ministry of guidance and illuminating the minds of God's people (e.g., Rom 8:14; 1 Cor 2:13-16; Gal 5:25; Phil 1:9-11; Eph 1:17-19) strongly suggests that Paul believed he was led by the Spirit of the living Christ as he read and contemporized the ancient texts for the churches.

Paul's hermeneutic of Scripture is therefore "incarnational," first in its use of the interpretive methods available in his culture; second in that it is directed to the church for the purpose of transforming God's people; and third in its ability to address the life circumstances of Paul's readers. Paul recontextualizes the Scriptures of Israel for predominantly Gentile mission churches in a way that enables a biblical text or story to become a fresh, transforming message from God for the Christians of his day.

Contextualizing Scripture today. What can we learn from Paul's hermeneutical approach that might inform and instruct contemporary Christians as they read Scripture within their various life settings? First, Paul shows us that our

---

[49]Sylvia C. Keesmaat, "Paul and His Story: Exodus and Tradition in Galatians," in *Early Christian Interpretation of the Scriptures of Israel: Investigations and Proposals*, ed. Craig A. Evans and James A. Sanders (Sheffield: Sheffield Academic Press, 1997), p. 327.

[50]There are various ways to view the relationship between the original historical meaning of the Old Testament text and its New Testament interpretation. Walter C. Kaiser Jr. has consistently argued that there is a single meaning to any passage of Scripture, which is given by God and understood by both Old Testament author and New Testament interpreter (e.g., *The Uses of the Old Testament in the New* [Chicago: Moody Press, 1985]). Others hold to some type of *sensus plenior* in which the New Testament discloses a deeper meaning that is hidden from the Old Testament author but intended by God. See Raymond Brown, "The History and Development of the Theory of a *Sensus Plenior*," *CBQ* 15 (1953): 141-62; Douglas J. Moo, "The Problem of *Sensus Plenior*," in *Hermeneutics, Authority and Canon*, ed. D. A. Carson and J. D. Woodbridge (Grand Rapids, Mich.: Zondervan, 1986), pp. 176-211. The issues are complex, but I support the view that in some cases in light of Christ the New Testament reflects a fuller meaning than what could have been understood by the original author or readers—one that is complementary to, rather than in conflict with, the original meaning.

interpretation of Scripture, no less than our theologizing, must be *context-oriented*. As Paul recontextualized scriptural stories and texts for new circumstances, so must we. The Enlightenment myth that we can achieve an "objective" interpretation of the Bible has turned out to be an emperor with no clothes. Interpretation requires a conversation between the sacred text and our human contexts. The crucial point of departure for that conversation is our own life in the world. As William Dyrness insists, "We must begin here because we simply cannot begin anywhere else. We cannot jump to some privileged place of neutrality or complete objectivity."[51]

This does not invite us disregard the meaning of the text in its original setting. The biblical text and the contemporary context are not equal partners. Understanding Scripture's communicative intent (its sense and genre) within its own historical context constitutes the first horizon of meaning and holds the place of privilege for interpreting a text.[52] But Christians from different cultures and socioeconomic situations and faith traditions come to a biblical text with different questions and assumptions, which inevitably influence what they "hear" from it.[53] It makes a difference whether the book of James is read from a perspective of affluence or one of suffering and oppression. It matters whether Jesus' parable of the sower (Mk 4:3-9) is read by city dwellers or North American farmers or farmers from Southeast Asia. As Tom Montgomery-Fate observes, "Though most Bible study leaders would focus their interpretation on the soil as the problem, a rice farmer would rather look at the *sower* as the problem. From his point of view a responsible farmer would not just randomly scatter seeds."[54] Yet, bringing our own questions and life situations to the text is just the beginning, not the end, of the interpretive process. If biblical texts function as Scripture, we must allow the text to ask questions of *us*, to confront our cultural presupposi-

---

[51]See William A. Dyrness, "How Does the Bible Function in the Christian Life?" in *The Use of the Bible in Theology: Evangelical Options*, ed. Robert K. Johnston (Atlanta: John Knox, 1985), p. 161.

[52]For a well-nuanced defense of the priority of the author's discourse meaning, see Max Turner, "Historical Criticism and Theological Hermeneutics of the New Testament," in *Between Two Horizons: Spanning New Testament Studies and Systematic Theology*, ed. Joel B. Green and Max Turner (Grand Rapids, Mich.: Eerdmans, 2000), pp. 44-70.

[53]See Joel B. Green, "The Challenge of Hearing the New Testament," in *Hearing the New Testament: Strategies for Interpretation*, ed. Joel B. Green (Grand Rapids, Mich.: Eerdmans, 1995), p. 8. For examples of biblical interpretation from a variety of global perspectives, see R. S. Sugirtharajah, ed., *Voices from the Margin: Interpreting the Bible in the Third World* (Maryknoll, N.Y.: Orbis, 1991); Daniel M. Patte, ed., *Global Bible Commentary* (Nashville: Abingdon, 2004).

[54]Tom Montgomery-Fate, *Beyond the White Noise: Mission in a Multi-Cultural World* (St. Louis, Mo.: Chalice, 1997), p. 17. Cited in Clemens Sedmak, *Doing Local Theology: A Guide for Artisans of a New Humanity* (Maryknoll, N.Y.: Orbis, 2002), p. 58.

tions, to challenge and reshape our default readings. Like the Corinthians who are summoned to hear the Exodus story as a word of judgment (1 Cor 10:1-13), we must allow Scripture to address our contexts with a targeted and transforming word.

This means that in the second place, we can learn from Paul that our interpretation must be *community-directed*. Paul teaches us that the Scriptures were written for the church, with the goal of re-forming the community of faith. Understanding the Word of God involves more than simply deploying the right exegetical strategies. As Joel B. Green frames the issue, "Needed most are not good methods for reading the Bible, but good people reading the Bible—that is, people deeply embedded in faithful communities of discipleship, people in whom the Spirit is actualizing the Word of God and, thus, for whom the Word of God is authenticated."[55] Like Paul, we must embrace a hermeneutic of transformation. Scripture only fulfills its purpose when, through the ministry of the Spirit, it edifies, challenges and changes the people of God in the midst of their present experience.

Third, Paul models for us a hermeneutical approach that is *gospel-shaped*. If Paul's interpretive activity was context-oriented, it was surely not context-*driven*. Instead, it was guided by an unswerving conviction that the gospel, which focuses on the life, death and resurrection of Jesus as the revelation of God's eschatological salvation, provides the hermeneutical key to the meaning of Scripture. Granted, we do not share the same historical proximity to the saving events as Paul, nor can we claim an equal measure of authority in our interpretations of Scripture. Yet this "gospelized" perspective can help to shape our hermeneutical perspective in at least two ways. First, it enables us to interpret the Old Testament within its broader canonical context, as a witness to the God of Israel who has now revealed himself in Jesus Christ in the last days. Along with Paul, we can recognize a narrative unity between Israel's history and Jesus' messianic mission. We cannot perceive the meaning of the Old Testament *in its fullness* apart from the hermeneutical lens of the gospel. In a sense, the "old" meaning of the Old Testament is contemporized for us through God's new saving action in Christ.[56]

Second, a hermeneutic shaped by the gospel can help us to discriminate be-

---

[55]Joel B. Green, "Scripture in the Church: Reconstructing the Authority of Scripture for Christian Formation and Mission," in *The Wesleyan Tradition: A Paradigm for Renewal*, ed. Paul W. Chilcote (Nashville: Abingdon, 2002), p. 47.

[56]See Robert W. Wall, "Canonical Context and Canonical Conversations," in *Between Two Horizons: Spanning New Testament Studies and Systematic Theology* (Grand Rapids, Mich.: Eerdmans, 2000), p. 178.

tween legitimate and illegitimate readings of Scripture within our particular contexts. "The gospel" that narrates the death and resurrection of Jesus Christ as the climax of God's redemptive work serves as one primary arbiter for specific readings of Scripture today. To cite one example, African theologian Tite Tienou critiques the attempts by some African interpreters to read New Testament references to the church as a family or household (e.g., Gal 6:10; Eph 2:19; 1 Tim 3:15) in terms of the traditional African notion of the "Great Family," which includes both the Ancestors and those yet to be born. He insists that such attempts to contextualize Scripture in light of African cultural and religious notions fall short of Paul's understanding of the gospel, since salvation and membership in God's household come not through natural family relationships, but through trust in and obedience to Christ.[57] The question we must ask of any interpretation is not simply "Is it relevant to the context?" but also "Does it reflect the 'truth of the gospel'?" (Gal 2:5, 14).

PAUL AS INTERPRETER OF CHRISTIAN TRADITION

Paul did theology and engaged in mission as part of a community that had already formulated confessions of faith, which represented the corporate memory of the church. We saw in chapter three that these shared traditions were foundational for Paul's understanding of the gospel. In the course of his letter writing, Paul not only interprets the written text of Scripture, but at times he also recalls and reappropriates the mainly oral traditions of the church for new circumstances. J. Christiaan Beker stresses that Paul is not a dogmatic theologian, but rather an *intepreter* of the gospel tradition, which he reformulates in innovative and distinctive ways.[58] Beker sees Paul's role as interpreter chiefly in relation to the Antiochene kerygmatic (preaching) tradition, which proclaims Christ's death and resurrection (1 Cor 15:3-5). This is true as far as it goes, but it does not say enough. Paul, in fact, draws upon and interprets a number of strains of traditional material. These include confessional statements (e.g., 1 Cor 8:6; 15:3-5; Rom 1:3-4; 10:9; Gal 4:4-5), early Christian hymns (Phil 2:6-11; Col 1:15-20; cf. 1 Tim 3:16b), eucharistic tradition (1 Cor 11:23-25) and ethical instruction (e.g., 1 Cor 7:10; 9:14; cf. 1 Cor 11:2; Phil 4:9; 2 Thess 2:15; Rom 12).

Anders Eriksson has shown that such traditions fulfill an important rhetorical function in Paul's arguments. They often provide shared premises between Paul

---

[57]Tite Tienou, "The Church in African Theology: Description and Analysis of Hermeneutical Presuppositions," in *Biblical Interpretation and the Church: The Problem of Contextualization*, ed. D. A. Carson (Nashville: Thomas Nelson, 1984), pp. 151-65.

[58]J. C. Beker, *Paul the Apostle: The Triumph of God in Life and Thought* (Philadelphia: Fortress, 1980), pp. 33-35, 109-31.

and his audience which Paul can then interpret and apply in ways that speak to the situation at hand.[59] There is, of course, a difference between Paul's interpretation of Scripture and his hermeneutic of oral tradition. This is not least because the written text has a definite, authoritative character, unlike more pliable units of oral tradition. For this reason, it is often much harder to recognize traditional formulations in Paul's letters and to distinguish this material from Paul's interpretations of it. Nevertheless, it is clear that Paul frequently adopts and adapts familiar gospel traditions in order to bring a new word that is tailored to the concrete situations of his readers.[60]

Sometimes Paul draws upon brief affirmations about Christ. A foundational confession such as "Jesus is Lord" can speak to a variety of concerns, including Christian worship (1 Cor 12:3), ethical instruction (Col 2:6), the defense of Paul's ministry (2 Cor 4:5) and the universal offer of salvation to Jews and Gentiles (Rom 10:9). Likewise, in 1 Thessalonians, the formula "Jesus died and rose again"(1 Thess 4:14a) becomes a basis for the believer's hope in the resurrection of the living and the dead in Christ at the time of his return (cf. 1 Cor 15:3-5). Elsewhere, Paul can deal with the practical questions of marriage (1 Cor 7:10) and the financial support of apostles (1 Cor 9:14) by appropriating memories of the sayings of Jesus. It will be particularly instructive, however, to look at how Paul contextualizes two more substantial passages that can be identified as early church tradition.

Interpreting the Christ hymn: Philippians 2. Philippians 2:6-11 is most likely a hymn in praise of Christ that comes out of early Christian worship. Its focus is christological: the story of Jesus's preexistence, his self-humbling human life and death, and his heavenly exaltation. Yet nothing in the context hints that Paul scores this hymn within the letter simply for its own sake. Nor is he trying to address any specific christological misunderstanding within the church. Whatever the prior function of the hymn, here Paul gives it an *ethical*, rather than a christological, interpretation. The example of Christ portrayed in this wondrously lyrical passage provides a foundation for Paul's exhortations to the Philippians, particularly in 1:27—2:18. Paul exegetes a familiar hymn about Christ in terms these readers need to hear. Apparently, the Christians in Philippi were facing opposition and the possibility of suffering for the sake of the gospel

---

[59]Anders Eriksson, *Traditions as Rhetorical Proof: Pauline Argumentation in 1 Corinthians* (Stockholm: Almqvist and Wiksell International, 1998), pp. 299-302 and *passim.*

[60]For Paul's contextual interpretation of tradition, see especially Richard N. Longenecker, *New Wine into Fresh Wineskins: Contextualizing the Early Christian Confessions* (Peabody, Mass.: Hendrickson, 1999), pp. 6-63. Unfortunately, Longenecker tends to unduly restrict the gospel that Paul contextualizes to the confessional traditions he has received from others.

(Phil 1:27-30). What is more, their fellowship was plagued by selfish rivalries and interpersonal differences (Phil 4:2-3; cf. 2:1-4). In light of this situation, Paul is not content simply to give them a list of moral instructions. Rather, in a kind of early Christian "What would Jesus do?" argument, he appeals to the story of Christ, which lies at the heart of the gospel, as a concrete paradigm that reveals how they should live.

The first part of the hymn portrays Christ as one who empties himself and becomes obedient to God even to the point of suffering and death on a cross (Phil 2:6-8). Nowhere, however, does the tradition describe Christ's actions in explicitly ethical terms.[61] That is Paul's *interpretation* of the Christ story for the community. He expands the meaning of the familiar hymn by giving it the fresh significance of imitating Christ. Verse five, which introduces the hymn, leaves no doubt over the connection between Jesus' behavior and that of the church: the Philippians should emulate the same life attitude of obedience and voluntary self-sacrifice for the sake of others. Paul draws out the implications of adopting this mindset in the exhortations that precede and follow the hymn. In a highly rhetorical passage, he prefaces the hymn in Philippians 2:1-4 by calling the Philippians to unity by means of humility and self-giving love. The structural and thematic parallels between 2:3-4 and 2:6-8[62] confirm that what Paul says in verses 3 and 4 about forsaking selfish ambition and humbly looking first to the interests of others is nothing less than a contextualization of the self-denying story of Jesus narrated in the hymn. No doubt Paul's appeals in Philippians 2:3-4 would have carried powerful social implications for the Philippians within their setting.[63] In a status-conscious Roman colony like Philippi, Paul's admonitions would mean no longer thinking and acting according to the cultural scripts of hierarchy and self-promotion; the Philippians must instead embody the pattern of the one who "emptied himself" of his rightful status and chose a path of status reversal.

Furthermore, as Christ willingly embraced the course of suffering and death, the Philippians too must remain steadfast in the faith, for they have been granted the privilege of suffering for Christ and like Christ (Phil 1:27-30). Later, Paul points to his own life (Phil 2:16-17; cf. 3:17) and to that of two of his coworkers, Timothy and Epaphroditus (Phil 2:19-30), as further examples of those who have modeled the kind of humility and self-giving obedience portrayed in the hymn.

---

[61]Michael J. Gorman, *Cruciformity: Paul's Narrative Spirituality of the Cross* (Grand Rapids, Mich.: Eerdmans, 2001), p. 164.

[62]E.g., the use of *but* as a hinge term (Phil 2:3-4, 7). See ibid., p. 168.

[63]Ben Witherington III, *Friendship and Finances in Philippi: The Letter of Paul to the Philippians* (Valley Forge, Penn.: Trinity Press International, 1994), p. 63.

The second part of the hymn describes Christ's vindication and exaltation (Phil 2:9-11). Here the correspondence between the story of Christ and the story of those who are in Christ is not as direct. Yet the wider context implies that if they follow their Lord on the way of self-humbling love, they too will be vindicated and experience a resurrection (cf. Phil 1:28; 3:10-11, 20-21). By transposing the gospel narrative in 2:6-11 for a new setting, Paul inscribes the Philippians into the text of the hymn. They need to listen to its lyrics again with new ears. Michael T. Gorman summarizes the meaning of Paul's contextualization: "For Paul, to be in Christ is to be a living exegesis of this narrative of Christ, a new performance of the original drama of exaltation following humiliation, of humiliation as the voluntary renunciation of rights and selfish gain in order to serve and obey."[64] In Philippians 2, Paul sings the gospel story in a new key.

Remembering Christ's death: 1 Corinthians 11:17-34. We find Paul giving a pastoral interpretation to traditional material again when he discusses the Lord's Supper in 1 Corinthians 11:17-34. In the midst of taking the church to task for their social divisions, Paul rehearses the tradition concerning Jesus' Last Supper, which he had earlier communicated to the Corinthians when he was among them (1 Cor 11:23-25). Despite a long history of interpretation that has focused on trying to uncover the nuances of sacramental theology from the Lord's Supper tradition, this is not the main thrust of the passage. Instead, Paul builds upon the common ground that he shares with his readers in the eucharistic tradition in order to address a highly contingent situation that threatened the life and character of the community. What is behind Paul's distinctive contextualization of this tradition?

It is obvious from the power of Paul's rhetoric (e.g., 1 Cor 11:17, 22) and his repeated warnings of judgment (1 Cor 11:29-32) that he is alarmed about divisions in the church (1 Cor 11:18-19) which are linked to the community's partaking of the Lord's Supper. There is broad agreement now that socioeconomic and cultural factors, rather than theological ones, were mainly responsible for the Corinthians' fractured fellowship. Apparently some of the wealthier and socially superior members of the community were taking their cues from the status-obsessed culture of first-century Corinth. Following the customary practice at Greco-Roman banquets, well-to-do patrons or householders—those with homes large enough to host the communal meal—would have assigned the biggest and best portions of food to the more privileged. Social geography may also have played a part. The host apparently invited higher status church members to join him/her in the dining room *(triclinium),* creating a private supper. The rest were

---

[64]Gorman, *Cruciformity,* p. 92.

left outside in the larger entry courtyard *(atrium)* with the poorer quality fare (see 1 Cor 11:21). Superior food and a dining position near to the host were visible symbols of favor in an honor-driven society like Roman Corinth. We might find a contemporary analogy in the hierarchy of cuisine and table location within the modern restaurant culture. The result of these practices was a partitioning of the community between the "haves" and the "have-nots." No doubt this kind of discriminatory behavior against the poor and the social "nobodies" would have seemed quite natural within the stratified world of Paul's readers.

What may have been acceptable in Corinth, however, was in Paul's eyes deplorable in the church; the Corinthians' selfish thinking and behavior contradicts the meaning of the Supper and, ultimately, the gospel itself. With more than a sprinkling of irony, Paul repeatedly describes them as "coming together" (1 Cor 11:17-18, 20, 33-34) in one location, knowing full well that their eating was anything *but* "together" as a unified body. The very ritual that was intended to celebrate and symbolically act out their oneness in Christ had become an occasion for splitting the church on the basis of status. It was their "own" meal (1 Cor 11:21), not the "Lord's Supper" (1 Cor 11:20), that is, "a supper whose character is determined by the Lord."[65] Consequently, Paul sets out to redefine the meaning of the ritual and in the process to reimagine their identity as a truly Christian community.

To do so, he retells the foundational story that is the ground of their Christian unity:

> For I received from the Lord what I handed on to you, that the Lord Jesus on the night when he was betrayed took a loaf of bread, and when he had given thanks, he broke it and said, "This is my body that is for you. Do this in remembrance of me." In the same way he took the cup also, after supper, saying, "This cup is the new covenant in my blood. Do this, as often as you drink it, in remembrance of me." For as often as you eat this bread and drink the cup, you proclaim the Lord's death until he comes. (1 Cor 11:23-26)

Paul's narration of the authoritative tradition that institutes the ritual meal allows him to view the situation in Corinth through the lens of Christ's saving death. Paul quotes the tradition selectively, and he interprets it in order to address the specific problems at hand. Several elements are of key importance to the apostle. First, the language of the body of Christ taken from Jesus' words ("This is my body," 1 Cor 11:24) enables Paul to draw a connection between the bread, which represents the body of the crucified Christ (1 Cor 11:23-24, 27),

---

[65]Stephen Fowl, "The New Testament, Theology, and Ethics," in *Hearing the New Testament*, ed. Joel B. Green (Grand Rapids, Mich.: Eerdmans, 1995), p. 404.

and Christ's body, the church. In failing to "discern" the corporate body of Christ (1 Cor 11:29), the Corinthians have shown that they did not understand the meaning of Jesus' saving death that the bread and the cup commemorate. Paul draws the stunning conclusion ("therefore") that, by tearing apart the Christian body through their status-oriented eating of the Supper, they come under the same accountability as those responsible for Jesus' crucifixion ("the body and blood of the Lord," 1 Cor 11:27).[66] This dual sense of the body symbol—christological and ecclesiological—establishes an inseparable link between the death of Christ and the church, which it brought into being.[67]

Second, the words of the shared tradition call the Corinthians twice to "remember" the death of Christ (1 Cor 11:24-25). In the context, this involves not just thinking about, but also acting in ways that reflect Jesus' sacrificial love and his new covenant of salvation, graciously given. This anticipates Paul's own interpretation of the tradition in verse 26: through their shared celebration they "proclaim the Lord's death until he comes." In other words, the rite of eating and drinking itself "proclaims" the gospel by re-presenting the meaning of his saving death "for you." Yet, how can the Corinthians truly remember and proclaim that self-giving death without conforming to its pattern? They cannot. Their present conduct at the meal sabotages that proclamation. For Paul, the crucifixion of Jesus is not just about how people are individually saved; it is about transforming the community into the pattern of the cross.

Paul further contextualizes the tradition in 1 Corinthians 11:27-32 by spelling out for the Corinthians the dire consequences of failing to participate in the Supper in a way that is consistent with its content. The language of the ritual (eating and drinking) and of judgment dominates, and Paul directly links the two themes. The decisive test comes in whether or not they recognize the church as the one body of Christ (1 Cor 11:29) and thereby treat one another with the Christian love that is consistent with Christ crucified "for you." To deny the grace they have received by persisting in their egocentric actions is to invite judgment on themselves, both now and in the future.

Paul concludes by refashioning the church's praxis on the basis of his theological reflections on the meaning of the tradition ("So then," 1 Cor 11:33). When the community gathers for the Lord's meal, they are to "welcome" one another without status distinctions (1 Cor 11:33). Paul, as Stephen Barton has argued, is

---

[66]Eriksson, *Traditions*, pp 191-92. According to Erikkson, Paul's allusive use of the term "body" reflects the ancient rhetorical figure of *emphasis*, which reveals a deeper meaning for the audience to ponder than is actually expressed in the words.

[67]Raymond Pickett, *The Cross in Corinth: The Social Significance of the Death of Jesus* (Sheffield: Sheffield Academic Press, 1997), p. 121.

redrawing social and religious borders in relation to the sacred meal.[68] The more privileged Corinthians have raised social barriers that partition the community, but they have smudged the lines between the church and the world. They are treating the Christian meal like a pagan feast. Paul wants to reconstruct their social and moral world. The cross demolishes boundaries within the body of Christ (cf. Gal 3:28), but the memorial to his death makes the church different from the society at large. Paul accepts the reality of social differences and does not forbid the wealthy from banqueting at home (1 Cor 11:34). His primary concern is not to overturn the patterns of social life in the culture at large. But in the church things are different. What is of immediate and critical importance is to reshape the people of God into a new covenant community that will, by the way Christians love and treat one another, genuinely "proclaim the Lord's death until he comes" (1 Cor 11:26).

Paul thus retells the story contained in the early eucharistic tradition in order to highlight the death of Christ as the central meaning of the ritual.[69] The gospel that proclaims Christ crucified becomes the hermeneutical lens through which Paul contextualizes the tradition for the Corinthians. As a result, they hear a fresh interpretation of Christ's death that is tailored to their circumstances. Truly "remembering" Jesus' death means living sacrificially toward others in the community. In this passage, as well as in Philippians 2, Paul reappropriates the story of Christ he shares with his readers in order to confront cultural "default settings" and re-form attitudes and lifestyles.

Paul's concern for both fidelity to the tradition and contextual innovation is instructive for our own time. Lamin Sanneh offers a beautiful example of this kind of theologizing in the so-called African Creed of the Maasai people of East Africa. This creed does not try to imitate the sometimes abstract and philosophically laden language of the creeds that emerged out of the christological controversies of the Western tradition. Instead, it speaks simply and concretely of "a man in the flesh, a Jew by tribe, born poor in a little village, who left his home and was always on safari doing good, curing people by the power of God." It goes on to later describe Jesus' resurrection with understated power: "He lay buried in the grave, but the hyenas did not touch him, and on the third day he rose from the grave."[70] Such a context-sensitive expression of the Christian tradition not only sings the story of Jesus in an East African key, but it may also

---

[68]Stephen Barton, "Paul's Sense of Place: An Anthropological Approach to Community Formation in Corinth," *NTS* 32 (1986): 225-46.

[69]Hays, *First Corinthians*, p. 199.

[70]Lamin Sanneh, *Whose Religion Is Christianity? The Gospel Beyond the West* (Grand Rapids, Mich.: Eerdmans, 2003), pp. 59-60.

contribute a fresh perspective to the theological understanding of the wider community of faith.

CONCLUSION

New Testament writers like Paul interpreted the Jewish Scriptures and the Christian traditions they inherited for a variety of new circumstances. This is a form of early contextualization. Neither Scripture nor church tradition can address the people of God as something frozen in time. They speak as *interpreted* Scripture and tradition. Notwithstanding the clearly more authoritative character of the written text of Scripture for the people of God, our study has shown a number of common elements in Paul's interpretation of both the Old Testament and Christian tradition, which I will try to summarize:

- In neither case is Paul rigidly bound to a specific *form* of the "text." He shows a restrained measure of freedom in selecting and adapting both Old Testament passages and early Christian confessions in light of the issues at hand. Meaning takes precedence over form.

- Paul assumes that both Scripture and Christian traditions function as shared premises that are accepted to be authoritative by both himself and his audiences. On the basis of such "givens," he delivers a directed word to the community.

- Paul is willing to appropriate a variety of rhetorical and exegetical strategies from the culture of his day, whether Jewish or Greco-Roman, in an effort to effectively communicate to his readers. At the same time, Paul's approach to interpretation is more than a matter of aping the contemporary hermeneutical methods available to him. Ultimately the gospel, not any particular exegetical technique or local concern of his audience, propels the interpretive process.

- Paul's hermeneutic has an ecclesial direction. Both Scripture and tradition, rightly understood, are intended to edify and transform the community of faith.

- Paul's use of both the Old Testament and church tradition are context- and audience-oriented. His contemporizing hermeneutic allows him to contextualize either the story of Christ told in the tradition or the message of the biblical passage so that it becomes a living word that speaks to his readers where they are. He reappropriates the traditions of his Jewish and Christian heritage for new circumstances.

- For Paul, meaning is not static and entombed either in the past historical context of a Scripture passage or a previous setting of the church's faith confessions. Guided by the Spirit, the dynamic interaction of scriptural or early church traditions, the gospel, and the present experience of the community often produces a deepening and extension of original meaning and fresh applications. When Paul interprets Scripture and, even to some extent, Christian tradition, his primary interest is with its present significance for the church.

- The gospel also places constraints upon Paul's interpretive activity. Any interpretation that is inconsistent with the gospel of Christ crucified and risen, no matter how "relevant" it may be, is excluded. Alternate readings, like the Jewish Christian teachers' interpretation of the Genesis stories for the Galatians or the Corinthians' distortion of the Lord's Supper institution, subvert the truth of the gospel.

We have now examined Paul's activity as a contextual theologian, as an "anthropologist" who engages Jewish and Gentile culture, and as a context-sensitive interpreter of Scripture and tradition. Perhaps the best way to see how these activities might play out in a given context is to examine two of Paul's letters— 1 Corinthians and Colossians—as case studies in contextualization.

6. CASE STUDIES FROM CORINTH
The Gospel, Food and the Future

*So, whether you eat or drink, or whatever you do,
do everything for the glory of God.*

1 COR 10:31

Church quarrels, gross sexual misconduct, internal lawsuits, marital advice, dinner parties at pagan temples, speaking in tongues. Such is the stuff of Paul's first letter to the Corinthians. This letter, unlike any other that Paul wrote, is largely made up of the apostle's responses to reported problems and his answers to specific questions addressed to him by the church. As a result, 1 Corinthians features a series of what might be called "case studies" in doing contextual theology, in which we find the gospel speaking to a whole range of concrete issues. Understanding how Paul brings the gospel to bear upon questions that come directly out of the Corinthians' life situation and cultural world has the potential to illuminate not only Paul's own method of doing theology but also the task of contextualization as a whole. Rather than taking a broad, surface-level approach to the interaction between gospel and situation in 1 Corinthians, I will examine two representative cases in some depth. The first has to do with lifestyle contextualization in a culture that is pervaded with idolatry. In the second, the gospel speaks to a problem of wrong *thinking* about the future which results when Christian and Corinthian worldviews collide.

1 CORINTHIANS 8—10: TO EAT OR NOT TO EAT

I admit that Paul's teaching on food offered to idols in 1 Corinthians 8—10 was a rather theoretical issue for me until I taught a class on 1 Corinthians in an Asian seminary for the first time. In the course of discussing these chapters in class, a student from a tribal area of the Philippines related a personal narrative. As a Christian pastor, he had been asked to partake in and even pray a blessing over a close family member's funeral banquet. Knowing that the food that was about to be eaten had been dedicated to the local pagan gods, he faced a moral dilemma. If he refused to participate, he might alienate his non-Christian family members and lose any platform he had to positively influence them. At the same time, he recognized the danger of giving the appearance of condoning the pagan beliefs and worldview that lurked behind the meal. For my student—unlike most Christians in the West—this was not simply a passage whose underlying principles needed to be reapplied in order to have any contemporary significance. It spoke directly to issues of worldview and practice that paralleled his own life experience. How to live out the gospel in a culture of "many gods and many lords" (1 Cor 8:5), where to draw the boundaries, how far to accommodate without compromising—these were pressing questions for Paul and the Corinthians as well.

In 1 Corinthians 8—10 we find Paul the missionary-theologian's answer to the second in a series of problem issues that the Corinthians have addressed to him in a letter—the matter of "food sacrificed to idols" *(eidōlothyta)*. Paul devotes a good deal of attention in 1 Corinthians to food, eating, and meals (1 Cor 8:1-13; 10:1-31; 11:17-34), not least because "food and meals are a fundamental symbolic means by which a group or a society expresses its values and its identity.[1] In this case, however, it is the link between food and idolatry in Corinth that provides the springboard for Paul's theological reflection.

What specific problem is Paul addressing? Despite gaps in our understanding of precisely what lies behind Paul's responses, it appears that the fundamental concern in 1 Corinthians 8:1-13 and 10:1-22 is with Christians' participation in meals within the temple precincts where food offered to pagan gods was served (1 Cor 8:10; 10:14, 21).[2] It seems that some Corinthian believers had continued to attend temple feasts as they had always done, against Paul's earlier prohibition of it. In their letter to Paul, they defended their right to do so on the basis of their

---

[1]Stephen C. Barton, "Social-Scientific Approaches to Paul," in *Dictionary of Paul and His Letters*, ed. Gerald F. Hawthorne, Ralph P. Martin and Daniel G. Reid (Downers Grove, Ill.: InterVarsity Press, 1993), p. 897.

[2]For a thorough defense of this position, see Gordon D. Fee, *First Epistle to the Corinthians* (Grand Rapids, Mich.: Eerdmans, 1987), pp. 357-491, and Fee, "Εἰδωλόθυτα Once Again: An Interpretation of 1 Corinthians 8—10," *Bib* 61 (1980): 172-97. See also W. L. Willis, *Idol Meat in Corinth: The Pauline Argument in 1 Corinthians 8 and 10* (Chico, Calif.: Scholars Press, 1985), pp. 7-64; 265-68. The traditional view of 8:1-13 is that Paul is addressing the issue of sacrificial food being sold at the market or served in private homes—a different matter than the one he tackles in 10:1-22. For a defense of this position, see Bruce N. Fisk, "Eating Meat Offered to Idols: Corinthian Behavior and Pauline Response in 1 Corinthians 8-10 (A Response to Gordon Fee)," *TJ* 10 (1989): 49-70. Although there are problems with both interpretations of chapter 8, in my mind the overall exegetical and historical evidence supports the background of cultic temple meals.

knowledge that idols do not really exist (1 Cor 8:4) and that food is irrelevant to one's relationship with God (1 Cor 8:8). They may even have gone a dangerous step further, actually encouraging other believers ("the weak") to participate in such meals against their own scruples. As a result, the moral consciousness of these fellow Christians—probably recent converts from paganism—was defiled and their very spiritual welfare placed in jeopardy (1 Cor 8:7, 9-11).

We might ask why some Christians would continue to go to the temple to eat meals that involved idol food in the first place, when both Judaism and Christianity took such a clear stand against idolatry. The issue, however, is not nearly as clear-cut as it might appear from a modern Western perspective. In a highly religious city like Roman Corinth, where the various deities were pervasive and inescapable, temples were centers not only of religious but also of social life. Pagan temples functioned more or less as the restaurants and community centers of the day. All kinds of feasts in which gods were honored took place in the temple environs, including citywide festivals, meetings of voluntary organizations like clubs and trade guilds, private birthday parties and family gatherings. On such occasions, the *religious* and *social* functions of the meal were inseparable.[3] In addition, participating in temple banquets was an important means of maintaining social contacts and cultivating relationships with benefactors, particularly for higher status Corinthians.[4] Such feasts functioned as an important strand in the intricate fabric of power relations that sustained imperial society. What is more, the growing importance of the imperial cult in Roman Corinth would have put Christians under added obligation to share in the life of the city by attending festivals honoring the emperor. In short, the social, economic and family pressure against withdrawing from such a normal cultural activity as eating meals at the temple would have been enormous.[5] Those Corin-

---

[3]For specific evidence of the variety of ways in which communal meals at the temple could function and of the overlap between their social and religious functions, see Derek Newton, *Deity and Diet: The Dilemma of Sacrificial Food at Corinth* (Sheffield: Sheffield Academic Press, 1998), pp. 226-57.

[4]David G. Horrell, *The Social Ethos of the Corinthian Correspondence* (Edinburgh: T & T Clark, 1996), pp. 148-49.

[5]Derek Newton thinks that various ambiguities and gray areas (e.g., precisely what constituted an idol or idolatry; whether such meals involved actual *worship* of a *deity* [versus living or dead heroes or emperors]) surrounding the perception of cultic meals in the Greco-Roman world contributed to the misunderstanding between Paul and the Corinthians (*Deity and Diet*, especially pp. 115-74, 342-62). Newton may well be right that the very complexity of the issue makes it likely that Paul confronts a range of different interpretations and positions about sacrificial food and feasts within the church. If this is the case, then within the broader orientations of the "weak" and the "strong" in Corinth there may have been a variety of perspectives on what Christians could or could not participate in (see pp. 22-23 and *passim*).

thians who did not want to give up their civic and social connections made compromises (in Paul's eyes) with the idolatrous culture.

Christians in Corinth faced a second related question of what to do about meat that had been slaughtered in a religious ceremony at the temple but now was being sold to the public at the marketplace. Was it acceptable for Christians to eat such meat, given its previous associations with idols, or even to dine in a home where it might be served (1 Cor 10:23-30)? Paul's extended response to these practical issues facing the Corinthian body offers a fascinating example of his ability to read both Christian community and culture through the transforming lens of the gospel.

Paul begins by addressing the issue that was apparently at the top of the Corinthians' agenda in their communication to him about idol food—the question of eating at the temple of the pagan gods. His response to this problem comes in two stages. Remarkably, he does not immediately dispense with the issue by simply condemning the practice or forbidding them to go to the temples. Instead, Paul's persuasive strategy is to first address the attitude behind their actions, along with its destructive consequences for the Christian fellowship (1 Cor 8:1-13). As we saw in connection with Paul's Areopagus speech in Acts, such an indirect entry into a sensitive and contentious issue is a well-attested practice of Greco-Roman rhetoric. Paul's method is persuasion, not compulsion. The second part of Paul's answer is to denounce their behavior more directly as a compromise with idolatry that is equivalent to participating with demons (1 Cor 10:1-22). Between these two sections comes a vital interlude in the form of a rhetorical digression in which Paul points to his own example of laying down his rights for the sake of others (1 Cor 9:1-27). Finally, he addresses other scenarios involving idol food as illustrations of the guiding principle that Christians should use their freedom responsibly for the good of others (1 Cor 10:23—11:1). The interplay between Paul's ardent concern to steer the Corinthians away from idolatry and his equally great desire to demonstrate the priority of self-giving love over knowledge or personal rights determines to a large measure the shape of his "theology in context" in 1 Corinthians 8—10. Each stage of the argument is essential to Paul's "gospelized" response to the practical matters at hand.

Love for the weak: 1 Corinthians 8:1-13. Paul's opening argument in chapter 8 finds numerous points of contact with his audience. In order to expose the faulty assumptions of the so-called strong (a term Paul does not actually use) in Corinth, he adopts a "yes, but" strategy. This involves establishing common ground by quoting and partially endorsing slogans from the Corinthians' letter (1 Cor 8:1, 4, 8), only to drastically qualify their positions. He also employs the practice of adopting and redefining key terms that likely come out of the Corinthians' own mouths ("knowledge," "right," "conscience," "weak").

Making use of such rhetorical strategies, Paul gives the enlightened eaters' claims to superior knowledge and personal rights a profound ethical and theological reinterpretation, one that flows out of the gospel itself.

Ethically, Paul subordinates knowledge *(gnōsis)* to love and the building up of the community (1 Cor 8:1-3). He then provides the moral imperative with a theological foundation (1 Cor 8:4-6). Temporarily agreeing with the "knowledge" of the "strong," Paul denies that idols have any real existence as gods (1 Cor 8:4). But having accepted the theological premise of the "knowers," he goes on to qualify it in two ways that address their situation. First, even though for Christians idols are not true gods, there is an undeniable reality to pagan polytheistic worship (1 Cor 8:5; cf. 10:20-21) which still influences the conscience[6] of the weak in Corinth. By encouraging the weak to take part in temple feasts through their own example, or maybe even urging them to attend in order to build up their deficient awareness of "the way things are," the "strong" are actually leading their fellow Christians back into the world of paganism (1 Cor 8:10-11). Second, Paul expands the Jewish *Shema* that he has already quoted ("There is no God but one," 1 Cor 8:4) and reinterprets it christologically: "yet for us there is one God, the Father, from whom are all things and for whom we exist, and one Lord, Jesus Christ, through whom are all things and through whom we exist" (1 Cor 8:6). This in turn points to a new definition of the community.[7] Because there is "one Lord, Jesus Christ," and because we are in relationship with him, we have a responsibility toward others.

Paul extends this christological grounding for Christian identity in verses 7-13. Here he applies it specifically to the effect of the actions of the "strong" upon the weak of the community. Following his pattern throughout the chapter, he agrees with "those in the know"[8] that "food will not bring us closer to God" (1 Cor 8:8). But Paul affirms that while food may be morally neutral, their selfish

---

[6]There is general agreement that the term *conscience (syneidēsis)* has a Greco-Roman background, but debate continues over how Paul uses it in 1 Corinthians 8—10. The best solution is that *conscience* refers less to a type of inner guide for the rightness or wrongness of their conduct (a modern, introspective way of thinking) than a moral *consciousness* or *self-awareness*. Their consciences are "weak" (1 Cor 8:7, 10) because they are insecure, i.e., they do not have moral confidence regarding their new beliefs, making them vulnerable to the more self-assured "strong." See P. D. Gardner, *The Gifts of God and the Authentication of a Christian: An Exegetical Study of 1 Corinthians 8—11* (Lanham, Md.: University Press of America, 1994), pp. 42-48; Anthony C. Thiselton, *The First Epistle to the Corinthians* (Grand Rapids, Mich.: Eerdmans, 2000), pp. 640-44.

[7]N. T. Wright, "One God, One Lord, One People: Incarnational Christology for a Church in a Pagan Environment," *ExAud* 7 (1991): 48-49.

[8]I borrow this apt phrase from Ben Witherington III, *Conflict in Corinth: A Socio-Rhetorical Commentary on 1 and 2 Corinthians* (Grand Rapids, Mich.: Eerdmans, 1995), p. 187.

attitudes and actions are not. Knowledge apart from love, and rights divorced from responsibility to others have caused them to become a moral stumbling block, even to *destroy* those "for whom Christ died" (1 Cor 8:11). Crucially, it is to the story of Christ crucified that Paul appeals as the theological basis for how Christians should act toward one another. To sin against a weak member of the family of believers is to sin against Christ himself (1 Cor 8:12). The knowledge boasters may have labeled their fellow believers as "weak" in order to shame them, but for Paul the incarnate and crucified Christ stands in solidarity with weak ones (cf. 1 Cor 1:25, 27; 9:22; 2 Cor 12:9-10; 13:4).[9] As N. T. Wright puts the matter, Paul's "allowance for the weak is not a mere ad hoc concession. It arises from the heart of Christian theology itself.[10]

Dining with demons: 1 Corinthians 10:1-22. Paul continues his argument against the Corinthians' attendance of temple meals in chapter 10, but from a different perspective. Here he mounts a more direct assault on the problem of idolatry: first, he warns the Corinthians of the danger in which their flirtations with paganism have placed them by way of example from Israel's story (1 Cor 10:1-13); and second, he prohibits eating at the idols' temple as wholly incompatible with their exclusive relationship with the one Lord (1 Cor 10:14-22).[11]

In 10:1-13, Paul appeals to the story of Israel as a kind of negative example for the behavior of the Corinthians. We have already looked at the hermeneutical implications of this passage in chapter five, but now we need to see how it contributes to Paul's contextual theologizing about idol food. According to Quintilian, paradigms and examples *(paradeigmata)* functioned as important rhetorical proofs in order to persuade an audience of the truth of an argument.[12] Here Paul sees a direct analogy between what happened to the Israelites in the desert and the precarious position of the Corinthians who are sailing close to the wind of pagan worship.

How then does Israel's wilderness story function as a "paradigm" *(typos,* 1 Cor 10:6, 11) for first century Corinthians? Both the content of Paul's Scripture exposition and the wider context (cf. 1 Cor 10:14) indicate that his reason for appealing to the Old Testament narrative is targeted specifically at the problem of idolatry. The only direct Scripture quotation comes in 1 Corinthians 10:7, as Paul recalls a classic example of Israel's worshiping other gods—the infamous golden calf incident (Ex 32:6). Likewise, the verse's reference to Israel's sitting

---

[9]See Willis, *Idol Meat,* pp. 94-95. Willis goes too far, however, in importing Paul's full theological understanding of "weakness" into this context.

[10]Wright, "One God," p. 49.

[11]Fee, *First Epistle,* p. 441.

[12]*Inst. or.* 5.11.6; cf. Witherington, *Conflict and Community,* p. 217.

down to eat and drink clearly pertains to the problem that Paul is addressing of eating and drinking at the temple. This is followed by allusions to three other wilderness episodes that have analogies to the Corinthian situation: (1) sexual immorality (1 Cor 10:8)—something regularly linked to idolatrous worship in Greco-Roman culture, as well as the New Testament (cf. Acts 15:29; Rev 2:14, 20); (2) putting Christ to the test, which is just what those "in the know" are doing by abusing their freedom in Christ; and (3) grumbling, which may relate both to the Corinthian quarreling and to their complaining about Paul himself. These negative patterns from Israel's misadventures are designed to warn the Corinthians. If they persist in their sinful behavior, particularly their casual atti- tude toward idolatry, not only are they imperiling other Christians (1 Cor 8:11), but they themselves are in danger of being destroyed (1 Cor 10:10; cf. 9:27; 10:12). It is striking that here Paul does theology not by citing the command- ments but by retelling the Jewish story in a way that speaks directly to the Corin- thian context.[13]

Paul's warning to the "knowers" in the first part of the chapters prepares the ground for the imperative toward which the whole argument of chapters 8—10 has been building: "my beloved, flee from idolatry" (1 Cor 10:14, my transla- tion). At last, Paul lays his cards face up on the table. He explicitly redefines idol food eaten at a temple as "idolatry"—a definition the "strong" would no doubt have contested.[14] First Corinthians 10:14-22 thus brings Paul's concern all along over idol food to a climax. Once more he draws his audience into the central reality of the gospel, Christ's saving death on their behalf, but this time in the framework of the Lord's Supper (1 Cor 10:16-17; cf. 10:3-4). This is not a theol- ogy of the Eucharist. Rather, the Christian celebration of the sacred meal sup- plies Paul with a symbol that allows him to speak directly to the issue at hand. N. T. Wright's view has merit that Paul, somewhat daringly, offers the Christian celebratory meal as a decisive alternative to all pagan ritual meals.[15] The oper- ative term is *koinōnia* ("sharing," "participation," 1 Cor 10:16, 18, 20; cf. "par- take," 10:17, 21, 30), language that the Corinthians would likely have recognized from its association with pagan sacrificial meals. Paul, however, gives it a proper Christian baptism. His point is that when believers celebrate at the Lord's table, they *participate* in the blood and the body of Christ; that is, they experience a

---

[13]Richard B. Hays, "The Role of Scripture in Paul's Ethics," in *Theology and Ethics in Paul and His Interpreters: Essays in Honor of Victor Paul Furnish*, ed. E. H. Lovering Jr. and J. L. Sumney (Nashville: Abingdon, 1996), p. 41.

[14]Anders Eriksson, *Traditions as Rhetorical Proof: Pauline Argumentation in 1 Corinthians* (Stockholm: Almqvist and Wiksell International, 1998), p. 146.

[15]Wright, "One God," p. 52.

profound spiritual communion with the one Lord and with his people, the one body in Christ. It is this exclusive solidarity with Christ and with the redeemed community that makes all other unions and all pagan worship unthinkable.

In 1 Corinthians 10:19-21 Paul draws upon this participation motif, as well as the symbol of the meal, to persuade the Corinthians of the contradiction between their Christian experience and their trifling with idolatry. The new element here is the bond between pagan worship and demons. The "strong" had apparently argued that the knowledge that idols have no existence as such (1 Cor 8:4) made idols and the food sacrificed to them insignificant. What they had *not* considered, however, is that behind the worship of idols is the very real activity of hostile spiritual forces, which may gain power through pagan cultic practice. Paul insists that to feast at an idol's temple is in fact to participate in the worship of demons in analogous fashion to the Christian's sharing in the blood and body of Christ in the Lord's Supper. A person who is already united with Christ and with his people while participating at the table of the Lord simply cannot at the same time join in another partnership with idolaters at the table of demons (1 Cor 10:21). Given the religiously inclusive environment of Corinth, which generally allowed one to pick and choose from a whole smorgasbord of deities, powers and cultic practices, Paul's radically exclusive stance was countercultural to the core.

Paul thus depends on the familiar symbol of the sacred meal and its connection to idolatry to tie together his argument throughout chapter 10. Positively, Israel's partaking in "spiritual" food and drink (1 Cor 10:3-4; cf. 18) prefigures the Christian celebration (1 Cor 10:16-17). Negatively, their eating and drinking in connection with pagan worship (1 Cor 10:7) anticipates the Corinthians' indulging in the table of demons (1 Cor 10:21). Ritual symbols often function as cultural boundary markers. In this case, Paul unambiguously declares the idol/demon table out of bounds for the fellowship of the king.[16] The church's identity is profoundly redefined by the cross and the meal that celebrates it.

Responsible freedom: 1 Corinthians 10:23-30. Paul concludes his discussion of idol meat by addressing a different but related question: How should Christians respond when they encounter food sacrificed to idols quite apart from cultic meals at the temple? On this issue, unlike the typical Jewish attitude that required abstinence from all pagan sacrificial meat, Paul comes down firmly on the side of responsible freedom. He begins by resuming his familiar "yes, but . . ."

---

[16]On the role of idol food in defining boundaries, see Peder Borgen, " 'Yes,' 'No,' 'How Far?': The Participation of Jews and Christians in Pagan Cults," in *Paul in His Hellenistic Context*, ed. Troels Engberg-Pedersen (Minneapolis: Fortress, 1995), pp. 42-48, 56.

tactic of quoting a slogan (twice!) of the "strong" and then reinterpreting it. Their claim is that "all things are lawful" (1 Cor 10:23-24), which recalls the enlightened eaters' concern over their individual "rights" (1 Cor 8:9).[17] Paul fundamentally agrees with the premise that "food is food" (1 Cor 8:8), but he immediately qualifies the quotation in two ways: first, the greater priority for the Christian is edifying the community (1 Cor 10:23); and second, the Corinthians' self-interest needs to be replaced by self-sacrificing behavior that follows the Jesus pattern (1 Cor 10:24; cf. 11:1). This qualification recapitulates and reinforces for the present context what Paul has already argued in chapter 8.

Paul introduces two case studies of cultural situations outside of a cultic setting where Christians would likely encounter meat that has been offered on a pagan altar—when it is sold in the marketplace for private consumption, or when it is served in the home of a pagan acquaintance (1 Cor 10:25-27). In both cases, the answer is the same: "Eat!" Believers may need to surrender their rights for the sake of others, but Paul is convinced that they have genuine freedom (1 Cor 10:29) when it comes to morally neutral matters. Based on the scriptural principle that God is the source of all created things (1 Cor 10:26; Ps 24:1), Paul argues that consuming food having former connections with idol worship is not harmful in itself. To say otherwise would mean lapsing into a dualism that regarded some parts of God's creation as permanently taboo for the Christian.[18] One should eat such food freely and thankfully without inquiring into its prior history. This is plainly a more "liberal" position than that of Paul's pious Jewish contemporaries. It shows the extent to which he was willing to relativize nonessential Jewish cultural issues in order to become "all things to all people" (1 Cor 9:22).

This freedom, however, is not without restraint. Paul therefore qualifies the second example with a hypothetical scenario: if an unbelieving guest (or perhaps the host) at the meal cautions that what is being served is sacrificial meat, the believer should abstain from eating it for the sake of "the other's conscience" (1 Cor 10:28-29).[19] Paul's repeated use of the Hellenistic term "conscience" (syneidēsis) in 1 Corinthians 8:7-12 and 10:25-29 not only suggests his sensitivity to communicate to his Greco-Roman audience in culturally appropriate lan-

---

[17]*Exousia* ("right," "liberty") is the noun form for the verb *exesti* ("it is lawful").

[18]N. T. Wright, *The Climax of the Covenant: Christ and the Law in Pauline Theology* (Minneapolis: Fortress, 1991), p. 135.

[19]Commentators are divided over whether the "informer" is a fellow believer or a pagan (either the host or another guest). The strongest argument in favor of the hypothetical informer being an unbeliever is that Paul has him use the pagan term "sacrificial meat" *(hierothyton)* rather than the standard Jewish Christian term "idol meat" *(eidōlothyton)*, which occurs elsewhere in 1 Corinthians 8—10.

guage, but it also reflects his contextual response to the Corinthians, who probably introduced the term in their letter. Here it refers to the "moral awareness" the pagan informant has about Christians, believing that they, like Jews, would have scruples against eating such food. Precisely because food is *not* a matter of conscience for the Christian, Paul advises the believer to refuse the "meat course." Otherwise, the unbeliever might get the wrong message and think that the guest has reneged on his or her Christian principles. In this case, preserving one's witness to a pagan acquaintance takes priority over personal freedom to eat. Throughout the passage, Paul walks a tightrope between genuine freedom (1 Cor 10:23a, 23c, 25-27, 29b-30) and restraint for the good of others (1 Cor 10:23b, 23d, 24, 28-29a).

When we compare this passage to Paul's discussion of sacrificial food consumed in a temple in 1 Corinthians 8:1-13 and 10:1-22, we come to an inescapable conclusion: the context truly matters. In a cultural environment where pagan religion and the growing emperor cult pervade virtually all threads of life, there is no uniform solution. The gospel itself determines how a Christian must respond to that culture. On the one hand, the prohibition of eating sacrificial food in the context of cultic meals or celebrations at the temple is nonnegotiable. Paul's theological convictions regarding monotheism and the exclusive relationship believers have with their Lord and each other on the basis of Christ's saving death permit no compromise. In this case the *form* (the ritual of eating at the pagan temple) and the *meaning* (idolatry and the activity of demons) are intertwined. Missiologist Paul Hiebert cites the contemporary analogy of the use in Indian dramas of the color aqua blue, which traditionally symbolizes the Hindu god Krishna. Form and meaning are so integrated that to use the same color on an actor's face in a Christian drama would almost certainly evoke the meaning of the Hindu mythology behind it.[20] Similarly, for Paul, the idol's temple becomes a border that Christians must not cross.

On the other hand, Paul makes no attempt to isolate believers from ordinary contact with idolaters or idolatry. That would mean withdrawing from society as a whole and would strangle the church's witness to the world. Paul is not interested in erecting unnecessary obstacles to the Christian mission. Away from the idol's turf at the temple, the form (idol meat bought at the market or eaten in a pagan home) is distinct from the meaning of idolatry. Only when the greater gospel concerns of sacrificial love for others and the community's witness to an

---

[20]Paul G. Hiebert, "Form and Meaning in the Contexualization of the Gospel," in *The Word Among Us: Contextualizing Theology for Today*, ed. Dean S. Gilliland (Dallas: Word, 1989), p. 117.

unbelieving world come into play must Christian freedom regarding cultural matters be voluntarily curtailed.

"Food" is not "food": 1 Corinthians 8—10 and Romans 14—15. The extent to which Paul's theological reflection is related to the situation at hand comes into sharp focus when we compare 1 Corinthians 8—10 to Romans 14—15. Because of some definite parallels between the two passages,[21] it is sometimes assumed that they address the same problem of idol meat, or at least reflect the same basic perspective on the question of the "weak" and the "strong." Closer comparison, however, confirms that their differences outweigh their similarities. In Romans 14—15 Paul is addressing an internal debate within the community over whether believers are free to eat meat. In 1 Corinthians 8—10, the basic issue is dining at a pagan temple, which involves the Corinthians' relationship to the wider culture. In Romans, the dispute is rooted in differences between mainly Jewish Christians whose conduct regarding food was governed by ongoing loyalty to the law of Moses, and primarily Gentile Christians who saw themselves as free from the Torah's restrictions. In 1 Corinthians, the fundamental conflict is between those who claimed to be "in the know" and the apostle. In Romans, the issue is "unclean" food; in 1 Corinthians, it is idol food.

Because Paul faces distinct problems in the two cases, it is not surprising that his theological response varies significantly as well. The fundamental difference is that Paul's advice in Romans assumes throughout that eating or abstaining from meat is a matter of indifference to salvation (Rom 14:14, 20). Both those who eat and those who do not "honor the Lord" (Rom 14:5). The problem comes not in the object or mode of eating, but in the attitude of condemning their fellow Christians who believe differently (Rom 14:3-4, 10, 13). As a result, Paul urges strong and weak alike to stop passing judgment on other believers (Rom 14:1-12) and to "welcome" one other (Rom 15:7-13), even as he particularly warns the strong that their Christian freedom must be limited by love and concern for the weak (Rom 14:13—15:6). The primary goal of Paul's argument, then, is the "peace" and "mutual upbuilding" of the community (Rom 14:19; cf. 15:5). In contrast, the issue of eating idol meat at the temple is *not* an ethically neutral matter. Not only does attending temple meals put others at risk (1 Cor 8:7-13); it poses grave danger for the "knowers" themselves by drawing them back into idolatry (1 Cor 10:1-22). Here the call to change attitudes and behavior is not even-handed, but hones in on the self-assured "strong."

---

[21]For parallels, see David E. Garland, *1 Corinthians* (Grand Rapids, Mich.: Zondervan, 2003), p. 358.

Yet, in spite of Paul's different arguments in the two passages, he gives both of them a theological grounding in the story of Christ. In each case, Jesus' self-sacrificing death on the cross becomes the pattern for how the "strong" must behave toward the "weak" (Rom 14:15; 1 Cor 8:11-12; 11:1). In Romans 15:1-13, Paul expands the appeal and cites Psalm 69:9 ("The insults of those who insult you have fallen on me," Rom 15:3) to show that Christ's suffering on behalf of others provides an example for the Romans. For the strong to live out the significance of Jesus' self-giving death in their context means, quite remarkably, being willing to change their diet for the sake of the weak.

All things to all people: 1 Corinthians 9:19-23; 10:31—11:1. Sandwiched between Paul's discussions of idol food in chapters 8 and 10 lies his so-called defense (1 Cor 9:3) of his apostolic rights in chapter 9. The apparently sudden change of topic has led many to view this chapter simply as a detour on apostleship that interrupts his main path of thought. A closer look at its content and rhetorical function, however, reveals an underlying theological and ethical coherence that makes this chapter essential to Paul's contextual theologizing in 1 Corinthians 8—10.[22] His primary aim in the chapter is to hold up to the Corinthians his own example of the self-sacrificing behavior that is demanded by the gospel and sorely lacking in this church. Paul, as it were, points to his own conduct as "Exhibit A" of the kind of radical renunciation of personal rights for the sake of others (cf. 1 Cor 8:9-13; 10:23-24, 28-29a, 31-33) that the Corinthians themselves must imitate (cf. 1 Cor 11:1).[23] Furthermore, the matters of "eating and drinking" surface throughout Paul's argument from example, tying it closely to the question of participating in sacrificial meals that is the subject of chapters 8—10 (1 Cor 9:4, 7-11, 13).

We will focus our attention on 1 Corinthians 9:19-23 because of its critical importance to our understanding of Paul's contextualization of the gospel. In Paul's highly rhetorical argument in chapter 9 that leads up to this passage, he goes to great pains to defend his right to receive financial support from the Corinthians, only to turn an about-face and insist that he has chosen *not* to make use of his rights (1 Cor 9:12b, 15, 18). The subtext of this unusual approach is apparently a dispute between some of the Corinthians and Paul

---

[22]Chapter 9 serves a specific rhetorical purpose as a "digression" designed to support and amplify Paul's initial argument in chapter 8 and prepare for his more specific reflection on the matter of idol meat in chapter 10. On the rhetorical use of the digression *(egressio),* see Margaret M. Mitchell, *Paul and the Rhetoric of Reconciliation: An Exegetical Investigation of the Language and Composition of 1 Corinthians* (Louisville: Westminster John Knox, 1992), pp. 249-50.

[23]The rhetorical practice of offering living examples (including the orator's own) that the audience should imitate was characteristic of deliberative rhetoric. See ibid., pp. 39-46.

that relates to Paul's means of support and the Greco-Roman convention of patronage. Patron/client relationships, in which parties of unequal status and power would voluntarily bind together because they could benefit one another's interests, were essential to the fabric of life in Roman Corinth.[24] Evidently some leading members of the congregation wanted to be Paul's ongoing patrons and would have liked for him to become their "in-house" apostle. According to the protocol of patronage, Paul's refusal of such support would have been socially offensive, bringing public shame to the benefactor. To make matters worse, Paul's insistence at paying his own way by doing manual labor was considered demeaning within higher status Greco-Roman culture; it would not only have further humiliated Paul, but his potential patrons as well (cf. 1 Cor 4:12).

Why does Paul refuse the support of the Corinthian patrons? Above all, it was to avoid putting any "obstacle in the way of the gospel" (1 Cor 9:12b). Such an obstacle could come if he were charged with impure motives for preaching, similar to familiar cultural models such as the Sophists, whose trademark was their greed and propensity for bilking their patrons (cf. 2 Cor 2:17). A hindrance could also come from the patronage convention itself, which was loaded down with cultural baggage. Accepting patronage would place Paul in an inferior client status where he would be under a system of perpetual obligation to his well-off benefactors. Such a relationship could stifle his ability to preach the gospel with freedom (1 Cor 9:18) and to fulfill his calling as an itinerant church planter.

Paul, however, makes a deliberate countercultural move. By dodging the offer of patronage, choosing instead to make tents with his hands, Paul was in effect challenging the values that upheld the patronage system of the culture. Ben Witherington is no doubt correct that Paul does not reject the Greco-Roman convention of patronage as such. Rather, he radically reframes how his converts should view those social networks in light of the gospel. All human status hierarchies are turned on their head and subordinated to the one true patron or master, God in Christ (cf. 1 Cor 3:21-23).[25] Paul's refusal to become the Corinthians' client not only gives him the practical freedom to fulfill his gos-

---

[24]On patron-client relations, see John K. Chow, *Patronage and Power: A Study of Social Networks in Corinth* (Sheffield: Sheffield Academic Press, 1992), pp. 30-82; and David deSilva, *Honor, Patronage, Kinship and Purity: Unlocking New Testament Culture* (Downers Grove, Ill.: InterVarsity Press), pp. 94-156.

[25]Witherington, *Conflict and Community*, p. 418. That Paul did not reject the convention of patronage per se is supported by his acceptance of financial support from other churches (2 Cor 11:8-9; Phil 4:14-16)—for work done elsewhere.

pel mission; more importantly, his course of downward social mobility becomes an illustration of the gospel itself, an identification with his crucified Lord. The message is embodied by the messenger. The gospel thus transforms Greco-Roman systems of power and patronage from within.

This brings us to 1 Corinthians 9:19-23. This passage is often seen as a description of Paul's cultural adaptation for the sake of mission, and that it is. Its principal function in chapter 9, however, is to provide a further personal illustration of self-sacrificing behavior for the sake of the gospel.[26] Here the apostle moves beyond the specific question of support for ministry and offers a more general insight into his self-understanding as one under obligation to preach the gospel (1 Cor 9:16-17). He begins by stating the norm for his conduct. Renouncing his rights, he has become "free" from all human expectations and impositions on his ministry (1 Cor 9:19a). Yet, paradoxically, Paul has made himself a "slave to all" (1 Cor 9:19b). By cloaking himself with the metaphor of slavery, Paul sets his own mission in diametric contrast to the "strong" Corinthians' concern over personal liberty and status. In light of chapter 9 as a whole and the values of Roman culture, Paul's "self-enslavement" could not help but include a social dimension. He has modeled slavish behavior by voluntarily climbing *down* the ladder of status for the sake of others.[27] Yet being a slave means more than that. Paul's language also recalls the Christ hymn in Philippians 2:5-8, in which Jesus gave up his rights in his incarnation and took "the form of a slave." Jesus' humble, self-giving behavior set him on a course to the cross. That Paul sees his Lord's action as a paradigm for himself and for his converts is confirmed in his conclusion to the entire argument on idol meat in 1 Corinthians 11:1: "Be imitators of me, as I am of Christ." Paul looks once more to the story of Christ for the theological basis and model for the kind of self-renouncing service he commends in chapter 9. Hence Paul's motive for evangelistic flexibility is far more than pragmatic success; it is what it means to follow his Lord.

In 9:20-22, Paul spells out what the principle of "becoming a slave" in order to win more means for various concrete settings:

> To the Jews I became as a Jew, in order to win Jews. To those under the law I became as one under the law (though I myself am not under the law) so that I might win those under the law. To those outside the law I became as one outside the law (though I am not free from God's law but am under Christ's law), so that I might win

---

[26]Richard B. Hays, *The Moral Vision of the New Testament: Community, Cross, New Creation: A Contemporary Introduction to New Testament Ethics* (San Francisco: HarperCollins, 1996), p. 43.

[27]See Dale B. Martin, *Slavery as Salvation: The Metaphor of Slavery in Pauline Christianity* (New Haven, Conn.: Yale University Press, 1990), pp. 133-35.

those outside the law. To the weak I became weak, so that I might win the weak. I have become all things to all people, that I might by all means save some.

Here he points to three groups on behalf of whom he has been "free" to adapt his behavior (Jews, Gentiles, "the weak"), before summarizing his conduct with the famous dictum, "I have become all things to all people." Paul is willing to "contextualize" his own conduct for the sake of mission. Contextualization applies not just to the message, but also the messenger.

In the first two examples, becoming "all things" refers to adapting his actions to different cultural and religious settings. Because Paul considered Jewish practices such as food laws (1 Cor 10:23-31), calendar regulations (Col 2:16) and circumcision (1 Cor 7:19; Gal 6:15; cf. Acts 16:3) to be morally neutral, he could live "as a Jew" when it would serve to better evangelize people of his own culture. When he was among Gentiles, however, he was free to behave as an outsider to the Jewish law and eat whatever was set before him (1 Cor 10:27). In other words, he adapted his lifestyle to his Gentile context in order to win Gentiles, even to the point of showing respect for the cultural and moral sensitivities of pagans. Paul's third arena for lifestyle contextualization is not a cultural group, but rather, "the weak." In this case, his identification with those he is trying to win is even more radical—he *became weak*. In becoming weak Paul follows the pattern of the incarnation of Jesus, who so identified with those he came to save that he took on their weak humanity (Phil 2:6-7).

Who are "the weak" in this passage? In light of Paul's earlier discussion in chapter 8, he no doubt has "weak" Christians in mind. In contrast to the "strong" Corinthians who are destroying the weak (1 Cor 8:11), he stands in solidarity with them and is attempting to save them. Yet, since 1 Corinthians 9:19-23 is a more generalized statement of Paul's self-understanding and behavior as a minister, he may be talking about something broader, as well. He has already declared that he is willing to endure weakness and humiliation as a minister of the gospel (1 Cor 2:1-5; 4:9-13; cf. 2 Cor 4:7-18; 11:16—12:10) for the sake of the Corinthian Christians. By sacrificing his own power and social clout, Paul became for the Corinthians an exemplar of the gospel of God's powerful weakness in the cross (1 Cor 1:18-2:5).[28] In fact, "becoming weak" in conformity with the cross was the hallmark of Paul's ministry in Corinth.

---

[28]See Barbara Hall, "All Things to All People: A Study of 1 Corinthians 9:19-23," in *The Conversation Continues: Studies in Paul and John*, ed. Robert T. Fortna and Beverly R. Gaventa (Nashville: Abingdon, 1990), pp. 148-52. Paul cannot say, "To the strong I became strong in order to win the strong," since this would deny his identification with the "weakness" of the cross.

In each case, Paul has a singular aim for contextualizing his behavior: to "win" ("save," 1 Cor 9:22) those with whom he identifies. In the case of Jews and Gentiles, this is missionary talk referring to Paul's goal of winning potential converts to faith in Christ. Paul's ability, however, to speak of winning "the weak" shows that he does not limit it exclusively to nonbelievers coming to faith. For Paul, salvation was a process that was not complete until converts were "won" in a final sense on the last day (cf. 1 Cor 8:11). To "win the weak" involved bringing them to a full maturity of faith which has as a goal their final salvation.[29] Paul's contextualizing principle of becoming "all things to all" applies as much to his ministry toward believers who need to be strengthened and a community that needs to be reconciled as it does to outsiders coming to faith.

There are clear limits, however, to what Paul included in the "all things" which he could adapt. Witherington's comment is well put: "He does not say that he became an idolater to idolaters or an adulterer to adulterers. But in matters that he did not see as ethically or theologically essential or implied by the gospel, Paul believed in flexibility."[30] Paul is no Christian chameleon. Doing everything "for the sake of the gospel" (1 Cor 9:23) and "for the glory of God" (1 Cor 10:31) provides the key to determining what is acceptable identification with others and what is not. It is instructive to compare this passage with Galatians 2:11-21, where Paul sternly rebukes Peter for withdrawing from table fellowship with Gentiles at Antioch. Peter, as head of the Jerusalem church, might have defended his behavior as necessary to avoid causing a stumbling block to Jews putting their faith in Christ. In Paul's mind, however, this was more than a matter of flexibility for the sake of the Jewish mission. Peter's actions sent a strong signal to the Gentiles that they were "second class citizens" of the kingdom and that something more than faith in Christ was needed for their salvation. It threatened the very truth of the gospel (Gal 2:14).

Since Paul is appealing to his own example in 1 Corinthians 9, the principle of becoming "all things to all people to save some" becomes a pattern for the whole church (including the "strong") to follow. This is underscored as Paul sums up the entire argument of chapters 8—10 with a concluding exhortation in 10:31—11:1:

> So, whether you eat or drink, or whatever you do, do everything to the glory of God. Give no offense to Jews or to Greeks or to the church of God, just as I try to

---

[29]Peter T. O'Brien, *Gospel and Mission in the Writings of Paul* (Grand Rapids, Mich.: Baker, 1993), pp. 95-96.
[30]Witherington, *Conflict and Community*, p. 213.

please everyone in everything I do, not seeking my own advantage, but that of many, that they may be saved. Be imitators of me, as I am of Christ.

Two comprehensive principles must guide the Corinthians' attitude and conduct. First, their entire lifestyle should bring glory to God (1 Cor 10:31). Second, he urges them not to be a stumbling block to Jews, Gentiles or fellow Christians (1 Cor 10:32). This echoes the burden of 9:20-22 to clear the ground of all nonessential obstacles to the gospel, both for those outside and within the community. Finally, because Paul exemplifies self-sacrificing behavior so that others may be saved, "he can at last articulate the exhortation that underlies the entire idol-meat discussion: 'Be imitators of me, as I am of Christ'" [31] (1 Cor 11:1). What Paul has been advocating all along is cruciform contextualization. Voluntary enslavement, renouncing one's rights for others, becoming "all things to all people"—this is simply what it means to be like the one who gave up all for the salvation of others, even to the point of dying on the cross.

Paul's explicit concern in 1 Corinthians 9:19-23 is with lifestyle contextualization—he modifies his cultural and social practice. Is this all that the passage suggests,[32] or does being "all things to all people" pertain to adapting his *message* to the language and thought forms of his audience, as well? It seems to me that Paul's generalizing of the principle of becoming "all things to save some" (cf. 1 Cor 10:31—11:1) opens the possibility of a wider application that includes flexibility in his communication of the gospel to various groups of people. We have seen that this is his consistent practice, both in evangelistic preaching (Acts 13:13-41; 17:16-34) and in his letters to mission communities. The issue of being "all things to all" is not simply one of social behavior *versus* preaching and theology. Rather, it is whether one's conduct or communication is consistent with the gospel in its saving power and Christ-centered content. Theology and Christian action are married in the gospel. In his influential treatment of this passage, Günther Bornkamm is surely correct that "Paul could not modify the gospel itself according to the particular characteristics of his hearers. The whole of his concern is to make clear that the changeless gospel . . . empowers him to be free to change his stance."[33] Nevertheless, it is only when the form of the Christian message is incarnated into a particular life setting that its genuine content

---

[31]Hays, *Moral Vision*, p. 43.

[32]So e.g., Fee, *First Epistle*, pp. 432-33; cf. Günther Bornkamm, who overdraws the division between what he thinks are Paul's flexible practice and nonflexible preaching ("The Missionary Stance of Paul in 1 Corinthians 9 and in Acts," in *Studies in Luke-Acts*, ed. L. E. Keck and J. L. Martyn [Philadelphia: Fortress, 1966], p. 202).

[33]Bornkamm, "Missionary Stance," p. 196.

can be preserved. The man from Tarsus models this kind of flexibility for the sake of mission in *both* word and walk.[34]

Idol food and the gospel: Conclusion. As we conclude our study of Paul's practice of missional theology in 1 Corinthians 8—10, it might be instructive to consider how these chapters could inform the task of contextualizing the gospel today. From one perspective, this part of Paul's conversation with a young church presents us with a classic case of how the gospel engages a religiously plural environment. Many Christians, like the Asian pastor I described at the beginning of the chapter, live in settings that are in obvious ways analogous to that of Paul's readers, and they struggle with the kinds of issues that Paul addresses here. When, for example, is ancestor worship simply a matter of honoring and respecting deceased family members and when is it a form of idolatry? Yet pluralism and new forms of paganism are increasingly prominent features in Western societies as well.[35] What is more, churches in all settings grapple with questions about where to draw the boundaries between the church and the surrounding culture: whether this or that practice is morally neutral or whether it gives away too much of the gospel.

What implications does Paul's approach to a highly specific matter like Corinthian idol food carry for the contemporary encounter between Christian faith and culture? First, the gospel of "the one Lord, Jesus Christ" (1 Cor 8:6) still excludes compromise with idolatry in all of its forms. First Corinthians 8—10 reminds us that the powers that lie behind pagan worship are real and Christians who flirt with idolatry do so to their spiritual peril. Might this observation speak to a host of issues that Christians face today, whether they involve attempting to "contextualize" Christianity by embracing elements of traditional religious belief or practice, or heeding the siren song of more subtle contemporary idolatries like nationalism, materialism and self-gratification?

Second, Paul models responsible freedom and flexibility in matters where the integrity of the gospel is not jeopardized. He refuses to legislate a total ban on

---

[34]In his magisterial book *Transforming Mission*, David Bosch argues that 1 Corinthians 9:19-23 is about "Paul's sense of responsibility" to preach to all types of people rather than about offering a model for missionary methods (*Transforming Mission: Paradigm Shifts in Theology of Mission* [Maryknoll, N.Y.: Orbis, 1991], p. 136). True, Paul does not set out to provide guidelines for crosscultural missionary adaptation as such. But Bosch fails to recognize the paradigmatic function of the passage in the flow of Paul's overall argument in 8:1—11:1, which carries important implications for *how* believers go about their witness to various groups of people. This goes beyond merely stating Paul's sense of responsibility.

[35]For a provocative analysis of the neopaganism of the Western world as a context for the church's ministry, see N. T. Wright, *Bringing the Church to the World* (Minneapolis: Bethany House, 1992).

eating idol food when that might have been the simpler option. Instead, Christians are expected to discern when and where it is appropriate to eat and when it is not. Principled flexibility, not restrictive legalism, must still govern our approach to nonessential matters. When St. Monica asked St. Ambrose whether to fast on Saturdays, as in Rome, or not, as in Milan, St. Ambrose replied, "When I go to Rome, I do as Rome does." Furthermore, our missional task calls us to follow Paul's lead in adjusting our own behavior and forms of expression so as not to erect any unnecessary obstacles to the gospel's progress. There are times when, like Paul, we must identify with the culture in order to redeem it. Christians ministering in Islamic cultures, for example, may find it necessary to remove church pews for the sake of converted Muslims, or to take off their shoes for worship, or to pray in public rather than in private. The challenge, of course, comes precisely at the point of determining which cultural issues are redeemable and which are not. Should those same Christian workers use the Islamic name for Jesus *(Isa)* when addressing Muslims? Fast during Ramadan? Pray at a mosque facing Mecca?[36] Particularly in contexts in which religion and culture are intertwined, when does the effort to contextualize one's language and behavior in order to win others cross the boundary into "partaking of the table of demons?" There are no easy answers. The church in every local setting must engage in the demanding task, guided by the Spirit, of discerning when to be "all things to all people" and when to "flee from idolatry."

Third, the symbol that grounds Paul's theologizing, as well as the controlling pattern that guides Christian behavior, is the cross of Christ. Christ's self-giving love norms the choices Christians make, whether in a nonnegotiable issue like drawing weak believers back into idolatry (1 Cor 8:9-12) or a flexible one like whether or not to eat meat in a pagan home (1 Cor 10:27—11:1). The question is not, how far can we go in accommodating to the dominant culture? but rather, how can we live out the cross in life as the character of the church and as a witness to the world?

Finally, we can learn from Paul's *method* of theological engagement with the knowledge boasters in Corinth, which has several dimensions. First, he acknowledges areas of agreement between them concerning knowledge, monotheism, Christian freedom and the moral neutrality of food. In each case, however, he reframes the issues in light of the gospel and challenges their errant beliefs. Second, he points to living examples, either as warnings—as in the case of Israel's wilderness story—or patterns to imitate, such as those of Paul himself

---

[36]For a helpful discussion of these issues, see David Racey, "Contextualization: How Far Is Too Far?" *EMQ* 32 (July 1996): 304-9.

and ultimately Jesus Christ. For Paul, contextualizing the gospel is more than a matter of theological correctness or persuasive arguments—it has a profoundly personal component. Such lifestyle contextualization has the potential to speak winsomely to a postmodern world, in which the demonstration of self-giving love and Christlikeness will no doubt carry more weight than a bale of closely reasoned arguments.

Third, Paul responds to the problem of idol food with theological imagination and communicative skill. He draws upon a quiver full of persuasive strategies in order to call the Corinthians to reenvision their world in light of the gospel: quoting his opponents' terms and slogans; appealing to Scripture (1 Cor 9:9; 10:1-12, 22, 26); illustrations from common life (1 Cor 9:7-11, 24-27); concrete case studies (1 Cor 8:10; 10:27-29); rhetorical questions (1 Cor 9:1, 4-12) and direct commands (1 Cor 10:14), to name just some. What is more, Paul refuses to offer a single-note solution to the idol meat problem. He speaks of its effect on the weak and its danger for the strong, its connection to idolatry in some settings and its lack of idol involvement in others, and the need for both responsible freedom and self-renouncing servanthood. This ought to caution us against simplistic answers to contemporary cultural questions, especially those gray areas over which sincere Christians disagree. At the same time, it should challenge us to exercise theological imagination under the leadership of the Spirit, so that the story of God in Christ might engage the complex "idol meat" issues of our own world.

1 CORINTHIANS 15: THE RESURRECTION STORY

First Corinthians 15 presents another intriguing case study in contextualization. In contrast to chapters 8—10 and much of the rest of the letter, the target issue in chapter 15 is belief, not behavior. The theological springboard from which Paul enters his argument is the idea of "some" Corinthians that "there is no resurrection of the dead" (1 Cor 15:12). Precisely what this denial involved is not clear.[37] However, given the thrust of Paul's overall discussion in the chapter, most likely their errant thinking was rooted in a Hellenistic dualism that rejected the basic Jewish and Christian teaching of a *bodily* resurrection (cf. 1 Cor 15:35-49) while retaining belief in a spiritual and immortal life of the soul after death. Paul's repeated references to the dead (14 times in verses 12-52) suggest that these Corinthians probably understood resurrection as the resuscitation of dead

---

[37]For an overview of the major positions, see A. J. M. Wedderburn, *Baptism and Resurrection: Studies in Pauline Theology against Its Graeco-Roman Background* (Tübingen: Mohr, 1987), pp. 6-22; Thiselton, *First Epistle*, pp. 1172-76.

corpses—a prospect that would have sounded like anything *but* "good news" to the Greek or Roman mind (cf. Acts 17:31-32).[38] This, combined with what we know of the Corinthians' pride in their possession of higher "wisdom" and "knowledge" (e.g, 1 Cor 1—3, 8) and in their present level of spiritual attainment (e.g., 1 Cor 4:6-10; 12—14), resulted in a defective view of the future.

First Corinthians 15 thus reflects a classic clash of worldviews. The intellectually sophisticated deniers apparently thought of death as liberating the soul from the body, thereby enabling a continuation of their superior spiritual life. The notion of an end-time "resurrection of dead bodies" would have seemed both crass and unnecessary. Paul's eschatological teaching is fundamentally incompatible with such a dualistic outlook, and it could not be accommodated for the sake of pastoral or missionary success. In this case, becoming "all things to all people" was out of the question. So divergent were the worldviews of Paul and the Corinthian disbelievers that some interpreters have wondered where the points of contact between them might have been.[39]

A shared story: 1 Corinthians 15:1-11. Paul finds that common ground in the heart of the gospel itself—the story of salvation in the Christ event. Paul does not begin his theological discourse in 1 Corinthians 15 with the point of contention between himself and his audience over the resurrection of the dead. Instead, he reminds them of the foundational gospel he preached to them from the beginning, which they received and now share in common with the whole church (1 Cor 15:1-11). Paul believes that by denying the resurrection of Christians, the Corinthians have called the truth of the gospel itself into question. This may help to explain why he follows the unusual tactic of rehearsing the full gospel narrative that he has received as Christian tradition and faithfully transmitted to the Corinthians:

> For I handed on to you as of first importance what I in turn had received:
> that Christ died for our sins in accordance with the scriptures,
> and that he was buried,
> and that he was raised on the third day in accordance with the scriptures,
> and that he appeared to Cephas, and then to the twelve. (1 Cor 15:3-5)

His exhortation to hold fast to the very terms of the gospel (literally, "what word I preached to you," 1 Cor 15:2), a message that is "of first importance" (1 Cor 15:3), indicates how serious the matter is to Paul. Not only the gospel, but the Corinthians' very Christian existence, is at stake (1 Cor 15:2); they are in dan-

---

[38]See Dale B. Martin, *The Corinthian Body* (New Haven, Conn.: Yale University Press, 1995), pp. 107-36; Witherington, *Conflict and Community*, pp. 302, 306-7.

[39]Richard A. Horsley, *1 Corinthians* (Nashville: Abingdon, 1998), p. 218.

ger of believing "in vain" (1 Cor 15:2; cf. 10, 14, 58). Paul, in effect, announces the solution before he addresses the problem. The only answer to their denial of the resurrection of the dead is to rightly understand the gospel through which they are saved. This bedrock confession of the gospel story functions as the ground of Paul's theological response to the Corinthian error throughout the rest of the chapter.

Although the narrative confession announces both Christ's saving death and his resurrection from the dead, it is the latter that is critical to Paul at the moment. The christological base from which Paul argues in chapter 15 is the core belief that "he was raised on the third day" (1 Cor 15:4). After barely a mention of the resurrection in the first fourteen chapters of the letter, suddenly it dominates the horizon like a brilliant sunrise. Paul's citing of the early Christian creed (1 Cor 15:3-5) and the various resurrection appearances that follow, including his own experience (1 Cor 15:6-10), has at least four functions in Paul's contextual argument. First, it allows Paul to reestablish that the resurrection is central and nonnegotiable to the gospel and the Christian faith. Second, the confession's claim that Christ was "buried" and "raised on the third day," along with the validating witnesses, affirms the reality of Christ's resurrection from the dead. This provides the anchor for Paul's appeal for the certainty and necessity of the resurrection of dead believers in 15:12-34. Third, the evidence that Christ was not raised to some disembodied spiritual existence, but was corporally visible to human witnesses, prepares for Paul's argument for the bodily nature of the resurrection of Christians in verses 35-57. Fourth, rehearsing the common tradition enables him to correct the Corinthians' denial of the future resurrection on the basis of a shared presupposition ("he was raised"), which they have already accepted and believed (1 Cor 15:11).

Christ the firstfruits: 1 Corinthians 15:12-34. Having established the touchstone reality of the resurrection that the gospel story proclaims, Paul takes up his main theological burden in the chapter—to convince the Corinthians of their gravely inadequate eschatology and to offer an alternative interpretation of the resurrection story, one whose ending is still in the future. In the process, Paul once again deploys a variety of weapons from his persuasive arsenal, including logical proofs, analogies, examples, rhetorical questions, apocalyptic symbols, and quotations from both Scripture and pagan writings.[40] In 15:12-34

---

[40]Witherington, *Conflict and Community*, p. 292. First Corinthians 15 can be viewed as a coherent piece of deliberative rhetoric (persuading an audience to adopt a particular belief or behavior) in itself. See the analysis of the rhetorical structure of Paul's argument in chapter 15 by Anders Erikkson (*Traditions*, pp. 248-75; cf. Thiselton, *First Epistle*, pp. 1177-78).

Paul argues for the *reality* of the resurrection of the dead, contradicting the Corinthians' denial of it (1 Cor 15:12). This passage follows a familiar A-B-A pattern (see 1 Cor 8—10, 12—14). Both 1 Corinthians 15:12-19 and 1 Corinthians 15:29-34 negatively expose the absurdity of the Corinthians' position for Christian belief and practice. In contrast, verses 20-28 expound the positive gospel truth that the resurrection of Christ is no isolated event; it is the beginning of the resurrection of Christians.

Negative consequences. In 1 Corinthians 15:12-19, Paul takes his readers down a familiar rhetorical path in demonstrating that the logical consequences of the Corinthian position are completely unacceptable.[41] If the Corinthians' denial of the resurrection were true, it would decimate the gospel that Paul has preached and the church believed (1 Cor 15:1-11). Sharply put, no resurrection of the dead means no resurrection of Christ (1 Cor 15:13, 16). This in turn renders both Paul's preaching of the gospel and their own experience of faith, which was generated by that gospel message, futile and false (1 Cor 15:14-15, 17). The Corinthians' denial of the coming resurrection is more than a blind spot in their theology; it shatters the very axis of the Christian faith, the Christ event itself. Paul's ability to argue in two directions, both from Jesus' resurrection to the resurrection of the dead (1 Cor 15:12), and from the future resurrection to the resurrection of Christ (1 Cor 15:13, 16), underscores how completely they are united in Paul's thinking. The argument in this section works because Paul sees the resurrection of Christ as the "paradigm case" of the reality of resurrection to come.[42]

Verses 29-34 resume the argumentative strategy of exposing the disastrous consequences of denying the resurrection of the dead with three additional arguments, framed in a familiar diatribe (question and answer) style. Paul begins with a series of rhetorical questions that give "specific examples of practices that make no sense in a resurrectionless world."[43] First, the practice of proxy baptism on behalf of the dead by some Corinthians becomes absurd and pointless (1 Cor 15:29). Whatever the specific background of this elusive rite—and there has been a swarm of suggestions—it is striking that Paul can appeal to a local ritual that he does not necessarily endorse. Its function in the argument is simply to show that the Corinthians' actual behavior contradicts their own theology of doubting the resurrection of the dead. Second, Paul once again draws attention to his own experience of opposition and suffering on behalf of the gospel (1

---

[41]Eriksson, *Traditions*, pp. 255-56.
[42]Thiselton, *First Epistle*, p. 1214.
[43]Hays, *First Corinthians*, p. 266.

Cor 15:30-32a). Tapping a colorful metaphor from the Roman gladiatorial shows that was often used in Hellenistic moral teaching,[44] Paul insists that his struggle against "wild animals" would be meaningless if there were no future hope.

Paul then spotlights the *ethical* consequences of the Corinthians' denial (1 Cor 15:32b-34). To make the point that without a future eschatology people will live only to satisfy their present pleasure, he quotes a slogan from the prophet Isaiah (1 Cor 15:32b; Is 22:13), which also resembles popular critiques of the Epicurean philosophers ("Let us eat and drink, for tomorrow we die"). Next, he turns to a contemporary pagan proverb attributed to Menander (1 Cor 15:33). In effect, he condemns the Gentile Corinthians "out of the mouth of their own cultural heritage even apart from Scripture and apostolic tradition."[45] The section concludes with a forceful ethical exhortation targeted to the morally dysfunctional Corinthians: "Come to a sober and right mind and sin no more" (1 Cor 15:34; cf. 48). For Paul, it is not only the cross but the resurrection and its future implications for believers, that functions as a powerful motive for Christian conduct and service (cf. 2 Cor 5:9-10, 15; 1 Thess 5:23).

Positive affirmations. In contrast to the mainly negative arguments of verses 1 Corinthians 15:12-19 and 1 Corinthians 15:29-34 about the appalling effects of the Corinthians' wrong thinking, in 1 Corinthians 15:20-28 Paul unfolds the positive theological meaning of Christ's resurrection for the future of Christians. Verse 20 triumphantly declares the premise that undergirds his whole argument in 15:12-34: "But in fact Christ has been raised from the dead, the first fruits of those who have died." This resumes the story told in the gospel tradition of 15:3-5, but it expands the sacred story's horizon to the end-time future and shows how the Corinthians themselves are included in the plot line. The Old Testament image of the "first fruits" (1 Cor 15:20, 23) is particularly apt for Paul's contextual purpose, because it establishes an inseparable relationship between the resurrection of Christ and that of the church. Christ the first fruits guarantees the inevitable completion of the full harvest to come. The Corinthian deniers have missed the point that Jesus' resurrection is an unfinished story.

In verses 21-22 Paul turns from metaphor to typology to further explain the connection between the resurrection of Christ and that of his followers. Just as Adam, the representative head of the old humanity, was the agent of death, so Christ, the head of the new humanity, has overturned the death sentence, bringing the assurance of resurrection life for all who are represented by him. Paul's ability to use the Adam/Christ typology to make different points elsewhere (cf.

---

[44]See Abraham Malherbe, "The Beasts at Ephesus," *JBL* 87 (1968): 71-80.
[45]Witherington, *Conflict and Community*, p. 292.

1 Cor 15:45-49; Rom 5:12-21)[46] suggests that this analogy is for him a means of expressing the significance of the gospel that can be applied flexibly to a variety of contexts. Here he insists that because Christ has been raised as the *representative* of his followers, the resurrection of believers will take place through participating in the resurrection of Jesus.[47] The connection between the two could not be closer.

At first glance, 1 Corinthians 15:23-28 seems to be a detour in Paul's thought in which he gets caught up in explaining the sequence of end-time events. This is not the case, however. Although Paul, not surprisingly, makes use of apocalyptic motifs and categories from his Jewish heritage, it is still Christology that controls his theological reflection.[48] First, Paul emphatically links the resurrection of the dead to the second coming *(parousia)* of Christ (1 Cor 15:23). Joost Holleman is probably correct that in this way Paul counters the Corinthian perspective that spiritual immortality is something to be obtained directly upon passing through death.[49] Second, Paul uses the military imagery that dominates this section to show that Christ's reign (1 Cor 15:25), which begins at his resurrection, has the ultimate goal of destroying death itself, the "last enemy" (1 Cor 15:26). This enables God's redeeming plan for the universe to reach its intended end (1 Cor 15:27-28). If the Corinthian disbelievers conceived of death as simply a transition of the soul into a purely spiritual existence, his argument is particularly relevant. Death, Paul affirms, is a terrifying cosmic power that will only be defeated at the end of time, and the resurrection of the dead is the evidence of its final overthrow. Without the end-time resurrection, the sinister powers will not be silenced; death is not finally defeated; God cannot be "all in all" (1 Cor 15:28).

The resurrection body—continuity and transformation: 1 Corinthians 15:35-58. Up to this point, Paul has focused primarily on demonstrating the certainty of the future resurrection of the dead in Christ and how this is a necessary

---

[46]It is instructive to compare Paul's usage of the Adam/Christ typology in Romans 5 with that in 1 Corinthians 15. In Romans 5, Paul focuses on the soteriological, rather than the eschatological, results of the representative acts of Adam and Christ. He speaks of salvation as a present, and not simply a future, reality for the believer (Rom 5:15ff.) and emphasizes the cross, rather than the resurrection of Christ, as the supreme instrument of God's righteousness and grace (Rom 5:15, 18). This is another example of Paul doing contextual theology.

[47]Joost Holleman, *Resurrection and Parousia: A Traditio-Historical Study of Paul's Eschatology in 1 Corinthians 15* (Leiden: E. J. Brill, 1996), pp. 55-57.

[48]Martinus de Boer, *The Defeat of Death: Apocalyptic Eschatology in 1 Cor 15 and Rom 5,* JSNTSup 22 (Sheffield: JSOT Press, 1988), p. 120. Contra J. C. Beker, *Paul the Apostle: The Triumph of God in Life and Thought* (Philadelphia: Fortress, 1980), pp. 168-76.

[49]Holleman, *Resurrection and Parousia,* pp. 37-40.

sequel to the resurrection of Jesus proclaimed by the gospel. Lurking behind the Corinthians' denial of the resurrection of the dead, however, is the issue that may well have been their chief stumbling block—the baffling and distasteful prospect of the reanimation of mortal bodies. For ancient Greek and Roman thinkers, immortality did not—indeed it *could* not—involve the body. The Corinthians are in need of major "worldview surgery." Consequently, Paul turns his theological energies toward the problem of the resurrection body.[50] Continuing the rhetorical technique of the diatribe he began in verse 29, he poses two crucial questions that address the Corinthians' confusion: how are the dead raised, and what kind of body do they have (1 Cor 15:35)?

What kind of body? 1 Corinthians 15:35-49. Paul's initial response to these targeted questions stresses both continuity and discontinuity between the body of this life and that of the life to come. Because the whole notion of a bodily resurrection is so much nonsense to the Corinthian deniers, Paul begins by drawing upon familiar analogies from the natural world of God's creation (1 Cor 15:36-41). The dominant image is that of the seed that in God's created order must "die" for it to be raised by God to new life. Although there is genuine continuity between the seed (body) that is sown and the plant that is raised, Paul's application of the analogy to the resurrection body (1 Cor 15:42-44) centers on the *dissimilarity* between the body that is buried in decay, dishonor and weakness and that which is transformed into incorruption, glory and power. The series of opposites crescendos until it culminates in the final contrast between the "natural human body" *(sōma psychikon)* of the present life and the "spiritual body" *(sōma pneumatikon)* of the life to come (1 Cor 15:44). Did Paul borrow this natural-spiritual distinction from the Corinthians in order to subtly reinterpret their language in light of his understanding of the resurrection? Possibly. More likely, however, Paul has chosen the term *natural (psychikos)* because it occurs in Genesis 2:7, which he is about to cite (1 Cor 15:45). As for the word *spiritual (pneumatikon)*, this probably was language the Corinthians claimed for themselves in relation to an exalted spirituality that had little or nothing to do with the body. The phrase *spiritual body* would no doubt have clanged in the ears of the deniers as a shocking oxymoron. Their notion of the future had no room for a combining of the two ideas. Paul must reshape both their worldview assumptions about the "body" as well as their theology of what it means to be "spiritual."

---

[50]Gordon D. Fee notes that while the term *dead* occurs eleven times in 1 Cor 15:1-34 and only three times in the remainder of the chapter, the word *body* occurs ten times in the chapter, all of them in vv. 35-58 (*First Epistle*, p. 776). Recent rhetorical analysis of the chapter confirms this shift in emphasis. See Thiselton, *First Epistle*, pp. 1258-59.

To do this he returns to the gospel's Christ-center. Paul takes up the Adam/Christ analogy again in verses 45-49, but now with a somewhat different focus. Here the stress is not on Adam's agency of death and the reality of resurrection in Christ, as in 1 Corinthians 15:21-22, but rather on the nature of "bodily" existence, now and in the future. Just as Paul had earlier demonstrated that the resurrection of Christ is the ground of believers' resurrection from the dead, he now reveals that the risen Christ is the source of their spiritual body. Appealing to Genesis 2:7, Paul argues that human existence in the present age is "natural" because it is determined by the first man, Adam, who in creation received mortal life (1 Cor 15:45). In contrast, the resurrection life of believers is "spiritual" because it is patterned after the last Adam, Christ, who became "spirit." By calling Christ a "life-giving spirit" (1 Cor 15:45), Paul is saying that at his resurrection, Christ not only assumed his "spiritual" (glorified) body, but that he also became the giver of the life of the age to come—a life that will be animated and empowered by the Spirit. In the context, this means that Christ's "power is manifest in the transformation of our mortal bodies into spiritual bodies that are like Christ"[51] (cf. Rom 8:10-11; Phil 3:21). Paul thus draws upon the Adam/Christ contrast—on the basis of his fresh reading of the Genesis story—in order to redefine the Corinthians' faulty notion of "resurrection of the *dead*."

Paul drives home a similar point with the help of another theological theme, the "image of Christ" (1 Cor 15:49). Believers who presently share the bodily likeness of Adam, the earthly man, can anticipate being conformed to the image of the risen Christ, the heavenly man. Undoubtedly, it is Paul's eschatological concern in the context that leads him to envision the image of Christ as a *future* reality ("we *will* . . . bear the image of the man from heaven," 1 Cor 15:49; cf. Rom 8:29).[52] Elsewhere, it is the present experience of being transformed into God's image that comes to the forefront (cf. 2 Cor 3:18; Eph 4:24; Col 3:10). But here Paul identifies the image of Christ with the end-time bodily resurrection of believers (cf. 1 Cor 15:44).[53] Although earlier in the letter he accented the need for the Corinthians to imitate Christ in his servanthood and self-giving death (1 Cor 11:1), now he stresses that the goal of Christlikeness is to be transformed into his resurrection image.

---

[51]James D. G. Dunn, *Christology in the Making: An Inquiry into the Origins of the Doctrine of Incarnation* (London: SCM, 1980), p. 110.

[52]So most commentators, who accept the future tense reading "we will bear" (*phoresomen,* 1 Cor 15:49) on exegetical and contextual grounds.

[53]Paul seems to have in mind not a restoration to a pre-Fall state (the image of God), but rather the transformation believers will experience into something new, the resurrection image of Christ, which includes his moral, as well as his bodily likeness. Although Paul's contextual focus is on sharing Christ's bodily image, the *moral* likeness of Christ is by no means absent from view.

We will all be changed: 1 Corinthians 15:50-58. Paul's unpacking of the implications of the resurrection story for believers comes to a rousing rhetorical climax in verses 50-58. Traditional expressions and images from the Old Testament and Jewish apocalyptic literature abound (e.g., "flesh and blood," "kingdom of God," "mystery," "trumpet"), but Paul also seems to make an effort to translate Jewish notions into terms that could be easily understood by a Gentile audience.[54] The language of "imperishability" and "immortality" (1 Cor 15:50, 52-54) resonates with the philosophical and religious concerns of the Hellenistic world. In his very use of such terms, however, Paul cuts the legs off the Greek worldview that perceived immortality as a disembodied state. He reconfigures "immortality" in terms of a transformed, resurrected *body*. It is illuminating to compare this passage with 1 Thessalonians 4:15-17, where Paul also marshals traditional apocalyptic symbols to argue for the future resurrection of believers. In spite of a number of similarities, there are significant differences, which reveal how Paul tailors his eschatological teaching to the needs of his converts. In his letter to the Thessalonians, he is writing to reassure Christians who were grieving over the fate of some in their number who had died before the parousia had taken place. As a result, he focuses on the return of Christ and the sequence of those who will be raised to meet him—first the dead in Christ, then the living. In contrast, in 1 Corinthians 15:51-54, the second coming is not mentioned as such, and it is the sudden transformation of the mortal *body*, rather than the resurrection order, that commands center stage.

The chapter ends with an exhortation (1 Cor 15:58) that at first blush might seem like something of an anticlimax: "Therefore, my beloved, be steadfast, immovable, always excelling in the work of the Lord, because you know that in the Lord your labor is not in vain." In fact, it is a concluding summary *(peroratio)* and application of the whole theological argument ("therefore"). Paul began by urging the Corinthians to take their stand in the gospel that proclaims the resurrection, to hold firmly to it lest their believing and Paul's labor among them be in vain (1 Cor 15:1-2). He has repeatedly insisted that without the resurrection their faith and their Christian life in the world are worthless (1 Cor 15:2, 10, 14, 17, 19, 30-34). Now, in the end, he calls them once more to stand firm in that same gospel because with an assured hope in the risen Lord their labor "is not in vain" (1 Cor 15:58). Paul's denial of the deniers has come full circle.[55] Both the Corinthians' thinking and their conduct must conform to the gospel.

---

[54]Collins, *First Corinthians*, pp. 573, 579; T. Fornberg, *An Early Church in a Pluralistic Society: A Study of 2 Peter* (Lund: C. W. K. Gleerup, 1977), pp. 123, 134.
[55]De Boer, *Defeat of Death*, p. 95.

The resurrection story: A half truth? First Corinthians 15 reveals Paul's contextual theologizing at its finest. Throughout the chapter, his audience-specific argument is grounded in the normative story of Christ that he brings to speech in the form of the church's gospel tradition (1 Cor 15:1-11). At the same time, he can draw upon an array of theological motifs and images, as well as every manner of rhetorical device, in order to express the gospel's meaning for the future in a way that specifically targets the misunderstandings and needs of the community. If we see it anywhere in Paul's letters, this chapter reveals the rich interplay between the central convictions of the gospel and the concrete situation within and for which the gospel is interpreted.

It is striking that although the tradition that grounds Paul's theological reflection in 1 Corinthians 15 refers to both the death and the resurrection of Christ, it is the resurrection alone that becomes the focus throughout the chapter. After the confession in verse 3 that "Christ died for our sins," Jesus' death is never explicitly mentioned again. Just as remarkably, Paul speaks of the resurrection only once in the entire letter prior to this chapter (1 Cor 6:14). Not only when Paul elaborates his theology of the cross in chapters one and two, but throughout the first fourteen chapters, his appeals to the work of Christ concentrate almost exclusively on his saving death (e.g., 1 Cor 1:18—2:5; 5:7; 8:11; 10:16; 11:23-26; cf. 6:11, 20; 7:23). How do we account for this? Does it mean, as J. C. Beker has argued, that Paul's theology in 1 Corinthians is one-sided—that the diverse polemical situations of the letter force him to argue in such a way that "the death and resurrection of Christ are torn apart and the 'whole' gospel of Paul, that is, its coherent core . . . is thwarted."[56]

I cannot agree. We have seen that the framework of Paul's gospel is the grand story of God's saving activity in Jesus, which in its broadest sense encompasses the preexistence, incarnation, death, resurrection and return of Christ. Because in Paul's missionary preaching to the Corinthians this saving story was announced and accepted (1 Cor 15:1-3a, 11), there is no need to restate the whole gospel narrative each time he refers to it in the course of his pastoral arguments. Paul is able to focus on the particular aspect of the story and its meaning that speaks to his immediate concern. In each case, the rest of the story is assumed.[57] When Paul unfolds the meaning of Christ's resurrection for the future of his followers in 1 Corinthians 15, he has not forgotten that "Christ died for our sins." This is confirmed by Paul's references to Christ's victory not only over death

---

[56]Beker, *Paul the Apostle*, pp. 173-75, here p. 174.
[57]Charles B. Cousar, *The Theology of the Cross: The Death of Jesus in the Pauline Letters* (Minneapolis: Fortress, 1990), p. 107.

but also over sin (1 Cor 15:17, 56, cf. 34), which presupposes his atoning work on the cross. Likewise, Paul's theology of the cross in 1 Corinthians would have little value apart from the vindication of the resurrection. Paul's gospel therefore remains whole, but his choosing to feature certain elements of that gospel for particular situations makes doing theology truly incarnational.

The same principle might have a contemporary analogy. Initially, it may be the gospel of the risen Lord who is victorious over death and the hostile powers (cf. 1 Cor 15:23-28) that is needed in an animistic setting, where people live in fear of unseen forces and an uncertain future. On the other hand, Paul's "theology of the cross" that overturns human wisdom, hierarchies and power structures from below (e.g., 1 Cor 1:18—2:5) has consistently spelled hope for poor and disenfranchised people. Yet it is possible that today, as in Corinth, a distorted or one-sided understanding of the gospel needs to be corrected by looking at the Christian message through different lenses. For instance, the two most popular images of Christ among the Filipino people are the suffering or entombed Jesus (such as the famous *Santo Entierro* of Quiapo Church in Manila) and the *Santo Niño* (Holy Child).[58] These representations of Jesus as an innocent child and as the symbol of human suffering powerfully resonate with people who have endured centuries of colonial rule and an ongoing experience of physical and economic hardship. But such images tell a half-truth without a complementary understanding of Christ as risen and victorious Lord. Hear the plea of Filipina theologian Melba P. Maggay: "In our message we need to make the emphatic transition from the Cross to the empty tomb! . . . Failure to do so consigns our people to the subtle demonic lie of seeing the work of Jesus, and life itself, as an endless passion, a picture of eternal defeat and unrelieved tragedy.[59] On the other hand, Douglas John Hall argues that many North Americans have been quick to embrace a misguided theology of the resurrection that welcomes a risen, triumphant Jesus but sidesteps the way of the cross in their own Christian experience. This "gospel lite" message sees the cross simply as Jesus' "hardships" and the resurrection as his victory over them. "It is time now," urges Hall, "that North Americans in their churches and on their billboards and television screens should meet the Crucified."[60]

---

[58]See Allan J. Delotavo, "A Reflection on the Images of Christ in Filipino Culture," *AJT* 3 (1989): 524-29; Rodrigo D. Tano, "Theology in the Philippine Context: Some Issues and Themes," in *Theological Education in the Philippine Context*, ed. Lee Wanak (Manila: OMF Literature, 1993), pp. 8-9.

[59]Melba P. Maggay, *The Gospel in Filipino Context* (Manila: OMF Literature, 1987), p. 8.

[60]D. J. Hall, *Lighten Our Darkness: Toward an Indigenous Theology of the Cross* (Philadelphia: Westminster Press, 1976), p. 140.

CONCLUSION

Case studies reveal a *process* of dealing with difficult issues which carries implications beyond any specific answers to the problems they address. Our cases from 1 Corinthians not only give us theological and ethical content that can be applied to our own circumstances; they model the theological task. Although much could be said at this point, I will simply highlight several dimensions of Paul's missional theologizing in these two cases and 1 Corinthians as a whole that have implications for the challenge of telling and living out the good news today.

First, this letter spotlights the vital link between the gospel and holy living. Most of the contingent concerns that Paul must address in Corinth are, at least on the surface, matters of behavior and attitudes. But Paul is convinced that the Corinthians' ethical and interpersonal shortcomings betray a more fundamental failure—a deep misunderstanding of the gospel itself. So whether the immediate problem happens to be prideful boasting in status, sexual misconduct, attending parties at pagan temples, or social divisions at church "pot-luck" meals, Paul consistently appeals to the gospel to reshape the community's conduct. In a contemporary scene in which the compartmentalizing of belief and behavior seems to be no less common among Christians, it is essential that we allow the gospel to address and confront, when necessary, issues of everyday Christian conduct within our various cultural worlds. The gospel is not the gospel unless it is lived out.

Second, Paul consistently approaches the local struggles and questions of the Corinthians from the perspective of the center of the gospel, the saving story of Christ. In particular, Christ's loving self-sacrifice in the cross becomes the matrix for the story of Paul and of the Corinthians. Likewise, the reality that Christ "was raised on the third day" and its meaning for the future can serve as the basis and motive for both right thinking and right living. First Corinthians is essentially a call for Christians to become radically conformed to the gospel of Christ crucified and risen—in their way of being, believing and behaving. At the same time, the contingent situation in Corinth leads Paul to *frame* the gospel in particular ways. Thus, his reflections on Christ as "first fruits" (1 Cor 15:20, 23) or Christ as "last Adam" and as "life-giving spirit" (1 Cor 15:45) all come to speech because they enable the gospel of Christ to engage hearers with a powerful word that speaks to their circumstances. As we address our multiplex cultures and concerns today, we can only do so from the center of it all—the story of Jesus, our crucified and reigning Lord. But the gospel anthem must be sung in new keys if its majestic strains are to be heard in all their transforming power.

Third, the gospel calls the Corinthians to a countercultural view of the world. Although Paul recognizes the role of embracing aspects of his hearers' culture in order to advance the Christian mission (1 Cor 9:20-23), he takes a largely critical posture toward Greco-Roman culture in 1 Corinthians. Such a stance is necessary because Corinth, not Christ, shapes many of the Corinthians' basic assumptions, values and behaviors. Christians today also need a conversion of the imagination that will let them see their own social and cultural worlds in dramatically different ways.[61]

Finally, 1 Corinthians underscores the personal dimension of Paul's communication of the gospel. He not only proclaims the message of Christ crucified and risen. He also embodies it. Over and over Paul appeals to his own presence among the Corinthians as a living demonstration of the crucified life that the gospel calls them to embrace (1 Cor 2:1-5; 4:1, 9-16; 9:1-27; 10:32—11:1). Paul's verbalizing of the story of Jesus and its transforming implications rings true because the Corinthians have seen the Christ-drama reenacted in his own life and ministry. Will our efforts to communicate and contextualize the gospel today bear any authenticity unless our lives, too, incarnate the story of Jesus' self-giving love?

---

[61]Hays, *1 Corinthians*, p. 11.

7. COLOSSIANS

The Gospel and Syncretism

And you have come to fullness in him,
who is the head of every ruler and authority.

COL 2:10

One of my missionary colleagues in the Philippines described a chance encounter he had with a grandmother in a part of the country where the local animistic religion was widely practiced. He noticed a cross hanging around her neck and asked her if she was a Christian. "Yes," she assured him, "I am a follower of Jesus Christ." When she discovered that my friend was a Christian missionary, she invited him to visit her humble dwelling. To his surprise, she showed him a traditional spirit house behind her home that was intended to ward off the evil spirits. "If you are a Christian," he queried, "why do you still keep a spirit house?" Her matter-of-fact reply: "I just want to make sure that all of the bases are covered."

Syncretism—the mixing of incompatible religious ideas and practices—is a constant challenge to the gospel, particularly when converts have recently come out of a pagan religious background. Paul's letter to the Colossians reflects such a situation. He writes to a young and predominantly Gentile church (cf. Col 1:21-22, 27; 3:5-7) in a part of Asia where religious pluralism and syncretism were woven into the very fabric of life.[1] These believers were apparently under intense pressure to syncretize their new Christian faith by adding elements from other traditions and teachings, including their own past religious experience. News had reached Paul—presumably from the church's founder Epaphras—that a destructive error had emerged in the Lycus Valley,

---

[1]For evidence of the syncretistic character of the religious scene in the region of Phrygia, see especially Clinton E. Arnold, *The Colossian Syncretism: The Interface Between Christianity and Folk Belief at Colossae* (Grand Rapids, Mich.: Baker, 1996).

one that could compromise the very heart of the gospel the Colossians had received.[2] Paul's response to this threat is twofold. Negatively, he confronts the syncretistic teaching and exposes the dangers of submitting to it. Positively, Colossians affirms what is central to the gospel and offers a fresh contextualization of that gospel for a new life setting. This first-century encounter between the gospel and syncretism not only provides insight into the character of Paul's way of doing missional theology; it also has important implications for the church's theological task today.

THE COLOSSIAN CONTEXT: A SYNCRETISTIC "PHILOSOPHY"

What is the context for Paul's targeted message in Colossians? Unfortunately, answering that question is no simple matter. Consensus over the specific background and nature of the teaching Paul counters in the letter has been hard to come by. Scholars have tried to root the opponents' "philosophy" (Col 2:8)—a term that could be used in a fairly broad sense—in some form of early Gnosticism, in Greek philosophy, or in Jewish mysticism, all without full success.[3] No single religious movement we know of can account for the collection of polemical references in Colossians 2:8-23. It is better, therefore, to see the Colossian problem as a kind of syncretistic stew made up of a number of religious ingredients.[4] This is hardly surprising, given that the cities of the Lycus Valley in western Asia Minor were intersections of various crisscrossing cultures. By the first century, the indigenous Phrygian culture and religion had become well integrated with Greek and Roman influences, and a significant Jewish minority population added to the mix. What is more, there was a general openness among Hellenistic peoples to experimenting with different religious beliefs and prac-

---

[2]We cannot be certain whether the error emerged from within the congregation or was imposed from the outside, or even the extent to which it had already been adopted. See Victor Paul Furnish, "Colossians, Epistle to the," in *Anchor Bible Dictionary*, ed. D. N. Freedman (New York: Doubleday, 1992), 1:1091-92.

[3]For helpful summaries of the various possibilities, see Peter T. O'Brien, *Colossians, Philemon* (Waco, Tex.: Word, 1982), pp. xxx-xxxviii; John M. G. Barclay, *Colossians and Philemon* (Sheffield: Sheffield Academic Press, 1997), pp. 39-48.

[4]James D. G. Dunn has argued that the Colossian "philosophy" was not syncretistic, but was rather a Jewish "apology" that promoted the distinctive religious practices of the Jews, such as circumcision and sabbath observances (*The Epistles to the Colossians and to Philemon: A Commentary on the Greek Text* [Grand Rapids, Mich.: Eerdmans, 1996], pp. 29-35); idem, "The Colossian Philosophy: A Confident Jewish Apologia," *Bib* 76 (1995): 153-81. The lack, however, of a polemic against law observance such as we find in Galatians (the word *law* does not appear in Colossians) and the absence of Old Testament citations makes this highly unlikely. Furthermore, it fails to account for the pervasive concern in Colossians with the "philosophy's" deference to the cosmic powers.

tices, making pluralism and syncretism standard features of the religious scene.[5]

Clinton E. Arnold sharpens the question by drawing attention to the often underestimated role of folk religious belief for understanding the backdrop to Paul's theological reflection in Colossians.[6] Popular religion in Asia Minor was highly syncretistic and sprang out of a worldview that was conscious of a host of evil spirits, capricious gods and goddesses, and astral powers. All of these posed ever-present threats to daily life. Fear over the onslaught of the powers led people to try various means of counteracting them, including "magical" practices such as calling on divine intermediaries for protection, ritual acts of power and ecstatic forms of worship.[7] Arnold thinks that it is against this background that we may best be able to appreciate a number of the features of the Colossian "philosophy." He reads the difficult phrase, "the worship of angels" (Col 2:18), for instance, as the veneration of angels by invoking them for protection against the hostile spirits.[8] Whether or not we accept Arnold's whole picture of the false teaching, he seems to be correct in seeing it as a thoroughly syncretistic melange, one that drew heavily from the worldview and practices of Colossae's pluralistic environment and especially emphasized the need to come to grips with the powers that ruled the cosmos.

Because of the limited and often elusive nature of Paul's references to the Colossian syncretism, our attempts to be more specific in describing its origin and character must be tentative at best. Nevertheless, we can suggest a number of features that may well have been part of the opponents' hybrid version of Christianity: (1) elements of popular folk religion, notably fear of evil powers (Col 1:16; 2:10, 15), as well as practices such as invoking angels (Col 2:18), observing taboos (Col 2:21), and rigid asceticism (Col 2:23) as means of gaining protection from unseen forces; (2) a Jewish orientation toward legal ordinances (Col 2:21), regulations about eating and drinking (Col 2:16), and ritual observance of festivals and special days, including the Sabbath (Col 2:16); (3) ecstatic visionary experiences, possibly connected with ritual initiation from the pagan mystery cults (Col 2:18);[9] (4) a devaluing of the role of Christ, who may have

---

[5]See Walter T. Wilson, *The Hope of Glory: Education and Exhortation in the Epistle to the Colossians* (Leiden: Brill, 1997), pp. 4-5.

[6]Arnold, *Colossian Syncretism*. For a more popular summary of his position, see Arnold, *Powers of Darkness: Principalities and Powers in Paul's Letters* (Downers Grove, Ill.: InterVarsity Press, 1992), pp. 138-47.

[7]Arnold, *Colossian Syncretism*, pp. 229, 234-44.

[8]Ibid., pp. 8-102, 310-11.

[9]For the argument that the notoriously difficult expression, "entering the things he has seen" (*ha heoraken embateuōn*, Col 2:18) has a background in the initiation rites of the Phrygian mystery cult, see ibid., pp. 104-57.

been seen as an intermediary spiritual being and therefore unable to offer full deliverance from the fearsome forces that threatened peoples' daily lives. In addition, Paul's frequent and rather polemical references to "wisdom," "knowledge," "understanding" and "fullness" suggest that the false teachers may have seen their "philosophy" as a means of gaining access to a fuller knowledge of God than was available in the gospel they received from Epaphras.[10] In short, this teaching represented an "*over*contextualization" of the Christian gospel in light of the local religious environment.

In particular, the Colossian syncretism assumed that trusting Christ alone was not enough to deal with the vise-grip that the cosmic powers held on people. The gospel of Christ needed to be supplemented with additional "wisdom" (Col 2:23), with rituals and ascetic practices, and with mystical experiences in order to help people survive in a world dominated by forces beyond their control. In effect, the rival teachers were trying to "cover all the bases" by paying homage to both Christ *and* the powers. The strongly syncretistic character of popular religion in the Lycus Valley no doubt made this an alluring alternative for the Colossian converts. For Paul, however, such a message poses grave danger to the life of the community. On the one hand, it inflates the control of the supernatural powers over Christians. On the other, it drastically diminishes Christ's lordship over the cosmos and the scope of the salvation he offers to the church.

PAUL'S CONTEXTUALIZED GOSPEL IN COLOSSIANS

Paul responds to the threat of this "supplemental" Christianity as a missionary-pastor who is concerned for converts still struggling to fully make the shift from their old patterns of thinking and acting. The situation in Colossae calls for a new "translation" of the gospel into language and theological categories that speak to the vital issues at hand. Not only does Paul need to counteract the syncretistic tendencies of the false teaching, but he also wants to empower the community to change elements of their basic worldviews, beliefs and behavior patterns.[11] How does he accomplish this?

Part of Paul's strategy in Colossians is to expose the rival teaching for just what he believes it is—a "human tradition" that threatens to kidnap the Colossians through its "empty deception" (Col 2:8). From Paul's perspective, the very boundaries of the Christian community are at stake. To adopt the false teaching and its associated practices means living as though one is still a part of the un-

---

[10]Furnish, "Colossians," p. 1092.
[11]See Arnold, *Colossian Syncretism*, p. 245.

believing world (Col 2:20).[12] Paul's direct assault on the "philosophy" is mainly confined to Colossians 2:8-23. In this section, he apparently takes up a series of catchwords from the lips of his opponents, which he then turns against them like verbal boomerangs.[13] These references serve as warnings to the Colossians against getting caught up in specific practices that are incompatible with the Christ-centered message they have received (Col 2:6-7).

Paul's primary response, however, is not to refute the features of the philosophy point by point. Instead, he challenges its misunderstandings by focusing positively on the meaning of the gospel. The paramount danger of the false teaching for the Colossians is that it "downsizes" the lordship of Jesus Christ. It is on this bedrock concern that his exposition of the gospel concentrates. The Colossian syncretism offers Paul the occasion to reflect theologically on the supremacy of Christ and the sufficiency of his salvation in a way that becomes a word on target for the church. In this reframing of the Christian message, several closely related themes emerge, pertaining to the gospel, the all-encompassing role of Christ, the character of the Colossians' salvation, and the Christian lifestyle.

THE TRUTH OF THE GOSPEL

At the letter's outset, Paul reminds the Colossians that their hope is in "the word of the truth, the gospel" (Col 1:5). This phrase almost certainly implies a contrast with the rival teaching that, if left unchecked, would undermine the authentic gospel of Christ. In the same spirit, Paul urges the new converts to "continue securely established and steadfast in the faith," not shifting from the hope of the gospel they had heard (Col 1:23). Yet, "the gospel" in Colossians is more than simply a truth to be believed. Unlike the restrictive human traditions of the "philosophy," it is a dynamic agent of God's transforming grace with a universal scope (Col 1:5-6, 23).

Paul enlists a variety of terms to describe the gospel in Colossians, including "the word" (Col 4:3), "the word of God" (Col 1:25) and "of Christ" (Col 3:16), "the faith" (Col 1:23; 2:7), and "the truth" (Col 1:5), all of which recall for his readers the content of the genuine message they have received. Of special note

---

[12]Margaret Y. MacDonald, *Colossians and Ephesians* (Collegeville, Minn.: Glazier/Liturgical Press, 2000), pp. 12, 106.

[13]E.g., "philosophy" (Col 2:8); "the elemental spirits of the universe" (Col 2:8, 20); "insisting on self-abasement," "the worship of angels," "dwelling on visions" (Col 2:18); "Do not handle, Do not taste, Do not touch" (Col 2:21); "self-imposed piety," "humility," and "severe treatment of the body" (Col 2:23). See O'Brien, *Colossians, Philemon*, p. xxxii. Any identification of the language of the false teachers, however, must remain tentative, since it is not always clear if Paul is quoting or simply describing his perceptions of the error.

is Paul's identification of the gospel as the "mystery of Christ" (Col 4:3; cf. 2:2)—
a mystery that was formerly hidden but now has been revealed to the saints (Col
1:26). Paul's understanding of "mystery" *(mystērion)* is rooted in the Old Testament and apocalyptic Judaism, not in the Greek mystery religions of the day.
Nonetheless, Arnold plausibly suggests that some of the Colossian Gentile believers likely had a background in the mysteries that were related to local deities. Perhaps, he argues, the rival philosophy itself included elements of mystery
belief and practice and made use of the term *mystery*.[14] Arnold concludes that,
"given the nature of the situation at Colossae and the background of the Gentile
readers, it is surprising that Paul does not avoid using the term altogether."[15] Yet
Paul is willing to risk seizing a word that carries the baggage of local religious
overtones. We might find a contemporary analogy in Indian Christians' adoption
of the Sanscrit term *sac-cit-ananda,* taken from the Hindu scriptures, in order
to speak of the triune God of the Bible. Likewise, Paul redefines *mystery* to refer
not only to God's eschatological plan of salvation, but even to Christ himself.
The content of God's mystery that has been made known among the Gentiles
is "Christ in you, the hope of glory" (Col 1:27). As John Barclay observes, "it
seems to be no accident that Colossians portrays Christ as 'mystery,' since this
term represented the supreme commodity offered both by Jewish apocalyptic
theology and by Graeco-Roman mystery cults."[16] The Colossians need look for
no other "mystery," because according to God's eternal purpose they have received *the* mystery: Christ, who now indwells their lives and embodies their
hope for the future. What is more, they should abandon the search for any
higher form of spiritual truth, since "all the treasures of wisdom and knowledge"
are hidden in Christ, the mystery of God (Col 2:2-3).

THE SUPREMACY OF CHRIST

The most gaping flaw of the Colossian "philosophy" from Paul's vantage point
was that it subverted the supremacy of Christ. That is not to say it necessarily
denied Christ and his saving work. But it apparently reduced his role in regard
to creation and questioned his ability to fully protect believers from the influence of the unseen powers. Christ, in this shrunken state, becomes a part of the
cosmos, not lord over it. Consequently, Paul's theologizing in Colossians exalts
Jesus Christ as unrivaled Lord of everything; it proclaims him as the sole and
sufficient mediator of salvation between God and his people.

---

[14] Arnold, *Colossian Syncretism,* p. 272.
[15] Ibid.
[16] Barclay, *Colossians and Philemon,* p. 79.

Paul affirms the supremacy of Christ most clearly in the magnificent christological hymn of Colossians 1:15-20. The passage is not polemical as such; however, it speaks forcefully to the concerns of the context and lays a foundation for Paul's christological response to the Colossian syncretism in Colossians 2:8-23. Drawing on themes from the Old Testament and the Wisdom tradition of Hellenistic Judaism, the hymn praises Jesus Christ as sovereign Lord of both creation (Col 1:15-18a) and redemption (Col 1:18b-20). Paul uses the powerful language of worship and praise to give the Colossians an alternative vision of the world from that of the Christ-constricting philosophy.

The hymn extols Christ's cosmic dominion in a variety of ways. He is the preexistent "image of the invisible God" as well as the "firstborn of all creation" (Col 1:15), a phrase that asserts both his priority to and his sovereignty over the whole universe. In fact, he himself is the Creator of all things (Col 1:16a)—he is mediator ("through him"), goal ("for him," Col 1:16b) and sustainer of the whole created order (Col 1:17b). He has no rivals. The hymn gives special emphasis to Christ's preeminence over the cosmic powers, whether good or evil.[17] His lordship over "all things" includes things in heaven and things invisible—listed as "thrones," "dominions," "rulers" and "powers" (Col 1:16: cf. 2:10). Peter T. O'Brien is quite right that within the context of the letter "no doubt it is the hostile rather than the friendly powers Paul has particularly in view."[18] Given the fear and regard Paul's readers apparently held for the cosmic forces and the concern of the rival teaching to appease them, the hymn's creation emphasis is entirely appropriate. Paul deflates the power of the powers by insisting they are a

---

[17]There has been considerable debate over the meaning of the "powers" in Paul's thought. The trend in New Testament scholarship in the West has been to depersonalize the "powers," most often identifying them with the structures of human existence—social, political, intellectual, and so forth. Particularly influential is the work of Walter Wink, who tries to combine a structural interpretation of the principalities and powers with a recognition of an invisible "spiritual" dimension to all earthly institutions and systems (*Naming the Powers: The Language of Power in the New Testament* [Philadelphia: Fortress, 1984], p. 5). Cf. the recent attempt by Brian J. Walsh and Sylvia C. Keesmaat to identify the "powers" in Colossians with Caesar and the power structures of the Roman Empire (*Colossians Remixed: Subverting the Empire* [Downers Grove, Ill.: InterVarsity Press, 2004], pp. 91-93). Although Paul no doubt understood the influence of the powers to extend beyond individuals and the church to human social and political structures that oppose God and his purposes (cf. 1 Cor 2:8), both the historical context and exegesis of the text of Colossians support the primary identification of the powers with personal spiritual beings. See further, Peter T. O'Brien, "Principalities and Powers: Opponents of the Church," in *Biblical Interpretation and the Church: The Problem of Contextualization*, ed. D. A. Carson (Nashville: Thomas Nelson, 1984), pp. 110-50; Clinton E. Arnold, *Ephesians: Power and Magic. The Concept of Power in Ephesians in Light of Its Historical Setting* (Grand Rapids, Mich.: Baker, 1989), pp. 44-51, 129-34.

[18]O'Brien, *Colossians, Philemon*, p. 46.

part of the order that was created and is now sustained through Christ and are thereby subject to his sovereign rule. The Colossians need a redefined cosmology and a transformed worldview.

The hymn goes on to stress that Christ is supreme not only over creation, but also the *new* creation; he is the head of his body, the church (Col 1:18a). In 1 Corinthians 12:12-27 and Romans 12:4-5 the body metaphor primarily addresses the interrelationship between the members of the community as the body of Christ. In Colossians, however, the accent is on the relationship of Christ, the head of the body, to his church. This shift in focus to Christ's lordship over the universal church not only demonstrates the flexibility of the body image, but it is well-fitted to a context where the sufficiency of Christ is in question. When Christians are part of the body of which Christ is head, there is no need to fear or to try to manipulate any other spiritual beings.[19]

Furthermore, Christ is the one through whom God has reconciled all things, earthly or heavenly, to himself (Col 1:20). Christ's reconciling work is universal in its scope and encircles not only the church but even the heavenly powers that oppose it. In the latter case, however, reconciliation takes the form of "pacifying" (Col 1:20c) or subjecting all the malignant forces under the rule of Christ.[20] This cosmic reconciliation has already been set into motion (cf. Col 2:15). But in the wider horizon of Paul's thought, it anticipates a final restoration of harmony when everything "in heaven and on earth and under the earth" will unite to proclaim that Jesus Christ is sovereign Lord (Phil 2:10). God's reconciling work in Christ is thus enacted on a broader cosmic stage in Colossians than in either Romans 5:10-11 or 2 Corinthians 5:18-20, where the focus is on the reconciliation of the Christian community. In the present context, the hymn's all-embracing vision of Christ's victory resounds as a word of assurance to people for whom the supernatural powers loomed as constant threats to a tranquil and secure existence. The subjugated powers "cannot finally harm the person who is in Christ, and their ultimate overthrow in the future is assured."[21]

Vitally, the hymn anchors this cosmic Christology and redemption in the center of the gospel, Christ crucified and risen from the dead. He is preeminent over all things because he is the "firstborn from the dead" (Col 1:18b), and his uni-

---

[19]P. J. Achtemeier, J. B. Green and M. M. Thompson, *Introducing the New Testament: Its Literature and Theology* (Grand Rapids, Mich.: Eerdmans, 2001), p. 410.

[20]See Dunn, *Colossians*, pp. 102-3; F. F. Bruce, *The Epistles to the Colossians, to Philemon, and to the Ephesians* (Grand Rapids, Mich.: Eerdmans, 1984), pp. 75-76. This means that Colossians 1:20 does not support a universalism in which Christ will redeem all persons and cosmic hostile powers in the end.

[21]O'Brien, *Colossians, Philemon*, p. 56.

versal reconciliation is put into effect through "the blood of his cross" (Col 1:20). Colossians 1:15-20 sings the story of Christ as preexistent Creator, as the crucified and risen Redeemer, and as the exalted Lord, through whom God will reconcile the cosmos. This grand story of salvation provides a narrative substructure for Paul's entire argument in Colossians. Paul's readers are called to embrace the gospel story as a controlling narrative, one that subverts all other competing stories.[22]

The story of the unparalled Christ in the hymn is given concrete application to the needs of the congregation in chapter 2. Picking up language from 1:19, Paul declares that in Christ "all the *fullness* of deity dwells bodily" (Col 2:9). Paul's use of the key term "fullness" *(plērōma)* raises an intriguing question. Has he co-opted it from the rival philosophy and infused it with new christological content? Or has Paul himself drawn this language from the Old Testament to positively assert that the completeness of God's nature and power has taken up residence in Christ? The answer is not entirely clear. In either case, however, Paul counters a teaching that devalues the role and power of Christ by assuring his readers that Jesus is the full embodiment of all that God is and does. The Colossians have no cause to pay homage to any lesser supernatural beings or angel-intermediaries.[23] He is not just one among the many competing gods or powers. Christ reigns supreme over *every* ruler and authority (Col 2:10).

The theological argument of Colossians 2:8-15 reaches a fitting climax in verse 15 with a profound contextualization of the death of Christ. Three metaphors drafted from the Greco-Roman world paint in bold colors God's victory in Christ over the dominions of darkness. In the cross of Christ, God "disarmed" the rulers and authorities, stripping them of their power; he "publicly exposed" them as being shamefully weak and worthless; and he led them in triumphal procession, as a victorious Roman general parades his vanquished enemies in his train for all to behold. The Colossians could hardly have missed the audacity of such images. According to normal standards of judgment in the Roman world, it was Jesus—not the evil powers—who was subjugated, stripped and publicly humiliated when he was nailed to a cross. Instead of triumphing over his enemies, it looked for all the world as if he were the helpless victim of the fury and violence of the powers. But Colossians flips every human expectation on its head. As N. T. Wright puts it, "The cross was not the defeat of *Christ* at the hands

---

[22]Wilson, *Hope of Glory*, pp. 191, 261.
[23]N. T. Wright, *The Epistles of Paul to the Colossians and to Philemon: An Introduction and Commentary* (Grand Rapids, Mich.: Eerdmans, 1986), p. 103.

of the *powers*: it was the defeat of the powers at the hands—yes, the bleeding hands—of Christ."[24]

Due to the needs of the situation, the "powers" that Christ has defeated in Colossians are not explicitly those of sin, death and the law, as we find elsewhere in Paul's writings (e.g., 1 Cor 15:54-57; cf. Rom 6—8). Here it is the forces that ruled the cosmos that are overpowered by the cross. The Colossians no longer need be tempted to placate the powers or to live in fear of forces that have already been broken. F. F. Bruce summarizes well the hope that Paul's targeted message would have brought to the Colossian believers:

> Christ crucified and risen is Lord of all: all the forces of the universe are subject to him, not only the benign ones but the hostile ones as well. They are all subject to the one through whom they were created; the hostile forces are also subject to the one by whom they were conquered. Therefore, to be united to him is to be liberated from their thraldom, to enjoy perfect freedom, to overcome the powers of evil through participation in his victory.[25]

Only a cosmic Christology could answer the new concerns raised by the Colossian syncretism.

THE PRESENT SUFFICIENCY OF SALVATION

The Colossian "philosophy's" inadequate view of the role of Christ meant that it also lacked a proper understanding of the salvation that was available in him. Unlike the situation Paul addressed in 1 Corinthians, where he encountered Christians who claimed too much for their present salvation, defenders of the new teaching in Colossae claimed too little. In their thinking, redemption in Christ needed to be augmented with other means—ascetic and ritual practices, angel worship, legal regulations, visionary experiences—in order to be truly effective. Paul's response is that Christ is not only supreme; he is also wholly *sufficient* for the Colossians' present experience of salvation. No supplements are required.

As a result, in Colossians Paul spotlights the completeness of the reconciliation believers have received from Christ. As in Romans, Colossians affirms that Christians participate in the story of Christ's death and resurrection, but with a striking difference. Whereas Romans 6:4-8 and 8:11 state that Christians have died with Christ but still await their resurrection with him in the future (but see

---

[24]N. T. Wright, *Following Jesus: Biblical Reflections on Discipleship* (Grand Rapids, Mich.: Eerdmans, 1994), p. 19; cf. Andrew T. Lincoln, "The Letter to the Colossians," in *The New Interpreter's Bible*, ed. L. E. Keck (Nashville: Abingdon, 2000), 11:628.
[25]Bruce, *Epistles to the Colossians*, pp. 112-13.

Rom 6:4b), Colossians declares that they have not only died (Col 3:3) and been buried with him in baptism (Col 2:12), but they have *already* been raised with him to a new heavenly life (Col 2:12-13; 3:1). Paul, it seems, has shifted the weight of the tension between salvation already realized and salvation not yet obtained to the side of the "now" of God's empowering and transforming grace. This is a daring move and no doubt capable of being misunderstood. Nevertheless, it is precisely what the Colossians needed to hear. By participating with Christ in his resurrection they share in the fullness of resurrection life, in particular his deliverance from the tyranny of the unseen powers.

In Colossians 3:1-4, Paul says that Christians who have been raised with Christ can already participate in the heavenly dimension where Christ is exalted at the right hand of God. Here the introduction of spatial categories ("things above," Col 3:1-2) rather than temporal ones ("things to come") risks being misconstrued as a sellout to a Greek dualism in which Christians must escape their earthly bodily existence for a heavenly, spiritual one. Once again, however, this familiar language speaks directly to the concerns of the Colossians. Andrew T. Lincoln rightly insists that because the heavenly realm is the place where Christ is seated in a position of authority beside the Father, "nothing can prevent access to this realm and God's presence and there can be no basic insecurity about the salvation they have in him."[26] Their lives are now "hidden with Christ in God" (Col 3:3) in a place of security and safety, protected from any menacing forces.

The theme of the present appropriation of salvation in Christ runs throughout the letter like a golden thread, particularly in the heart of Paul's polemic against the syncretistic error in 2:8-15. The section is peppered with Paul's characteristic "in Christ" and "with Christ" language, highlighting the church's ongoing participation in Christ and the fruits of his salvation. This *participatory* Christology is no less significant than Paul's *cosmic* Christology in Colossians.[27] In 2:9-10 he applies the remarkable affirmation that all of the divine "fullness" dwells bodily in Christ to the situation of the church: "and you have come to fullness in him." As a result, "The fullness of God—his power and grace—are bestowed on believers by virtue of their incorporation into Christ."[28] This is Paul's counterpunch to the opponents' apparent suggestions that fullness of salvation could not be secured by Christ or Christ alone. Lincoln says it well: "Because of their link with

---

[26]Andrew T. Lincoln, *Paradise Now and Not Yet: Studies in the Role of the Heavenly Dimension in Paul's Thought with Special Reference to His Eschatology* (Cambridge: Cambridge University Press, 1981), p. 125.

[27]Robert W. Wall, *Colossians and Philemon* (Downers Grove, Ill.: InterVarsity Press, 1993), p. 26.

[28]Arnold, *Colossian Syncretism*, p. 295.

the fullness of deity through Christ, by definition there can be nothing lacking about their relation with God, no deficiency that needs to be filled by further teachings and practices offered by the philosophy."[29] An immediate corollary of the believers' partaking in Christ's fullness is that they also share in his "headship," particularly his ongoing authority over the cosmic powers (Col 2:10b; cf. 1:18; 2:19). Christ is altogether sufficient to deliver God's people from whatever threatens their lives.

In Colossians 2:11-15, Paul marshals a medley of images to interpret Christ's atoning death and resurrection and their present meaning for those who are in him, some of which we have already noted. He describes the Colossians' salvation in 2:11 as a "spiritual circumcision" (literally, "a circumcision not made with hands"). Although the language of verse 11 is difficult to decipher, it is best to see it as a reference to the inward heart circumcision (cf. Deut 10:16; 30:6; Jer 4:4; Ezek 44:7) effected by Christ ("the circumcision of Christ") in his dying and rising and actualized in the believer's union with him.[30] It is possible that the syncretists promoted circumcision among the Colossian Gentiles as a rite of entry into the group, but Paul's failure to directly condemn the practice as he does in Galatians makes this less than certain. Even if circumcision was not touted in Colossae, the Jewish input into the false teaching, along with Paul's desire to explain metaphorically the fullness of the salvation the Colossians have received, would have made this appropriate language. Being incorporated into Christ brings about a radical inward purification. This involves the stripping off of the old sinful self, in contrast to the outward physical circumcision of Judaism.

Another colorful metaphor from the financial world of the day expresses the meaning of Christ's death in Colossians 2:14. The "certificate of indebtedness"— a kind of commercial bond or IOU—that was incurred by their transgressions has been publicly displayed as canceled through God's "nailing it to the cross." The appearance of the term "legal demands" in the same verse suggests that Paul may have specifically been thinking of the kind of ascetic and ritual requirements that the opponents were trying to impose upon the Colossian Christians (Col 2:16, 20).[31] The cross of Christ has truly liberated them from the condemnation associated with such external and legalistic obligations.

Paul's portrayal of the present reality and scope of redemption in Christ also addresses the Colossians' concerns about the hostile powers. At the conclusion of his

---

[29]Lincoln, "Letter to the Colossians," p. 623.
[30]Bruce, *Epistles to the Colossians*, p. 104.
[31]So Petr Pokorný, *Colossians: A Commentary*, trans. S. S. Schatzmann (Peabody, Mass.: Hendrickson, 1991), pp. 138-39.

opening prayer for the Colossian church (Col 1:12-14), Paul assures them that they have not only been rescued from the dominion of darkness, but they have also been transferred into the kingdom of God's Son (Col 1:13). Here Paul draws upon Exodus language from the Old Testament ("rescue," Col 1:13; "redemption," 1:14) to describe their present deliverance from bondage to the evil domain over which the powers rule (cf. Eph 6:12). A robust strain of already realized salvation runs through 1:12-14, as well. Believers in Christ even now share in the end-time inheritance of the saints (Col 1:12). They have already been uprooted from the old realm and transported into the new kingdom (Col 1:13). Whereas elsewhere in the Pauline letters believers' full participation in the kingdom of God usually has a decidedly future cast (1 Cor 6:9-10; 15:50; Gal 5:21; 1 Thess 2:12; 2 Thess 1:5; 2 Tim 4:1), here the emphasis is on their present share in the blessings and resources of the still-coming kingdom. What this means practically for the Colossians, Bruce explains, is that "no longer was there any need for them to live in fear of those forces which were believed to control the destinies of men and women: their transference to the realm of light had been accomplished once for all."[32] Later in a polemical context, Paul reminds the Colossians that they have died to the "elemental spirits of the universe" *(stoicheia tou kosmou)*. In light of the Colossian philosophy, this term probably refers to the astral and cosmic powers that were thought to hold a sinister influence over the daily lives of human beings.[33]

This deliverance does not exhaust the present benefits of God's transforming grace. Believers have appropriated the reconciling work of Christ on the cross lauded in the Christ hymn (Col 1:20-22). Christ's death has brought them forgiveness of sins (Col 1:14; 2:13; 3:13), an aspect of salvation that receives special attention in the letter.[34] They have already stripped off the old self and put on the new self that is now being transformed into the Creator's image (Col 3:9-10). Their lives are currently indwelt by the presence of Christ (Col 1:27). This accent on the indwelling of Christ rather than the indwelling Spirit (as e.g., Rom 8:9-11) fits the context of the letter. Paul apparently felt that stressing the present ministry of Christ offered a stronger defense against the particular Colossian menace than talking about the work of the Spirit.[35] Furthermore, the community

---

[32]Bruce, *Epistles to the Colossians*, pp. 51-52.

[33]See Eduard Lohse, *Colossians and Philemon*, trans. W. R. Poehlmann and R. J. Karris (Philadelphia: Fortress, 1971), pp. 96-99; Arnold, *Colossian Syncretism*, pp. 158-94.

[34]David M. Hay may be correct that Paul's emphasis on the forgiveness of sins in Colossians "suggests that the Colossian philosophy induced great fear that Jesus had not brought full forgiveness" (*Colossians* [Nashville: Abingdon, 2000], p. 98).

[35]Bruce, *Epistles to the Colossians*, p. 28. There is only one explicit reference to the Holy Spirit in the letter (Col 1:8).

is strengthened with the enabling and overcoming power of God (Col 1:11; 2:10; cf. 1:29). Paul's prayer for the Colossians in 1:11 conspicuously piles up the language of "power." The Colossians need divine strengthening not only for fruitful Christian living and service (Col 1:10), but also for endurance in the face of all opposition (Col 1:11b). That resistance includes "the pressure of evil forces in the Lycus valley that would lead them astray as well as make them dispirited."[36]

Given this pervasive emphasis on the *now* of salvation in Christ, we might be tempted to think that Paul's contextualizing of the gospel in Colossians has spun out of control, that the Pauline tension between the "already" and the "not yet" has collapsed and the future has been swallowed up by the present. But this is not the case. For all of its emphasis on the Christian's present experience of resurrection life, Colossians retains a clear vision of the future hope. When Christ returns, Christians "*will be* revealed with him in glory" (Col 3:4; cf. 1:5, 22, 27, 28; 3:6, 24). Christ's victory over the powers is decisive (Col 2:15), but its consummation is yet to come.

THE TRANSFORMED LIFE

The context-sensitive translation of the gospel in Colossians would be incomplete without Paul's unfolding its meaning for Christian discipleship and the formation of the community. Beginning with chapter three, he shifts his main focus to the practical holiness that is demanded by the gospel. The ethical teaching in Colossians reveals a profound interaction between the constant gospel and the contingent situation being addressed.

In the first place, Paul grounds the call to live in a way that is worthy of the Lord (Col 1:10) in the reality of God's gracious and saving action in Christ. As they "received Christ Jesus the Lord," they are now to "walk" in him (Col 2:6). Since they have been reconciled to Christ, they must continue on in holy living or else risk falling back into their old evil way of life (Col 1:21-23). In Colossians, as elsewhere in Paul's letters, theology and ethics are interwoven. Nowhere is this more apparent than in Colossians 3:1-4, which provides a christological foundation for Paul's instruction in chapter 3 on living as a transformed community. Paul calls the Colossians to a new moral vision, one that is determined by their solidarity with the triumphant, exalted Lord and their experience of dying and being raised with him (Col 3:1, 3). Consequently, they are to seek the "things that are above" and exchange what is earthly for what is heavenly (Col 3:1-2, 5). This vision entails a complete reorientation of their existence, a radically different way of imagining the world. They must live no longer by the norms and values

---

[36]O'Brien, *Colossians, Philemon*, p. 24.

of the world, but by those of God's future heavenly kingdom (cf. Col 2:20). The story of Christ, his death, resurrection, exaltation and return (Col 3:4), thus becomes foundational not only for their redemption, but also for living a holy life.

Paul adapts the concrete instructions for Christian living that follow to his cultural setting, incorporating a number of standard conventions found in the Hellenistic moral teaching of the day.[37] These include traditional motifs ("put off/put on"), lists of vices and virtues, and the so-called household codes. Yet he recasts each of them christologically, thereby giving them a distinctively Christian basis and motivation. The list of vices to avoid (Col 3:5-9) concludes with the theme of inward moral transformation into God's image and the confession that "Christ is all in all" (Col 3:9-11). The ensuing code of virtues (Col 3:12-17) calls believers to forgive one another on the basis of their experience of Christ's forgiving grace (Col 3:13); it then grounds community conduct in the ruling peace and the indwelling word of Christ (Col 3:15-16). The virtue list reaches a pinnacle in verse 17, where the church is urged to do "all things" under the lordship of Christ. And as we saw in chapter four, the household code's (Col 3:18—4:2) sevenfold appeal to "the Lord" transforms the relationships described, reimagining them in terms of service to the divine Master. A household that is "in the Lord" will be a visible alternative to the dominant cultural model. The claim that "Christ is all in all" means that every household role, every social condition, every cultural situation, becomes an expression of allegiance to Christ.

At the same time, Paul's moral teaching, like his theological exposition of the gospel, speaks to the concrete issues facing the community. Paul's polemic in Colossians 2:16-23 is directed in part against a bogus form of holiness that embraced human regulations and taboos, "self-imposed piety," "severe treatment of the body" (Col 2:23), and possibly visionary experiences such as those found in the rites of the mystery religions (Col 2:18). Paul considers such practices to be of the world (Col 2:20) and the flesh (Col 2:18) and completely useless in restraining sinfulness (Col 2:23). They are a part of the "earthly things" that Christians must put to death (Col 3:2, 5). At stake in Colossae is not only a false theology, but also a wrongheaded perception of what constitutes holy living. Robert Wall is right to insist that Colossians 3:1—4:6 is "an integral part of Paul's polemic, setting forth the moral flip side of his theological argument against the 'hollow and deceptive philosophy.' "[38] The household codes, for example, seem to challenge the asceticism and visionary experiences of the false teaching by

---

[37]For the appropriation in Colossians of forms and strategies that are characteristic of popular Hellenistic moral exhortation, see Wilson, Hope of Glory.

[38]Wall, Colossians and Philemon, p. 129.

engaging the everyday institutions and kinship relations of Greco-Roman society in a transforming way. Although Paul's ethical exhortations in Colossians are not limited to a specific response to the heresy, they offer a radical alternative to the kind of external religious piety promoted by the opponents' philosophy. N. T. Wright makes the point with characteristic verve:

> The old taboos put the wild animals of lust and hatred (see 3:5, 8) into cages: there they remain, alive and dangerous, a constant threat to their captor. Paul's solution is more drastic: the animals are to be killed (3:5). The old method of holiness attacked symptoms: the true method goes for the root.[39]

The goal of Christ's redeeming work in Colossians is no less than genuine perfection *(teleios)* in Christ (Col 1:28; cf. 1:22): a radical renewal into the image of the Creator (Col 3:10).

For Paul, the praxis of the errant teachers is simply an extension of their bad Christology. It represents bowing to the cosmic powers (Col 2:20) and demoting Christ from his lordly rank (Col 2:17, 19). The Colossians do not need the "shadow" of ritual observances demanded by the philosophy; they already have the "real thing" that belongs to the one and only Lord (Col 2:16-17).[40] This is by no means an outright condemnation of religious ritual, or even regulations about special days and diet within Judaism as such. Rather, such practices, apparently motivated out of deference to the elemental spirits (Col 2:20), become transitory and irrelevant in light of the coming of God's salvation in Christ. Given this connection between belief and behavior, it is surely no coincidence that Paul begins his moral exhortations with an echo of Psalm 110:1, which calls believers to share the heavenly life of the Lord who has defeated all his adversaries, including the powers (Col 3:1; cf. 2:10, 15). Later, the notion of the renewed creation where Christ is "all and in all" (Col 3:10-11) recalls the cosmic Christology of the hymn in chapter one. Christ's reconciliation of "all things" (Col 1:20) includes the tearing down of national, cultural and social barriers within the one new humanity that is being recreated in the image of its Lord (Col 3:11). Eduard Lohse is surely right that the entire ethical section of Colossians "is stamped with the leitmotif that runs throughout the letter from beginning to end: Christ is Lord over everything—over powers and principalities, but also over the Christian's daily life" (see Col 3:15, 17; 3:18—4:1; 2:6).[41] In Colossians, exalted Christology and Christ-centered living walk hand in hand.

---

[39]Wright, *Colossians*, p. 128.
[40]The contrast between "shadow" *(skia)* and "substance" *(sōma)* reflects familiar language that Paul apparently draws from Plato and Hellenistic Judaism. See e.g., Philo *De migratione Abrahami* 12, *De confusione linguarum* 190.
[41]Lohse, *Colossians*, p. 178.

CONCLUSION

Paul's letter to the Colossians bears importance well beyond its size for our understanding of contextualization in the New Testament. It gives us a glimpse of how the gospel comes to grips with the challenge of a new situation, one that is colored by a syncretistic onslaught that threatens to undermine the life of a young Asian church. Above all, the alluring mixture that was brewing in Colossae tried to supplement the converts' faith and offer them substitutes for an exclusive allegiance to Jesus Christ. Paul tailors his new translation of the gospel to address this countermessage with both fidelity and imagination. On the one hand, the truth of the gospel sanctions no compromise with syncretism or a religiously plural environment. Although Paul is more than willing to become "all things to all people" in matters that are nonessential, he draws a "line in the sand" before anything that challenges the unique supremacy of Jesus Christ, his sole sufficiency to mediate salvation, or his lordship over Christian conduct. If Jesus is Lord, he can have no rivals.

On the other hand, Paul's expression of the Christian message in Colossians shows a remarkable sensitivity to the context. Writing out of a missionary-pastor's heart, he seeks not only to turn the Colossians away from the errant teaching, but also to reshape some of their fundamental worldview assumptions in light of the gospel. This leads him to elaborate more profoundly on the cosmic dimensions of Christ's lordship and redemption than we find in his earlier letters. Furthermore, the need to assure believers of the present sufficiency of their salvation from sin and the forces of evil calls forth a daring vision of the Christian's co-resurrection with Christ as something already available.

Paul's approach to the Colossians is one of sensitive engagement, not heavy-handed intrusion. Characteristically, he persuades, but he does not coerce. He encounters the rival teaching on its own turf, both by citing catchwords from his opponents (see Col 2:16-23) and by apparently taking over familiar language from the syncretistic religious culture of the day (e.g., "wisdom," "mystery," "power," "fullness") and imbuing it with new Christ-centered meaning.[42] He adopts familiar ethical conventions like the "household code" only to recast existing social relationships in light of the lordship of Christ. And while Paul characteristically grounds both theology and ethics in the death and resurrection of

---

[42]Strikingly absent from Colossians is any sustained argument based on the Jewish Scriptures or, for that matter, any explicit citation from the Old Testament at all. Perhaps in a letter written to ex-pagans which repeatedly stresses the universal implications of the gospel (e.g., Col 1:5-6, 15-20, 23, 28; 3:11) in response to a particular form of errant teaching, Paul feels less need to make direct appeal to the Scriptures of Israel or to spotlight the Jewish background of his readers' faith. See Hay, *Colossians*, p. 33.

Jesus, the particular images he adopts from his world (see especially Col 2:11-15) enable the Christ event to speak a fresh word that resonates with his readers.

Perhaps not surprisingly, the distinctive thrust of the language and theology in Colossians is often taken as an example of *post*-Pauline innovation, rather than of Paul's contextualization.[43] J. C. Beker, for one, thinks that the "realized eschatology" of Colossians and its consistent christological focus do not ring true to the apostle's thought. For Beker, they collapse Paul's future-oriented, "theocentric" theology into a vertical conception of the church being raised with Christ into heaven that is inconsistent with the genuine Paul.[44] Though this is not the place for a full discussion of the question of who wrote Colossians, our study suggests that apparent theological differences between Colossians and the undisputed Pauline letters may be better explained in terms of a versatile author attempting to reframe the gospel in context-appropriate ways.[45] Both the cosmic Christology and the presently realized eschatology of Colossians stand in continuity, not in conflict, with Paul's earlier teaching (cf. 1 Cor 8:6; Phil 2:9-11; 3:21; Rom 6:4; 2 Cor 4:4, 16). It seems that the Colossian syncretism functioned as a catalyst for Paul's reflection on the deeper implications of Christ's universal lordship and its saving meaning for believers. At the same time, innovations such as the church's sharing in Christ's resurrection are not merely ad hoc rhetorical strategies drummed up to give the false teachers a black eye. Rather, they give expression to elements of Paul's theological convictions that are coherent with what he says elsewhere. Colossians, viewed in this light, gives us another striking example of Paul's ability to hold firmly to his Christ-centered gospel even while creatively doing theology for a new mission context.

Finally, Colossians offers us an instructive pattern for the church's encounter with syncretism today. It is hard to miss the similarities between the context Paul addressed in Colossae and that of many non-Western worldviews and cultures, where established religions, popular folk beliefs and Christianity routinely share

---

[43]See the arguments, e.g., of Lohse, *Colossians*, pp. 177-83; Furnish, "Colossians," pp. 1092-94.

[44]See, e.g., J. C. Beker, *Paul the Apostle: The Triumph of God in Life and Thought* (Philadelphia: Fortress, 1980), pp. 163, 214, 278.

[45]The issue of the authorship of Colossians is by no means settled. While the majority opinion among scholars favors a deutero-Pauline origin, a significant cadre of interpreters continue to support the Pauline authorship of the letter. See, e.g., the arguments of P. T. O'Brien, *Colossians*, pp. xli-xlix; N. T. Wright, *Colossians*, pp. 31-34; Luke Timothy Johnson, *The Writings of the New Testament: An Introduction*, rev. ed. (Minneapolis: Fortress, 1999), pp. 393-95. The issues are complex and involve not only vocabulary and theology, but also style of writing, historical concerns and Colossians' literary relationship to Philemon and Ephesians. Although I find no compelling reason to overturn the authenticity of the letter, ultimately, the issue cannot be proven one way or the other, and our observations about contextual theology in Colossians hold in either case.

the same quarters. The message of this ancient correspondence speaks with un-common force to contemporary cultures where animism inspires fear or venera-tion of the destructive powers, or where idolatry pits rivals against the lordship of Christ. But it is not only in Asia or Africa that we find analogous contexts to that of Colossians today. Paul's firm but flexible approach to syncretism has growing relevance for the West, as well. The societies of North America, Europe and Australia live in a world that is increasingly postmodern (characterized by a relativizing of values and a splintering of truth), "post-Christian" (where the Christian story no longer has a privileged role in shaping the life or values of the culture), and religiously plural. In this climate, the celebrity who wears a cross around her neck, keeps a Buddhist statue on her bedroom nightstand, consults a spiritist medium for life decisions, and engages in sexual relations with a variety of people, possibly of different genders, is not an altogether far-fetched image. Even in the church, there is a momentum toward a willingness to adopt a "mix and match" theology. According to one survey in the United States, one in ten "born-again Christians"—people who claimed a personal commitment to Jesus Christ as their savior—believed in reincarnation after death.[46] Syncretism also masquerades in more subtle forms, like the "gospel" of materialism and consum-erism that is all too prevalent in the churches of the North and West.

In practice, the lines between syncretism and cultural relevance are not al-ways easy to draw. Yet, we must seek the Spirit's "eye surgery" so that we can learn to recognize when the gospel cannot be bent without breaking. Through-out the worldwide community of faith, the unflinching christocentrism of Colos-sians needs to be voiced again and again. Paul's penetrating polemic against syncretistic error stands cross-grained to a contemporary spirit of flabby reli-gious tolerance. The unique and universal lordship of Jesus Christ must remain the anchor of any theology that calls itself "Christian."

At the same time, Paul's context-sensitive and noncoercive way of doing the-ology in Colossians offers a paradigm for the church's theological task in every generation and culture. Remarkably, Paul does not respond to the threat of syn-cretism by imposing upon the Colossians a pre-packaged, "one-size-fits-all" the-ology, as sometimes happens in mission settings today. Instead, he allows the gospel to speak directly to their fears and felt needs, and to address their par-ticular worldviews and behaviors. We might find a contemporary parallel in the gospel's encounter with worldviews that are burdened with a fear of unseen powers thought to exercise control over practical concerns like crops, flocks,

---

[46]"Americans Describe Their Views About Life After Death," *The Barna Update,* n.p. (October 21, 2003).

health and family relations. Too often the form of Christian theology that has been imported to these settings from the West has failed to address such issues, giving people the impression that God is powerless to overcome the fears and forces that touch their daily lives. Unless we proclaim Christ as the One who has defeated the powers and is able to free people from fear, they, like the Colossian syncretists, may turn to other answers—amulets, rituals, shamans, occult practices—for protection against the enslaving spirits. A gospel that neglects such worldview issues and their practical outworkings will not only fail to be truly liberating; it may end up actually promoting syncretism rather than preventing it.[47] Hwa Yung makes a convincing case that a contextualized theology for Asia (and elsewhere in much of the non-Western world) must take seriously the demonic and spirit world or it will be evangelistically powerless and pastorally irrelevant.[48]

Still, the contextualizing of the gospel in Colossians does not dwell on the threats to Christ's lordship. Although Paul warns his readers of the dangers of the syncretistic error, he concentrates his energies on lifting up Christ, the all-encompassing and all-sufficient Savior, in comparison to whom every human and cosmic alternative pales. He is the sun that trivializes the output of every tiny candle. Such a positive reformulation of the gospel, then and now, leaves no valid reason to syncretize the faith.

---

[47]For an insightful elaboration of these issues, see Neville R. Bartle, "Developing a Contextual Theology in Melanesia with Reference to Death, Witchcraft, and the Spirit World" (D.Miss. diss., Asbury Theological Seminary, 2001).

[48]Hwa Yung, *Mangoes or Bananas? The Quest for an Authentic Asian Christian Theology* (Oxford: Regnum Books International, 1997), pp. 72-75.

8. THE GOSPELS

Contextualizing the Story for a Target Audience

But these are written that you may believe
that Jesus is the Christ, the Son of God,
and that by believing you may have life in his name.

JN 20:31 NIV

The Gospels tell the defining story of Jesus, sent by God, crucified, risen. Everything else in the New Testament in some way assumes and interprets this master narrative. But why does it take *four* Gospels to tell the story? Indeed, the very plurality of the Gospels has sometimes been an embarrassment to Christians, both ancient and modern. As early as the second century, Tatian produced the *Diatessaron*, the forerunner to all subsequent harmonies of the four Gospels. But compressing the Gospel writers' different renditions of the story into a single, generic tale defies the very dynamic by which the Gospels bear witness to and interpret Jesus for the church. If modern Gospel studies have taught us anything, it is that the four Evangelists have narrated the story of Jesus according to their own theological and literary concerns and in light of how they perceived the needs of their readers. We might even say that the four Gospels are four "contextualizations" of the one story. The Gospels, then, form an important piece of the total picture of how the Christian message is reexpressed for new audiences in the New Testament. That is the subject I want to explore in this chapter.

"GOSPEL COMMUNITIES" OR "TARGET AUDIENCES"?

Like preachers today, the Gospel writers interpreted the traditions they received—whether in the form of oral community memories about Jesus or written sources (see Lk 1:1-4)—in a way that best engaged the pastoral and cultural settings of their readers. But how narrow an audience were they targeting? It has become almost axiomatic in Gospel studies to talk about "communities" of

Christians that gave rise to each of the Gospels and to which the writings were addressed. Interpreters thus speak of a "Matthean community" or a "Lukan community," by which is usually meant a specific church or group of churches. From this perspective, the text of the Gospel can become a mirror of this hypothetical community, allowing scholars to reconstruct its specific theological views or conflicts (as in earlier redaction criticism), or to profile its particular "social location" (the main concern of social-science approaches to the Gospels).[1] Thus, Mark's rather negative portrayal of Jesus' disciples is said to expose a community embroiled in a christological controversy with the leaders of the Jerusalem church, whom the disciples allegorically represent.[2] Or the social status of the characters in Mark's story becomes a reflection of readers who are from the same rural peasant background.[3] Examples of this kind of "mirror reading" of the Gospels are legion.

The whole notion that the Gospels were shaped by and addressed to narrowly defined "communities" has in my mind been successfully challenged by a ground-breaking collection of essays on the Gospel audiences.[4] Richard Bauckham rightly criticizes the tendency "to treat Gospels hermeneutically as though they were Pauline epistles."[5] Texts vary in the extent to which they are context-specific. The fact that we may be able to reconstruct in a fair amount of detail the problems and social location of the Corinthian community from the text of 1 Corinthians does not mean that the same method can be applied equally well to the Gospels. Beyond the simple lack of data for such reconstructions, an even more serious hermeneutical problem arises when the Evangelist's hypothetical community becomes the filter through which virtually everything in the text is read. For example, J. Andrew Overman interprets Jesus' Sermon on the Mount (Mt 5—7) as simply an attempt to shore up the collective identity of Matthew's local Jewish Christian community, which is engrossed in a fierce conflict with a group of rival Jewish leaders.[6] In effect, the person and teaching

---

[1]See Richard Bauckham, "For Whom Were the Gospels Written?" in *The Gospel for All Christians: Rethinking the Gospel Audiences*, ed. Richard Bauckham (Grand Rapids, Mich.: Eerdmans, 1998), p. 22.

[2]T. J. Weeden. *Mark—Traditions in Conflict* (Philadelphia: Fortress, 1971).

[3]Richard L. Rohrbaugh, "The Social Location of the Markan Audience," *Int* 47 (1993): 80-95.

[4]Richard Bauckham, ed., *The Gospel for All Christians: Rethinking the Gospel Audiences* (Grand Rapids, Mich.: Eerdmans, 1998).

[5]Bauckham, "For Whom?" p. 26; cf. G. N. Stanton, "Revisiting Matthew's Communities," in *Society of Biblical Literature Seminar Papers 1994* (Atlanta: Scholars, 1994), p. 11.

[6]J. Andrew Overman, *Church and Community in Crisis: The Gospel According to Matthew*, The New Testament in Context (Valley Forge, Penn.: Trinity Press International, 1996). "The Sermon articulates the character of a follower and their relationships within the Matthean community, no more and no less" (p. 22).

of Jesus are relegated to a supporting role as a device through which the Evangelist speaks to the specific problems of his church. Francis Watson is quite right to insist that "[a]ny interpretation of the Gospels that overlooks the obvious fact that the subject of the gospels is the particular historical existence of Jesus of Nazareth, believed by Christians to be the Christ, the Son of God, is simply misinterpretation."[7] If the Gospels are to have any transcultural significance for our lives, they must be able to transcend the parochial concerns of a single first-century community.

Now if the Gospels are not like Paul's letters in trying to address the specific problems of a narrowly defined church, should we view them as contextual documents at all? Bauckham, I believe, goes too far in trying to decontextualize the Gospels. He describes the audience of the Gospel writers as an "open category," which includes any and every church of the ancient Mediterranean world.[8] If, however, the Evangelists were all addressing an identical and undefined readership, we have trouble accounting for their distinctive emphases and portraits of Jesus. Closer to the mark is Richard A Burridge's suggestion that, rather than for specific communities, we ought to think of the Gospels being written for something more like the modern notion of a "target audience."[9] Matthew, say, might have a target audience of Jewish Christians with a high regard for the Mosaic law, whereas Luke was aiming his Gospel at a mainly Gentile constituency. The Gospel writers' intended audience would therefore not necessarily be confined to a specific locale or a small group of people along with their immediate problems; it could include a wider range of readers in various communities who fit the profile of the Gospel's projected readership and pastoral concerns.[10] This does not rule out the possibility that the Evangelists could have addressed their Gospels in the first place to those individuals or churches

---

[7]Francis Watson, "Toward a Literal Reading of the Gospels," in *The Gospel for All Christians: Rethinking the Gospel Audiences*, ed. Richard Bauckham (Grand Rapids, Mich.: Eerdmans, 1998), pp. 195-217.

[8]Bauckham, "For Whom?" p. 46.

[9]Richard Burridge, "About People, by People, for People: Gospel Genre and Audiences," in *The Gospel for All Christians: Rethinking the Gospel Audiences*, ed. Richard Bauckham (Grand Rapids, Mich.: Eerdmans, 1998), p. 143.

[10]Ibid., pp. 143-44. The image of a Gospel "target audience" fits well with the notion used by contemporary narrative critics of the "implied reader," i.e., the imaginary reader who has the competence to respond to the expectations of the text in an ideal way; in short, the "ideal interpreter" of the text. This does not mean, however, that we can simply set aside questions relating to the social and historical context of the original readers, as if the Gospels had no connection to the world in which they were produced. Rather, "implied readers" can help to serve as pointers toward a sketch of the "real readers" for whom the Gospels were actually written. See Jack Dean Kingsbury, *Matthew as Story* (Philadelphia: Fortress, 1986), p. 120.

that they knew best (see Lk 1:1-4). However, the relatively less context-specific character of these writings, along with the likelihood that good networks of communication among churches operated in early Christianity,[11] means that the Gospel audiences were apparently a broader group than the Evangelists' own local communities.

THE QUESTION OF GENRE

Thinking about the Gospel audiences and how the Evangelists contextualized the story of Jesus for those people raises the question of how the Gospels functioned as literary works within their first century Mediterranean setting. In recent years, there has been a growing recognition that the Gospel writers were strongly influenced by the literary models and conventions of their day. In particular, the Gospels share many common features with Greco-Roman popular biographies *(bioi)*, and they would probably have been seen in that light by their first readers.[12] Unlike modern biographies, ancient *bioi* (including the Gospels) generally did not cover the whole life of their subject. What is more, writers of ancient Lives had the freedom to rearrange their sources thematically rather than in strict chronological sequence, allowing the life and teachings of their subjects to have the greatest impact on their readers.[13]

Viewing the Gospels within the broad genre of ancient biographies means first of all that what they are "about" is the person of Jesus—his words and deeds, his story—not the specific problems or ideas of the Evangelist's community. Furthermore, recognizing that the Gospels function within the category of ancient biographies (and not letters) reinforces the expectation that they would address a wider readership than a small group of people facing highly localized issues. At the same time, ancient biographers often had certain types of people in mind (target audiences?) and wanted their Lives to achieve particular functions, such as apologetic or polemic or teaching. One of the stated purposes of Luke and John, for example—to inform and instruct their readers about Jesus (Lk 1:3-4; Jn 20:30-31)—corresponds to the expressed intention of biographers like Philostratus and Philo to correct their readers' ignorance about their subjects.[14]

---

[11]See Bauckham, "For Whom?" pp. 30-44; Michael B. Thompson, "The Holy Internet: Communication Between Churches in the First Christian Generation," in *The Gospel for All Christians: Rethinking the Gospel Audiences*, ed. Richard Bauckham (Grand Rapids, Mich.: Eerdmans, 1998), pp. 49-70.

[12]See especially Richard A. Burridge, *What Are the Gospels? A Comparison with Graeco-Roman Biography* (Cambridge: Cambridge University Press, 1992).

[13]See Craig S. Keener, *A Commentary on the Gospel of Matthew* (Grand Rapids, Mich.: Eerdmans, 1999), pp. 17-18.

[14]Burrridge, "About People," p. 137. See Philostratus *Vita Apollonii* 1.2-3; Philo *De Vita Mosis* 1.1.

In addition to ancient biography, the four Gospels reflect the influence of other forms of contemporary literature. Since ancient biographers wrote with historical intentions, we should not be surprised that the Gospels have features in common with Greco-Roman historiography.[15] This is most evident in the Gospel of Luke. We noted in chapter one that the Third Gospel is part of a two-volume work, Luke-Acts, that has striking affinities with historical writings of the Hellenistic world. Nevertheless, the fluidity of genres such as "biography" and "historiography"and their considerable overlap in antiquity mean that we should not be too rigid in defining the genre of Luke's Gospel.[16] It shares characteristics with both biographies and historical writings. Moreover, the Gospels also bear the stamp of Old Testament and later Jewish historical works, which feature biographical narratives (e.g., the Former Prophets, 1 and 2 Chronicles, Ezra, Nehemiah, Maccabean literature). The Gospels (especially Matthew and Luke) are saturated with the language and style of the Greek Bible.

All of this suggests that the Gospels participate in the popular literary forms of the world in which they were born. This participation is but one evidence of their being incarnated in a particular cultural context. That they are closer to Greco-Roman models than Jewish ones is hardly surprising, given that they are written in Greek and were probably all addressed to people living outside of Palestine.[17] At the same time, however, the Evangelists transcend the patterns of their general culture in the writings they produced. These narratives are not *simply* a type of ancient biography or history. They are also *Gospels*, which means that their primary reason for being, their aim and their character, are derived from the needs and mission of early Christianity, not from their literary environment. The Gospels proclaim the church's good news by narrating the story of Jesus of Nazareth (Mk 1:1).

PERSUADING THE AUDIENCE

If we are correct that the Gospels were targeted to different groups of people

---

[15]See David E. Aune, *The New Testament in Its Literary Environment* (Philadelphia: Westminster Press, 1987), pp. 29-30, 64-65.

[16]Larry Hutardo, "Gospels (Genre)," in *Dictionary of Jesus and the Gospels*, ed. Joel B. Green, Scot McKnight and I. Howard Marshall (Downers Grove, Ill.: InterVarsity Press, 1992), p. 281; Burridge, "About People," pp. 244-46.

[17]It is difficult to be certain about the extent to which the Gospel writers *consciously* adopted Greco-Roman literary models. Richard Burridge thinks that Mark—generally thought to be the first Gospel writer—may have written in a way that was similar to popular biographies, or he may have done so unconsciously "simply because it is the natural genre for any text concentrating on the deeds and words of a single person" ("About People," pp. 248-49). A conscious patterning after literary forms of the period seems easiest to establish with Luke's Gospel (e.g., Lk 1:1-4; Acts 1:1).

within the Greco-Roman world, then the relationship between the Evangelist and his audience becomes a key to understanding how the Gospel writers contextualized their christological story. Lately, the role of the audience in the communication process has been taken much more seriously in Gospel studies. Rhetorical critics have made us aware that the Gospels function as "audience-oriented" communication.[18] Like other ancient writings, they are intended not simply to provide information but to persuade their readers and move them to action. Luke tells us that he writes "in order that you may know the assurance *(asphaleia)* about the things which you have been taught" (Lk 1:4, my translation). The Fourth Gospel candidly declares its purpose: "that you may come to believe that Jesus is the Messiah, the Son of God, and that through believing you may have life in his name" (Jn 20:31).

Like Paul, the Evangelists, consciously or unconsciously, drew upon rhetorical conventions and strategies that would have been appealing and persuasive to audiences in the Greco-Roman world. The Synoptic Gospel writers, for example, made extensive use of the ancient form of *chreia*, the kind of concise, character-revealing anecdotes about historical persons that were a particular feature of ancient biographies.[19] The Gospels also vary in the levels of literary and rhetorical competency they expect from their audiences. Thus, Luke shows a higher degree of literary sophistication and mastery of Greek style (e.g., Lk 1:1-4) than Mark.

If Whitney Shiner is right that Gospel writers like Mark primarily intended their works to be orally recited or performed in a communal setting—most likely a house church—then the Gospel's ability to target and shape an audience becomes even more compelling.[20] In the culture of the day, oral delivery would have been quite dramatic and spirited, emphasizing the emotional impact of the Gospel on the hearers. This enables the Gospel to become not just a story but an event which directly involves the listeners. Thus, in Mark's story of the con-

---

[18]For the importance of the effect of oratory upon the audience in Greco-Roman rhetorical theory, see Mary Ann Beavis, *Mark's Audience: The Literary and Social Setting of Mark 4:11-12* (Sheffield: JSOT Press, 1989), pp. 18-19.

[19]See Ben Witherington III, *The Gospel of Mark: A Socio-Rhetorical Commentary* (Grand Rapids, Mich.: Eerdmans, 2001), pp. 9-16; D. F. Watson, "Rhetorical Criticism," in *Dictionary of Jesus and the Gospels*, ed. Joel B. Green, Scot McKnight and I. Howard Marshall (Downers Grove, Ill.: InterVarsity Press, 1992), p. 700.

[20]See Whitney Shiner, *Proclaiming the Gospel: First-Century Performance of Mark* (Harrisburg, Penn.: Trinity Press International, 2003). Contra Ben Witherington III, who argues that Mark's Gospel was intended to be privately read (out loud), but not orally performed for an audience (*Gospel of Mark*, pp. 14-16). As Shiner points out, when Mark addresses the "reader" (Mk 13:14), in the ancient world this could include those listening to a performance of a literary work (pp. 176-77).

fession at Caesarea Philippi (Mk 8:27-33), the Christian audience is able to identify positively with Peter's confession, "You are the Christ." This only intensifies
the emotional shock of Jesus' dramatic rebuke of Peter that so quickly follows,
"Get behind me, Satan!" In an oral setting with a dramatic delivery, "the listeners
suddenly find themselves addressed as "Satan!"[21] In my own experience of reciting Jesus' Sermon on the Mount (Mt 5—7) before an audience, I find that
something similar happens as the sermon builds to an emotional climax. Immediately after the listeners are led to identify with those who say to Jesus, "Lord,
Lord, did we not prophesy . . . and do many deeds of power in your name?"
comes Jesus' stunning retort, "I never knew you. Go away from me, you evil-
doers!" (Mt 7:21-23). The audience is visibly moved by the profound emotional
impact and the challenge to change.

The four Gospels are therefore contextual documents in that they narrate the
gospel story for distinct "target audiences" within the first century Mediterranean
world. In addition, they draw upon popular literary and rhetorical conventions
from that world in order to persuasively communicate the good news of Jesus
and transform their audiences. Yet in order to better understand why we have
four versions of the story of Jesus in the New Testament and how each one is
sculpted for a somewhat different audience, we need to consider each of the
Gospels as a contextualized narrative.

THE GOSPEL OF MARK

I will begin with the Gospel of Mark because it is widely thought to be the original Gospel written. Mark's opening line is crucial: "the beginning of the gospel
of Jesus Christ, the Son of God" (Mk 1:1). Mark is the only Evangelist to explicitly
connect his story with "the gospel"—the church's proclamation of God's salvation through Jesus. As narrative, Mark's "good news" focuses not only on Jesus
the Messiah's redemptive death and resurrection, but also his earthly life and
kingdom-inaugurating ministry (Mk 1:14-15). Yet Mark has a distinctive way of
telling the story. Unlike Matthew and Luke, who introduce their protagonist with
birth narratives, Mark seems to be little concerned with Jesus' earthly origins.
Jesus appears abruptly on the scene, fully grown, and launches immediately
into his fast-paced, almost breathless ministry of teaching, preaching and healing. The action unfolds like a collage of images flashing in rapid succession on
a video screen, with little time to take in the details.

Mark portrays Jesus as a figure cloaked in mystery. Jesus acts with great
power and authority, performing miracles, rebuking diseases and casting out

---

[21]Shiner, *Proclaiming the Gospel*, p. 180; see also pp. 4-5, 192.

demons, yet he binds people to keep it secret. He is frequently called a "teacher," but Mark presents less of his teaching than the other Gospels, and it is often deliberately difficult to grasp. This paradoxical prophet is misunderstood by virtually everyone, including his closest followers, and he lives in constant conflict with demonic powers, religious authorities and even his own family members. He is the powerful, divine Son of God, yet he is also the suffering Son of Man who must die, humiliated, abandoned even by God himself, on a Roman cross. Mark's ending only adds to the enigma. Jesus is raised from the dead, but instead of Jesus appearing to his disciples and commissioning them to mission, as in the other Gospels, Mark's story closes with a response of fear, amazement, and silence (Mk 16:1-8), leaving readers with unanswered questions and unfulfilled promises.[22]

Mark's audience. Why does Mark shape the "gospel" about Jesus Christ into this mysterious and compelling form? No doubt Mark's particular approach to the Jesus story is largely related to the target audience he is addressing and his concerns for them. But compared to the other Gospels, Mark gives us few direct clues about the character of his readers and his purpose in writing. We must therefore approach the task of drawing up a profile of Mark's audience and contextual aims with great care. Nevertheless, when we examine factors such as recurring themes and emphases, differences from Matthew and Luke, and narrative characteristics such as the comments of the narrator or the actions of the characters, a number of features emerge. In the first place, Mark's Gospel has an intercultural character.[23] Its roots are thoroughly Jewish. Many traits of the Gospel bring this out, including quotations and allusions from the Hebrew Scriptures, familiarity with Jewish customs and religious sects, Jewish apocalyptic notions and symbols (e.g., Mk 13) and traditional Jewish titles for Jesus, like Messiah, Son of David, Son of Man. At the same time, there are strong indications that Mark was writing primarily to *Gentiles* of the Greco-Roman world. In addition to telling the story as a type of Greco-Roman biography, Mark writes in Greek and pauses to translate Aramaic words and phrases (e.g., Mk 5:41; 7:11; 14:36; 15:22, 34). Furthermore, he infuses his Gospel with numerous untranslated Latin loanwords and has to explain certain Jewish beliefs and customs to his audience (Mk 7:3-5; 12:18; 14:12). Mark renarrates a gospel story anchored

---

[22]The oldest and best manuscripts of Mark's Gospel end at 16:8. This is best understood as the way Mark intended it, rather than assuming that an additional ending was lost. For an illuminating and creative treatment of Mark's distinctive portrayal of Jesus, see Richard A. Burridge, *Four Gospels, One Jesus?* (Grand Rapids, Mich.: Eerdmans, 1994), pp. 33-63.

[23]Vernon K. Robbins, *New Boundaries in Old Territory: Form and Social Rhetoric in Mark* (New York: Peter Lang, 1994), pp. 219-23.

in a Palestinian Jewish heritage for a Greco-Roman cultural setting.

Second, the striking emphasis on suffering, persecution and the cost of discipleship in the Second Gospel implies that Mark was writing to people who were facing times of testing for their allegiance to Christ and their mission to proclaim the good news. This comes through most vividly in chapter 13, where Mark reminds his audience that Jesus had predicted suffering and social alienation for his followers (Mk 13:5-23; cf. 9:49; 10:30). They would be arrested, beaten, betrayed and killed (Mk 13:9-13). Such words would have been heard with forceful relevance if the immediate setting for Mark's readers was the brutal persecutions of Nero at Rome or the tumultuous period of the Roman-Jewish war leading up to the fall of Jerusalem (see Mk 13:14-20). From start to finish, Mark's portrayal of Jesus and his followers would have offered hope to hard-pressed Christians, encouraging them to stand firm in their faith.

A crucified Messiah and cross-bearing disciples. How does Mark portray the subject of his story? On the one hand, he assures his audience of the "good news" that Jesus is indeed the Spirit-anointed Messiah and God's powerful Son (Mk 1:1, 11; 3:11; 5:7; 9:7). Jesus is pictured as the one who ushers in God's reign, defeats Satan and the cosmic forces, has authority over nature, heals diseases, forgives sins and raises the dead. Such a figure might well have reminded Mark's Gentile readers of a Greco-Roman miracle-worker or magician. Moreover, he is the eschatological Son of Man who is risen (Mk 16:1-8) and will soon return in glory (Mk 8:38; 13:24-27). On the other hand, what is truly remarkable about this Gospel's portrait of Jesus is how keen Mark is to reveal him as the kind of Messiah and Son who serves, suffers and dies. Not only does Mark allot a disproportionate amount of his story to the narrative of Jesus' passion, but everything that leads up to it falls under the shadow of the cross.[24] Thus, the thread of secrecy that runs through the Gospel at least in part signifies that Jesus' true mission can only be understood in light of his suffering and death as a ransom for many (Mk 10:45). Little by little, Mark pulls back the curtain over Jesus' identity until at last a lone Roman centurion, with face toward the cross, declares him publicly to be the Son of God (Mk 15:39). Only then does Jesus' question to his disciples, "Who do you say that I am?" (Mk 8:29) find its final answer.[25] Beginning with Peter's confession of Jesus as

---

[24]See Jack Dean Kingsbury, "The Significance of the Cross within Mark's Story," in *Gospel Interpretation: Narrative-Critical and Social-Scientific Approaches*, ed. J. D. Kingsbury (Harrisburg, Penn.: Trinity Press International, 1997), pp. 95-105.

[25]Richard B. Hays, *The Moral Vision of the New Testament: Community, Cross, New Creation: A Contemporary Introduction to New Testament Ethics* (San Francisco: HarperCollins, 1996), p. 80.

Messiah in chapter 8, Mark spotlights three predictions of the passion on the road to Jerusalem that define the suffering character of Jesus' mission (Mk 8:31; 9:31; 10:32-34). In each case, however, the teaching that follows reveals that Jesus' disciples must *also* travel the way of the cross. They, too, must deny themselves, bear a cross, lose their lives in order to save them, and become servant of all (Mk 8:34-35; 9:35; 10:42-45). Easy, triumphalistic notions of God's kingdom shatter. Mark consistently presents Jesus as a paradigm for people to follow on the path of persecution, obedience, and suffering. The narrative of the cross is the norm for the disciple. This speaks a powerful and relevant word to readers who are facing stern trials.

Perhaps the clearest insight into how Mark shapes his good news story for his audience emerges from his treatment of Jesus' disciples. Once again, the picture is riddled with ambiguity. Positively, the disciples are called by Jesus and leave all to follow him (Mk 1:16-20; 2:14). They are chosen to be with him (Mk 3:13-19), commissioned to do his work (Mk 3:14; 6:7-13), and given the mystery of the kingdom (Mk 4:11-12). On the other side, the disciples almost monotonously miss the point of Jesus' teaching (Mk 4:13; 7:17-18), his miracles (Mk 4:40-41; 6:50-52; 8:21), and especially his passion predictions (Mk 8:32-33; 9:32; 10:32-40). What is more, their denseness is coupled with failure, particularly as Jesus approaches the cross. Peter, James and John sleep through Jesus' hour of decision in Gethsemane (Mk 14:32-42), Judas betrays (Mk 14:10-11, 44-45), Peter denies (Mk 14:66-72), and they all flee at his arrest (Mk 14:50). In fact, Mark paints the disciples in such inky tones that Matthew and Luke repeatedly "touch up" the picture so that it is not so harsh. When, for instance, in Mark the disciples are said to have "no faith" (Mk 4:40), Matthew softens it to "you of *little* faith" (Mt 8:26; cf. 6:30; 14:31; 16:8), and in Luke, the *disciples* implore Jesus, "*Increase* our faith" (Lk 17:5).

Although it is hard to be sure of the extent to which Mark wants his readers to see themselves in Jesus' disciples, it seems that he uses their story to instruct, warn and encourage his audience. Mark's portrayal of the disciples cautions his readers that following Jesus is not something easy or automatic. It warns them not to imitate the disciples in adopting the values of their culture regarding power and honor, values that bypass the way of suffering and servanthood, the way of true discipleship (Mk 9:33-37; 10:42-45). No doubt many of Mark's readers who faced the prospect of persecution and rejection were tempted, like the disciples, to succumb to failure and fear. But Mark's story also offers hope of Jesus' continued faithfulness in the present in spite of their failures (cf. Mk 14:27-28), and it promises deliverance in the future with the coming of the triumphant Son of Man. Mark's readers are exhorted to "endure to the end" (Mk 13:13), whatever it costs. They are to "keep alert" (Mk 13:33; cf. 13:23), living in watchful readiness for Jesus' eschatological return. Even Mark's enigmatic ending, which remains unresolved where the other Gospels are not, masterfully draws readers into the story and confronts them with a decision. Will they shrink in fear like the women at the tomb (Mk 16:8), or will they pursue the one who has promised to go ahead of them to Galilee (Mk 16:7; 14:28)? Will they submit to worldly standards of status and power, or will they take up his cross and follow? Once again Mark's audience is faced with the ambiguity of the present age. The ending of the story is still being written in the lives of the readers.[26]

Mark, then, shapes the gospel story for a new audience. Whatever other goals his Gospel may have, it engages a predominantly Gentile church of beleaguered believers. Mark's story is artfully crafted for Christians who need to hear both a word of encouragement and a call to walk faithfully in Jesus' steps in the midst of difficulties, dangers and fears.

THE GOSPEL OF MATTHEW

Matthew's audience. The author of the First Gospel is a Jew who contextualizes his story about Jesus primarily for fellow Jews. Nothing has been more widely recognized about the Gospel of Matthew than its overtly Jewish character, both in the material it includes and in the way the story is told. At the same time, however, Matthew contains some of the harshest critique of Jewish leaders in all of the New Testament (see Mt 23), and it embraces a universal perspective that culminates in Jesus sending his followers to make disciples of all nations (Mt 28:19-20). These well-known tensions may suggest that Matthew is directed in the first place to Jewish Christians who were facing a painful time of transition, perhaps not long after the Roman-Judean War (A.D. 66-70).[27] Although still culturally and religiously rooted in Judaism, their faith in Jesus as Messiah inevitably was pulling them in a different direction from the majority of their fellow Jews. This growing separation apparently provoked opposition or persecution from other Jewish groups, especially their leaders (Mt 10:17-25; cf. 24:9). At the same time, these Christians would have been confronted with the dual realities of the overall failure of the Jewish mission and the increasingly Gentile character of the church. As Donald Hagner observes, they were in a kind of "no-man's

---

[26]See Burridge, *Four Gospels*, p. 62.

[27]On the arguments for dating Matthew in the seventies A.D. after the destruction of Jerusalem and the Temple, see Keener, *Gospel of Matthew*, pp. 42-44. As with all of the Gospels, however, any assigning of specific dates must be tentative.

land," caught between their Jewish heritage and identity on one side and God's new work among non-Jews on the other.[28]

As a result, an important purpose of Matthew is to provide his readers with an account of the story of Jesus that could address these crucial issues of identity and mission. Matthew reassures his audience on the one hand that in following Jesus the promised Messiah "they were being completely faithful to their Jewish heritage and would find in Jesus' teaching and example the embodiment of all that God had promised Israel."[29] On the other hand, Matthew's story proclaims that in the life, death and resurrection of Jesus, God has brought about a turning point in the history of salvation. Israel's rejection of its King and the church's mission to the Gentiles (Mt 24:14; 28:18-20) mean that God is calling non-Jews to be a part of a new people of the kingdom; the future of Matthew's Jewish Christian readers is with the Gentiles. Matthew's story of Jesus would thus provide his audience with resources to better answer their critics from the synagogue, as well as an impetus for engaging in both Jewish and Gentile missions. Although Matthew may have had specific Christian communities that he knew well in mind, he probably wrote his Gospel for a broader target audience of largely Jewish believers in Jesus—Christians who were both concerned about their connection to their Jewish past and anxious about their future.[30]

Jesus, the Jewish Messiah. How does Matthew re-present Jesus and his mission in a way that engages the culture and concerns of his mainly Jewish Christian audience? On the most obvious level, Matthew tailors his Gospel to Jews by assuming his readers will be familiar with Jewish language and culture. Unlike Mark, Matthew is free to interject untranslated Aramaic words (Mt 5:22; 6:24; 27:6) and make reference to details of Jewish customs—hand washing at meals (Mt 15:2; cf. Mk 7:3-4) or the wearing of phylacteries and fringes (Mt 23:5)—without explanation. Matthew alone regularly substitutes the term *kingdom of heaven* for *kingdom of God* in deference to Jewish sensibilities. He features material on such Jewish concerns as fasting, Sabbath observances, temple offerings and the payment of the temple tax. Jewish readers would also have noticed Matthew's references to Jerusalem as the "holy city" (Mt 4:5; 27:53) and

---

[28]Donald Hagner, *Matthew*, vol. 1 (Dallas: Word Books, 1993), p. lxx. For other treatments of the setting for Matthew's Gospel similar to the one advanced here but with some variations, see Donald Senior, *The Gospel of Matthew* (Nashville: Abingdon, 1997), pp. 72-84; Keener, *Gospel of Matthew*, pp. 45-51.

[29]Senior, *Gospel of Matthew*, p. 84.

[30]See Senior, *Matthew* (Nashville: Abingdon, 1998), p. 24. This is not to say that issues such as the continuity of the church with Israel and the relationship of Jews and Gentiles in the Christian community would have no interest for Gentile Christians. I do not see Gentiles, however, as Matthew's main target audience.

his structuring of his opening genealogy into sets of *fourteen*—the numerical value of the Hebrew letters in David's name (Mt 1:17).

More significantly, Matthew presents a more "Jewish" Jesus than we find in Mark. The Jesus we encounter in the First Gospel is "the Jewish messiah sent by the Jewish God to the Jewish people in fulfillment of the Jewish Scriptures."[31] As Craig Keener notes, it seems that Matthew repeatedly "re-Judaizes" Mark's picture of Jesus for a Jewish Christian audience.[32] Nowhere is this more visible than in Matthew's overture to the Gospel. With his opening words, literally, "the book of genesis" (*biblos geneseōs,* Mt 1:1; cf. Gen 2:4; 5:1), he immediately echoes the beginning of the Torah. The genealogy that follows traces Jesus' Jewish roots back to Abraham and David, the father of the faith and the head of the royal line. The title "Son of David" (Mt 1:1) comes to special prominence in Matthew (e.g., Mt 9:27; 12:23; 15:22; 20:30-31), identifying Jesus as a Davidic messiah. From the very outset, Matthew hooks the Jesus narrative onto a previous story, the story of Israel.[33]

Jesus fulfills Scripture. One way that Matthew contextualizes his story for a Jewish Christian audience is through hailing Jesus as the fulfillment of Israel's Scriptures. The Gospel is teeming with Old Testament allusions, quotations and typology.[34] Above all, on at least ten different occasions Matthew splices a Scripture citation to the story of Jesus by means of a formula that goes something like, "this happened to fulfill what was spoken by the prophet." All of them are unique to Matthew, and they reveal how intent this writer is to demonstrate to his Jewish audience that Jesus is the Messiah who fulfills all of the promises of sacred Scripture. Especially in the first half of the Gospel, where Matthew introduces his readers to his understanding of Jesus, the fulfillment citations undergird the narrative, demonstrating that the events of Jesus' life are part of the divine plan. It is important to note, however, that the interpretive process moves in two directions. Not only do the Scriptures reveal the true meaning of Jesus' life and mission, but God's climactic work in Jesus Christ brings out the fuller intent and meaning of the Old Testament. Thus Matthew can reread Hosea 11:1 ("Out of Egypt I called my *son*"), which originally has to do with the exodus of the children of Israel from Egypt, from a christological perspective. Matthew

---

[31]Bart D. Ehrman, *The New Testament: A Historical Introduction to the Early Christian Writings,* 2nd ed. (New York: Oxford, 2000), p. 97.

[32]Keener, *Gospel of Matthew,* p. 13.

[33]N. T. Wright, *The New Testament and the People of God* (Minneapolis: Fortress, 1992), p. 385.

[34]For Matthew's use of the Old Testament, see Robert Gundry, *The Use of the Old Testament in St. Matthew's Gospel with Special Reference to the Messianic Hope* (Leiden: Brill, 1967); G. N. Stanton, "Matthew," in *It Is Written: Scripture Citing Scripture,* ed. D. A. Carson and H. G. M. Williamson (Cambridge: Cambridge University Press, 1988), pp. 205-19.

finds a correspondence between the ancient experience of Israel and that of God's true *Son* Jesus (Mt 2:15), who ultimately embodies Israel's redemption.

Matthew seems to practice a pesherlike handling of Old Testament texts in the fulfillment citations, as he interprets them from an eschatological perspective and directly applies them to events in Jesus' life.[35] This hermeneutical strategy, although strange to most modern readers, would no doubt have resonated with many from Matthew's intended Jewish audience. We saw in chapter five that Paul could use similar means of contemporizing Israel's Scriptures for his readers. Matthew's handling of Old Testament texts has a different focus, however. Whereas Paul mainly reads Scripture as a prefiguration of salvation and the church, Matthew's hermeneutic is thoroughly christocentric. Matthew's readers needed to know that the entire story of Jesus ultimately fulfills what God had promised by the prophets. Not only would this lead them to a deeper understanding of Jesus' messiahship; it would also provide them with apologetic answers to their Jewish critics and a basis for evangelizing their fellow Jews.[36]

Jesus fulfills and interprets the Law. In addition to fulfilling the promises of the Hebrew prophets, Matthew also underscores that Jesus is the fulfillment of the Torah, the core symbol of Judaism. The First Gospel alone records Jesus' programmatic claim that he has come to "fulfill," not abolish, the law. Immediately following are statements that declare the ongoing validity of the law, which must be obeyed by Jesus' followers (Mt 5:17-20). In other cases, Matthew re-Judaizes Mark's narrative, making it more appropriate to Jewish believers who still practice the law. For example, where Mark's version of the apocalyptic discourse has Jesus telling his disciples to pray that the end will not come "in winter," Matthew adds the phrase, "or on a sabbath" (Mt 24:20; cf. Mk 13:18).

At the same time, Jesus not only appropriates the Torah; he reinterprets it.[37] This is most obvious in the Sermon on the Mount (Mt 5—7), where Jesus radicalizes and internalizes the law. Adopting the role of a Jewish teacher, six times he quotes legal texts from Scripture and then interprets them (Mt 5:21-48), supplanting the authority of traditional understandings of the law. Because he is the Messiah and Son of God, Jesus can truly "fulfill" the Torah precisely by revealing its ultimate meaning and intention. Accordingly, in matters of human relationships Jesus' disciples must go beyond the letter of the law to embrace the radical principle of perfect love for others (Mt 5:38-48). Elsewhere, all of the require-

---

[35]See Richard N. Longenecker, *Biblical Exegesis in the Apostolic Period*, 2nd ed. (Grand Rapids, Mich.: Eerdmans, 1999), pp. 124-35.

[36]See Senior, *Gospel of Matthew*, p. 36.

[37]See Luke Timothy Johnson, *The Writings of the New Testament: An Introduction*, rev. ed. (Minneapolis: Fortress, 1999), pp. 197-204.

ments of the Torah are subsumed under the two greatest commandments, love for God and love for one's neighbor (Mt 22:34-40). Matthew drives home the point when he adds to Mark's account, "On these two commandments hang all the law and the prophets" (Mt 22:40; cf. 7:12; Mk 12:29-31). Jesus transforms the Torah by establishing love as the lens through which the entire law is truly perceived and practiced.

Matthew thus addresses the concerns of his audience by spotlighting the relationship between the gospel and the Torah. The law is not rejected, but rather fulfilled and reinterpreted for a new situation in light of Jesus and his teaching. What is true of the central symbol of the Torah is also true of other Jewish symbols: Jesus is greater than the Jewish *temple* (Mt 12:6); he is lord of the Jewish *sabbath* (Mt 12:8); he promotes a redefined *righteousness* that is "greater" than that of the Jewish leaders (Mt 5:20-48); he affirms the practice of *tithing*, but subordinates it to "the weightier matters of the law: justice and mercy and faith" (Mt 23:23). This christological reappropriation of the core symbols of Judaism establishes continuity with the Jewish heritage of Matthew's readers. At the same time, it affirms—in contrast to all other rival interpretations—that the focus of their symbolic world is no longer the Torah but the person of Jesus Messiah, the *one* teacher of Israel (Mt 23:10).

A Gospel for all nations. The tension in Jesus' mission statements in Matthew is well-known. On the one hand, Jesus instructs the Twelve to "Go nowhere among the Gentiles . . . but go rather to the lost sheep of the house of Israel" (Mt 10:5-6; cf. 10:23; 15:21-28).[38] On the other hand, the Gospel concludes with Jesus commissioning his followers to go and "make disciples of all nations" (Mt 28:19-20; cf. 24:14). And in response to a Roman centurion's faith that is like "no one in Israel," Jesus prophesies that many Gentiles will enter the kingdom of heaven, "while the heirs of the kingdom" (the Jews) "will be thrown into the outer darkness" (Mt 8:10-12; cf. 21:43). Matthew, in fact, prepares for the Gentile mission from the beginning—whether by naming Gentile women in Jesus' family line (Mt 1:5-6), by telling the story of the visit of Persian Magi at Jesus' birth (Mt 2:1-12), or by citing scriptural prophecies that include Gentiles in the Messiah's mission (Mt 4:15; 12:18-21).

How do we account for this approach to mission that seems to run on two different tracks—one particularistic, the other universal? I would argue that Matthew retains both emphases, at least in part because both were relevant to his readers' situation. The mission statements that focus on Israel seem to have a

---

[38]For other passages in Matthew that put Gentiles in a negative light, see Mt 5:47; 6:7, 32; 10:18; 18:17; 20:19, 25; 24:9.

twofold function for Matthew's audience. First, we noted that in light of the widespread rejection of the gospel by the Jews, Matthew's Jewish Christian readers needed to be reminded that God had been faithful to his promises to Israel, offering the messianic salvation first to his covenant people. This is an issue of identity. But there is also the question of mission. The church's calling to "the lost sheep of the house of Israel" (Mt 10:6) has not been repealed. What *has* been revoked is the prohibition that limited the scope of the mission to Israel during Jesus' lifetime (Mt 10:5).[39] Matthew's readers also need to look beyond their own horizons and embrace the mission to the Gentiles. Matthew wants these Jewish Christians to understand that Jesus is no longer simply the Messiah of the Jews; he is the Savior of the world. Matthew's audience must adopt a new identity, as God's new people from "all nations" (*panta ta ethnē,* Mt 24:14; 28:19), made up of Jews and Gentiles. These two aspects of mission in Matthew, the *contextual* dimension that focuses on one's own culture and society (Mt 10:5-6), and the *global* dimension that reaches out to peoples and cultures beyond one's own (Mt 28:19-20), are both integral to the church's mission in every generation.[40]

Jesus, the teacher of the church. Matthew adapts the traditions available to him for his audience in a way that accents the role of Jesus as the teacher of the church. Perhaps this is most obvious in how Matthew inserts five extended teaching discourses of Jesus into Mark's narrative framework. It is also communicated through an emphasis on the presence of Jesus in the Christian community. Unlike Mark, who paints Jesus as a figure of mystery and hiddenness, Matthew bookends his narrative with promises of Jesus' abiding presence with his people: he is Emmanuel, "God with us" (Mt 1:23), and he will *always* be with the church, to the end of the age (Mt 28:20; cf. 18:20). Jesus speaks beyond his own Palestinian audience directly to the church of Matthew's day. He is *still* teaching the church as the risen, living Lord.

Much of Jesus' instruction in Matthew seems to be targeted toward a community of believers that needs to be discipled. Jesus' teaching in chapter 18 presupposes a "church" (Mt 18:16; cf. 16:18) that has definite boundaries and a shared life.[41] Although what Jesus says about the disciplining of unrepentant of-

---

[39]Keener, *Gospel of Matthew*, p. 719.

[40]See Johannes Nissen, "Mission and Globalization in New Testament Perspective," in *For All People: Global Theologies in Contexts*, ed. E. M. W. Pedersen et al. (Grand Rapids, Mich.: Eerdmans, 2002), pp. 40-41.

[41]David B. Howell, *Matthew's Inclusive Story: A Study of the Narrative Rhetoric of the First Gospel* (Sheffield: JSOT Press, 1990), p. 218. The term "church" *(ekklēsia)* occurs only in Matthew (Mt 16:18; 18:20) among the Gospels.

fenders and the need for forgiveness within the community (Mt 18:15-35) could apply more universally, it is likely that Matthew directs this teaching in the first place to divisive tendencies within the church of his time (cf. Mt 7:1-5).[42] Take the parable of the lost sheep. In Luke, it reveals God's compassion for sinners *outside* the fellowship (Lk 15:1-7). For Matthew, however, the same parable speaks of the *church's* care for straying fellow-disciples (Mt 18:10-14). In the same vein, Matthew's warnings that the disciples should expect rejection and persecution (Mt 10:16-25; 24:9), or that false prophets and messiahs will invade the church (Mt 7:15-23; 24:4-5, 11, 23-26), directly address the life situation of his audience.

Once again, we find a Gospel writer who consistently contextualizes his narrative in order to shape a particular audience, in this case made up largely of Jewish Christians who are apparently caught in an inter-Jewish conflict. In this Evangelist's retelling of the story, Jesus is the Jewish Messiah and Teacher who fulfills the Scriptures and traditions of Israel, but who also redefines Israel's law and her key symbols in light of the new realities of the gospel. But Matthew's story also moves his readers beyond Jewish parochialism. They must embrace a new inclusive identity and a mission that knows no bounds.

THE GOSPEL OF LUKE

Luke's audience. Unlike Matthew—a Jew writing to Jews—Luke was likely a Gentile who targeted his Gospel to a predominantly Gentile Christian audience. The Gospel of Luke reflects a Gentile orientation in a variety of ways. Of all the Gospels, Luke shows the strongest influence from Greco-Roman literary forms and conventions, with features of both Hellenistic biographies (e.g., the extended narrative of Jesus' birth and infancy) and historical writings of the time (see the Greco-Roman prologue in Lk 1:1-4). Luke, among the Evangelists, takes the greatest care to relate the story of Jesus to the larger setting of world history, including contemporary Roman rule (Lk 1:5; 2:1; 3:1). A dominantly non-Jewish audience might also explain why Luke's genealogy of Jesus goes back to Adam and God (Lk 3:23-38) instead of to Abraham, the father of Israel, as in Matthew. In addition, Luke sometimes uses the term "Judea" to represent all of Palestine (Lk 1:5; 4:44; 6:17; 7:17; 23:5), thus presenting Judaism as a single, identifiable category to non-Jews. Finally, Luke's Gospel is addressed to Theophilus, who is in all likelihood a Gentile.

Luke's Gentile readers were probably for the most part city dwellers outside

---

[42]Hays, *Moral Vision*, p. 108; R. T. France, *Matthew: Evangelist and Teacher* (Grand Rapids, Mich.: Zondervan, 1989), pp. 252-53.

of Palestine. In a number of places, Luke apparently "Hellenizes" and "urbanizes" a Palestinian tradition to make it more relevant to urban Gentiles. Luke's descriptions of houses, for example, reflect a different cultural setting than that of a Palestinian village (e.g., Lk 5:19, cf. Mk 2:4; Lk 6:47-49, cf. Mt 7:24-27; Lk 8:16 and 11:33, cf. Mt 5:15).[43] Elsewhere Luke portrays Jesus as a teacher who sits and talks at dinner parties, reminding his readers of the symposia of urban Greco-Roman society (e.g., Lk 7:36-50; 14:1-24).

At the same time, Luke presupposes an audience that is familiar with the Greek Bible. In contrast to Matthew, Luke's Gospel has fewer direct quotations and is less concerned to show how Jesus fulfills specific prophecies. Nonetheless, language, allusions and echoes from the Old Testament abound. In the birth and infancy stories of Luke 1 and 2, the reader is immediately plunged into the world of the Greek Bible as Luke consciously imitates the style and setting of the Septuagint. Luke's opening scenes resonate with echoes of the stories of Abraham and Sarah from Genesis and of Hannah from 1 Samuel, which would only be heard by ears tuned to the wavelength of the Scriptures. In light of this influence from the biblical tradition, Luke's target audience may have included former "God-fearers" with synagogue connections (Theophilus?) who could serve as an interpretive resource for the wider community.[44] At the very least, Luke's implied readers appear to be Gentile *Christians* (see Lk 1:1-4) who had been sufficiently instructed in the Greek Bible to begin to appreciate the scriptural fabric of the Gospel.

Luke's Gospel seems to be directed to a socially diverse audience as well.[45] The relatively high level of Greek style in Luke's prologue suggests that the narrative may have been intended at least in part for educated readers. Indeed, Theophilus—addressed as "most excellent" (Lk 1:3)—was likely a highly placed person. Nevertheless, Luke's presentation of Jesus is sufficiently broad to address both poor and rich, elite and marginalized, women and men. We should therefore not limit his audience to any narrow social or economic group.

---

[43]See Joseph Fitzmyer, *The Gospel according to Luke, I-IX* (New York: Doubleday, 1981), pp. 58, 644, 719; Halvor Moxnes, "The Social Context of Luke's Community," *Int* 48 (1994): 380. See also Luke's use of language that applies to authorities in a Hellenistic city (Lk 12:11-12) in contrast to rulers in Roman Palestine (Mt 10:18).

[44]Although it is attractive in some ways to identify Luke's primary or ideal reader as a Gentile God-fearer (see John Nolland, *Luke* [Dallas: Word, 1989], 1:xxxii-xxxiii; Herman Hendrickx, *The Third Gospel for the Third World* [Collegeville, Minn.: Michael Glazier/Liturgical Press, 1996], 1:xi-xii), it is not necessary to assume this is the only kind of reader that Luke was addressing.

[45]Robert C. Tannehill, *Luke* (Abingdon: Nashville, 1996), pp. 24-25; Moxnes, "Social Context," pp. 379-89.

Good news for the marginalized. The Third Gospel recontextualizes a
story that is set mainly in rural Palestine for a largely urban Gentile audience.
As Luke tells the story afresh, certain distinctive themes emerge. First, Luke sets
his narrative within the wider backdrop of God's plan to bring salvation to the
world. He is keen to show Gentile believers that the "new" story of Jesus is
rooted in God's ancient plan.[46] The biblical language of Luke's opening chapters
alerts his readers that Jesus stands in continuity with Israel's history and fulfills
God's promises of salvation to his people (e.g., Lk 1:54-55, 68-77; 4:21; 24:44-
49). At the same time, only Luke among the Gospel writers connects his story
of Jesus to a sequel—the story of the early church in Acts. This connection enables him to more fully demonstrate that it is part of God's ancient plan to include the Gentiles in the people of God. Already in Luke's Gospel, we encounter foreshadowings of universal salvation and the Gentile mission that will move
to center stage in Acts. These include Simeon's prophecy of "a light for revelation to the Gentiles" (Lk 2:32), the Roman centurion who has faith like none in
Israel (Lk 7:1-10), and Luke's version of Jesus' "great commission" to preach repentance and forgiveness of sins to all nations (Lk 24:47; cf. 3:6; 4:24-27; 8:26-
39; 13:22-30; 21:24). Although references to the Gentiles are not numerous, they
are important. This is not only because they prefigure the Gentile mission of the
church, but also because Gentiles are just one evidence of Jesus' boundary-
breaching mission in Luke.[47]

Luke demonstrates the inclusiveness of God's saving plan by spotlighting
Jesus' compassion for groups of people who were on the margins of society:
the poor and the oppressed, the sick and the lepers, "sinners" and tax collectors,
women and children, Samaritans and Gentiles. Pivotal to the emphasis is Jesus'
dramatic announcement of his mission manifesto at his hometown synagogue
in Nazareth (Lk 4:16-30). By moving an episode that Mark and Matthew record
much later in their stories (Mk 6:1-6; Mt 13:53-58) to the very beginning of Jesus'
ministry, and by expanding it to include the content of Jesus' message, Luke
gives it a programmatic character. For Luke, Jesus is the Spirit-anointed prophet
who arrives to preach good news to the poor and release to the captives, the
blind and the oppressed (Lk 4:18). Indeed, bringing "good news to the poor" is
the hallmark of Jesus' mission in Luke (cf. Lk 7:22). Just who, then, are the
"poor" from Luke's perspective? Joel B. Green has made a compelling case that
it is important not to define the "poor" exclusively along economic lines. Rather,

---

[46]Joel B. Green, *The Theology of the Gospel of Luke* (Cambridge: Cambridge University Press,
1995), p. 30.
[47]Ibid., p. 126.

the term embraces all those who are on the outside according to normal criteria of status and acceptability in the Mediterranean world.[48] Consequently, "in the Third Gospel, 'good news to the poor' is preeminently a gracious word of inclusion to the dispossessed, the excluded."[49] At the same time, Luke is not solely concerned about economic and social status, since the people who constitute the "poor" in the Gospel are those who also acknowledge their utter dependence on God and receive him.[50]

Themes heralded in Jesus' sermon in Nazareth continue to reverberate throughout the Gospel. Luke's account of Jesus' Beatitudes pronounces blessing on the poor and the hungry, in contrast to Matthew's more "spiritualized" version, where those who are "poor in spirit" and who "hunger and thirst for righteousness" receive God's favor (Lk 6:20; Mt 5:3, 6). In Luke's Gospel, meals—thick with social significance in the Mediterranean world—become a symbol of God's embrace of the outsider. Jesus urges people not to invite the rich to their dinners, but those of low status, "the poor, the crippled, the lame, and the blind" (Lk 14:13). Jesus himself dissolves boundaries by eating with the "wrong" people such as the sinners and tax collectors like Levi and Zacchaeus (Lk 5:27-32; 7:34; 15:1-2; 19:1-10). In reply to the Pharisees' mumblings and grumblings over such scandalous activity, Luke's Jesus tells three distinctive parables that demonstrate God's rejoicing over the restoration of the lost (Lk 15:1-32; cf. Mt 18:12-14). Luke also shows a special interest in Samaritans—ethnic and religious pariahs in Jewish eyes—and twice portrays them in a positive light (Lk 10:26-37; 17:11-19). Even in his crucifixion, Jesus shows compassion on the women of Jerusalem (Lk 23:27-31) and offers forgiveness to the penitent criminal (Lk 23:43; cf. 23:34). Jesus' boundary-shattering ministry in Luke serves not only to anticipate the universal mission of the church; it also calls Luke's audience to embody a gracious and inclusive fellowship that reaches beyond ethnic, religious, or status lines. The Lord exhorts his church, "Be merciful, just as your Father is merciful" (Lk 6:36).

---

[48]Joel B. Green, "Good News to Whom? Jesus and the 'Poor' in the Gospel of Luke," in *Jesus of Nazareth: Lord and Christ. Essays on the Historical Jesus and New Testament Christology*, ed. Joel B. Green and Max Turner (Grand Rapids, Mich.: Eerdmans, 1994), pp. 59-74; idem, *Theology*, pp. 79-84.

[49]Green, "Good News," p. 69. See also Mary Ann Beavis, "Expecting Nothing in Return: Luke's Picture of the Marginalized," in *Gospel Interpretation: Narrative-Critical and Social-Scientific Approaches,* ed. J. D. Kingsbury (Harrisburg, Penn.: Trinity Press International, 1997), p. 144.

[50]Craig L. Blomberg, " 'Your Faith Has Made You Whole': The Evangelical Liberation Theology of Jesus," in *Jesus of Nazareth: Lord and Christ. Essays on the Historical Jesus and New Testament Christology*, ed. Joel B. Green and Max Turner (Grand Rapids, Mich.: Eerdmans, 1994), pp. 88-89; I. Howard Marshall, *Luke: Historian and Theologian* (Grand Rapids, Mich.: Zondervan, 1971), pp. 122-23.

Comprehensive salvation. Whereas Matthew reveals Jesus as the one who brings true righteousness, Luke portrays Jesus as the bearer of God's *salvation,* an idea with Jewish roots, but that also was familiar to the Greco-Roman world. The language of salvation comes to particular prominence in Luke's Gospel. Early on, Jesus is announced as a "Savior" (Lk 2:11; cf. 1:47)—a title sometimes ascribed to the Roman emperor—who is destined to bring "salvation" to Israel and to all people (e.g., Lk 1:77; 2:30; 3:6; 19:9). Luke can summarize Jesus' ministry as coming "to seek out and to save the lost" (Lk 19:10). In fact, it has been widely recognized that *salvation* is the overarching theme of Luke-Acts.[51]

Luke's understanding of salvation cannot be confined to the terminology itself or to any narrow concept of what divine deliverance entails. More explicitly than the other Evangelists, Luke unveils an all-encompassing salvation that is for all people. It involves repentance and forgiveness of sins (Lk 1:77; 3:3; 5:20-24, 32; 7:47-49; 24:47) and is dependent on faith (Lk 7:50; 8:48; 17:19; 18:42). At the same time, Jesus offers liberation from whatever forces create brokenness and exclusion in the human situation, and whatever tries to frustrate God's redemptive purpose.[52] We can see this especially in the way that Luke handles Jesus' healing ministry. Repeatedly, Jesus declares to suffering people, "Your faith has made you *whole*" (literally "*saved* you," Lk 8:48; 17:19; 18:42; cf. 7:50), signaling both physical and spiritual restoration. Part of this wholeness involves freedom from diabolic cosmic powers. Thus Jesus interprets the healing of a woman crippled for eighteen long years as release from the bondage of Satan (Lk 13:10-17). Yet salvation as wholeness has *social,* as well as physical and spiritual, consequences. Disease in the Mediterranean world brought shame along with social and religious exclusion. Deliverance of this "daughter of Abraham" (Lk 13:16) from her crippling ailment meant restoration to the community of God's people.[53] Indeed, Jesus' announcement in Nazareth of a permanent Jubilee year, the "year of the Lord's favor" (Lk 4:19), promises release in a fully orbed sense—economic, social, religious—to God's people. Salvation in Luke's narrative can also carry political undertones, as in Zechariah's prophecy that Israel would be "saved from our enemies and from the hand of all who hate us" (Lk 1:71; cf. 1:74).

An important dimension of Luke's comprehensive view of salvation is the notion of the eschatological reversal of fortunes. Early in the Gospel, Mary's song rings out:

---

[51]I. Howard Marshall has in particular demonstrated the centrality of the notion of salvation for Luke-Acts. See his *Luke: Historian and Theologian,* especially chapters 4-8.
[52]Green, *Theology,* p. 136.
[53]Ibid., p. 97.

> He has brought down the powerful from their thrones,
>   and lifted up the lowly;
> he has filled the hungry with good things,
>   and sent the rich away empty. (Lk 1:52-53)

The theme of salvation as reversal plays out in the Third Gospel in a host of ways (see e.g., Lk 6:20-21, 24-25; 7:11-17; 7:36-50). Here I will simply point out how it is reflected in Jesus' parables in Luke: a profligate son returns home and has a party thrown in his honor, while a dutiful son stands outside and complains about his mistreatment (Lk 15:11-32); an extravagant rich man goes to torment in Hades, and a poor beggar is carried by angels to Abraham (Lk 16:19-31); a despised tax collector who mourns his sinfulness is justified, but a prideful Pharisee who rejoices in his righteousness is not (Lk 18:9-14). In Luke's eyes, God's salvation means that "some are last who will be first, and some are first who will be last" (Lk 13:30).

Luke and Hellenistic culture. In addition to considering particular themes and emphases in the Third Gospel that were appropriate to its readers, it is important to ask how Luke's story interacts with the cultural and social environment of its world.[54] This question has special relevance to Luke's Gospel, not least because Luke among the Evangelists seems most obviously concerned to unfold for his audience the broader social, economic and cultural implications of Jesus' message.

On the one hand, Luke articulates the Christian story within the language and conventions of his cultural environment. From a literary perspective, Luke tells his tale with an elegance and rhetorical skill that would have been appreciated by an educated Greco-Roman audience.[55] More significantly, he situates the saving events he narrates within the context of the social institutions and conventions of first-century Mediterranean life. This is in the first place the world of Roman Palestine, the sociohistorical setting for his story. It is a world of Roman occupiers and subjects (Lk 2:1-2; cf. 1:52, 71), of social elite and nonelite, of patrons and clients (Lk 7:1-10; 22:25), of religiously pure and unclean, of patriarchal family systems and of Jewish piety. All of these features and others are reflected in the Gospel. Luke's Jesus is at home in his own cultural environment. Yet Luke is not interested in simply describing the way things are in first-century Palestinian society. Green is right that Luke's Gospel "is not a neutral, disinter-

---

[54]For this section, I am particularly indebted to Joel B. Green, *Theology*.

[55]On rhetorical features in Luke, see e.g., Philip L. Shuler, "The Rhetorical Character of Luke 1-2," in *Literary Studies in Luke-Acts: Essays in Honor of Joseph B. Tyson*, ed. R. P. Thompson and T. E. Phillips (Macon, Ga.: Mercer University Press, 1998), pp. 173-89.

ested chronicle but a partisan narrative shaping of the story of Jesus." Luke's purpose is "to engage his audience in discourse and so to shape them by his work."[56] This means that while Luke embraces cultural conventions at one level in order to convey the story of salvation, he often does so with the intention of challenging and subverting the status quo.[57] In part because many of the cultural realities of the Palestinian world of Luke's narrative have relevance within the wider Mediterranean context, Luke's "partisan narrative" is able to address and transform the Gospel's mainly non-Jewish audience.

Two examples will illustrate Luke's model of cultural engagement. First, Luke's "good news for the poor" challenges the system of patronage, which was pervasive in the Roman world. As we have seen in our discussion of Paul's interaction with the Corinthians, the convention of patronage assumes a large degree of inequality, or "power distance,"[58] between higher-status patrons and their clients. Benefactors bestowed favors on clients in order to raise their own status in the community. This, in turn, placed clients under debt to their patrons and obligated them to return expressions of loyalty and honor. As a result, self-serving exploitation by the wealthy and powerful of their social inferiors was pandemic. For Luke's Greco-Roman readers, Jesus' command that people should "lend, expecting nothing in return" (Lk 6:35) would have come as a countercultural shock. Likewise, in the Third Gospel Jesus gives instruction to invite to dinner not those who can repay in kind, but rather the poor and the outcasts: precisely those who are *unable* to enhance a patron's social position by reciprocating (Lk 14:12-14). In such teaching, Jesus engages the patronage system of his culture in order to transform it.[59] In the economy of the kingdom, patrons are liberated to give freely to the needy without expectation of return or of higher status. Instead, God, the supreme Benefactor, is rewarder of all (Lk 6:35; 14:14).

Luke's narrative thus contrasts two competing models of "greatness" (Lk 22:24-27). One is that of the rulers of the Roman world (only Luke among the Evangelists calls them "benefactors"), who promote their own prestige through wielding power over their clients and acquiring their praise (Lk 22:25). The other is that of Jesus, who challenges the very premise of the Roman patronage

---

[56]Green, *Theology*, p. 123.

[57]Ibid., p. 141.

[58]For the notion of "power distance," see Geert Hofstede, *Cultures and Organizations: Software of the Mind* (New York: McGraw-Hill, 1991), esp. pp. 23-48. In societies with a high degree of power distance, the less powerful members "expect and accept that power is distributed unequally" (p. 28).

[59]Green, *Theology*, pp. 115-21; Halvor Moxnes, "Patron-Client Relations and the New Community," in *The Social World of Luke-Acts: Models for Interpretation*, ed. J. H. Neyrey (Peabody, Mass.: Hendrickson, 1991), pp. 264-65.

system by voluntarily demoting his own status and serving his followers (Lk 22:26-27). No doubt Luke's critique of the status-seeking Roman social order would have been particularly uncomfortable for the higher-placed members of his Gospel audience.

A second example relates to the role of women in Luke's narrative. Women come to special prominence in the Third Gospel. They are key players in Jesus' ministry, from Elizabeth and Mary in the infancy stories to the women who discover the empty tomb of Jesus and bear witness to the disciples (Lk 24:1-10). This is all the more remarkable given the inferior status of women in both Jewish and Greco-Roman society. Luke's cast of characters features women who interpret the significance of Jesus' coming (Lk 1:42-45; 2:38), receive his healing (Lk 4:38-39; 8:41-56; 13:10-17), travel with him and support his ministry (Lk 8:1-3), provide models of faith (Lk 1:26-38; 2:36-38; 7:36-50; 8:42-48; 18:1-8) and mourn for Jesus at his passion when the disciples had deserted him (Lk 23:27).

Nevertheless, Luke's portrayal of women has been criticized for promoting traditional, supportive female roles that merely reinforce a patriarchal social structure.[60] It is important, however, that we view Luke's story against the backdrop of *his* culture, not *ours*. As Green notes, Luke "faced the necessity of working *within* the constraints of one's historical particularity while at the same time calling (some of) those constraints into question."[61] For example, when Jesus' praises Mary, who sits and learns at his feet, instead of her sister Martha, who fulfills her domestic duties, he turns the normal role of women on its head (Lk 10:38-42).[62] Luke transcends his sociocultural context in his treatment of women not because he is a modern feminist, but because God in Jesus is in the process of upending conventional estimates of status and inclusion, of lowering the mighty and lifting up the marginalized.

In these and other ways, Luke both represents and challenges his world. And all the time, he does so by retelling the story of a Savior who lived and died in Palestine for a largely urban Greco-Roman audience. This is narrative theology at its finest.

THE GOSPEL OF JOHN

John sings the gospel story in a new key. Although his essential storyline is like that of the other Gospels—Jesus' ministry from baptism to death and resurrec-

---

[60]See e.g., Beavis, "Expecting Nothing," p. 148; Janice Capel Anderson, "Mary's Difference: Gender and Patriarchy in the Birth Narratives," *JR* 67 (1987): 200.

[61]Green, *Theology*, pp. 143-44.

[62]Jonathan Knight, *Luke's Gospel* (New York: Routledge, 1998), p. 158.

tion, with some believing and following and others rejecting his God-given mission—John reinterprets the narrative and the traditions upon which it is based in a creative and compelling way. Differences between John's presentation of Jesus and that of the three Synoptic Gospels are well-known, and several examples will suffice. John writes in a distinctive style with his own vocabulary that repeats the same theologically-charged words again and again, words like *love, light, life, word, world, witness, know, believe,* and *abide.* In contrast to the Synoptic emphasis on the "kingdom of God," especially as a coming eschatological reality, the Fourth Gospel highlights the theme of "eternal life" as something those who believe in Jesus experience now. In John, Jesus teaches in extended discourses about himself rather than in parables and terse sayings about the kingdom of God. Instead of Jesus performing "mighty works" and exorcisms that point to the arrival of the kingdom (e.g., Lk 11:20), the seven miracles in John are "signs" that provide insight into the identity of Jesus and call people to believe in him. All in all, the Fourth Gospel inhabits a quite different symbolic world from that of the Synoptics.

John's audience. What accounts for this radical recontextualization of the story of Jesus? Scholars continue to debate the extent to which John's Gospel reflects the specific historical situation and needs of its readers. In an effort to account for John's distinctiveness, complex and innovative theories have emerged about various stages of development in a "Johannine community," each of which can be uncovered in the text of the Gospel itself.[63] But neither the Gospel genre nor the overall coherence of John's telling of the story support such detailed reconstructions of a hypothetical community whose ongoing conflicts and concerns determine the specific shape of the Gospel.[64] What is more, if we listen to John's own statement of purpose for his Gospel, we get the clear impression that he had a readership in view that extends beyond a narrowly defined community of Christians:

> Jesus did many other miraculous signs in the presence of his disciples, which are not recorded in this book. But these are written that you may believe that Jesus is the Christ, the Son of God, and that by believing you may have life in his name (Jn 20:30-31 NIV).

---

[63]E.g., R. E. Brown, *The Community of the Beloved Disciple* (New York: Paulist, 1979); J. Louis Martyn, *History and Theology in the Fourth Gospel,* 2nd ed. (Nashville: Abingdon, 1979); R. A. Culpepper, *The Gospel and Letters of John* (Abingdon: Nashville: 1998), pp. 42-61.

[64]This does not exclude the possibility that the Fourth Gospel was edited over a period of time, as most scholars now hold. Nevertheless, the Gospel in its canonical form represents a narrative with an overall literary and theological unity. I will therefore refer to "John" as the Evangelist who is responsible for the Gospel in its final form.

Once again, it is better to think in terms of John's target audience. I agree with Marianne Meye Thompson that the Gospel is in the first place addressed to a second (and subsequent) generation of believers who were not eyewitnesses to Jesus' "signs" (Jn 20:26-31), an audience that includes both Jewish and Gentile Christians.[65] Accordingly, a number of features in the narrative suggest that John is addressing people of Jewish background (whether Jews or Gentile synagogue adherents). John makes extensive use of Old Testament images and themes (Abraham, Moses, the exodus, Wisdom traditions). He often refers to Jewish practices and institutions (Passover and other Jewish festivals, the temple). Jesus in John is repeatedly identified as the Jewish Messiah (e.g., Jn 1:41; 20:31), and John portrays his ministry and death as the fulfillment of Scripture (Jn 12:14-15, 37-41; 19:24, 28). In addition, John's sharp polemic against "the Jews" (used some 70 times) and the theme of expulsion from the synagogue (Jn 9:22; 12:42; 16:2) may point to a situation in which at least some of his Jewish Christian readers are facing conflict with the Jews of the synagogue in their own time. At the same time, John finds it necessary to explain Hebrew terms like *Messiah* and *rabbi*, as well as common Jewish practices such as the lack of sharing food and water between Jews and Samaritans (e.g., Jn 4:9; cf. 2:6; 5:16, 18). This surely implies that there were Gentiles, the "other sheep that do not belong to this fold" (Jn 10:16; cf. 11:52; 12:20-21), in his intended audience, as well.

Furthermore, these were Christians who faced ongoing pressures of existence in this world such as persecution (Jn 15:18-24; 16:1-4) and anxiety (Jn 14:1-7, 18-21; 16:16-24), believers who needed to be reminded of Jesus' words to the church about the character of its life and mission. Above all, John wants to strengthen and encourage this new generation of believers by making clear the identity of Jesus and the salvation he brings (Jn 20:30-31).[66] Whatever specific issues or polemics may have influenced the shape of the Fourth Gospel, John's basic concern is to repreach the gospel events and message for the church of his time. To do so, he uses images and categories that are anchored in Judaism but that also speak to an audience with a broader cultural and religious background.[67] In one sense the entire Gospel is a case study in how John recontextualizes the story of Jesus for a new audience and a new generation.

---

[65]Marianne M. Thompson, "John, Gospel of," in *Dictionary of Jesus and the Gospels*, ed. Joel B. Green, Scot McKnight and I. Howard Marshall (Downers Grove, Ill.: InterVarsity Press, 1992), pp. 372-73.

[66]This is by no means incompatible with a secondary evangelistic purpose for the Gospel. For a discussion of the textual and interpretive issues surrounding the phrase "that you may believe" (Jn 20:31) and its bearing on the purpose of John, consult the major commentaries.

[67]Thompson, "John," pp. 372-73.

Here I will simply highlight several representative examples of that process.

The Word was God. John, among the Evangelists, is most intentionally doing narrative *Christology.* He consciously interprets the life and teaching of Jesus in light of later theological reflection on their meaning (e.g., Jn 2:22; 7:39; 12:16). Nowhere is this clearer than in how the Fourth Gospel answers the question, "Who is Jesus?" John offers an almost dizzying array of responses. Jesus is the preexistent Word, the Son of God, the Lamb of God, the Messiah, the King of Israel, the Prophet, the Savior of the world. He is the one who comes from heaven, the "I am," the bread of life, the light of the world, the good shepherd, the resurrection and the life, the true vine, Lord, God, and so on. Some of these images are unique to John. Others he shares with his fellow Gospel writers but applies them in distinctive ways. Unlike Mark, there is nothing secretive about Jesus' true identity in the Fourth Gospel. John broadcasts Jesus' exalted and divine status from the opening prologue ("the Word was God," Jn 1:1) to Thomas's postresurrection confession, "My Lord and my God" (Jn 20:28). What is left implicit in the Synoptics, John ushers into full light.[68] In the Gospel of John, Jesus "exegetes"—both in the sense of revealing and interpreting—the Father (Jn 1:18).

No designation for Jesus better captures John's creative theological genius than the first one the reader encounters: the Word, the *Logos.* The Fourth Gospel introduces Jesus to its audience with the image of the *Logos* who was with God "in the beginning" (echoing Genesis 1:1). We can begin to see why when we recognize that *logos* was a notion with a rich heritage in the religious and philosophical traditions of the day. For the Greek Stoic philosophers it represented the principle of divine reason that stood behind the cosmos. For the Jewish wisdom tradition it paralleled the preexistent Wisdom of God. In the Greek Old Testament, it was the powerful Word of Yahweh that spoke the world into existence and that accomplished what God said through the prophets. For the Hellenistic Jewish writer Philo the *logos* was the bridge linking God and his creation. John thus embraces a familiar term that resonates with both Jewish and Hellenistic cultures and carries undertones of divinity. But he proceeds to melt it down and recast it with a new meaning that explodes the symbolic worlds of his contemporaries: the preexistent divine Word became finite human *flesh* in the historical person of Jesus of Nazareth (Jn 1:14). The Logos "lived among us." George R. Beasley-Murray is quite right that "John's employment of the concept to introduce the story of Jesus was a master-stroke of communication to the world of his day."[69]

---

[68]Johnson, *Writings of the New Testament,* pp. 531-32.

[69]George R. Beasley-Murray, *John* (Waco, Tex.: Word, 1987), p. lxvi.

Image-rich communication. John retells the story of Jesus and the salvation he brings with an abundance of symbols and images from his world. Nearly all of them have deep roots in Jewish thought. Some, like the symbols of the temple (Jn 2:19-21), the tabernacle (Jn 1:14), and the slain lamb (Jn 1:29, 36; 19:36), originate directly from Jewish religious life. Images, however, like life, light, darkness, water, bread, wine, birth, growth, and so on, are universal symbols that are found not only in Judaism, but also in various other religious and philosophical traditions of the time. John draws upon a whole range of symbols that enable him to communicate theologically to Jews and non-Jews alike.

Furthermore, John consistently pictures Jesus as one who uses images that are appropriate to the situation and the people he is addressing. In John, a conversation beside a well and a woman's felt need for a constant source of fresh water become the occasion for a theological exposition on "living water" (Jn 4:4-15). Jesus follows up a miracle of feeding bread to a multitude by proclaiming *himself* as the bread of life from heaven (Jn 6:1-15, 22-59). A Jewish feast that celebrates God's provision of water becomes the backdrop for Jesus imaging the Spirit as a river of living water that flows from within (Jn 7:37-39). The "sign" of restoring sight to a blind man (Jn 9:1-34) is interpreted by a pair of theological bookends—Jesus' claim to be the "light of the world" (Jn 8:12) and his teaching on spiritual blindness (Jn 9:35-41). Later, Jesus turns the somber scene of Lazarus's entombment into an opportunity to assure Mary and Martha that Jesus himself is the resurrection and the life, the one who bestows eternal life on all who believe in him (Jn 11:1-44). And following an encounter with Greek Gentiles (Jn 12:20-26), Jesus declares that his being lifted up on the cross will draw *all people* to himself (Jn 12:32; cf. 12:47). In John, Jesus uses different approaches with different people. He tailors the particular language and imagery that communicate the offer of salvation to the occasion. I suspect that Ben Witherington is right that John highlights Jesus' ability to speak to the concerns of a whole parade of different sorts of people, at least in part to provide a model for the church's mission to various kinds of people in his own day.[70] Indeed, John's flexible and image-rich approach continues to speak to the church's task today of leading people from different life circumstances into fullness of faith in Christ.

In but not of the world. One striking aspect of John's theological outlook has to do with his perception of the unbelieving world. It is often claimed that the Fourth Gospel reflects a strong sectarian perspective—the "us-versus-them" mentality of an embattled community that has been alienated from its social en-

---

[70]Ben Witherington III, *John's Wisdom: A Commentary on the Fourth Gospel* (Louisville: Westminster John Knox, 1995), pp. 31, 36.

vironment.[71] According to Robert Gundry, John uses an "antilanguage" which radically separates Christ's community from the hostile world around it:

> John not only leaves the world outside the scope of Jesus' praying and loving. He also describes the world as full of sin; as ignorant of God, God's Son, and God's children; as opposed to and hateful of God's Son and God's children; as rejoicing over Jesus' death; as dominated by Satan; and as subject to God's wrath. In the only one of the four gospels to mention the incarnation, then, the world looks wholly negative. . . . The Fourth Gospel is unalterably countercultural and sectarian.[72]

I would go part way, but only part way, with such readings of John. It is true that John establishes definite boundaries between the church and the world outside, which he reinforces with the dualistic language of light and darkness, above and below, truth and falsehood, God and Satan. Jesus in John builds a sturdy security fence around his own special flock who have been chosen by God. Unbelievers who do not recognize his voice are excluded from the fold (Jn 10:25-27; cf. 6:65). John assures his readers:

> If the world hates you, be aware that it hated me before it hated you. If you belonged to the world, the world would love you as its own. Because you do not belong to the world, but I have chosen you out of the world—therefore the world hates you. (Jn 15:18-19)

Such language serves to reassure Christians that hostility from the dominant culture is not a source of shame, but rather a badge of honor, as it was for Jesus. No doubt it also helps to dissuade them from trying to relieve the animosity of the world by compromising with its values and perspectives.[73]

But that is only one side of the story. John's wariness of the world does not translate into a "circle the wagons" mentality or an absence of responsibility toward unbelievers, as is sometimes suggested. Rather, there is a tension in John's Gospel between separation from the world and missional involvement in the world, a tension faced by the church in every generation. True, the world is a dangerous place and Satan is its ruler (Jn 12:31), but it is also the object of God's redemptive love (Jn 3:16). The disciples do not belong to the world, but

---

[71]See e.g., David Rensberger, *Johannine Faith and Liberating Community* (Philadelphia: Westminster Press, 1988); W. A. Meeks, "The Son of Man in Johannine Sectarianism," in *The Interpretation of John*, ed. J. Ashton (Philadelphia: Fortress, 1986), pp. 141-73.

[72]Robert H. Gundry, "Jesus the Word According to John the Sectarian: A Paleofundamentalist Manifesto for Contemporary Evangelicalism, Especially Its Elites in North America" (paper presented to the Annual Meeting of the Institute for Biblical Research, Nashville, Tenn., Nov 17, 2000), p. 7.

[73]David A. deSilva, *The Hope of Glory: Honor Discourse and New Testament Interpretation* (Collegeville, Minn.: Michael Glazier/Liturgical Press, 1999), p. 84.

they are sent into the world on Jesus' own saving mission (Jn 17:15, 18; 20:21). The community of believers is summoned to solidarity and unity through loving one another, but that very oneness becomes a light of witness to an unbelieving culture (Jn 17:21, 23; cf. 13:35; 15:26-27). This creative theological tension at least in part reflects John's sensitivity to Christians who are facing exclusion and persecution from a world that hates them, yet who also need to be encouraged, in the midst of such opposition, to participate in Jesus' own redeeming mission in their society. Like their Master, they must be "in" but not "of" the world, carrying out their missionary task without compromising their fundamental christological identity.[74]

Ultimately, John's theological understanding of the incarnation of Jesus insures that the need to paint bold borders between the church and the surrounding culture does not lapse into a world-despising dualism. Richard B. Hays makes a keen observation:

> at the level of deepest theological conviction, the Word made flesh affirms the goodness and significance of creation. All creation breathes with the life of the Logos, apart from whom there is no life (1:1-4). This conviction finds subliminal expression in John's masterful use of elemental, earthy symbols to articulate the Word: water, wine, bread, light, door, sheep, seed, vine, blood, fish. . . . No other New Testament writing so vividly visualizes the eternal in, with, and under the ordinary.[75]

John's persecuted readers must take a countercultural stance. Accommodation with the unbelieving world isn't an option. But the Fourth Gospel also declares that the Son of God has entered the world in human flesh, and he has given his own flesh for the life of the world (Jn 6:51). Incarnation and dualism are like oil and water.

He will give you another Paraclete. For a new generation of believers who were not eyewitnesses to Jesus' life and teaching and who may have struggled with the delay of Jesus return (e.g., Jn 21:21-23), John provides a fresh theological language and emphasis. Jesus' departure will not leave the church "orphaned" (Jn 14:18). The Holy Spirit, the *Paraclete*, will mediate Jesus' presence and ministry to his church. Unlike in Mark and Matthew, the Spirit is a key player throughout John's Gospel. It is not, however, until Jesus' farewell discourse in chapters 14—16 that the Paraclete takes center stage. The Paraclete's ministry is multifaceted, and each of those roles speaks to the new situation of

---

[74]Witherington, *John's Wisdom*, pp. 39-41, 276. For the missionary character of John's Gospel, see Eckhard Schnabel, *Early Christian Mission, Vol. 2: Paul and the Early Church* (Downers Grove, Ill.: InterVarsity Press, 2004), pp. 1502-12.

[75]Hays, *Moral Vision*, p. 156.

John's readers. The Paraclete functions as the presence of Jesus during the time of his absence (*another* Paraclete, Jn 14:16), as his disciples continue to live in a world that opposes them. The Spirit will assist the church in carrying out its mission by convicting and condemning an unbelieving world and testifying about Jesus, especially when his disciples face opposition in their witness (Jn 15:18—16:11). Above all, the Paraclete is the church's teacher and guide, both in terms of bringing remembrance of what Jesus said (Jn 14:26) and of continuing revelation for Jesus' followers (Jn 16:12-13). Indeed, in important ways, John's interpretation of the Jesus traditions in his Gospel is evidence of the Spirit's role of leading the church into inspired truth. Surely one reason that the Fourth Gospel features such a distinctive retelling of the story of Jesus is that John has "homiletically" reworked the Jesus tradition and spun out its meaning for a new situation and time with the aid and guidance of the Spirit.[76]

The Gospel of John, then, is a shining example of an effort to reexpress the story of Jesus in a new theological idiom and language, thereby enabling it to speak afresh to a new audience and their needs. It draws upon a kaleidoscope of images—some from religious and philosophical traditions, others from earthy everyday life—to try to communicate the height and depth and breadth of who Jesus is and to engender a deeper faith in him. To Christians who are under pressure from the surrounding culture, it sends out the strongest call in the Gospels for separation from the dark world. But it also assures its readers of Jesus' continued presence through the Paraclete, who will enable the church to extend the witness of the living Word in the world.

CONCLUSION

The New Testament includes not one, but four narrative accounts of the "gospel" that focuses on the life, ministry and passion of Jesus of Nazareth. Each Evangelist has distinctively contextualized the Jesus tradition under the inspiration of the Spirit. The story must be articulated for new audiences and settings which are in many ways different from the original Palestinian context of Jesus and his hearers. The Gospels, we could say, represent four examples of doing narrative theology. Clearly, these are not impartial accounts, such as might be attempted by a modern journalist. The Evangelists' interpretations of the gospel story are *ecclesial*, in that they are addressed to the needs of the church and seek to shape the identity of communities of faith; they are *missional*, not so much in the sense of functioning as missionary documents per se, but rather in motivating and providing resources for the church's mission to its world; and they are *transformational*: they inten-

---

[76]Witherington, *John's Wisdom*, p. 101; Thompson, "John," p. 376.

tionally draw their readers into the story of Jesus for the purpose of empowering a change in behavior and creating deeper faith in him.

The church today has much to learn from the Gospel writers' audience-sensitive way of doing theology. As Scripture, each of the Gospels represents an authoritative witness to Jesus, who he is and what he means for the church and its mission. Because the Gospels addressed different audiences and needs originally, they will no doubt speak with special relevance to different Christian communities and contexts today. For example, Luke's emphasis on Jesus' ministry to the marginalized and dispossessed might be a sorely needed prophetic word for affluent and individualistic churches. On the other hand, Mark's portrayal of Jesus' suffering and the ambiguity of the life of discipleship still offers hope to persecuted and fearful Christians, as well as a validation of their struggle.

But it is not only the theological message of the Gospels that is able to inform the contemporary church. Once again, we must pay close attention how the Gospel writers carry out the theological task, how they engage their audiences and cultures in order to transform them. The Gospels give us precedents and models for what it means to retell the story of Jesus for new target audiences. Joel B. Green rightly perceives that "[i]n order to hear and communicate the gospel today, we must become 'evangelical' in the sense of immersing ourselves in these accounts and by learning from them how to convey this gospel in our own world."[77] How, for instance, might Luke's strategy of co-opting the cultural language of patron-client relations in order to reshape the convention of patronage challenge us to see ways that we can engage our own cultural institutions and values while at the same time calling them into question? How might John's image-rich portrayal of the person and mission of Jesus encourage us to look for fresh metaphors, symbols and stories from our own traditions and cultures? Might such discoveries enable us to better communicate the wonder of Jesus among, say, non-Western peoples whose thinking tends to be concrete and pictorial, or to an image-driven postmodern world? Does not the very plurality of the four Gospels prompt us to find new pictures of the one Jesus and fresh ways of narrating the one gospel story? The twenty-first-century church in its abundantly varied cultural manifestations is called to continue the task of doing theology in an "evangelical" way. Like the Gospel writers before us, we must learn to sing the gospel story in new keys so that people might encounter Jesus in life-changing ways. We have the assurance that the same Paraclete who guided John's authoritative contextualization of the Jesus story for his own world will again help the church as it enunciates God's good news in diverse and changing circumstances today.

---

[77]Green, *Theology*, p. 133.

9. REVELATION

The Gospel and the Empire

*Let anyone who has an ear listen to
what the Spirit is saying to the churches.*

REV 2:7

It may seem a bit strange to single out the book of Revelation as an example of doing contextual theology. After all, for many Christians, Revelation is the least *contextual* book of the New Testament. Popularly, it is often viewed as a book of visions and prophecies about the *future*—a kind of predictive blueprint for what will take place in the last days. Other than perhaps the messages to the seven churches in chapters two and three, Revelation's weird and wonderful (or terrible) images are sometimes thought to have little connection with the circumstances and cultural world of John's first-century audience. What, for instance, do John's visions of the great battle at Armageddon (Rev 16:16) or of Christ's millennial reign (Rev 20:1-6) have to do with the life experience of Christians in the late first century?

This "noncontextual" approach to Revelation, however, obscures the reality that John, no less than any other New Testament author, is doing theology within the concrete life world he shares with his readers. Whatever Revelation might tell us about future events related to the return of Christ, it was not written in the first place to twenty-first-century people. First and foremost the Apocalypse was intended to be a "word on target" for seven churches in Asia Minor—churches that were struggling with what it meant to live Christianly in a world dominated by an empire that claimed ultimate allegiance for itself. It is only when we appreciate how rooted the message of Revelation is in its political and literary context that we can begin to grasp its compelling and relevant word for the church in every generation, including our own. In this chapter, I will focus on understanding how Revelation engaged its own first-century world and how that engagement models the task of doing theology in context.

THE CONTEXT

The theological character of Revelation is closely related to the concrete circumstances in human history that it addresses. The evidence points to a setting near the end of the reign of Emperor Domitian (A.D. 81-96), when the influence of the imperial cult in Western Asia Minor was on the rise.[1] These were difficult times to be a Christian in Roman Asia. Although a systematic, official persecution of Christians by Rome seems unlikely during this period, it was a time of sporadic local oppression.[2] Antipas had already been martyred (Rev 2:13), John himself was probably in exile (Rev 1:9), and other Christians were under pressure to deny the name of Christ (Rev 2:3, 13; 3:8). Moreover, John sees the present trials of his readers as a foretaste of an intensifying persecution and suffering for God's people that was about to come (e.g., Rev 2:10; 3:10; 6:9-11).

Revelation suggests that Christians were being pressured from two sources: Judaism and Rome. First, because Christians were considered a sect of Judaism up through the Jewish War (A.D. 66-70), they enjoyed the special exemption from practicing the emperor cult that Roman law had given to the Jews. After the war, however, Judaism began to close ranks and tried to disassociate itself from the Christian movement. As a result, Jews at times "slandered" Christians (Rev 2:9), denouncing them to Roman authorities as not being part of Judaism. Practically, this meant that Christians would lose any legal right to practice their religion or to abstain from giving homage to the emperor. Even more, they would no longer benefit from the protection and tolerance that Rome often exercised toward the Jewish people.

Second, Christians faced the daily social and economic pressure to participate in Roman cultural life, which was tightly bound to the emperor cult and the worship of various traditional gods.[3] It was almost impossible to enter into a city's public life without getting involved in some form of imperial worship, especially in Asia, where devotion to the emperor was exceptionally strong. Occasions like civic festivals or meetings of the trade guilds regularly included

---

[1]See the discussion and references in Greg K. Beale, *The Book of Revelation* (Grand Rapids, Mich.: Eerdmans, 1999), pp. 5-12.

[2]See the balanced discussions of Thomas B. Slater (*Christ and Community: A Socio-Historical Study of the Christology of Revelation* [Sheffield: Sheffield Academic Press, 1999], pp. 22-46), and Ben Witherington III (*Revelation* [Cambridge: Cambridge University Press, 2003], pp. 4-10), both of whom take issue with L. L. Thompson's thesis that there was no significant external persecution of Christians during Domitian's reign (L. L. Thompson, *The Book of Revelation: Apocalypse and Empire* [Oxford: Oxford University Press, 1990]).

[3]See Wes Howard-Brook and Anthony Gwyther, *Unveiling Empire: Reading Revelation Then and Now* (Maryknoll, N.Y.: Orbis, 1999), pp. 102-11, 115-18; David A. deSilva, "The Social Setting of the Revelation to John: Conflicts Within, Fears Without," *WTJ* 54 (1992): 286-96.

homage to the emperor or to pagan deities. Refusal to partake in the Caesar cult would be viewed as politically disloyal and unpatriotic. David A. deSilva is no doubt correct that "[b]y withdrawing from cultic expressions of solidarity with the citizenry and loyalty and gratitude toward those who secured the well-being of the city, Gentile Christians especially were at risk of being viewed as subversive, unreliable, and even dangerous elements of society."[4] With economic hardship, social ostracism and perhaps some form of local persecution awaiting those who spurned the normal cultural expectations, the temptation to accommodate would have been intense.

Christians in Roman Asia responded to this opposition in different ways. Not all resisted. In fact, Revelation's prophetic messages to the seven churches in Revelation 2 and 3 reveal that for many of John's readers the problem was not so much persecution as it was cozying up to the dominant Roman culture. Since the letters to the churches are crucial for understanding how John contextualizes his message for his various Asian audiences, they are a good place to begin.

A MESSAGE FOR SEVEN CONTEXTS

John tells us at the outset that this book is addressed "to the seven churches that are in Asia" (Rev 1:4). He does not, however, simply treat these communities as a monolithic group. Instead, each of the seven Spirit-inspired messages in chapters 2 and 3 is carefully tailored to the specific church in question.[5] John is speaking as a pastor to churches he knows well, and a stock sermon will not suffice. Each church requires a contextualized word that fits its own situation. This is immediately evident from the frequent references in the letters to events or images that have local significance. For instance, "Satan's throne" in the letter to Pergamum (Rev 2:13) likely refers to the city's primacy in the emperor cult in Asia. Likewise, the "lukewarmness" of Laodicea (Rev 3:16) is an allusion to the tepid and undrinkable water supply of this city, in sharp contrast to the "hot" medicinal springs of Hierapolis and the "cold" pure waters of Colossae nearby.[6]

These targeted letters do not only show points of contact with the historical circumstances of the churches. More importantly, they also address different spiritual conditions and needs. Contrary to a common interpretation of Revela-

---

[4]David A. deSilva, *The Hope of Glory: Honor Discourse and New Testament Interpretation* (Collegeville, Minn.: Michael Glazier/Liturgical Press, 1999), p. 180.

[5]For a discussion of the messages to the churches in light of their historical circumstances, see especially William M. Ramsay, *The Letters to the Seven Churches in Asia and Their Place in the Plan of the Apocalypse* (London: Hodder and Stoughton, 1904), and Colin J. Hemer, *The Letters to the Seven Churches of Asia in Their Local Setting* (Grand Rapids, Mich.: Eerdmans, 1986).

[6]See Hemer, *Letters to the Seven Churches*, for these (pp. 82-84, 186-91) and numerous other possible local references.

tion, John's purpose in writing was not simply to give consolation and encouragement to Christians who were suffering persecution.[7] Only two of the churches, in fact—Smyrna and Philadelphia—seem to be facing open hostility at the time. In both cases, it is Jewish opposition—the "synagogue of Satan" (Rev 2:9; 3:8)—that is singled out. This local harassment was especially strong in Smyrna, where Christians experienced economic persecution (Rev 2:9), and where Jewish denunciations of Christians to local Roman authorities might result in imprisonment or even death (Rev 2:10). These believers have the promise, however, that if they remain faithful until death, they will be granted the crown of eternal life (Rev 2:10). Likewise, the powerless and persecuted Christians in Philadelphia, though excluded from the synagogue, have been given an "open door" to the kingdom (Rev 3:8). If they patiently endure, they will find protection in the coming hour of trial (Rev 3:10) and in the end bear the name of the New Jerusalem (Rev 3:12). For these beleaguered but faithful churches, the message of the exalted Christ does indeed come as a word of comfort and hope for the future.

But John's contextualized messages are different for the other five churches, where the greatest dangers loom less from the outside than from within. These letters make it clear that John is addressing multiple contexts, not a single one. For the churches of Pergamum and Thyatira, the chief problem was tolerating false teachers who preached a doctrine of accommodation to the dominant culture. Christ's address to Pergamum praises this church for its faithfulness in the wake of persecution (Rev 2:13). But it also warns them of a group called the Nicolaitans, who apparently taught that compromising a bit with imperial worship and pagan society was the best formula for survival in the Roman world. The specific practices John targets are eating food sacrificed to idols and fornication (Rev 2:14).[8] The former likely involved eating sacrificial food at pagan festivals honoring the emperor in this center of the imperial cult. Perhaps these teachers were saying that Christians could join in such occasions as a civic duty without surrendering their loyalty to Christ.

The same two sins—idol food and immorality—were problems in Thyatira as well. Here they were being promoted within the fellowship by a female

---

[7]This reading of Revelation is often based on the assumption that offering comfort for persecuted and alienated people is the function of apocalyptic literature as a whole.

[8]It is difficult to be certain as to whether "fornication" in Revelation 2:14 and 20 should be taken literally or as a figure for religious infidelity and idolatry, as is often the case in the Old Testament. Since fornication is typically used figuratively elsewhere in Revelation, this meaning is more likely. But idolatry and sexual sin were often connected in the Roman world, and an antinomian element to this teaching cannot be ruled out.

prophetess, appropriately nicknamed "Jezebel" (Rev 2:20) after the idolatrous Israelite queen. Given the pervasive influence of the trade guilds in Thyatira, it is plausible that the issue of idolatry centered on Christians' participation in guild feasts, which inevitably involved the worship of patron gods.[9] For Christians to opt out of joining the guilds and participating in their celebrations would have carried serious economic and social repercussions, not least a potential loss of livelihood. John sees Christians in both Pergamum and Thyatira in danger of imbibing practices that were quite normal in Roman culture but would involve them in a syncretistic compromise with paganism. As a result, the exalted Christ's message to these churches is not one of consolation, but rather of stern warning and a call to repent (Rev 2:16, 21-23).

The church in Ephesus, while sharing a common problem with the communities in Pergamum and Thyatira, reacts to it in an altogether different way. This church is praised for its aggressive stance against false "apostles" (Rev 2:2-3, 6). But the Ephesians' intolerance of error and their hatred of heresy had left them with a gaping hole in their congregational life—they had abandoned their first love for God and for others. As G. B. Caird elegantly comments, "They had set out to be defenders of the faith, arming themselves with the heroic virtues of truth and courage, only to discover that in the battle they had lost the one quality without which all others are worthless."[10] Consequently, Christ's targeted word for the Ephesians is to remember, repent and return to the love they had lost (Rev 2:5).

Finally, the letters to Sardis and Laodicea address a somewhat different situation. Here Christians are apparently facing neither an external threat in the form of persecution nor internal pressure from false teachers. The great pitfall for these churches is their own material success and self-sufficiency. In both cases, a chasm separates outward appearance and reality. The congregation at the prosperous city of Sardis has a reputation ("a name") for being alive but is in fact more of a corpse than a living church (Rev 3:1). The church in Laodicea— a city that prided itself on being wealthy enough to rebuild after an earthquake without any help from Rome—thought it was rich and needed nothing. In truth, it is poor and wretched. Famed for its superior wool and production of high quality clothing, it stands shamed and naked (Rev 3:17-18). Like the city's insipid water supply, the Laodiceans' complacency makes Christ sick (Rev 3:16). In contrast to the other letters, there is little to commend in these churches. They

---

[9] For the importance of trade guild feasts as a background for the letter to Thyatira, see Hemer, *Letters to the Seven Churches*, pp. 107-9, 120-23; Beale, *Book of Revelation*, pp. 30, 261.

[10] G. B. Caird, *The Revelation of St. John the Divine* (New York: Harper and Row, 1966), p. 31.

had assimilated to the values, lifestyle and affluence of the cities around them so fully that they were oblivious to their danger. Christ's message to Sardis and Laodicea comes not as a comforting balm but as a jolt, like an electric shock. Their material well-being and comfort had lulled them into a false sense of security. They need to "wake up," open their eyes and repent (Rev 3:2-3, 18-19)— or face Christ's judgment.

Seven churches, seven distinct messages. We might call them seven Spirit-mediated "contextualizations," for each letter includes a call to "listen to what the Spirit is saying to the churches." How then do these various prophetic words for the churches with their different contexts and needs relate to the rest of the book of Revelation? As John's Spirit-inspired visions unfold in Revelation, it becomes clear that each of these churches is a part of a common situation in a world dominated by an oppressive Roman system of power near the end of the first century.[11] More than that, they are enlisted in the eschatological battle between God and evil that the rest of the book describes. This is the significance of the promises to "the one who conquers" that are given at the end of each of the letters (Rev 2:7, 11, 17, 26; 3:5, 12, 21). Despite their different situations, the churches are all called to be victorious in the cosmic conflict to come and to share in the end-time destiny that God has planned for all of his creation. Richard Bauckham is right that "while the book as a whole explains what the war is about and how it must be won, the message to each church alerts that church to what is specific about its section of the battlefield."[12]

As a result, each of the churches must hear and respond to the message of the rest of the book from the perspective of its own need, whether that message comes as a word of consolation or as a warning of judgment. Although the message of Revelation 4—21 speaks to all the churches, parallels between the exalted Christ's messages in chapters 2 and 3 and the following description of a world under Satan's power enables each church to see itself and its problems as part of the wider cosmic struggle. Thus the persecution that even now threatens Smyrna and Philadelphia prefigures the oppression of the faithful that is to come and the need for the church to patiently endure, even to the point of death (Rev 6:9-11; 7:14; 9:5-6; 12:11; 13:7, 10, 15; 16:6; 17:6; 18:24; 19:2; 20:4). Again, the specific sins associated with the Nicolaitans and Jezebel—idolatry and fornication— typify pagan society as a whole (Rev 9:20-21) as well as the beast (Rev 13:4, 8) and Babylon the harlot (Rev 17:1-2, 5; 19:2). Jezebel's efforts to "deceive" the

---

[11]Richard Bauckham, *The Theology of the Book of Revelation* (Cambridge: Cambridge University Press, 1993), pp. 14-15.
[12]Ibid., p. 14.

church in Thyatira are echoed in the deceptions of Satan (Rev 12:9; 20:3, 8, 10), the false prophet (Rev 13:14; 19:20) and Babylon (Rev 18:23). The warning for the believers in Pergamum and Thyatira is clear: through their cozy compromise with Roman religion, they are themselves in danger of worshiping the beast. Furthermore, the smug affluence of the church in Laodicea is mirrored in the picture of Babylon in chapter 18 as the very image of arrogance and self-indulgent consumption. For these Christians, the road to riches has been paved with easy accommodation and a collusion with the exploitative economic system of Rome. Their repentance "will be equivalent to coming out of Babylon, as God's people are urged to do, renouncing her sins lest they share her judgment."[13]

We see, then, that the letters to the seven churches, brimming with local allusions and focused on the issues that were specific to each congregation, allow John to contextualize his prophetic message to the situation at hand. At the same time, each of the churches must hear and apply John's visions of God's coming salvation and judgment in the rest of the book in a somewhat different way, depending on its own failings and needs. Might not a similar process continue to guide our reading of Revelation today? For example, Christians who are facing persecution and oppression may particularly need to hear Revelation's message of consolation to Smyrna and Philadelphia, and to receive strength to endure from the rest of the book. On the other hand, Christ's words of warning against complacency to Sardis and Laodicea may speak with uncommon power and relevance to Christians living in affluent societies, giving them an arresting perspective from which to read Revelation as a whole.

FAMILIAR FORMS AND SYMBOLS

Seven-headed beasts and bottomless pits. Locusts with human faces and tails like scorpions. The often bizarrely symbolic and imaginary character of Revelation has contributed much to its being read noncontextually. There is no doubt that this is a different literary landscape than the occasional arguments of Paul's letters or the historical narratives of the Gospels and Acts. John has chosen to place his message to the churches in the *form* of an apocalypse (Rev 1:1), a highly visionary type of religious literature that would have been quite familiar to people of his time. Revelation shares many of the standard features that readers of apocalypses would have come to expect, such as the communication of heavenly mysteries to a human seer and the extensive use of symbols. It also reflects in many ways an apocalyptic mindset. We witness, for example, an acute contrast between the present evil age and the age to come, when God's final

---

[13]Ibid., p. 123. See also deSilva, *Hope of Glory*, pp. 181-82.

victory over Satan will vindicate the saints, bring judgment on the wicked, and usher in a new heaven and a new earth.[14] An apocalypse provides John with an appropriate literary vehicle for addressing a context in which the people of God and the hostile pagan world, embodied by Rome, are on a collision course. John, however, alters and adapts this common literary form in light of his own Christian theology and his immediate pastoral concerns.

Crucially, this book is not only an "apocalypse"; it is also a "prophecy" (Rev 1:3). John sees himself standing in the Old Testament and Christian prophetic tradition, delivering God's authoritative messages to a concrete historical situation—the churches in Asia Minor in the late first century. Unlike other apocalyptists, John writes under his own name, not that of an ancient figure such as Enoch or Moses. His visions are not sealed up for some distant future time, when people would finally be able to understand them (Rev 22:10; cf. Dan 12:4, 9). Instead, he self-consciously speaks as a Christian prophet to his contemporary fellow believers in the seven churches in Asia (Rev 1:4, 11). What is more, this prophetic apocalypse as a whole appears in the format of a letter (Rev 1:4-6; 22:21), which allows John to address the concrete needs of his audience with prophetic wisdom and pastoral concern.

The knowledge that John's book is oriented toward a specific context and audience bears profound implications for how we read it. It means that the mysterious images of Revelation cannot be viewed as a secret code that was unintelligible to John's contemporaries but waits to be "cracked" by Christian readers at some later point in time, thereby unveiling a script for end-time history. Nor are they simply timeless symbols of the eternal struggle between good and evil. In the first place, the visionary imagery of Revelation enables John's audience to see their own concrete situation from a new transcendent vantage point. Richard Bauckham captures this well:

> John (and thereby his readers with him) is taken up into heaven in order to see the world from the heavenly perspective. He is given a glimpse behind the scenes of history so that he can see what is really going on in the events of his time and place. He is also transported in vision into the final future of the world, so that he can see the present from the perspective of what its final outcome must be, in God's ultimate purpose for human history.[15]

---

[14]For more on the characteristics of apocalyptic literature, see David E. Aune, *Revelation 1-5* (Dallas: Word, 1997), pp. lxxvi-xc; L. J. Kreitzer, "Apocalyptic, Apocalypticism," in *Dictionary of the Later New Testament and Its Developments*, ed. Ralph P. Martin and Peter H. Davids (Downers Grove, Ill.: InterVarsity Press, 1997), pp. 55-68.

[15]Bauckham, *Theology of the Book*, p. 7.

Sharply put, John's visions are intended to create a new symbolic world for his readers, one that opposes the Roman imperial worldview that dominated their horizon.[16]

In order to do this, John taps a common reservoir of symbols from the cultural world he shares with his audience—images from the Old Testament and Judaism as well as the Greco-Roman world. As G. B. Caird observed some time ago, many of these images would have been quite recognizable to John's readers, just as modern readers are able to understand conventional symbols they encounter in political cartoons.[17] Revelation co-opts and reworks familiar symbols *from* its readers' world in order to provide an alternative vision *of* their world. For example, in chapter 17 John pictures Rome as a woman who is seated on many waters and on a scarlet beast full of blasphemous names, with seven heads and ten horns. She is adorned with fine clothing and jewels, and the name "Babylon the great" is written on her forehead (Rev 17:1-5). Even though Rome is never actually named, this woman's identity for John's audience would have been unmistakable. Rome was well known for its command of the seas (many waters), its worship of emperors (blasphemous names), and its ostentatious wealth and luxury. Later, an angel tells John that the seven heads of the beast on which the woman is "seated" are actually seven mountains—a clear allusion to the seven hills on which Rome was built (Rev 17:9). Moreover, the wicked Old Testament city of Babylon frequently symbolized Rome in Jewish and Christian writings. John paints Rome as a woman—but not as the familiar goddess Roma, the mother figure who personified Roman power and dignity and who was worshipped in the temples of Asia Minor. Instead, she is "the mother of whores and of earth's abominations" (Rev 17:5), besotted with her own prosperity and committing fornication in her idolatrous worship. This debauched whore, John announces, is the *true* portrait of the great and glorious city. When Revelation envisions Rome as a grotesque beast rising from the sea (chapter 13), or as a cruel and seductive harlot, or as the fallen and desolate city of Babylon, it invites its readers to reimagine the political and religious realities of their world from a transformed, heavenly perspective.

At times, John's images draw upon the popular myths and fears of his contemporary world, thereby connecting his descriptions with his readers' experience. The picture of armies attacking from across the Euphrates in the east, for example, suggests the paranoia people felt in the Roman Empire concerning a

---

[16]Ibid., p. 8; Elisabeth Schüssler Fiorenza, *The Book of Revelation: Justice and Judgment* (Philadelphia: Fortress, 1985), pp. 187-92.

[17]Caird, *Revelation*, p. 6.

Parthian invasion, which would shatter Rome's peace and prosperity (Rev 9:13-19; 16:12). Likewise, Revelation's vision of the beast that is healed from a mortal wound and rises from the abyss to make war is an allusion to a contemporary myth in which the ruthless emperor Nero one day returns to reclaim his throne and avenge his enemies (Rev 13:3; 17:8, 11).[18] John's picture of Christ holding "the keys of Death and Hades" (Rev 1:18) may also tap into popular pagan mythology. Various pagan deities, especially the goddess Hekate (who was called the "keybearer"), were thought to hold the keys to the gates of Hades, symbolizing control of the underworld.[19] Revelation assures Hellenistic readers, however, that Christ alone has power to release people from the realm of death through his resurrection from the dead.

A fascinating example of John's reworking of pagan myths in the service of the gospel unfolds in the story of the pregnant woman and the dragon in Revelation 12:1-6. Various ancient cultures had similar stories, including Egypt, Mesopotamia and the Greco-Roman world. In the latter version, which would have been most widely known in Roman Asia, the goddess Leto, pregnant with Apollo, is pursued by the great dragon Python in order to kill both her and her child. But Leto is rescued by Poseidon, who hides her on a remote island under the water. Four days after Apollo is born, he avenges his mother by slaying the dragon. Roman imperial propaganda milked the myth to its own advantage, portraying the woman as the goddess Roma, who was the queen of heaven, and Apollo as the divine emperor, the world's savior. John, however, recontextualizes the pagan myth (using elements from the Jewish tradition[20]) and gives the story a new, distinctively Christian interpretation. As Craig R. Koester explains:

> [I]n [John's] version the woman in labor is not a pagan goddess, but the people of God; the child is not the emperor but Christ; and the dragon represents the forces that oppose Christ and threaten his church. In the end, a story that was used to celebrate the popular culture is now transformed in a way that helps readers resist being assimilated to that culture.[21]

We might say that Revelation "demythologizes" the myth by finding its ulti-

---

[18]Richard Bauckham, *The Climax of Prophecy: Studies on the Book of Revelation* (Edinburgh: T & T Clark, 1993), pp. 407-52.

[19]See David E. Aune, "The Apocalypse of John and Graeco-Roman Revelatory Magic," *NTS* 33 (1987): 484-89.

[20]See Beale, *Revelation*, pp. 624-25. E.g., the figure of the dragon is also familiar in the Old Testament, where it symbolizes evil kingdoms that oppress God's people (e.g., Ps 74:13-14; Is 27:1; Ezek 32:2-3; Dan 7:1-7).

[21]Craig R. Koester, *Revelation and the End of All Things* (Grand Rapids, Mich.: Eerdmans, 2001), p. 118.

mate fulfillment in the history of Jesus of Nazareth, who is the true conqueror of evil and the one Savior of the world.[22] Such visions find points of contact with the beliefs, images and myths of the pagan world in order to drive home the seer's prophetic message. John knows his world intimately, and he perceptively uses that insight both to communicate truth in a culturally compelling way and to subvert the worldview of the dominant culture.

Above all, John dips deep into the image pool of the Hebrew Scriptures in order to help his audience see their own situation in a new light. Although the Old Testament is never directly quoted, the Apocalypse is drenched with scriptural allusions and echoes from beginning to end. In general, Revelation does not see the events and realities it describes simply as the fulfillment of prophecy. Rather, it creatively reworks and adapts Old Testament language, images and symbols and applies them to the new eschatological context of John and his readers.[23] Thus the plagues of Exodus against Egypt—hail, water made blood, sores, darkness, locusts, frogs, death—are recast in God's end-time plagues of the trumpets (Rev 8:6—9:21) and the bowls (Rev 16:1-21) on the whole earth. Old Testament prophecies that foretold the doom of proud and oppressive Tyre and Babylon prefigure God's certain judgment on Rome, the present embodiment of wicked "Babylon" for John's readers. The church's faithful and prophetic witness to the world is foreshadowed in the ministries of the Old Testament figures of Moses and Elijah (Rev 11:3-13). The biblical city of Megiddo—scene of Old Testament battles in which Israel's enemies are defeated—is transformed into "Armageddon" (which plays on its name), the place where the kings of the earth gather in anticipation of God's final judgment on his foes (Rev 16:16).

There is perhaps no more striking example of Revelation's reinterpretation of Old Testament images than John's treatment of the symbol of the temple in his vision of the New Jerusalem. In Ezekiel's vision of the Jerusalem to come, which serves as a precedent, the temple was the dominant feature (Ezek 40—48). John, however, transforms the image by eliminating it from the holy city altogether. He immediately clarifies, however, that the city's temple is actually "*the Lord God the Almighty and the Lamb*" (Rev 21:22). Ezekiel's temple morphs, so to speak, into the Almighty's throne. In reality, the entire New Jerusalem, with its perfect cubic shape, becomes a sanctuary like the holy of holies that is filled with the glory and unimpeded presence of God.[24] John repeatedly, under the

---

[22]Grant R. Osborne, *Revelation* (Grand Rapids, Mich.: Baker, 2002), p. 454.

[23]Paul J. Achtemeier, Joel B. Green and Marianne Meye Thompson, *Introducing the New Testament: Its Literature and Theology* (Grand Rapids, Mich.: Eerdmans, 2001), p. 563.

[24]Koester, *Revelation*, p. 198.

influence of the Spirit, recycles familiar events and images in ways that transcend the old meaning and frame of reference. This is not only an imaginative way of doing contextual theology, but it also lets John draw back the curtain on the eschatological realities that provide his readers with a new lens through which to envision their world.

Re-imagining the Gospel Story

No less than Paul's letters or Acts, Revelation is concerned with the gospel of God's saving designs for humanity and all of creation in Jesus Christ. But that gospel story is transposed into a new apocalyptic key. John does theology in light of his contextual aim to call his readers to resist compromise with the earthly powers and to motivate them to endurance and faithfulness in light of God's ultimate purpose for the world. I will highlight several distinctive emphases of John's theological vision.

A sovereign God.

> Holy, holy, holy,
> the Lord God the Almighty,
>   who was and is and is to come. (Rev 4:8b)

Revelation's prophetic vision is unashamedly *theocentric*. Perhaps more than any other New Testament book, it spotlights God as the sovereign Ruler of the universe, the Creator and Judge, who is Lord over all of history. Bauckham is on target that Revelation's entire theological vision might be seen as a fulfillment of the first three petitions of the Lord's prayer: "God's name be hallowed, his kingdom come, his will be done, on earth as it is in heaven" (Mt 6:9-10).[25] This is a highly relevant emphasis, since the Roman Empire propagated its power in religious terms and claimed ultimate sovereignty over the world.[26] John's vision of a transcendent and sovereign God is reflected first of all in the distinctive names for God in Revelation. He is the "Almighty" *(pantokratōr)*, a word found almost exclusively in this book within the New Testament (Rev 1:8; 4:8; 11:17; 15:3; 16:7, 14; 19:6, 15; 21:22). He is the "Alpha and the Omega" (Rev 1:8; 21:6; cf. 22:13) and "the One who is, was, and is to come" (Rev 1:4, 8; 4:8; 11:17; 16:5); his power embraces history from beginning to end. Revelation sees God's salvation and judgment from a cosmic perspective. God is before all things, he is their creator (Rev 4:11), and he will bring all things to their fulfillment in the end.

---

[25]Bauckham, *Theology of the Book*, p. 40.
[26]Ibid., p. 34.

Second, in the theological heart of the book, chapters 4 and 5, John is taken up into the heavenly throne room, where he sees God in all of his divine majesty and sovereign splendor. The picture of the throne, which appears no less than forty-six times in the book, is one of the key symbols of Revelation. The seer's vision of the Almighty One on the throne in chapter four carries political as well as religious implications for the Christians of Asia Minor. David Aune has shown that Revelation's description of the heavenly throne room scene bears so many resemblances to the ceremonial practice of the Roman imperial court and cult that John's readers couldn't help but make the connection.[27] The message is clear: if God is on the throne reigning over the world, then Caesar is not. Domitian, the current emperor, claimed the title "our Lord and God."[28] But John proclaims that there is only one "Lord and God," and he alone is worthy of glory and honor (Rev 4:11). Every earthly power is doomed, and in the end the enthroned One will overcome all resistance to his rule. Koester well perceives that "[t]he heavenly throne is the vantage point from which John wants readers to look out upon the world of human affairs."[29] John is taken up into heaven in order to see and relate what must become true on earth.

Third, the appropriate response to this sovereign and holy God and to Christ is *worship*. Worship is a central theme not only in chapters 4 and 5, but throughout Revelation. Accompanying and interpreting God's triumphs, scenes of heavenly worship break out repeatedly at critical junctures in the remainder of the book (e.g., Rev 7:11-17; 11:16-18; 15:3-4; 19:1-8). For the churches of Roman Asia, worship is both a political and a religious act. The worship of the one true God in heaven is set in sharp conflict with the idolatrous worship of the beast on earth (Rev 13:4, 8, 12, 15; 14:9, 11; 16:2; 19:20), which is embodied for John's Asian readers by the pervasive imperial cult. When the community sings Revelation's songs of worship, it declares that God, not Caesar, is Lord. The beast's throne may appear to be mighty and eternal, but it cannot survive; it is but a whimpering parody of God the Almighty's sovereign rule. This is a note that John's readers, whether threatened by Roman power or tempted through their own compromise to honor the beast, need to hear like a trumpet's blare.

A slaughtered Lamb. We have seen that Paul's letters presuppose a sacred story about God and Christ and that the Gospels and Acts communicate their Christology in narrative form. Revelation also tells stories. Typical of apocalyptic

---

[27]See David E. Aune, "The Influence of Roman Imperial Court Ceremonial on the Apocalypse of John," *BR* 28 (1983): 5-26. Common practices included the presentation of gold crowns, prostration, torchbearers and the singing of hymns.

[28]Aune, *Revelation 1-5*, pp. 310-11.

[29]Koester, *Revelation*, p. 75.

literature, John narrates his own experiences (e.g., Rev 1:9-11) as a framework for his visions, and the visions themselves appear in story form. But beneath the various tales the Apocalypse tells—stories of heavenly throne rooms, breaking open of seals, bowls of judgment and cosmic wars—is an underlying macronarrative about the sovereign God acting to redeem all things in Christ.[30] It is a story that spans the entire horizon of sacred history from God's act of creation to consummation, from beginning to end. This story incorporates the previous biblical story of God and Israel, but it also reconfigures it. Once again, the crucial and defining narrative for God's saving purpose is the story of Christ.

The Christ story that underlies Revelation has a past, a present and a future. Looking to the past, John refers to Jesus' preexistence (Rev 1:17-18; 3:14; 13:8) and alludes symbolically to his birth (Rev 12:1-5). But neither Jesus' prehistory nor his earthly life is emphasized. The focal point of Jesus' messianic career for John, as it was for Paul, is Christ's death, resurrection and exaltation. This is the saving event by which all of history is to be understood. It is in the vision of the heavenly throne room in chapter 5 that the significance of the Christ event comes into sharpest focus. The seer begins to weep when no one is found who is worthy to open the scroll and to break its seals. John, however, is consoled by one of the twenty-four elders: "Do not weep. See, the Lion of the tribe of Judah, the Root of David, has conquered, so that he can open the scroll and its seven seals" (Rev 5:5; cf. 22:16). The titles Lion of Judah and Root of David evoke nationalistic Jewish hopes for a Davidic Messiah who would defeat all of Israel's enemies. We expect to encounter a glorious figure like the one John describes in Revelation 1:12-20, with eyes like a flame of fire, feet like bronze, a voice like the sound of many waters, and a two-edged sword coming from his mouth. Instead we see "a Lamb . . . as if it had been slaughtered" (Rev 5:6). Through this sacrificial Lamb—which recalls the Passover lamb of Exodus (Ex 12:1-27; 1 Cor 5:7) and Isaiah's picture of the Servant as a lamb led to the slaughter (Is 53:7, 10)—people are redeemed from all nations (Rev 5:9-10). With this penetrating symbol of the slain Lamb, Revelation completely transforms the Jewish notion of what the Messiah of David would be like. True, he is a conqueror, but he conquers through *suffering* and *death*, not by force. This Lamb

---

[30]On the role of narrative in Revelation, see M. Eugene Boring, "Narrative Christology in the Apocalypse," *CBQ* 54 (1992): 702-23, to which I am indebted for some of the following discussion. Boring sees four layers of narrative in Revelation: (1) John's account of his own experiences and their bearing on the churches; (2) the visions of God, Christ, and the heavenly throne room; (3) the dramatic stories that unfold within the heavenly visions; and (4) the comprehensive narrative world presupposed by each of the first three; i.e., the underlying story. Our primary concern in this context is with levels (2) and (4).

also turns Rome's notions of power and militaristic conquest on their head. The very One who was crucified at the hands of brute Roman might vanquishes all of God's enemies by submitting to death. A more countercultural perspective within the world of John's readers could hardly be imagined.

Christ as the slain but conquering Lamb becomes the master symbol for the whole story of Jesus in Revelation. In the "present" time of John and the church, the story of Christ is intertwined with that of his followers. As he conquers, they too must defeat the enemies of God (Rev 3:21; 12:11; 15:2). As he suffered and died, so they must be ready to face suffering and martyrdom (Rev 1:9; 2:10; 6:9-11; 12:11; 13:7-10). The pattern of Christ functions as a call to discipleship for John's audience. But victory for God's people is assured, because in Jesus' sacrificial death Satan has already been vanquished; the faithful "have conquered him by the blood of the Lamb" (Rev 12:11). This is a word of hope to Christians in the midst of crisis. As Grant R. Osborne reminds us, "the great victory in the Apocalypse occurs not at Armageddon but at the cross."[31]

Nevertheless, the stories of the Lamb and his followers are unfinished stories. Christ's victory still awaits its goal. In contrast to, say, Colossians, where we saw a prominent emphasis on the salvation already realized in Christ, the distinctive focus of Revelation is on the end of the story, which remains in the future. Satan and the self-deifying power of Rome continue to rebel against God and to oppose his people. A final showdown is yet to come. And so when the earthly political powers represented by the beast and the ten kings wage war against the Lamb in John's vision of the future, they are "conquered" (Rev 17:14). Christ is pictured as a divine Warrior on a white horse leading his followers ("the armies of heaven") to victory in the final battle against the beast and its allies. The name blazoned on his robe is "King of kings and Lord of lords" (Rev 19:16; 17:14). He judges and utterly crushes the "kings of the earth" (Rev 19:19). Revelation's focus on Christ's final defeat of the political forces that oppose him is somewhat different than in 1 Corinthians 15:24-25, where his "enemies" are in the first place death and the cosmic powers (cf. Col 2:15). John, in contrast, stresses that the coming victory of Christ will unmask every earthly authority that opposes God's reign. This raises a direct challenge to Rome's claim to eternal rule, a myth proclaimed by poets and pictured on the coins of the day. John's readers need to see Roman imperial power for what it truly is and to recognize the danger of accommodating to a doomed force.

But not only does the eschatological Lamb conquer and judge. In the end, he will come for his people (Rev 22:7, 12, 20) and take them as his bride (Rev 19:7,

---

[31]Osborne, *Revelation*, p. 34.

9; 21:9). Along with God he will welcome and care for them in the New Jerusalem, and they will worship him forever (Rev 21:22-23; 22:1, 3). The Christ who will come in the future is the same slaughtered Lamb who has in love redeemed his people through his death on the cross (Rev 1:5; 5:9). At the conclusion of the book, the One who is faithful and true gives them his personal promise: "Surely I am coming soon" (Rev 22:20). The story has a blessed consummation.

John's theologizing in Revelation is therefore anchored in the gospel story, which tells of a Creator God who reasserts his sovereignty over all of his creation. But God acts through Christ, and the story of Jesus is the crucial story line in John's prophetic vision. Revelation retells this tale in an apocalyptic form, borrowing traditional symbols that challenge readers to reimagine their world. At the same time, apocalyptic images and timetables are reinterpreted in light of John's conviction that Christ died, was raised and is now alive. The militaristic lion of Judah is transformed into a sacrificial Lamb (Rev 5:5-6). The Son of Man comes not only as a future judge (Rev 14:14); he is present now among the churches and calls them to repent (Rev 1:13, 20; 2:1, 5). He himself is the bridegroom, the temple and the lamp of the New Jerusalem (Rev 21:9, 22-23). Revelation's particular emphasis on the conclusion of the story—Jesus' final victory over God's enemies—is essential to its rhetorical purpose. For as we have seen, the end of history provides the field of vision from which the truth about the present comes to light. Jesus' promise to come again soon functions both as an encouragement to be faithful and as an urgent "wake up call" to the church.

A witnessing community. Revelation's contextualized expression of the gospel about God and Christ demands a response from John's hearers. Above all, they are called to be faithful witnesses to God's truth, following the "faithful and true" witness of Jesus (Rev 3:14; cf. 1:5; 19:11). This witness *(martys)* in the first place means bearing verbal testimony to the word and truth of God, as well as obedience to God's commands (Rev 12:17). But Jesus' testimony led him to the cross, and those who follow him must also bear witness and suffer. They are to hold fast to the "testimony of Jesus" (Rev 2:17; 19:10; cf. 1:2, 9), which means not only their testimony *to* Jesus, but also their bearing Jesus' own testimony to the truth through their words and through their lives.[32]

In the world in which John and his readers live, bearing witness to Jesus is a costly business (cf. Rev 2:13). John is convinced that when the church prophetically testifies to God's truth against the idolatry and injustice of Rome, against its claims to ultimate allegiance, the result may be the shedding of the

---

[32]See A. A. Trites, *The New Testament Concept of Witness*, Society for New Testament Studies Monograph Series 31 (Cambridge: Cambridge University Press, 1977), pp. 156-64.

blood of the saints. John beholds in heaven "the souls of those who had been slaughtered for the word of God and for the testimony they had given" (Rev 6:9). But through their very suffering and death they participate in Christ's triumph over Satan and evil: "they have conquered him [Satan] by the blood of the Lamb and by the word of their testimony, for they did not cling to life even in the face of death" (Rev 12:11). Here the church overcomes the Devil by two means: first, by the atoning death of Christ on the cross,[33] which has already defeated Satan; and second, by the witness of their own martyrdom. In other words, to follow Jesus on the way of the cross, the path of powerless suffering and death, *is* their victory.[34]

Yet the language of "conquering" through martyrdom poses a dilemma for John's audience. The deaths of the faithful saints have already been described as a victory for the beast (Rev 11:7). From the standpoint of the "earth-dwellers" who worship the beast, the exercise of political and military power against the witnesses of Jesus looks for all the world like an utter triumph (Rev 13:7-8; cf. 13:15). Even the Christians to whom John is writing—a largely powerless and marginalized community that is seemingly at the mercy of the overwhelming force of the great empire—might be tempted to see things from that perspective.[35] Why should they resist accommodation when resisting would make them even more weak and vulnerable? Why should they continue to bear witness when it will only turn them into victims? Is the fate of God's faithful a victory for the Lamb or for the beast? This is the critical question that John raises for his readers. Bauckham's insightful analysis is worth quoting at length:

> Is the world a place in which military and political might carries all before it or is it one in which suffering witness to the truth prevails in the end? Thus Revelation offers its readers prophetic discernment guided by the core of Christian faith; that Jesus Christ won his comprehensive victory over all evil by suffering witness. . . . Whereas modern terminology calls martyrdom 'passive resistance', John's military imagery makes it just as active as any physical warfare. While rejecting the apocalyptic militancy that called for literal holy war against Rome, John's message is not, 'Do not resist!' It is, 'Resist!—but by witness and martyrdom, not by violence.' On the streets of the cities of Asia, John's readers are not to compromise but to resist the idolatry of the pagan state and pagan society. In so doing they will be playing an indispensable part in the working-out of the Lamb's victory.[36]

---

[33]This is a more natural interpretation of the phrase "by the blood of the Lamb" than as a reference to the death of Christian martyrs (as e.g., Bauckham, *Theology of the Book*, p. 75).
[34]Osborne, *Revelation*, p. 43.
[35]Bauckham, *Theology of the Book*, p. 90.
[36]Ibid., pp. 91-92.

We see then that the militaristic language and imagery that plays such a large role in Revelation is resignified in light of the gospel paradox of conquering through suffering, victory through defeat, and overcoming through sacrificial love. God's holy warriors "follow the Lamb *wherever* he goes" (Rev 14:4). Although not all will be required to die, all must be *prepared* to die. This is the call to "endurance and faithfulness of the saints" (Rev 13:10; cf. 14:12). But Revelation also gives its readers the confidence that the saints' faithful testimony even to the point of death will have the magnetic effect of drawing people from the world's nations to worship the one true God (Rev 11:3-13; 15:1-4; cf. 5:9; 7:9; 14:6; 21:3, 24, 26). Courageous witness is a powerful instrument of mission.

Even as I write these words, I have received a report from South Asia of a Christian witness who has laid down his life because of his testimony to the truth. For a host of Christians in our own world, suffering for the sake of Christ is a present experience and martyrdom a real possibility. Yet Revelation also asks Christians who live in relative comfort to stand in solidarity with history's vulnerable victims, as it did in John's day. Revelation takes the perspective of the powerless and the persecuted, against the sinful use of wealth and might. Richard B. Hays recalls that the anthem of the U.S. civil rights movement, "We shall overcome," was based on the King James Version's translation of God's promise to those who "conquer" through their faithful witness, which comes at the end of each of the seven letters (Rev 2:7, 11, 17, 28; 3:5, 12, 21). "As freedom marchers from the black churches joined hands and sang 'We shall overcome someday,' " writes Hays, "they were expressing their faith that, despite their lack of conventional political power, their witness to the truth would prevail over violence and oppression."[37] This is a poignant illustration of how John's call to his first-century readers to be part of a sacrificial resistance movement against all idolatries and injustices is capable of being recontextualized in our own time.

RE-IMAGINING THE WORLD

Revelation addresses Asian churches that are living under the pressure of the pagan onslaught by calling them to an alternative vision of their world. This apocalyptic vision challenges what is normal in John's world—the status quo of the Roman Empire and its prevailing worldview—and replaces it with a new understanding of how Christians should think, believe and live in their context. One way that Revelation creates such a counterimagination is to sharpen the

---

[37]Richard B. Hays, *The Moral Vision of the New Testament: Community, Cross, New Creation: A Contemporary Introduction to New Testament Ethics* (San Francisco: HarperCollins, 1996), p. 184.

boundaries between the church and the world. Neutrality is not an option. The choices are clear: either worship the one true God who reigns on the heavenly throne or honor the earthly beast; either buy into the dominant ideology of the culture or recognize it as a diabolical deception.

As a result, the portrait of Rome that Revelation paints is entirely unflattering. Rome is vilified for its unrestrained violence against the people of God. John believes that God's designs for the world will inevitably collide with those of the Empire, and as a result, faithful servants of God will suffer. The goddess Roma, who is really a wanton whore, is "drunk with the blood of the saints and the blood of the witnesses to Jesus" (Rev 17:6; cf. 18:24). But it is not just for persecuting Christians that Revelation censures Rome. As Bauckham notes, John critiques the entire Roman system of power, which has political, economic and religious dimensions.[38] In chapter 13, the formidable beast, representing Rome's tyrannical political and military might, is worshiped by "the whole earth" (Rev 13:3). The blasphemous beast usurps the honor and allegiance that belong alone to God and to the Lamb (Rev 13:1, 5). Likewise, the image of the harlot Babylon (chapters 17—18) especially symbolizes Rome's economic wealth, gained through corruption and the exploitation of the empire. She exercises economic as well as political dominance over "the kings of the earth" (Rev 17:18)—perhaps the first century equivalent to economic globalization.[39] At the expense of others, she indulges her insatiable lust for luxury (Rev 18:3, 7). This is the point of the long list of actual Roman imports, most of them destined to feed the expensive tastes of the rich, in Revelation 18:11-13.[40] Ironically, at the very bottom of the list of cargoes is "slaves—and human lives." What should have been of greatest worth, Rome values the least. Revelation's prophetic critique scorns the Roman order for its oppressive and self-glorifying abuse of wealth and power.

From Revelation's heavenly perspective, however, the power and prosperity of Rome are all smoke and mirrors. She extends her tyranny and influence by means of a demonic sham (Rev 18:23), following the dragon Satan, "the deceiver of the whole world" (Rev 12:9). The beast from the sea is a counterfeit messiah, a demonic counterpart to Christ the Lamb. Revelation's beast parodies the Lamb's death and resurrection when it is healed of a mortal wound (Rev 13:3, 14). Its description as the one that "was and is not and is to come" (Rev

---

[38]See Bauckham, *Theology of the Book*, pp. 35-39.

[39]See Richard Bauckham, *The Bible and Mission: Christian Witness in a Postmodern World* (Grand Rapids, Mich.: Baker, 2003), p. 108.

[40]See Bauckham, *Climax of Prophecy*, pp. 350-71.

17:8; cf. 17:11) reveals a feeble attempt to mimic the Lord God, "who is and who was and who is to come" (Rev 1:4, 8; 4:8). And the beast from the land, the false prophet, deceives the "earth-dwellers" with its miracles and propaganda, which advance the divine pretensions of the beast in the form of the imperial cult (Rev 13:11-15). Using the tools of parody and irony, Revelation calls its readers to see reality as it *really* is, from God's perspective. Not surprisingly, then, we find a contrast throughout John's visions between deceit and truth, between the bogus claims to divinity of the beast and the God whose judgments and words are righteous and true (Rev 15:3; 16:7; 19:2, 11; cf. 3:14; 6:10; 21:5; 22:6).

Part of Rome's deception is tied up in a complex of popular myths that served to legitimize the ideology of Rome. Wes Howard-Brook and Anthony Gwyther have shown that one way by which Revelation tries to give its readers a radically different perception of the truth is by exposing and opposing the myths of the Roman Empire.[41] Thus Rome's claim to be the provider of peace to the world (the *Pax Romana*) is countered by Revelation's picture of the beasts and Babylon as shedders of blood (Rev 13:15; 16:6; 17:6; 18:24); the myth of Roman "Victory" *(Victoria)* through imperial conquest is debunked by the insight that true "victory" comes only to the slaughtered Lamb and those who follow him in nonviolent witness; the myth of Rome's status as the "eternal city" *(urbs aeterna)* deconstructs under the picture of endless smoke rising from Babylon's ruin (Rev 19:3: cf. 14:11; 20:10) and the vision of God and the Lamb reigning for ever and ever in the true eternal city, which comes down from heaven (Rev 22:5; cf. 1:6; 5:13; 11:15). With Rome fixed in his crosshairs, John rehearses the language and ideals of the Empire in order to subvert them. His readers must decide which "gospel" to believe: the gospel of Caesar or the gospel of Christ?

A TALE OF TWO CITIES

Another way that Revelation tries to reshape its readers' theological imagination is through giving them a picture of the alternative cities of Babylon and the New Jerusalem. In many ways, Revelation is "a Tale of Two Cities." "Babylon the great" (Rev 18:2) represents the fallen human city, embodied in the Old Testament by cities like Babel, Sodom, Tyre and especially the empire of Babylon that destroyed Jerusalem. But it is presently incarnated in the city of Rome, whose evil outstrips them all.[42] John's audience must resist the siren call of

---

[41]Howard-Brook and Gwyther, *Unveiling Empire*, pp. 113-15, 223-35.
[42]See M. Robert Mulholland Jr., *Revelation: Holy Living in an Unholy World* (Grand Rapids, Mich.: Francis Asbury Press, 1990), pp. 46-50; Bauckham, *Theology of the Book*, p. 130.

Babylon's materialism, power and idolatry, which had infiltrated their own cities of Asia Minor. Not only that, but the letters to the seven churches make it clear that agents of Babylon and the spirit of fallen Babylon were already present in their own congregations (e.g., Rev 2:14, 20; 3:17-18). Some of John's readers were in danger of becoming accomplices to the harlot's shameful deeds and thereby sharing her impending doom. They are warned to "come out of her" (Rev 18:4) and to leave Babylon behind or risk being seduced by her charms. But where should they go? They need another city to call their home.[43]

Revelation provides that alternative city in its stunning vision of the New Jerusalem, the "holy city" that descends from heaven (Rev 21:2). This image fulfills not only the Jewish and Christian vision of a heavenly Jerusalem (e.g., Is 52:1; 65:17-18; Ezek 40—48; 2 Esdras 10:27-28; Heb 11:10, 16; 13:14), but also current Greco-Roman aspirations for an ideal city where the human community lives in continuous peace and prosperity.[44] Unlike John's picture of the present "holy city," which represents the faithful saints who are oppressed by the worldly powers (Rev 11:1-3), chapters 21 and 22 offer a vision of the eschatological city that is filled with God's glory and where opposition to the Lamb and to his people has ceased. The tears of the present will be wiped away and God will make his home with humanity on earth (Rev 21:3-4). Those now dominated and dehumanized by Babylon will reign with God forever (Rev 22:5). Above all, the New Jerusalem symbolizes the immediate and uninterrupted presence of God. The heavenly throne of chapters 4—5 comes down to earth, and humans at last will see the very face of God (Rev 22:4; cf. Ex 33:20-23). This is a city worth living for, and, if need be, worth dying for.

Although the New Jerusalem belongs to the future, it stands for a vision of reality that needs to shape the church's present experience.[45] Only by "entering" God's future city will John's readers gain the proper perspective to recognize the lies and the illusions of the dominant culture. Only when their theological

---

[43]See Bauckham, *Theology of the Book*, p. 129.

[44]Harry O. Maier, *Apocalypse Recalled: The Book of Revelation after Christendom* (Minneapolis: Fortress, 2002), pp. 191-96. J. Nelson Kraybill shows that many of the physical features of the New Jerusalem (e.g., foursquare layout, water, inscriptions) mirror those of the ideal Roman city (*Imperial Cult and Commerce in John's Apocalypse* [Sheffield: Sheffield Academic Press, 1996], pp. 211-14).

[45]Bauckham, *Theology of the Book*, pp. 129-30. In spite of many valuable insights on the significance of the New Jerusalem for John's audience in the Roman empire, I cannot agree with Howard-Brook and Gwyther's reduction of the New Jerusalem to a symbol of God's activity in *present* human history (*Unveiling Empire*, pp. 158-59, 184; cf. William Stringfellow, *An Ethic for Christians and Other Aliens in a Strange Land* [Waco, Tex.: Word, 1973], e.g., 48-58). John's vision of the New Jerusalem (e.g., "death will be no more," Rev 21:4) will not be fully realized until the coming of "a new heaven and a new earth."

imaginations are captured by a vision of the life to come can they faithfully endure the trials of the impending crisis. Embracing the future will mean receiving the grace to live out the values of New Jerusalem citizenship in a world that is ruled by the power and perspective of Babylon. The force of such imagery would surely not have been lost on Christian urban dwellers in Asia. For them, allegiance to Christ would have required distancing themselves in part from the normal public life of their cities, with its unavoidable ties to idolatry.

John spotlights the competing alternatives facing his readers with numerous parallels and contrasts between the two cities. One is the "great whore," decked out in seductive luxury (Rev 17:1, 4), the other, the chaste bride of the Lamb, adorned in righteous deeds (Rev 19:8; 21:2, 9). Babylon is the dwelling place of demons (Rev 18:2), but the New Jerusalem the home of God (Rev 21:3). The harlot's splendor comes from exploiting her subjects (Rev 17:4; 18:12-13), while the bride's radiance is from the glory of God in her midst (Rev 21:11-21). Wicked Babylon is filled with abominations, impurities and illusion (Rev 17:4-5; 18:23), but the new holy city banishes everything false and unclean (Rev 21:27). Babylon the prostitute intoxicates the nations with her wine of immorality and idolatry (Rev 14:8; 17:2; 18:3), but in the heavenly Jerusalem the nations are beckoned to drink from the water of life and to be healed by the tree of life that grows beside the river (Rev 21:6; 22:1-2).[46]

John's readers must decide: which city will determine their lives in the present and shape their destiny for the future? "Those who conquer" by being part of the Lamb's resistance movement against evil will inherit the glorious blessings of the New Jerusalem (Rev 21:7). Those, however, who share in the sins of Babylon will be excluded from the holy city that is filled with God's holy presence (Rev 21:8, 27; 22:3). By offering its readers an alternate view of what is true and real—a vision of God's new world—Revelation at the same time summons God's people to live counterculturally. Resisting captivity to fallen Babylon means that they must sacrificially challenge the cultural ideologies that dominate their world. It might be a mild overstatement to call Revelation a "political resistance document,"[47] but surely part of the theological burden of John's vision is to give Christian communities that lack worldly power the courage and confidence to swim against the stream in a world that has succumbed to the beast. It is no less vital that the contemporary church has ears to hear that challenge.

---

[46]Koester, *Revelation*, p. 196. For a more extensive list of contrasts between the two cities, see Howard-Brook and Gwyther, *Unveiling Empire*, p. 160.
[47]Hays, *Moral Vision*, p. 170.

RADICAL CONTEXTUALIZATION

Revelation gives us the most consistently countercultural theological perspective of any of the New Testament writings we have examined in this study. By and large, John describes the relationship between the gospel and the dominant Roman culture, with its ideologies and institutions, in either-or categories. Revelation seems a long journey distant from Luke's description of Paul recognizing the touch of God's grace in the religious longings of the Greeks in Acts 17. For John, imperial religion is the sinister tool of Satan. It is a blockade, not a steppingstone, to the truth. Likewise, we find little in Revelation that corresponds to Paul's positive use of the Greco-Roman convention of the household code, in which he exhorts Christians to participate in existing social structures, but with a transforming difference (Col 3:18—4:1). John the seer calls his readers to separate from significant aspects of ordinary public life in the Roman Empire which he believed had been thoroughly infested with idolatry and oppression. The issue of eating idol food is a concrete example of this difference. Unlike Paul's more nuanced argument in 1 Corinthians 8—10, Revelation does not consider any possible scenarios where eating sacrificial food might *not* involve idolatrous worship (cf. 1 Cor 10:23-30). For Paul, whether to eat or not to eat idol meat depends to a large measure on the context. John, however, views the practice as a touchstone of the church's whole relationship to pagan society; he uniformly portrays it as a cold compromise with state-sponsored idolatry (Rev 2:14, 20-21).

Revelation's more radical stance in relation to the dominant culture is undoubtedly linked to the context in which John does theology. The Roman imperial cult was expanding its visibility and influence in late first-century Asia Minor. As we have seen, the majority of the churches to which John writes were under intense pressure to accommodate with the idolatrous culture around them. This was due not only to external social and economic pressures but also to groups like the Nicolaitans within their own number. Such teachers presented an alternative approach to the social order. They urged Chrisitians to "inculturate" through joining in such common social practices as those involving idol food. Thus, in response to a setting in which communities of believers were perceived to be under grave threat, either from imminent persecution or from syncretistic compromise with the pagan world, Revelation magnifies the boundaries between the church and the world to the tenth power.

Perhaps most striking of all is the tension between Revelation and other New Testament writings in their respective attitudes toward the Roman "powers-that-be." Revelation's call for Christians to "come out" of oppressive Babylon seems to be a far cry, say, from Peter's advice to "accept the authority of every human institution" and to "honor the emperor" (1 Pet 2:13, 17). And John's parody of Roman power as a diabolical beast (Rev 13) cuts a bold contrast with Paul's teaching that Roman authorities are "instituted by God" (Rom 13:1) and function as "God's servants" for the church's good (Rom 13:4, 6).

Once again, different contexts call for different responses to Roman power. A comparison between Revelation 13 and Romans 13 will illustrate the point. Revelation, we have seen, presupposes a situation in which Rome has hijacked the claim to ultimate sovereignty that belongs to God and Christ alone. As a result, John finds precious little room for common ground between the evil empire of Caesar and the glorious kingdom of Christ. Romans 13:1-7 addresses a very different situation. Apparently, Paul is concerned that if Christians refuse to pay taxes or if they engage in antisocial behavior, they would bring reproach on the church and its public witness.[48] At least in part, this passage is intended to ensure that the Christians, who are a community lacking sociopolitical power, do not jeopardize their mission in Rome, let alone their very existence, through disobedience to the civil authorities. An unstable Christian community in Rome could have the further negative effect of disrupting Paul's plans to use Rome as a base for his intended mission to Spain (Rom 15:22-24). Paul is therefore speaking to a setting in which, as James Dunn puts it, "good citizenship was also a missionary strategy which commended the gospel to those of good will."[49] Romans 13:1-7 assumes a kind of best-case scenario of Roman authorities who will execute justice and fulfill their God-established role in a generally responsible way, even to the point of commending the church for doing good (Rom 13:3).[50] This stands oceans apart from the situation envisioned by Revelation, in which obedience to Christ will inevitably set Christians on a collision course with a self-deifying power. Neither Revelation 13 nor Romans 13, then, tries to give a carefully balanced treatment of how Christians should relate to Roman rule. Rather, these are

---

[48]I agree with N. T. Wright that the passage makes good sense when it is read against the background of the recent expulsion of the Jewish community (with whom Christians would still have been largely identified) from Rome by Emperor Claudius ("Romans and the Theology of Paul," in *Pauline Theology, Volume 3: Romans*, ed. D. M. Hay and E. E. Johnson [Minneapolis: Fortress, 1995], p. 62). Christians would automatically have been suspected of antisocial behavior by the Romans, and Paul no doubt wanted to avoid another expulsion that could negatively affect Jewish Christians or the community as a whole.

[49]James D. G. Dunn, *The Theology of Paul the Apostle* (Grand Rapids, Mich.: Eerdmans, 1998), pp. 679-80.

[50]Philip H. Towner, "Romans 13:1-7 and Paul's Missiological Perspective: A Call to Political Quietism or Transformation?" in *Romans and the People of God: Essays in Honor of Gordon D. Fee on the Occasion of His 65th Birthday*, ed. S. K. Soderlund and N. T. Wright (Grand Rapids, Mich.: Eerdmans, 1999), p. 169.

contextualized theological responses to the dominant political order, each appropriate to its particular audience, circumstances and literary form.

Nevertheless, I see these two quite different responses as complementary, not mutually exclusive. Both, in fact, engage their public worlds with a missional goal, but they do so from alternative angles. Romans 13:1-7 seems to reflect the broader concerns of the New Testament household tradition to encourage Christians to positively participate in the life of society in redemptive ways.[51] Furthermore, Philip H. Towner has shown that when Paul urges Christians to "do what is good" in verse three, he co-opts the language of the cultural convention of benefaction. In the Greco-Roman world, "doing good" would normally be the obligation of the powerful and well-to-do to promote the city's welfare. But Paul turns cultural expectations upside down by encouraging the powerless and marginalized Christian community to take on the role of the noble benefactor. "Doing good," redefined in terms of Christians performing acts of humble service in love, becomes part of the church's transforming witness in its world.[52] Thus, Paul can recognize God's grace and judgment at work even through political power structures, and he sees the Christian community as a leavening influence from within its social world.

Revelation clearly takes a more "sectarian" stance toward the world and its political structures. It calls its readers to an exodus from a demonic order of idolatry and oppression (Rev 18:4) and launches a countercultural critique against it. But does John expect Christian communities simply to withdraw from their public world and passively wait for God to destroy Babylon in the end, as is sometimes assumed? On the contrary, Revelation's vision for the church is not to retreat into a cocoon of pious irrelevance, but to resist Rome's dominant ideology through its prophetic and costly witness. What is more, Revelation's bold vision of the heavenly Jerusalem *coming down* to a redeemed and sanctified creation shows that John's message is not about world denial. In the New Jerusalem even the political rulers of the nations—the "kings of the earth" who formerly cohabited with the harlot and the beast (Rev 17:2, 18; 18:3, 9; 19:19)—will bring their glory into the city and worship God and the Lamb (Rev 21:24). This is a radical optimism in the ultimate triumph of God's grace, which reframes the possibilities of grace for God's people and his creation even now. Revelation's transforming vision of the future summons the church to be an agent for the "healing of the nations" (Rev 22:2), in anticipation of the time when peoples from every language, tribe and nation will worship the holy God and the Lamb around the

---

[51]Ibid., pp. 156-60.
[52]Ibid., pp. 164-69.

throne (Rev 5:9; 7:9; 15:4; 21:3). Christians are called to embody the purity and wholeness of the life to come in their everyday world. Within the cities of Roman Asia, Christian communities resist the empire of Caesar by being outposts of another kingdom, the empire of God and the slain Lamb.

Hence in Romans 13 and the book of Revelation we discover two different but complementary theological visions. Each spotlights one side of the church's relationship to the Empire; each shows sensitivity to the particular needs of the communities they address. Surely both of these perspectives are still needed today. There are times when the Christian community must take a costly prophetic stand over against the dominant order. And there are also times when Christians are called to live within the institutions of their culture, recognizing their positive, God-given role and serving as yeast that will bring about their ultimate transformation. How these responses are practically worked out will depend much upon the given political realities and options that are available to God's people. But the variety of perspectives we find in the New Testament reminds us that the church must continually discern and reassess its relationship to the power structures of its world. It likewise illustrates the broader concern of this book that the New Testament writers do not do theology in a uniform way, marching in step like an army. Instead they play different variations on the one gospel of God in Christ, each allowing the theme to be heard, but in fresh and appropriate forms.

CONCLUSION

Revelation offers a highly contextualized theological response to the situation of Christians living in a pagan society who are besieged by the oppressive engines of Roman power and idolatry. Part of that response is to demolish its readers' current attitude toward the status quo and replace it with a radically transformed vision of the world. The Apocalypse thus gives us a distinctive perspective within the New Testament on the relationship between the gospel and the dominant culture. I have intentionally concentrated on Revelation's contextual message for its first readers rather than the present and future implications of that prophetic message. Nevertheless, Revelation's apocalyptic images and perspective on the world transcend first-century Asia and Rome. How, then, might Revelation's re-visioning of reality inform the church's theological task today?[53]

First, our theologizing can still be shaped by John's alternative vision of the world. Revelation's powerful and evocative images force us to see things in a new

---

[53]See especially the valuable discussion in Bauckham, *Theology of the Book*, pp. 159-64, some of which informs the following discussion.

light. They call us to experience no less than a renewed theological imagination. Images that spoke so forcefully to John's contemporaries deal with ultimate issues that continue to find fresh analogies today. Rome was only one of many actors to play Babylon's part.[54] Babylon and her sins are recast in new roles again and again in human history, including on our own world stage. The Lamb's end-time victory over the beast calls us to expose and resist the commercial, political or military empires that oppose God's rule in every generation. Revelation's transformed world of vision can therefore give us a perspective from which to do theology in our own world. It grants us eyes to challenge the worldviews and symbols of the dominant culture that enthrone corrupt power and glorify materialism. What shape this cultural critique takes must, of course, always be contextualized, but Revelation gives us a vantage point from which to reimagine our world.

Second, Revelation teaches us that authentic contextual theology must challenge the *church*, as well as the world.[55] As in the first century, churches today all too often compromise with fallen Babylon. Modern-day Laodicean churches can be deceived into becoming enamored with their own numerical success, buildings, budgets and influence. Too often boundaries are blurred between Christians and non-Christians in their values and behaviors. Doing theology in light of John's prophetic vision involves calling God's people to genuine holiness. The church's contextual response to its culture must be constantly shaped and renewed by its vision of the thrice-holy God who is seated on the throne and by the sacrificial love of the Lamb who was slain.

Third, John's Spirit-inspired prophecy draws upon the language, literary forms and images of its world even as it challenges that world to change. This involves both recontextualizing traditional Old Testament and Jewish apocalyptic symbols for a new setting and co-opting pagan images and myths from political, economic and religious life. Revelation frequently borrows the language of the Roman Empire, but not so much to build bridges as to unmask and dethrone. John's example ought to once again encourage us to make use of all of the resources that are available to us—from Scripture and church tradition, as well as from the wider culture—in order to speak a prophetic word to our contexts as the Spirit guides today.

Fourth, Revelation models a concern for both the particular and the universal in its prophetic message. In the letters to the Asian churches (chapters 2 and 3), we discover carefully targeted messages that feature local points of contact and

---

[54]Craig Keener, *Revelation*, NIV Application Commentary (Grand Rapids, Mich.: Zondervan, 2000), p. 434.

[55]See Bauckham, *Theology of the Book*, pp. 162-63.

speak to each church's own strengths and shortcomings. On the other hand, the rest of the book narrates more generally the cosmic struggle between God and Satan's forces that leads to God's ultimate triumph, a conflict in which every church is called to take part. Taking our lead from John, we need to ensure that our theological reflection is not only truly contextualized to our particular audience, but that it also enables each local or national church to see its role in the establishing of God's universal kingdom to come.

Fifth, we can learn from Revelation that our theological response to the sovereign God and the slain Lamb must always bear faithful witness to God's truth. In many settings in our world this witness of word and life is still carried out in the presence of structures of power that absolutize their own ideology and try to squelch the truth of the gospel. In the West, however, commitment to any ultimate vision of the truth is rapidly going out of fashion, and the church faces a postmodern reduction of truth to a matter of personal style and preference. What is more, false teaching still menaces the church throughout the world. Too often Christians lack the discernment to distinguish God's truth from, say, watered-down versions of Christianity that promise easy answers and uninterrupted blessings. Revelation's portrayal of the truth is anchored in a vision of a God who reigns over history and the story of a victorious Lamb who has redeemed a people of all nations through his sacrificial death and will return bearing both judgment and salvation. John's theologizing in Revelation flows out of this vision, and ours must as well. All of our contextualized theological reflections must conform to the bedrock truth about God and Christ.

Sixth, Revelation also invites us to do theology from the perspective of the persecuted and the powerless. John speaks as a pastor/theologian who does his thinking about God and God's designs for the world while in the trenches. He addresses his audience from the rough rock of Patmos as a "companion in the suffering . . . and patient endurance that are in Jesus" (Rev 1:9 my translation). For those who do theology from such a stance, Revelation continues to proclaim a message of hope. Yeo Khiok-khng thus witnesses to the theological and pastoral importance the book of Revelation has had for persecuted believers in the Chinese house church movement: "The theology of the Lamb as One who suffers and the One who controls history speaks to the Chinese Christians the assured victory of the faithful despite the apparent domination of the evil power. It is the hope portrayed in the Book of Revelation that sustains Chinese Christians to endure to the end."[56] But it is not just oppressed and marginalized be-

---

[56]Yeo Khiok-khng, *What Has Jerusalem to Do with Beijing? Biblical Interpretation from a Chinese Perspective* (Harrisburg, Penn.: Trinity Press International, 1998), p. 234.

lievers who are called to share this vantage point. When Christians from more comfortable settings incarnate the gospel in their world, they must do so in a way that identifies with the weak and challenges abusive and idolatrous power. This identification is no less than the way of the slain Lamb.

Seventh, Revelation teaches us that theology only has true meaning in relation to *doxology*. The heavenly vision that shapes our theological reflection focuses on the worship of God the Almighty and the Lamb who was slain. As Bauckham insists, "The truth of God is known in genuine worship of God."[57] The book of Revelation is an act of worship that calls us into a life of worship. It is out of that worship that our theological perspective on the world must flow. When God's people truly worship, they proclaim that the powers and idols of the dominant culture are dethroned. Such idols can take many forms, such as success, hedonistic pleasure, nationalism, consumerism, celebrity or technology. Worship of the one holy God excludes all competing affections and all other allegiances. Without this experience of worship, our theology may be contextual, but it will be too flabby to face the injustice, the relativism and the religious pluralism in our world.

Finally, John's apocalyptic and prophetic vision reminds us of the power of imagery and imagination to communicate theological truth. Eugene Peterson describes the book of Revelation as *theological poetry*.[58] At the outset, it pronounces blessing on "the one who *reads aloud* the words of this prophecy" and "those who *hear* and who *keep* what is written in it" (Rev 1:3). Its impact is greatest when it is performed, heard and experienced, rather than simply read as a written work. The most powerful rendering of Revelation I have encountered was that of an aged preacher who acted out the Apocalypse by memory from beginning to end.

Revelation is like a cosmic musical drama, teeming with imagination, interactivity and sensation. We hear the sounds of trumpets, thunders, and worship hymns; we see the sights of multiheaded animals and mighty angels, of golden lampstands and glorious cities; we taste scrolls that are sweet in the mouth and bitter in the belly and smell fragrant incense that is the prayers of the saints.[59] Doing theology involves more than formulating rational arguments. Particularly in the world's South, the church has learned that symbols, ritual, drama and colors often express the realities of the gospel more fully and forcefully than propositional theological language. Both are needed, true. But our efforts to

---

[57]Bauckham, *Theology of the Book*, p. 162.
[58]Eugene Peterson, *Subversive Spirituality* (Grand Rapids, Mich.: Eerdmans, 1994), p. 93.
[59]On the sensory character of Revelation, see ibid., pp. 91-100.

contextualize the gospel must follow Revelation's appeal to the theological imagination and utilize a full range of images and media from our own traditions and cultural worlds. This is especially crucial in cultures that give priority to concrete thinking and to aural and nonverbal forms of communication. At the same time, Revelation might provide a first-century model for communicating theology to a twenty-first-century postmodern generation that is shaped largely through media, images and sensory experiences. Do we have ears to hear and eyes to see what and how the Spirit would speak to the churches in Asia, Africa and America today?

10 Contextualizing the Gospel Today

You ransomed for God saints from
every tribe and language and people and nation.

Rev 5:9

The gospel is a rich and compelling song capable of being sung in many variations and in different keys. Any attempt to reduce the gospel to a set of prefabricated formulations that can be carried about and unpacked for all situations runs contrary to both the spirit of the New Testament and the nature of the Christian mission. Furthermore, I have tried to show that the New Testament writings do more than give us a finished theological product. They also model for us a process of doing theology in context, of engaging their cultures and offering their audiences a fresh and fitting articulation of the good news. While we must recognize the distinctive and authoritative character of New Testament theologizing as the expression of divine revelation, the church today is called to the same essential theological task. The contemporary church must therefore be shaped not only by what the New Testament *says* (the message), but also by what it *does* (the *process* of doing theology). This does not mean that we can imitate the contextualizing activity of the New Testament apostles and theologians in a direct cookie-cutter fashion. They articulated the good news in specific historical and sociocultural circumstances that are quite different from our own. Rather, the New Testament precedents function for us primarily in an analogous and exemplary sense. I am convinced that such biblical resources are vital for our time. This final chapter will seek to build on what we have learned from our study of New Testament patterns of contextualization as a whole and apply those insights to the church's theological task in the early twenty-first century. First, I will reflect on how Scripture models for us the need to give diverse theological expression to the one gospel story, as well as to provide constraints and limits to theological innovation. I will then ask what resources the New Testament might offer us for addressing such complex issues as globalization, post-modernity, and how the gospel engages our cultural worlds. Finally, I will consider the critical role of the church as the agent for incarnating the gospel within a host of challenging contexts today.

SINGING THE STORY IN DIVERSE KEYS

There is a delightful diversity to the New Testament. All of its writings in one way or another bear witness to the transforming story of God's self-giving love, revealed above all in the life, death and resurrection of Jesus Christ. But that gospel is too pregnant with meaning to be confined to a single set of terms or images, or to one way of telling the story. The four Gospels give us four different versions of the story, each with its own theological interpretation of the gospel narrative for a target audience. The book of Acts narrates how that decisive story continues to be retold and reappropriated as it crosses new cultural and social barriers. The rest of the New Testament writings interpret and expand the gospel story by drawing out its theological and ethical implications for different audiences and communities of believers. The New Testament writers articulate the good news in distinctive ways, with their own styles, literary genres, vocabularies, perspectives and persuasive strategies. Even a single author such as Paul is capable of tailoring his theological reflection to the circumstances and pastoral needs of particular churches, so that in each case it becomes a word on target for his audience.

Although this book has concentrated on representative writings rather than the New Testament as a whole, I believe the same pattern of contextualizing the gospel could also be demonstrated in the remaining books. When we listen to the New Testament witness to Christ, what we hear is not a theological monotone but a chorus of different voices, or, as David Hesselgrave and Edward Rommen put it, "Holy Spirit-inspired 'contextualizations.'"[1] These allow the one gospel to be expressed and applied in a variety of ways, using language, images and ideas that make sense to the audience. This pattern of context-sensitive theologizing legitimates—even mandates—appropriate theological diversity in our own time. The multitextured gospel story must be told and lived out in flexible forms as it engages new contexts. Otherwise, it will never truly be understood or embodied.

To be sure, contextualization always involves a risk. When theologians in the New Testament like Paul and John incarnated the gospel for people in the Helle-

---

[1]David J. Hesselgrave and Edward Rommen, *Contextualization: Meanings, Methods, and Models* (Grand Rapids, Mich.: Baker, 1989), p. 236.

nistic world, they sometimes co-opted "dangerous new language."[2] Terms like "mystery" *(mystērion)*, "transformation" *(metamorphōsis)* or "word" *(logos)* had long-standing associations with Greek religion and philosophy; they carried the potential of being confused with their pagan meanings. What is more, the process of doing theology in the early church was at times a messy business. Groups of Christians disagreed over a whole variety of matters, such as circumcision or sacrificial food or whether or not to be a vegetarian, resulting in competing interpretations of the gospel and its ramifications. There is still a real risk that attempts at doing contextual theology will result in something other than a genuine representation of the gospel. Indeed, it might be "safer" to resist diversity altogether—to simply memorize and recycle specific formulations of Christian doctrine that were developed for another time and place. We might even be tempted to think that our tried and true ways of telling the story are timeless expressions of the "pure" gospel. But we would only be fooling ourselves. *All* theology is *contextual* theology, from the creeds of the early church to the modern "Four Spiritual Laws." All theologizing is done from a particular location and perspective whether we are conscious of it or not. Contextualized theology is not just desirable; it is the only way theology can be done. This insight ought to give us pause that, whatever rich gifts the church has received from a particular historical expression of theology (for instance, Martin Luther's understanding of "justification by faith," or John Wesley's insights into sanctification, or liberation theology's concern for socioeconomic justice), we cannot simply import these interpretations of Scripture into a new cultural setting without considering how they might need to be recontextualized.

We have much to learn from the ways that Matthew, Luke and Paul appropriated concepts and images from their world in order to shape their audiences. Some of their language was biblical and traditional, which they recast for new circumstances. Other images were creatively drawn from everyday realities in their cultural world. Both forms of appropriation are needed today. First, the New Testament writers' theological reflections, as Scripture, continue to carry foundational significance for our own theologizing. Certain metaphors and ideas, however, may speak more clearly than others to a particular setting. Thus, the Synoptic Gospels' image of Jesus as Exorcist and the emphasis on Christ's victory over the powers in Colossians and Ephesians will be especially relevant among traditionally animistic peoples, for whom the issue of freedom from evil spiritual forces is of paramount concern. On the other hand, a biblical metaphor like rec-

---

[2]Brian D. McLaren, "The Method, the Message, and the Ongoing Story," in *The Church in Emerging Culture: Five Perspectives*, ed. Leonard Sweet (Grand Rapids, Mich.: Zondervan, 2003), p. 209.

onciliation, which focuses on the restoring of broken relationships, connects with the experience of a wide range of people. It speaks with a clarion voice to the increasingly postmodern European context in which I now live, where people have a deep longing for community and authentic relationships. At the same time, Joel Green and Mark Baker wisely caution against "the temptation simply to read [the New Testament writers'] words and metaphors into our contemporary world."[3] Sacrificial language, for example, evoked deep religious associations for ancient Mediterraneans, as it still does in many cultures today. But that same language may need careful translation for many contemporary Westerners, for whom an act of "sacrifice" could mean giving up desserts to lose weight.[4]

Second, as Christians seek a language in which to communicate the saving story to their specific contexts, fresh images need to be found that can relate the gospel to life as people know it. African theologian P. O. Iroegbu relates one example:

> Among the Gbaya people of Cameroon and Central African Republic, there is a tree: the *Soreh*. . . . It is not extraordinary in size or appearance. But it is so in the reality that it portrays, and in the symbols it represents. . . . The *Soreh* cools hot situations: murder, conflicts and wars. When somebody is killed, willfully or accidentally, if the perpetrator party wants to prevent the offended party from savagely avenging, they will plant a branch of *Soreh* in between their border. On seeing that, the offended party will await a serious, quick and effective reconciliation. . . . Jesus becomes . . . *Jesus Soreh-ga-mo-kee*: Jesus our *soreh*-cool-thing. Like the *Soreh*, Jesus is for making new villages, new families, new alliances and friendships. Like the *Soreh* also, Jesus becomes an antidote against death, suffering, disease and eternal loss. Above all, the *Soreh* creates the lieu [place] for life-together, for dialogue, for communication, for communion. It is a tree of life.[5]

Here the symbol of the *Soreh* tree is highly evocative for a specific cultural group, but its explanation of the person and ministry of Jesus coheres well with the biblical witness to Christ. Such efforts to locate apt forms of telling the good

---

[3]Joel B. Green and Mark D. Baker, *Recovering the Scandal of the Cross: Atonement in New Testament and Contemporary Contexts* (Downers Grove, Ill.: InterVarsity Press, 2000), p. 111.

[4]In some cases, in order for the power of biblical images to be grasped we may need to find "dynamic analogies," in which we "discern dynamic equivalents in our own cultural context to that which is addressed in the text." (Brian J. Walsh and Sylvia C. Keesmaat, *Colossians Remixed: Subverting the Empire* [Downers Grove, Ill.: InterVarsity Press, 2004], p. 136). See pp. 137-39 for one creative attempt of this kind of reading of Colossians 2:8—3:4 for a postmodern context.

[5]P. O. Iroegbu, *Appropriate Ecclesiology: Through Narrative Theology to an African Church* (Owerri, Nigeria: International Universities Press, 1996), p. 96. Cited in Clemens Sedmak, *Doing Local Theology: A Guide for Artisans of a New Humanity* (Maryknoll, N.Y.: Orbis, 2002), p. 149.

news from the everyday lives of people can be reenacted for each culture, each generational group and each linguistic community across the globe.

The dynamic and context-specific way that Jesus and the apostles do theology, then, should encourage us that diversity in the way we think about and live out the gospel is not a problem to be avoided but a gift to the church. Such diversities "are a stimulus and aid disclosing more deeply the inexhaustible mystery and power of the gospel."[6] When we hear the gospel being sung in its varied harmonies, we can discern more fully the richness of the song. Yet, theological diversity also raises important questions: first, is there not a danger of Christian theology splintering into a thousand different pieces? What holds these variegated theological reflections together? Second, how do we know which contextual expressions are authentic and which have distorted the gospel? The next two sections will explore how the New Testament witness helps us to address such concerns.

CONTEXTUALIZING A COHERENT STORY

Our study has shown that although there are many diverse voices, the gospel itself provides coherence to the New Testament witness. Fundamentally the gospel is news of what has happened. It proclaims what God *has done* in Jesus' life and ministry, death and resurrection, and what God *will do* to bring Jesus' saving mission to a consummation. This Christ-centered story of God's intervention in human history is told explicitly in the Gospels and is assumed, interpreted and expanded in the other New Testament writings. We find the one coherent story running through the Gospel passion narratives, Paul's bedrock confession that Christ died for our sins and was raised according to the Scriptures (1 Cor 15:3-4), Peter's witness to the Roman God-fearer Cornelius (Acts 10:34-43) and Revelation's song in praise of the Lamb who was slain to redeem the nations (Rev 5:9). This gospel story becomes the lens through which the New Testament writers view all other stories, whether the story of Israel, with which it stands in continuity, or the story of humankind in the world, or the ongoing stories of Christians and the church. The gospel of Christ that Scripture proclaims is *the* defining and norming story.

The gospel, of course, is more than *just* a story. Paul's understanding of the gospel, for instance, embraced foundational convictions about the gospel's saving effects "for us": justification by faith, reconciliation, sanctification, liberation from sin, the gift of the Spirit, and so forth. But such notions all flow out of the central narrative of God's gracious and loving act of salvation in Christ and un-

---

[6]"On Intercultural Hermeneutics: Report of a WCC Consultation, Jerusalem, 5-12 December 1995," *IRM* 85 (1996): 244.

fold its meaning for humanity and the cosmos. Furthermore, the New Testament response to false teaching and sinful behavior makes it clear that there are certain nonnegotiables that all Christians must believe and live out. When Christians confess that there is one sovereign God and that Jesus Christ is Lord (1 Cor 8:4-6; Phil 2:10-11; Rev 1:8; 4:8; 11:17), this excludes all other loyalties and deposes all idols. Again, however, such gospel truths are inseparable from the narrative of how this sovereign God has exalted Jesus as Lord by raising him from the dead (Rom 10:9; Phil 2:9-11).

Just as the gospel story offers coherence to the various stories and theological reflections in the New Testament, which take shape in both narrative and nonnarrative forms, so it grounds and forms our theologizing within our particular cultural worlds today. This has several important implications for the ongoing task of contextualization. First, it means we should not seek the heart of the gospel that we are trying to contextualize in any core of doctrines or in a set of timeless propositions that can be abstracted from Scripture. The danger is that when it comes to actually defining a gospel core (and what is *not* the core), it is hard to avoid remaking the gospel in line with our own cultural and doctrinal biases. The gospel announces in the first place a living story, not a cluster of abstract theological ideas.

Second, focusing on the narrative of what God has done allows us to engage the gospel in a way that shapes our own contexts and stories. Christians affirm that the biblical story of God's saving purpose that climaxes in the Christ event is truly a metanarrative, that is, a story that gives meaning to all of reality and the whole of human history. As Richard Bauckham explains, "If the Bible offers a metanarrative, a story of all stories, then we should be able to place our own stories within that grand narrative and find our own perception and experience of the world transformed by the connexion."[7] Instead of standing outside of the story in order to simply analyze it and then apply it to our context, the gospel invites us to become a part of the biblical story. Brian McClaren keenly observes that entering into God's story in Christ will lead people to abandon competing narratives—stories of idolatry and oppression, greed and corruption, power and domination, despair and self-destruction.[8]

Third, a grasp of the coherent biblical narrative points the way to finding unity in the midst of our theological diversity. Although people in various life circumstances talk about and embody their commitment to Christ in multiplex

---

[7]Richard Bauckham, *Bible and Mission: Christian Witness in a Postmodern World* (Grand Rapids, Mich.: Baker, 2003), p. 12.
[8]McClaren, "Method," p. 206.

ways, they all take part in the larger story of God's loving purpose for the world in Jesus Christ. Just as the biblical writings, with all of their differences in form and content, participate in telling the single overarching story, so that defining story continually draws us back to the shared understanding of our faith. The story is bigger than any particular cultural expression of it.

Fourth, understanding that the gospel proclaims a defining story encourages a way of doing theology in our diverse settings. Stories are basic to human experience, and cultures throughout the world are teeming with stories and proverbs, myths and metaphors that help people understand and order their world. Christians in Asia, Africa, Oceania and Latin America have long been using stories as cultural bridges to link the larger biblical story with their own life worlds. This kind of narrative theology, which is modeled by Jesus and occurs throughout Scripture, is especially important for communicating Christian truth in predominantly oral cultures like those of the New Testament world and of much of the world's South today.

DISCERNING THE LIMITS

The second question raised by the need to enunciate the gospel in diverse ways for different circumstances has to do with the matter of authenticity. Where do we draw the line of demarcation between genuine contextualization and inappropriate syncretism that compromises the "truth of the gospel" (Gal 2:5, 14)? How do we recognize when the story being told is no longer the gospel story? It is not always easy to discern when theological innovation is healthy and when it is not. As Richard Cunningham affirms, "Our challenge is always to remain open to a new word from God or a new breeze of the Holy Spirit without being enticed by every siren's song that catches our ears. Throughout the universal church, we must learn how to say 'no' as well as how to say 'yes' to local theologies and how to achieve the wisdom to know when to do which."[9]

So when do we "just say no"? Once again, the process of doing theology we observe in the New Testament provides important precedents. At times the apostolic church says "no" to the *unwillingness* to contextualize the gospel. In Acts, we see the people of God struggling to keep pace with what the Spirit of God is doing, as reactionary elements of the church resist Spirit-led interpretations of the gospel for the Gentiles (Acts 10—11; 15). Paul reserves some of his harshest rhetoric for the Jewish Christian teachers in Galatia who were trying to force an ethnocentric version of Christianity on Gentile believers, which in-

---

[9]Richard B. Cunningham, "Theologizing in a Global Context: Changing Contours," *RevExp* 94 (1997): 359.

cluded practicing circumcision and kosher food laws. He calls this constriction of the faith a "different gospel," a perversion of the true gospel of Christ (Gal 1:6-9). In modern times, missionaries and mission organizations have sometimes imposed an imported brand of theology and Christian behavior on younger churches in a well-meaning effort to prevent heresy or syncretism. But short-circuiting the development of a contextualized theology has often had the opposite effect. When the Christian message appears to be irrelevant to peoples' lives and worldview questions, they will likely turn elsewhere for answers, especially to traditional religious beliefs and practices.

At the same time, we have seen that the New Testament writers are profoundly concerned over cultural accommodation and syncretistic compromises of the gospel's integrity. To recall just one example, Paul shows in 1 Corinthians 15 that the Corinthians' defective thinking about the future, which is anchored in the dominant cultural worldview, is not only incompatible with the gospel Paul delivered to them (1 Cor 15:3-5) but places their very salvation at stake (1 Cor 15:2, 14-19, 58). Throughout the New Testament, the authenticity of the gospel is of highest priority, and it should be for us as well. In general, however, the New Testament writers do not seem to be interested in precisely defining the boundaries of what is genuine theology and what is not. They offer no definitive articulation of the gospel to use as a template and no single attempt to summarize the gospel story as a whole. Rather, the dynamic theological activity modeled in Scripture reveals both a range of acceptable contextualizations and parameters that bind all theological reflection to the central gospel proclamation of what God has done in Christ. Bauckham points out that we can recognize limits to theological diversity when we compare the Fourth Gospel, for instance, with the Gnostic gospels from Nag Hammadi: "The Gospel of John tells recognizably the same story as the Synoptics, whereas the gnostic gospels do not."[10] Likewise, the Jerusalem Council affirms the understanding that all peoples are saved on the basis of grace through faith without distinction, but it rejects the alternate interpretation of the gospel by the Pharisaic group that would require "add-ons" like circumcision for membership in the people of God.

At least four criteria seem to emerge from the New Testament witness that can guide us as we seek to recognize both the possibilities and the parameters of contextualization.[11] First, the biblical witness to what God has done in Jesus Christ is fundamental. Paul, we have seen, affirms that there is *one* gospel,

---

[10]Richard Bauckham, "Reading Scripture as a Coherent Story," in *The Art of Reading Scripture*, ed. Ellen F. Davis and Richard B. Hays (Grand Rapids, Mich.: Eerdmans, 2003), p. 43.

[11]Cf. Paul G. Hiebert, "Critical Contextualization," *IBMR* 11 (1987): 110-11.

which has been attested by Scripture and given to himself and the other apostles (e.g., 1 Cor 15:3-5, 11; Gal 1:6-9; 2). All theologizing in the New Testament church had to be tested against that revealed gospel. "The gospel," insists Lesslie Newbigin, "is not an empty form into which everyone is free to pour his or her own content."[12] Theological reflection that is context or culture-driven rather than rooted in Scripture runs a high risk of moving beyond the limits of acceptable diversity. For example, when Sri Lankan theologian S. Wesley Ariarajah tries to contextualize the gospel within the Hindu and Buddhist contexts of South Asia, he consciously plays down the biblical witness to the uniqueness of Jesus Christ. In light of the present context of religious pluralism, Ariarajah advocates a rethinking of New Testament Christology and a movement toward a more "theocentric" theology.[13] If, however, we acknowledge that a biblical witness such as the letter to the Colossians, also addressed to a pluralistic context, has any normative significance as God's Word for us, then the uniqueness and supremacy of Christ are simply off the negotiating table. Whenever the voice of the interpreter or the contemporary context drowns out the voice of Christ as revealed in Scripture, that interpretation moves "out of bounds."

Second, our theologizing must be guided by the Spirit, who leads the community into all truth (Jn 16:13). The book of Acts makes it clear that "the Holy Spirit was active both to push the early Christian community beyond its structures and commitments . . . *and* to close the door to certain innovations in the mission."[14] The church's explanation of the theological process in Acts 15 is that "it has seemed good to the Holy Spirit and to us" (Acts 15:28). The people of God must continually be open to the check of the Spirit on their theological reflection.

Third, Christians in different local settings must be willing to test their theologies in light of the wider Christian community. This includes a dialogue with both the historic tradition of the church through the ages and with today's global community of Christians in other cultures and life circumstances. We saw in the example of the Jerusalem Council that one part of the church was able to help another to recognize areas in which their thinking or practice had strayed from its roots in Scripture and the gospel of Christ. One question that must be asked regarding the legitimacy of any contextual theology or reading of Scripture is, does it ring true for the church in settings different than my own? This kind of intercultural critique must always be done in a spirit of love, humility and mu-

---

[12]Lesslie Newbigin, *The Gospel in a Pluralist Society* (Grand Rapids, Mich.: Eerdmans, 1989), pp. 152-53.

[13]S. Wesley Ariarajah, *The Bible and People of Other Faiths* (Maryknoll, N.Y.: Orbis, 1992), e.g., pp. 68-69.

[14]Green and Baker, *Recovering the Scandal*, p. 219.

tual edification. Too often the charge of "syncretism" has been wielded by the traditionally powerful churches in the West as an instrument of theological control over younger churches. We must be willing to recognize the weeds of syncretism that are growing in our own garden as well as that of our neighbor.

A fourth test of authentic contextualization is that it bears fruit in the furtherance of the Christian mission and the transformation of individuals and the community. Throughout the New Testament, both theological innovation and the critique of unacceptable thinking and behavior have a common goal—that the people of God might be increasingly conformed to the pattern of the Crucified in their attitudes, thinking, and living. Orlando Costas grasps this well:

> I submit that the ultimate test of any theological discourse is not erudite precision but transformative power. It is a question of whether or not theology can articulate the faith in a way that it is not only intellectually sound but spiritually energizing, and therefore, capable of leading the people of God to be transformed in their way of life and to commit themselves to God's mission in the world.[15]

This criterion will protect our theological efforts from being self-serving or manipulative. Authentic reflection on the gospel for our particular context will lead us deeper into a life of self-giving service and a more faithful worship of God within that context. Any theology, however "relevant," that does not help to shape God's people in their shared life of discipleship and their participation in God's kingdom mission is unworthy of the gospel.

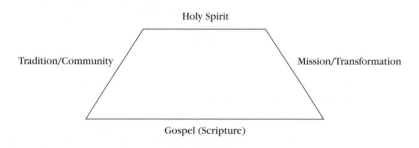

Figure 10.1. Tests of authentic contextualization

We can picture these criteria for authentic contextualization as a kind of trapezoid (figure 10.1). The gospel and Scripture are foundational but never isolated from the other tests of the Spirit's guidance, tradition and the wider Christian community, and the capacity to promote transformation in the people of God.

---

[15]Orlando E. Costas, "Evangelical Theology in the Two Thirds World," *TSFBul* 9 (1985): 12.

ENGAGING OUR CULTURES

We cannot talk about contextualization in the first century or today without considering how the gospel engages the human cultures in which it comes to life. What light does our study shed on the task of *inculturating* the gospel? First, we cannot know the gospel apart from culture, either in Scripture or in our present world. Newbigin is quite right that "[e]very statement of the gospel in words is conditioned by the culture of which those words are a part, and every style of life that claims to embody the truth of the gospel is a culturally conditioned style of life. There can never be a culture-free gospel."[16] This means that when the gospel enters a particular culture, it is never simply a matter of adapting a "pure" gospel to that setting. Indeed, sometimes the task of contextualization has been described as a process of decoding a "supracultural" message from its original biblical cultural forms and then reclothing it in a new cultural garb without loss of meaning.[17] The problem comes, however, when we try to isolate and identify this decontextualized gospel essence. A supracultural gospel may be a theoretical possibility, but we have no access to it. Cultural forms and supracultural content cannot be easily separated like oil and water. When New Testament writers like Paul or Mark or Luke articulated the gospel message for communities of Gentile believers, they told a particular story about what God had done in history through Jesus Christ, a story that was thoroughly immersed in Jewish culture and the tradition of Israel. But they told that story in ways that would make sense within the cultural world of their audiences.

Second, the relationship between the gospel and culture is complex and multidimensional. The gospel is both at home in every culture and alien to every culture. The New Testament bears witness to the gospel engaging its cultural and social world at a variety of levels. Different circumstances require different approaches (compare, e.g., Rom 13 and Rev 13). The kinds of cultural engagement we discover in the New Testament can serve as precedents for how Christians respond to various facets of a given culture today.

In Acts 17, for example, we find a striking example of Paul the evangelist respecting and listening to Athenian culture by drawing upon its language, im-

---

[16]Lesslie Newbigin, *Foolishness to the Greeks: The Gospel and Western Culture* (London: SPCK, 1986), p. 4.

[17]This is the "translation" or "transculturation" model of contextualization popularized by anthropologist Charles H. Kraft (*Christianity in Culture: A Study in Dynamic Biblical Theologizing in Cross-Cultural Perspective* [Maryknoll, N.Y.: Orbis, 1979]). For a critique of Kraft's approach to the relationship between the gospel and culture, see my "The Third Horizon: A Wesleyan Contribution to the Contextualization Debate," *WesTJ* 30 (1995): 151-54.

ages, and literary forms and concepts in order to tell the gospel story in a way that would make an impact on his audience. Christians must still look for ways to utilize the internal resources of a culture in order to connect the biblical story to particular cultural stories. To cite one case, Martin Goldsmith describes how the method of "parabolic preaching" used by Jesus can help to communicate fundamental theological ideas to Islamic peoples. It does so in a nonconfrontational and dialogical way that is appropriate to the culture. Here Goldsmith retells Jesus' story of the Pharisee and the Tax Collector (Lk 18:9-14):

> Two men went up to the mosque to pray. One was a good Muslim who knew all the right actions for his ritual lustrations; his Arabic was perfect . . . and he was accomplished in the words and movements of the *salat*. He therefore went confidently to the centre of the mosque and prayed, but his mind wandered to think about the pretty girl next door! . . . The second man was a real sinner who had led a rather corrupt life (easily described!) and had not prayed for many years. He could not remember how to perform the lustrations and therefore just gave his face and hands a quick wash. He also could not remember in detail how to perform the *salat*, so he was shy to enter the mosque. On doing so, however, he went diffidently behind a pillar, squatted down and began to pray in his own words: "O God, forgive me; I have made a complete mess of my life, but I long to follow and serve you . . ." Local people recognize the characters of both men as typical of the hearts of many around them and they make suitable comments! I then ask the Biblical question as to which man's prayer God approved of.[18]

Although many Muslims may not get the point of the story immediately upon hearing it (similar to Jesus' hearers), this approach provides a point of contact with people in a traditional story-telling culture and can spur further reflection on what truly pleases God.

At other times, however, the gospel says "no" to cultural stories, ideas and behaviors. The gospel judges as well as affirms. We have seen many occasions where Jesus or a New Testament writer takes a countercultural stance. New Testament reflection on the practice of eating food offered to idols is but one notable example. Eating idol food during religious or social occasions at the temple was normal cultural behavior in the Roman world. Both Revelation and 1 Corinthians, however, perceive this activity as an unacceptable form of idolatry. It seems clear that Christians in the churches in question sharply disagreed over how to relate to the surrounding culture in this matter. We still need the Spirit's wisdom in order to discern when to affirm the culture and when to confront it, when to participate and when to withdraw. This is no simple task. I recall a sem-

---

[18]Martin Goldsmith, "Parabolic Preaching in the Context of Islam," *EvRT* 15 (1991): 275-76.

inary student from Korea struggling over the relationship of the gospel to Korean traditional religion. "Shamanism is part of my culture, my heritage," she agonized. "How can I be Korean and reject my heritage?" Ultimately, she came to believe that there were dimensions to her cultural heritage that were incompatible with her new commitment to Christ. With disarming candor, Nigerian theologian Teresa Okure singles out aspects of her own culture that need to be challenged by the gospel, including the practice of witchcraft and sorcery, the cult of secret societies, endemic bribery and corruption, and the cultural oppression of women.[19] When the gospel is truly contextualized, it will oppose oppressive and sinful elements in *every* culture.

Perhaps the most characteristic and suggestive response to the gospel's encounter with first-century Mediterranean culture is that of *transforming engagement*. New Testament writers sought to shape and reshape not just their readers, but dimensions of their cultural and social worlds as well. We have seen, for instance, how both Paul and Luke engaged the cultural conventions of benefaction and patronage in order to transform them. While living in the Philippines, I encountered a modern-day parallel in the Filipino cultural value of *utang na loob* (debt of gratitude). Negatively, *untang na loob* can take the form of an enslaving compulsion, such as when a father demands his son's exclusive loyalty, affection and service for raising him and sending him to school, or when the poor are caught in a perpetual snare of obligation to reelect a corrupt politician in return for services rendered to the community. But the gospel can liberate this same cultural value from the chains of a manipulative, unequal relationship. When this happens, *utang na loob* becomes an expression of the Christian virtues of gratitude, loyalty, and willingness to care for someone in need.[20]

Jesus and the New Testament writers model a delicate dance between formulating the gospel in terms that make sense in their cultural worlds and at the same time calling those worlds into question in order to re-form them. Today it is possible to lose this balance in either direction. On the one hand, when we become too much at home in our culture we can begin "to transform the gospel in light of cultural values instead of the reverse."[21] The gospel of health and prosperity that is often preached in North American pulpits and propagated over

---

[19]Teresa Okure, "Inculturation: Biblical/theological Bases," in *32 Articles Evaluating Inculturation of Christianity in Africa*, ed. Teresa Okure and P. van Thiel et al. (Eldoret, Kenya: Gaba Publications, 1990), p. 78.

[20]See Evelyn Miranda-Feliciano, *Filipino Values and Our Christian Faith* (Manila: OMF Literature, 1990), pp. 69-75.

[21]Henry H. Knight III, *A Future for Truth: Evangelical Theology in a Postmodern World* (Nashville: Abingdon, 1997), p. 165.

the global media is an especially blatant example of such an uncritical accommodation to culture; it is syncretism dressed in a Sunday suit. On the other hand, failing to tell and live out the sacred story in forms that both reflect and speak to a given culture will trivialize the good news and cause it to be perceived as irrelevant. The task of every Christian interpreter and communicator is to enable the Word of God, which is incarnated within particular cultural worlds in Scripture, to speak once again in ways that are both relevant to our own cultures and faithful to the biblical message.[22]

Third, although to this point we have been talking about the gospel's engagement of specific cultures, the New Testament also offers some perspectives for inculturating the gospel and embodying God's mission in multicultural settings today. The first-century Roman world was a multicolored mosaic featuring interacting cultures, complex societies and religious pluralism. The churches Paul established were heterogeneous communities which embraced Jew and Greek, barbarian and Scythian, male and female, slave and free (Gal 3:28; Col 3:11). Paul himself, although retaining his primary identity as a "Hebrew of Hebrews," had a rich and multifaceted cultural background, which equipped him to become "all things to all people" for the sake of the gospel. What is more, many of the New Testament writings—the Gospels of Mark and Luke, Acts, Paul's letters, 1 Peter and Revelation, to name some—are themselves intercultural documents rooted in a Jewish heritage but retelling this "Jewish" story for predominantly non-Jewish audiences.

The mission of the church to which the New Testament bears witness, then, is not simply a monocultural or even a classic "crosscultural" mission, in the sense of moving directly from one culture into another target culture. It is an *intercultural* mission, which requires enormous creativity, flexibility, and Spirit-inspired wisdom. This has obvious implications for contextualizing the gospel within our increasingly multicultural and pluralistic ministry settings today. On the one hand, the New Testament writings show respect for the particular cultural identities of believers. As C. Norman Kraus notes, the gospel does not recruit believers to a particular cultural (Jewish) form of Christianity, but it allows them to do theology and live out their faith within their own culture.[23] At the same time, however, the gospel relativizes all cultures and demolishes the old cultural lines of division and ethnocentrism in favor of a common identity "in Christ" (Acts 10:34-35; Gal 3:26-28; Col 3:11). This is part of the transforming na-

---

[22]See Green and Baker, *Recovering the Scandal*, pp. 210-11.
[23]C. Norman Kraus, *An Intrusive Gospel? Christian Mission in the Postmodern World* (Downers Grove, Ill.: InterVarsity Press, 1998), p. 114.

ture of the gospel. In the many-cultured and multilingual setting in which I currently teach and worship, we are learning (often painfully) that the gospel does not erase our differences. But it repeatedly challenges us to lay aside our particular cultural preferences and our ethnocentric perspectives in order to "maintain the unity of the Spirit in the bond of peace" (Eph 4:3).

"GLOBALIZING" THE GOSPEL

How do we contextualize the gospel in a globalized world? Although "globalization" has become something of a buzzword, its impact on contemporary life is indisputable. Due to the barrage of Western media influences and a globalized world economy, throughout the planet people eat McDonald's fast food, wear name-brand gym shoes, watch Hollywood (and Bollywood) blockbusters and listen to the same rock and rap music. In a positive sense, globalization means an increasing interconnectedness of all cultures and parts of the world, along with a greater awareness of one another. But it also has a seamy side. Today vast numbers of people—mostly in the South—feel excluded from the benefits of global capitalism and are suspicious of the creeping encroachment of an emerging world culture. The movement toward globalization has been accompanied by a countertrend toward a renewal of tribalism and nationalism, as smaller ethnic and cultural communities assert their autonomy and try to clutch on to their particular cultural and religious identities. Bridges and barriers stand side by side.

How does this tension between the global and the local, the universal and the particular, affect our efforts to contextualize the gospel? In the first place, contextualization resists the oppressive dimension of globalization; it affirms the necessity of doing theology in a particular, local context. As a result, many Christians in the South and in groups outside the mainstream within the North have questioned the dominance of classic Western theologies, with their heavy dependence on Greek metaphysics and Enlightenment rationality.[24] The voices of the traditionally marginalized, the "vernacular" theologies of powerless local Christian communities, need to be heard.[25]

> When the church's faith is genuinely contextual, the shame and stigma imposed on oppressed people begins to be lifted. They find a new dignity as they see not only their own lives but also their culture in God's redeeming light. When faith is contextual, there is a recognition that the gospel speaks to Christians in their

---

[24]See Cunningham, "Theologizing in a Global Context," p. 357.
[25]On vernacular theologies, see William A. Dyrness, *Invitation to Cross-Cultural Theology* (Grand Rapids, Mich.: Zondervan, 1992).

language, connects with their symbols, addresses their needs and awakens their creative energies.[26]

In some ways, the current phenomenon of globalization recalls the dream of ancient Babel: to create unity and power through one language and one culture (Gen 11:1-4). But that arrogant vision was reversed on the day of Pentecost, when local languages and identities were affirmed within the context of the new unified community of faith (Acts 2:1-13).[27] The biblical story upholds the theological and cultural integrity of all peoples.

Second, however, in the shadows of contextualization lurks the danger of what Max L. Stackhouse calls "contextualism"—a belief that none of our theological reflections have the ability to transcend a particular context.[28] In recent decades we have seen a deluge of contextual theologies emerging from different quarters and cultures of the global Christian community: liberation, feminist, black, African, *Minjung*, Hispanic, Chinese, *Mujerista* theologies, and many more.[29] Although these diverse voices offer many positive theological insights, there is a risk that in trying to sing the gospel in multiple variations we will forget the song we share. The result will be theological dissonance rather than harmony. "Contextualizing theology," insists Richard B. Cunningham, "that does not exercise self-criticism and submit itself to the judgment of the gospel can so celebrate the variety of contextualizations that theology slips into relativism, in which any contextual theology is as good as any other."[30]

In contrast to either a homogenizing globalization on the one hand or an atomizing relativism on the other, Scripture models a dynamic interaction between the local and the global which has important implications for our time. The biblical story is both particular and universal. God is revealed in the particular stories of Abraham and Israel and Jesus of Nazareth with the purpose of bringing about the universal realization of the kingdom of God in all creation.[31] Jesus "became flesh and lived among us" (Jn 1:14) in a specific local culture. Yet

---

[26]"On Intercultural Hermeneutics," p. 245.

[27]Johannes Nissen, "Mission and Globalization in a New Testament Perspective," in *For All People: Global Theologies in Contexts*, ed. E. M. W. Pedersen, H. Lam and P. Lodberg (Grand Rapids, Mich.: Eerdmans, 2002), p. 42.

[28]Max L. Stackhouse, *Apologia: Contextualization, Globalization, and Mission in Theological Education* (Grand Rapids, Mich.: Eerdmans, 1988), p. 10.

[29]For a helpful overview of the variety of theological developments in a global context, see Virginia Fabella and R. S. Sugirtharajah, ed., *Dictionary of Third World Theologies* (Maryknoll, N.Y.: Orbis, 2000). See also John Parrott, ed., *An Introduction to Third World Theologies* (Cambridge: Cambridge University Press, 2004).

[30]Cunningham, "Theologizing in a Global Context," p. 359.

[31]Bauckham, *Bible and Mission*, p. 13.

as the eternal Word, he has a universal significance that transcends all cultures. The Jesus movement, which begins with a handful of messianic Jews in Palestine, is driven by the Spirit to cross one cultural boundary after another and to witness to the good news to the ends of the earth. This global mission anticipates the heavenly gathering of saints from all the world's diverse cultures, tribes and nations in the end (Rev 5:9; 7:9). Furthermore, the New Testament writings themselves illustrate the mediation between the specific and the universal. Each saying, story, letter, sermon or apocalyptic vision participates in the larger metanarrative of God's dealings with the world without sacrificing its own particularity or contextual focus.[32]

Our efforts at contextualization today must likewise embrace the movement from the local to the global. Does this mean that our goal is to produce a single "global theology," one way of articulating the gospel to be applied everywhere without adaptation? Certainly not. Yet if we partake in a common story that is bigger than our local stories, then we must learn to think not just in contextual, but also *transcontextual* categories. This involves allowing our various contextual insights and interpretations of the gospel to contribute toward a richer, fuller, more adequate grasp of the Word of God and its implications for people. Local groups of Christians must envision themselves as part of a global interpretive community. Churches throughout the world must take on the roles of both teacher and learner, interacting with the church in its cultural multiplicity as well as the tradition of the church throughout its history. C. René Padilla is surely right that

> every culture makes possible a certain approach to the gospel that brings to light certain of its aspects that in other cultures may remain less visible or even hidden. Seen from this perspective, the same cultural differences that hinder intercultural communications turn out to be an asset to the understanding of the many-sided wisdom of God.[33]

At the same time, Christians from another setting will often be able to see my theological weaknesses and cultural blind spots more clearly than I can from within my own culture.

This kind of intercultural conversation has roots in the early church. Johannes Nissen observes that "[t]he Book of Acts as a whole is the story of the gospel being unfolded, opened up, its beauty increasingly revealed as it is appropriated

---

[32]See Knight, *Future for Truth*, p. 101.
[33]C. René Padilla, *Mission Between the Times: Essays on the Kingdom* (Grand Rapids, Mich.: Eerdmans, 1985), p. 89.

and reappropriated by culture after culture."[34] The encounter between the kosher Peter and the Gentile "outsider" Cornelius transformed both of their theological visions (Acts 10—11). In the Jerusalem Council, the church functioned as an intercultural hermeneutical community (Acts 15). The outcome was a new and fuller understanding of the Spirit's work. Paul's interaction with the pagan cultural and religious world in Athens (Acts 17) undoubtedly deepened his own grasp of the gospel and how to proclaim it.

When we consider today's theological landscape, particularly Christians in the North must be willing listen to the voices of Jesus' disciples from the world's South and from minority communities—voices that have historically been muffled or marginalized. Three factors make this intercultural exchange all the more imperative. First, the New Testament invites us to be open to the voices of outsiders. In Luke's Gospel, for example, Jesus repeatedly recognizes the spiritual insight of peripheral people like Samaritans (Lk 17:11-19), Gentiles (Lk 7:1-10), women (Lk 7:36-50) and even a criminal hanging with Jesus on a cross (Lk 23:39-43).[35]

Second, we are currently witnessing a massive shift in the center of gravity of global Christianity from the North to the South. The majority of followers of Jesus Christ now live south of the equator. Christian historian Philip Jenkins estimates that by the year 2050 the proportion of Christians who are non-Latino whites will have fallen to perhaps one in five or less.[36] If we consider sheer demographics alone, the theological contributions of Third World churches can no longer be ignored.

Third, since Christians in the South and in minority or immigrant communities in the North often are a part of cultures that are closer to those of the biblical world, they are in a position to offer needed contributions and critiques to the global Christian conversation. For example, Christians from Africa might help to correct North American interpretations of Scripture that reflect an unbiblical individualism. Believers from Asian shame-based cultures might have a clearer insight into the meaning of the cross as God's ultimate identification with human shame, leading to freedom from shame's fear and exclusion. Such perspectives on Christ's atonement can help to balance more individualistic and legal understandings like the penal substitution theory, which has played a dominant role

---

[34]Nissen, "Mission and Globalization," p. 42.

[35]See Joel B. Green, "The Practice of Reading the New Testament," in *Hearing the New Testament: Strategies for Interpretation*, ed. Joel B. Green (Grand Rapids, Mich.: Eerdmans, 1995), pp. 418-19.

[36]Philip Jenkins, "After the Next Christendom," *IBMR* 28 (2004): 20. Cf. idem, *The Next Christendom: The Coming of Global Christianity* (Oxford: Oxford University Press, 2004).

in Western theology.[37] I have personally gained much insight into the role of genealogies in Scripture—largely ignored in my own interpretive community— from Christians who live in cultures that have a deeper regard for the role of kinship and ancestral relations. Likewise, I only came to realize how incomplete was my own understanding of the New Testament passages dealing with perse- cution while teaching a class on the Gospels for Middle Eastern pastors, for some of whom persecution was a fact of everyday life. At the same time, the Western theological tradition and the wisdom of the church down through the ages has much to teach Christians throughout the world. Western traditions of spirituality and holiness, for example, might expose a one-sided emphasis on sociopolitical and material concerns in some Third World liberation theologies.

All local theologizing, then, must be done in the context of the global church. Doing transcontextual theology takes an attitude of humility and what John Wesley called a "catholic spirit."[38] We need to recognize that all of our the- ologies or readings of Scripture are partial and imperfect understandings of God and his revelation in Christ (1 Cor 13:12). Are we willing to allow our cher- ished interpretations and theologies to be challenged by the insights of fellow Christians in Pune or Perth or Prague? Not long ago I witnessed the possibilities of this kind of intercultural listening and sharing at a global theology confer- ence of my own denomination held in Guatemala City. For the first time, theo- logians, educators, pastors, students and denominational leaders from the con- fessional community throughout the world were able to sit down together, not simply to listen to presentations from "experts," but to carry on intercultural conversations about concerns of mission and theology that we shared. In the discussion group of which I was a part, each participant brought to the table the unique insights she or he had gained through a particular cultural, life and church experience. We tried to lay aside issues of distribution of power and past histories, which often cloud such conversations between Christians from different cultures and socioeconomic backgrounds. Repeatedly I felt checked and challenged by others' experiences and theological insights. For each of us,

---

[37]See Green and Baker, *Recovering the Scandal*, pp. 153-70; see also C. Norman Kraus, *Jesus Christ Our Lord: Christology from a Disciples' Perspective* (Scottdale, Penn.: Herald, 1990), esp. chapters 12-13.

[38]John Wesley, "Sermon XXXIX: Catholic Spirit," in N. Burwash, *Wesley's Doctrinal Standards: I. The Sermons* (Salem, Ohio: Schmul; repr. 1967), pp. 379-89. For an analysis of Wesley's un- derstanding of the "catholic spirit," see Randy L. Maddox, "Opinion, Religion and 'Catholic Spirit': John Wesley on Theological Integrity," *AsTJ* 47 (1992): 63-87. Maddox concludes that the mature Wesley steered a middle course between doctrinal indifference and theological pluralism on the one hand and a dogmatic zeal that fails to recognize the fallibility of human perceptions of theological truth on the other.

this intercultural exchange resulted in Spirit-graced enrichment and a deeper grasp of the gospel in its multitextured expression. "After this experience," reflected one group member from Latin America, "I feel *liberated.*" When churches in various cultural and historical settings are willing to truly listen to one another, not only will their own grasp of the gospel be strengthened, but the international Christian community as a whole will come to a deeper, more *transcontextual* understanding of the faith.

THE GOSPEL IN A POSTMODERN KEY

The context for articulating and embodying the gospel, particularly in Western societies, is in the throes of a seismic shift. It is not only more global; it is also increasingly postmodern. One of the profound challenges facing the church in the current generation is how to come to grips with the transition from a twentieth-century world dominated by modernism, with its faith in radical individualism, rational and objective knowledge, and scientific progress, to a postmodern world that questions the entire modern project. Many churches in historic "Christendom" have begun to recognize that, just as missionaries contextualize the gospel in order for it to be meaningful in a new cultural situation, so the Christian message must be transposed into a new key for a postmodern world. Especially for Christians like myself who have been shaped by the culture of modernity and are accustomed to articulating the Christian faith in ways that fit that mentality, this will take no less than a form of intercultural communication. If we are going to meaningfully address the emerging culture, we must be willing to intentionally release our theology from its enculturation for a modern worldview rooted in the Enlightenment and recontextualize it for a profoundly different situation.[39] According to Robert Webber, this new culture "is shaped by globalization; historical nostalgia; spiritual hunger; mystery; oral, visual and interactive forms of communication; the longing for community; and the fear of terrorism."[40] What is more, it is a world of constant change and multiple perspectives, a world in which "difference" is awarded celebrity status. As Brian Walsh and Sylvia Keesmat describe it, "Lacking any unifying story, rational justifications and normative anchors, postmodern culture fills the boredom of our time with a carnival of worldview options and consumer-directed faiths."[41] Faced with this reality, the church must learn to speak a new language for a new postmodern world.

---

[39]See Robert E. Webber, *The Younger Evangelicals: Facing the Challenges of the New World* (Grand Rapids, Mich.: Baker, 2002), p. 17.

[40]Ibid., p. 242.

[41]Walsh and Keesmat, *Colossians Remixed*, p. 24.

What will it mean to proclaim and live out the gospel in a postmodern context? Once again, under the Spirit's guidance, we must enable the gospel to come to life within postmodern categories while at the same time challenging them. One of the discoveries I have made in the course of this study is that New Testament examples of doing theology and evangelism resonate in some profound ways with the realities of a postmodern world. In many ways, the new world of postmodernity in North America and Europe, with its high level of biblical illiteracy, its greater openness to spirituality, and its religious and philosophical pluralism, is much closer to the world in which the apostles communicated the gospel than was the twentieth-century world. The postmodern challenge affords churches a fresh opportunity to revisit New Testament texts and to learn from how the first Christian witnesses and theologians engaged a pluralistic world. I do not have space here for a full discussion of the matter. I will therefore simply mention several potential points of contact for our attempts to contextualize the gospel for an emerging postmodern culture.[42] Although this speaks most directly to the churches of the North, the influence of postmodern attitudes is growing in wider global contexts as well.

1. Community. In contrast to modernity's radical focus on individual autonomy, postmoderns yearn for an experience of genuine community and connectedness. A gospel for a postmodern context must recover the New Testament emphasis on individuals finding a new identity within a loving and healing community of faith. This suggests, for instance, a more corporate theology of evangelism, enacted by the entire community into which women and men are invited to participate. A gospel that is plausible to the postmodern world will be one that is "preached" by the shared life of the people of God. Genuine loving relationships will give our message a stamp of authenticity. This dovetails closely with the story told in Acts of a church whose loving embodiment of the gospel and care for one another became a compelling form of evangelism (Acts 2:43-47).

2. Story. A gospel contextualized for a postmodern world will concentrate on telling the biblical story. This is an obvious touch point between the New Testament message and postmodern thought, which recognizes that narratives

---

[42]There has already been a good deal of creative and valuable theological reflection on relating the gospel to a postmodern setting. See, e.g., Webber, *Younger Evangelicals;* Knight, *Future for Truth;* Brad J. Kallenberg, *Live to Tell: Evangelism for a Postmodern Age* (Grand Rapids, Mich.: Brazos, 2002); Leonard Sweet, *Postmodern Pilgrims: First Century Passion for the 21st Century World* (Nashville: Broadman and Holman, 2000); Bauckham, *Bible and Mission.*

give meaning and direction to our lives. It is also consistent with New Testament patterns of doing apologetics and theology. When Paul addressed the biblically illiterate Athenians (Acts 17), he did not offer rational proofs for God's existence or present the gospel as a string of logical propositions. Instead, he narrated the grand story of a God who has revealed himself to humanity in creation and, above all, in Jesus Christ. We, too, must tell this life-yielding story. But we must insist that the story we tell is not just one choice at a buffet of optional narratives. Here the gospel must confront postmodern thinking. Postmodernists like Jean-François Lyotard have rejected overarching metanarratives as being inherently oppressive and authoritarian.[43] Yet the grand narrative of the Bible, far from being an instrument of oppression, is a story of a compassionate God who repeatedly chooses and uplifts the lowly, a story that is centered in the humility, shame and vulnerability of the cross (1 Cor 1:18—2:3; Phil 2:6-8). A message for a postmodern culture will invite people to see the world through the biblical story and to allow that story to reshape their lives. It will also lead us to communicate the gospel through telling our own stories—with vulnerability and integrity—as witness to the experience of the compassion and transforming grace of God.

3. Imagination. Marshall McLuhan taught us that the medium and the message are inseparable,[44] and this is especially the case for communicating the gospel to a postmodern culture. In contrast to the word-and-reason-based modern world, postmodernity easily embraces more imaginative, emotive and aesthetic forms of communication. The church today must speak the language of metaphor and symbol. It must supplement verbal communication with various forms of audio, visual, and interactive media, ceremony, and the practice of the arts. It must portray the beauty and mystery of the gospel. "The story of Christ," writes Mark Filiatreau "is a feast for the imagination. Why not serve it this way to those who are starving?"[45] We have seen that the New Testament supplies ample provisions for such an imaginative feast. Jesus was a wielder of metaphors and parables. Paul understood the power of the symbol of the cross. Revelation challenges our perspective on the world through apocalyptic symbols and multisensory visions. As the New Testament writers found imaginative bridges for communicating the Christian message to their world, so we

---

[43]Jean-François Lyotard, *The Postmodern Condition*, trans. G. Bennington and B. Massumi (Minneapolis: University of Minnesota Press, 1984).

[44]Marshall McLuhan, *Understanding Media: The Extensions of Man* (New York: McGraw-Hill, 1974).

[45]Mark Filiatreau, "Make It Real: The Imagination's Role in Living Our Beliefs," *Re:generation Quarterly* 2 (1996): 23, cited in Webber, *Younger Evangelicals*, p. 69.

will need to draw on a whole variety of media and images. Dennis Haack makes the point that

> Story, song, and image can be used as points of contact to explore the big issues of life without compromising the integrity of the gospel. Popular culture (TV, film, pop music), the very heart of the postmodern ethos, can become the beginning point for exploring the claims of Christ, and thus serve as the postmodern equivalent of the Athenian altar to an unknown god. . . . A postmodern apologetic needs to be essentially rooted in glory, with a greater emphasis on art, narrative, and image.[46]

Contextualizing the gospel for a postmodern world will require a rekindling of the church's theological imagination.

THE ROLE OF THE CHURCH

Everything I have said in this chapter to this point assumes that for the gospel to be contextualized within our social and cultural worlds, there must be a contextualizing agent. Although we might say that the Holy Spirit is the *ultimate* agent of contextualization, the *visible* agent is the church. Wherever it happens to be situated, the church is a local, particular embodiment of the gospel story. Consequently, contextualization is inherently an *ecclesial* activity; it is done *by* the church and *for* the church. This carries several important implications for the task of incarnating the gospel.

First, biblically informed contextualization calls for *communal* hermeneutics and theologizing. We find a magnificent example of this way of doing theology in Luke's narrative of the Jerusalem Council in Acts 15 (cf. Acts 10—11). The whole community, including its leaders, is involved in the theological reflection that results in the reconciling of a divided church. Today doing theology and interpreting the Word of God within a particular context is not something reserved solely for academic "experts" or for church officials. It is the responsibility of the whole people of God. It is done best when a faithful community of cultural insiders can dialogue and wrestle with how the gospel intersects their world. At the same time, those with theological and biblical training, such as pastors, theological educators or missionaries, can play a key role in guiding and providing critical input to the process. In the New Testament, figures like James at the Jerusalem Council, Paul in his letters to communities

---

[46]Dennis Haack, "The Glory of God and Human Culture: How Do We Influence Postmodern Society?" (Paper, Gospel and Society Conference, Bratislava, Slovakia, June, 1996): 7, cited in Brian McClaren, *The Church on the Other Side: Doing Ministry in the Postmodern Age* (Grand Rapids, Mich.: Brazos, 2002), p. 181.

of converts, and John in his messages to the seven churches in Asia (Rev 2—3) all served as catalytic agents who spurred the community to rethink its theological perspectives and come to a clearer understanding of the gospel for their situation.[47]

Second, in the practice of ecclesial contextualization, the *unity* and *up-building* of the church is a primary goal. When Paul does theology in light of divisive issues like the matter of what to eat and what not to eat, he repeatedly stresses the priority of ecclesial unity and the community's responsibility to the weak. Christians are to "pursue what makes for peace and for mutual upbuilding" (Rom 14:19; cf. 14:15) and to "give no offense to Jews or to the Greeks or to the church of God" (1 Cor 10:32; cf. 8:9-13). Although the New Testament recognizes a range of acceptable diversity, theological or ethical innovations must not be allowed to fracture the church that is one body under one Lord (Eph 4:4-6; cf. 1 Cor 1:10).

Third, contextualization is also profoundly *missional*. The New Testament's example shows us that contextual evangelism, interpretation of Scripture and theologizing are essential components of the church's mission in the world. Jesus did theology in a way that was appropriate to diverse people and situations in order to advance his kingdom mission. Acts tells the story of a church whose boundary-breaking mission is linked to its willingness to tailor its ministry of the word to fit new audiences and contexts. Paul adapts his way of living out the gospel and enslaves himself to all in order to win more to Christ (1 Cor 9:19-23). He writes context-sensitive letters in fulfillment of his missionary calling in order to shape and equip churches for their ongoing mission. Contextualizing the gospel is more than a pragmatic methodology; it is part and parcel of what it means to be a missionary church.

Fourth, contextualizing the gospel not only involves the church's *telling* the story but also *embodying* the kingdom of God within its particular circumstances. If I have learned anything from the Wesleyan theological tradition in which I have been nurtured, it is that we cannot meaningfully talk about doing evangelism and theology apart from living and "loving" the faith. As Jesus "exegeted" (Jn 1:18) the compassionate heart of God when he entered our concrete world and lived among us, so the church must continually incarnate God's holy love within the specificity of our many cultures and contexts.

We must also recognize the tension in the church's relationship to the world it is called to serve. Too often, the church in the modern world, particularly in

---

[47]C. Norman Kraus talks about those involved in intercultural mission and service ministries as "catalytic change agents" (*Intrusive Gospel?* pp. 42-44).

the West, has tried to be relevant to its culture by accommodating to its ideas and practices. Stanley Hauerwas and William Willimon state the problem this way: "Alas, in leaning over to speak to the modern world, we had fallen in. We had lost the theological resources to resist, lost the resources even to see that there was something worth resisting."[48]

Alternatively, the relationship of the church to its cultural world has sometimes been described by the image of "resident aliens" or of "exiles" in a foreign land.[49] There is some validity to this picture. Within the New Testament it probably comes closest to the perspective of the book of Revelation, where John addresses churches under intense pressure that must radically disengage from their dominant political and social order. Nevertheless, I do not think this is the best way of imaging the New Testament's understanding of the church's relationship to culture in general. The missional church does not seek to create an alternative culture that is external to the alien land of its cultural world. Miroslav Volf thoughtfully describes the position of the church in the world:

> Christians do not come into their own social world from the outside seeking either to accommodate to their new home (like second generation immigrants would), shape it in the image of the one they have left behind (like colonizers would), or establish a little haven in the strange new world reminiscent of the old (as resident aliens would). They are not outsiders who either seek to become insiders or maintain strenuously the status of outsiders. Christians are the *insiders* who have diverted from their culture by being born again.[50]

As I mentioned in chapter four, the church carries dual citizenship. It lives both "in Corinth" and "in Christ." Perhaps the picture of the church as a "mission outpost" is closer to the broader New Testament perspective.[51] The church engages its culture missionally from within, speaking the language in order to be plausible but embodying a radically different set of values, from the vulnerable position of the cross.

Like the Christian communities to which the New Testament was written, churches today struggle to find the right balance between identifying with the

---

[48]Stanley Hauerwas and William H. Willimon, *Resident Aliens: A Provocative Christian Assessment of Culture and Ministry for People Who Know That Something Is Wrong* (Nashville: Abingdon, 1989), p. 27.

[49]E.g., ibid., pp. 11-12.

[50]Miroslav Volf, "Soft Difference: Theological Reflections on the Relation between Church and Culture in 1 Peter," *ExAud* 10 (1994): 18-19 (emphasis Volf's).

[51]See Craig van Gelder, "Defining the Center—Finding the Boundaries: The Challenge of Re-visioning the Church in North America for the Twenty-first Century," in *The Church Between Gospel and Culture: The Emerging Mission in North America*, ed. George R. Hunsberger and Craig Van Gelder (Grand Rapids, Mich.: Eerdmans, 1996), p. 46.

culture and distancing from it in order to make an internal difference. This is nowhere more evident than in the debate over the so-called user-friendly mega-churches in North America, which practice needs-oriented and market-driven models of ministry. Granted, such churches score high marks for contextual relevance and have shown impressive success in reaching their target audience with the gospel message. But they must also wrestle with the question of whether they have so embraced the American cultural values of consumerism, individualism and materialism that they have become all too enmeshed with that culture. Have they maintained the *difference* of the gospel and its *countercultural* implications? The New Testament model of the church is ever mission-directed, but never market-driven.

CONCLUSION

If we are to fulfill our calling as a missional church in the twenty-first century, we must reenact the task of singing the gospel in new keys that we see modeled in the writings and stories of the New Testament. Although the modern interest in contextualization emerged out of missiological discussions, I have sought to show that the concerns of this study have a broader scope than the activity of crosscultural missionaries alone. Every church in every setting, every preacher or teacher of the Word, must consider how to articulate the gospel in ways that allow it to come to life for their particular audience. While this book has focused especially on biblical patterns of doing contextual theology, the issues it raises have clear implications for other aspects of the church's life and mission in the world—preaching, apologetics, theological education, evangelism and church growth, worship, leadership styles, organizational structures, social and political witness, and spiritual formation, among them. How, for instance, might theological education change if it were to go beyond simply mastering the content of a theological system and focus more on learning *how* the biblical writers did theology, as a model for theologizing today? Or what shape should church leadership take in a setting in which culturally accepted styles of leadership are in tension with the gospel pattern of Christ crucified? Such questions deserve further exploration.

Although the activity of reappropriating the gospel is integral to the church's identity and mission, it is not easy to do it well. There are no "five-step formulas." This is all the more reason to be mentored by the biblical writers. They show us the need for a sensitive balance in our approach. We must exercise freedom and imagination under the guidance of the Spirit as we enunciate the gospel in response to particular needs. However, our theology must also remain anchored in the one normative gospel that centers on God's loving and saving action in Jesus Christ. This will help us to steer a middle course between resisting contextualization on the one hand and overcontextualization on the other. The theologians of the New Testament teach us as well that the gospel must shape not only the content of our theological reflection, but also the way that we carry out the task. Authentic contextualization is incarnational and cruciform. As Paul modeled himself after the self-emptying Jesus in his service of the gospel, we must do theology in an attitude of self-giving love and humble identification with others. Our communication of the gospel must be more than just relevant; it must be *real*. Christian witness that is reduced to marketing a religious product or that imposes a foreign theology on a less powerful church has little to do with the gospel of the crucified and risen One.

Contextual theology is never a finished product. We may attain clear theological understandings for a particular time and place as a result of critically reflecting on the gospel. But cultures and societies change. New questions arise. We must remain open to the need to reevaluate and reformulate our theology in light of fresh insights into Scripture and altered external circumstances. Like the book of Acts, contextualizing the gospel is an open-ended story.

Lest we become discouraged by the difficulty of the task, we would do well to heed Richard Bauckham's reminder that the church's mission "is God's work before and after it is ours. . . . God continually makes more of what we do for him than we can make of it ourselves, and God continually prevents the harm our foolishness and failures would do."[52] The Holy Spirit, who led the New Testament church in its interpretation of Scripture and inspired fresh appropriations of the gospel for its world, continues to guide the church's mission today. All of our efforts to do context-sensitive theology have little value unless the Spirit is our source of wisdom and power. The task takes a prayerful mind and a humble heart. May faithful communities of disciples in a multitude of local settings purpose to truly listen to Scripture, to the Spirit, to Christians through the ages, and to one another, as they learn to sing the old, old story in new keys.

---

[52]Bauckham, *Bible and Mission*, pp. 91-92.

SELECT BIBLIOGRAPHY

Aageson, J. W. *Written for Our Sake: Paul and the Art of Biblical Interpretation*. Louisville: John Knox, 1993.

Arnold, Clinton E. *The Colossian Syncretism: The Interface Between Christianity and Folk Belief at Colossae*. Grand Rapids, Mich.: Baker, 1996.

Bassler, Jouette M., ed. *Pauline Theology, Volume 1: Thessalonians, Philippians, Galatians, Philemon*. Minneapolis: Fortress, 1991.

Bauckham, Richard. *The Bible and Mission: Christian Witness in a Postmodern World*. Grand Rapids, Mich.: Baker, 2003.

———. *The Climax of Prophecy: Studies on the Book of Revelation*. Edinburgh: T & T Clark, 1993.

———. *The Theology of the Book of Revelation*. Cambridge: Cambridge University Press, 1993.

Bauckham, Richard, ed. *The Gospel for All Christians: Rethinking the Gospel Audiences*. Grand Rapids, Mich.: Eerdmans, 1998.

Beale, G. K. *The Book of Revelation*. New International Greek Testament Commentary. Grand Rapids, Mich.: Eerdmans, 1999.

Beker, J. Christiaan. *Paul the Apostle: The Triumph of God in Life and Thought*. Philadelphia: Fortress, 1980.

———. "Recasting Pauline Theology: The Coherence-Contingency-Scheme as Interpretive Method." In *Pauline Theology, Volume 1: Thessalonians, Philippians, Galatians, Philemon*, edited by Jouette M. Bassler, pp. 15-24. Minneapolis: Fortress, 1991.

———. *The Triumph of God: The Essence of Paul's Thought*. Minneapolis: Fortress, 1990.

Bevans, Stephen B. *Models of Contextual Theology*. Maryknoll, N.Y.: Orbis, 1992.

Bevans, Stephen B., and Roger P. Schroder, eds. *Constants in Conflict: A Theology of Mission for Today*. Maryknoll, N.Y.: Orbis, 2004.

Boring, M. Eugene. "Narrative Christology in the Apocalypse." *Catholic Biblical Quarterly* 54 (1992): 702-23.

Bosch, David. *Transforming Mission: Paradigm Shifts in Theology of Mission.* Maryknoll, N.Y.: Orbis, 1991.

Boyarin, Daniel. *A Radical Jew: Paul and the Politics of Identity.* Berkeley: University of California Press, 1994.

Brownson, James V. *Speaking the Truth in Love: New Testament Resources for a Missional Hermeneutic.* Harrisburg, Penn.: Trinity Press International, 1998.

Bruce, F. F. *The Epistles to the Colossians, to Philemon, and to the Ephesians.* New International Commentary on the New Testament. Grand Rapids, Mich.: Eerdmans, 1984.

Burridge, Richard A. "About People, by People, for People: Gospel Genre and Audience." In *The Gospel for All Christians: Rethinking the Gospel Audiences,* edited by Richard Bauckham, pp. 113-45. Grand Rapids, Mich.: Eerdmans, 1998.

———. *Four Gospels, One Jesus? A Symbolic Reading.* Grand Rapids, Mich.: Eerdmans, 1994.

———. *What Are the Gospels? A Comparison with Graeco-Roman Biography.* Cambridge: Cambridge University Press, 1992.

Caldwell, Larry W. "Cross-Cultural Bible Interpretation: A View from the Field." *Phronesis* 3 (1996): 24-30.

Carson, Donald A., and H. G. M. Williamson, eds. *It Is Written: Scripture Citing Scripture.* Cambridge: Cambridge University Press, 1988.

Charles, J. Daryl. "Engaging the (Neo)Pagan Mind: Paul's Encounter with Athenian Culture as a Model for Cultural Apologetics (Acts 17:16-34)." *Trinity Journal* 16 (1995): 47-62.

Cousar, Charles B. *The Letters of Paul.* Nashville: Abingdon, 1996.

Cunningham, Richard B. "Theologizing in a Global Context: Changing Contours." *Review and Expositor* 94 (1997): 351-62.

Davis, John R. "Biblical Precedents for Contextualization." *Asia Theological Association Journal* 2 (January 1994): 10-35.

deSilva, David A. *Honor, Patronage, Kinship and Purity: Unlocking New Testament Culture.* Downers Grove, Ill.: InterVarsity Press, 2000.

———. *The Hope of Glory: Honor Discourse and New Testament Interpretation.* Collegeville, Minn.: Michael Glazier/Liturgical Press, 1999.

Dibelius, Martin. *Studies in the Acts of the Apostles.* Edited by Heinrich Greeven. Translated by Mary Ling. London: SCM Press, 1956.

Dollar, Harold E. *A Biblical-Missiological Exploration of the Cross-Cultural Dimensions in Luke-Acts.* San Francisco: Mellen Research University Press, 1993.

Dunn, James D. G. *The Acts of the Apostles.* Valley Forge, Penn.: Trinity Press International, 1996.

———. *The Epistles to the Colossians and to Philemon: A Commentary on the Greek Text.* New International Greek Testament Commentary. Grand Rapids, Mich.: Eerdmans, 1996.

———. *The Theology of Paul the Apostle.* Grand Rapids, Mich.: Eerdmans, 1998.

Dyrness, William A. *The Earth Is God's: A Theology of American Culture.* Maryknoll, N.Y.: Orbis, 1995.

Ellis, E. Earle. *Paul's Use of the Old Testament.* Grand Rapids, Mich.: Eerdmans, 1957.

Eriksson, Anders. *Traditions as Rhetorical Proof: Pauline Argumentation in 1 Corinthians.* Stockholm: Almqvist and Wiksell International, 1998.

Evans, Craig A., and Stanley E. Porter, eds. *Dictionary of New Testament Background.* Downers Grove, Ill.: InterVarsity Press, 2000.

Fee, Gordon D. *The First Epistle to the Corinthians.* New International Commentary on the New Testament. Grand Rapids, Mich.: Eerdmans, 1987.

———. *Paul's Letter to the Philippians.* New International Commentary on the New Testament. Grand Rapids, Mich.: Eerdmans, 1995.

Fernando, Ajith. *Acts.* NIV Application Commentary. Grand Rapids, Mich.: Zondervan, 1998.

Fitzmyer, Joseph. *The Acts of the Apostles.* Anchor Bible 31. New York: Doubleday, 1998.

Flemming, Dean. "Contextualizing the Gospel in Athens: Paul's Areopagus Address as a Paradigm for Missionary Communication." *Missiology* 30 (2002): 199-214.

———. "Foundations for Responding to Religious Pluralism." *Wesleyan Theological Journal* 31 (1996): 51-75.

———. "The Third Horizon: A Wesleyan Contribution to the Contextualization Debate." *Wesleyan Theological Journal* 30 (1995): 139-63.

Gallagher, Robert L., and Paul Hertig, eds. *Mission in Acts: Ancient Narratives in Contemporary Context.* Maryknoll, N.Y.: Orbis, 2004.

Geertz, Clifford. *The Interpretation of Cultures.* New York: Basic Books, 1973.

Gilliland, Dean S. "New Testament Contextualization: Continuity and Particularity in Paul's Theology." In *The Word Among Us: Contextualizing Theology for Today,* edited by Dean S. Gilliland, pp. 52-73. Dallas: Word Books, 1989.

Gilliland, Dean S., ed. *The Word Among Us: Contextualizing Theology for Today.* Dallas: Word Books, 1989.

Gorman, Michael J. *Apostle of the Crucified Lord: A Theological Introduction to Paul and His Letters.* Grand Rapids, Mich.: Eerdmans, 2004.

———. *Cruciformity: Paul's Narrative Spirituality of the Cross.* Grand Rapids, Mich.: Eerdmans, 2001.

Green, Joel. "Acts of the Apostles." In *Dictionary of the Later New Testament and Its Developments,* edited by Ralph P. Martin and Peter H. Davids, pp. 7-24. Downers Grove, Ill.: InterVarsity Press, 1997.

———. *The Gospel of Luke.* New International Commentary on the New Testament. Grand Rapids, Mich.: Eerdmans, 1997.

———. "Scripture in the Church: Reconstructing the Authority of Scripture for Christian Formation and Mission." In *The Wesleyan Tradition: A Paradigm for Renewal,* edited by Paul W. Chilcote, pp. 38-51. Nashville: Abingdon, 2002.

———. *The Theology of the Gospel of Luke.* Cambridge: Cambridge University Press, 1995.

Green, Joel B., and Mark D. Baker. *Recovering the Scandal of the Cross: Atonement in New Testament and Contemporary Contexts.* Downers Grove, Ill.: InterVarsity Press, 2000.

Green, Joel B., and Max Turner, eds. *Between Two Horizons: Spanning New Testament Studies and Systematic Theology.* Grand Rapids, Mich.: Eerdmans, 2000.

Green, Joel B., Scot McKnight, and I. Howard Marshall, eds. *Dictionary of Jesus and the Gospels.* Downers Grove, Ill.: InterVarsity Press, 1992.

Hauerwas, Stanley, and William H. Willimon. *Resident Aliens: A Provocative Christian Assessment of Culture and Ministry for People Who Know That Something Is Wrong.* Nashville: Abingdon, 1989.

Hawthorne, Gerald F., and Ralph P. Martin, eds. *Dictionary of Paul and His Letters.* Downers Grove, Ill.: InterVarsity Press, 1993.

Hays, Richard B. "Crucified with Christ." In *Pauline Theology, Volume I: Thessalonians, Philippians, Galatians, Philemon,* edited by Jouette M. Bassler, pp. 227-46. Minneapolis: Fortress, 1991.

———. *Echoes of Scripture in the Letters of Paul.* New Haven, Conn.: Yale University Press, 1989.

———. *First Corinthians.* Interpretation. Louisville: Westminster John Knox, 1997.

———. *The Moral Vision of the New Testament: Community, Cross, New Creation: A Contemporary Introduction to New Testament Ethics.* San Francisco: HarperCollins, 1996.

Hemer, Colin J. *The Letters to the Seven Churches in Their Local Setting.* Grand Rapids, Mich.: Eerdmans, 2001.

———. "The Speeches of Acts II. The Areopagus Address." *Tyndale Bulletin* 40 (1989): 239-59.

Hengel, Martin. *The Pre-Christian Paul.* Translated by John Bowden. Philadelphia: Trinity Press International, 1991.

Hesselgrave, David J., and Edward Rommen. *Contextualization: Meanings, Methods, and Models.* Grand Rapids, Mich.: Baker, 1989.

Hiebert, Paul G. *Anthropological Insights for Missionaries.* Grand Rapids, Mich.: Baker, 1985.

———. "Critical Contextualization." *International Bulletin of Missionary Research* 11 (1987): 104-12.

———. "Form and Meaning in the Contextualization of the Gospel." In *The Word Among Us: Contextualizing Theology for Today,* edited by Dean S. Gilliland, pp. 101-20. Dallas: Word, 1989.

Hilary, Mbachu. *Inculturation Theology of the Jerusalem Council in Acts 15: an Inspiration for the Igbo Church Today.* Frankfurt: Peter Lang, 1995.

Horsley, Richard A., ed. *Paul and Politics: Ekklesia, Israel, Imperium, Interpretation.* Harrisburg, Penn.: Trinity Press International, 2000.

Howard-Brook, Wes, and Anthony Gwyther. *Unveiling Empire: Reading Revelation Then and Now.* Maryknoll, N.Y.: Orbis, 1999.

Hundley, R. C. "Towards an Evangelical Theology of Contextualization." Ph.D. diss., Trinity Evangelical Divinity School, 1993.

Hunsberger, George R., and Craig Van Gelder, eds. *The Church Between Gospel and Culture: The Emerging Mission in North America.* Grand Rapids, Mich.: Eerdmans, 1996.

Johnson, Luke Timothy. *The Acts of the Apostles.* Sacra Pagina. Collegeville, Minn.: Liturgical Press, 1992.

———. *Scripture and Discernment: Decision Making in the Church.* Nashville: Abingdon, 1983.

———. *The Writings of the New Testament: An Introduction.* Rev. ed. Minneapolis: Fortress, 1999.

Kallenberg, Brad J. *Live to Tell: Evangelism for a Postmodern Age.* Grand Rapids, Mich.: Brazos, 2002.

Keener, Craig S. *A Commentary on the Gospel of Matthew.* Grand Rapids, Mich.: Eerdmans, 1999.

Kim, Seyoon. *Paul and the New Perspective: Second Thoughts on the Origin of Paul's Gospel.* Grand Rapids, Mich.: Eerdmans, 2002.

Knight, Henry H., III. *A Future for Truth: Evangelical Theology in a Postmodern World.* Nashville: Abingdon, 1997.

Koester, Craig R. *Revelation and the End of All Things.* Grand Rapids, Mich.: Eerdmans, 2001.

Kraft, Charles H. *Anthropology for Christian Witness.* Maryknoll, N.Y.: Orbis, 1996.

———. *Christianity and Culture: A Study in Dynamic Biblical Theologizing.* Maryknoll, N.Y.: Orbis, 1979.

Kraus, C. Norman. *An Intrusive Gospel? Christian Mission in the Postmodern World.* Downers Grove, Ill.: InterVarsity Press, 1998.

Larkin, William J. "The Contribution of the Gospels and Acts to a Biblical Theology of Religions." In *Christianity and the Religions: A Biblical Theology of World Religions,* edited by Edward Rommen and Harold Netland, pp. 72-91. Pasadena, Calif.: William Carey, 1995.

Legrand, Lucien. *The Bible on Culture: Belonging or Dissenting?* Maryknoll, N.Y.: Orbis, 2000.

Lincoln, Andrew T. "Letter to the Colossians." In *The New Interpreter's Bible,* edited by Leander E. Keck, 11:551-669. Nashville: Abingdon, 2000.

Longenecker, Bruce W., ed. *Narrative Dynamics in Paul: A Critical Assessment.* Louisville: Westminster John Knox, 2002.

Longenecker, Richard N. *Biblical Exegesis in the Apostolic Period.* 2nd ed. Grand Rapids, Mich.: Eerdmans, 1999.

———. *Galatians.* Word Biblical Commentary 41. Dallas: Word Books, 1990.

Longenecker, Richard N., ed. *The Road from Damascus: The Impact of Paul's Conversion on His Life, Thought, and Ministry.* Grand Rapids, Mich.: Eerdmans, 1997.

McLaren, Brian D. "The Method, the Message, and the Ongoing Story." In *The Church in Emerging Culture: Five Perspectives,* edited by Leonard Sweet, pp. 191-230. Grand Rapids, Mich.: Zondervan, 2003.

Marshall, I. Howard. *The Acts of the Apostles.* Tyndale New Testament Commentaries. Grand Rapids, Mich.: Eerdmans, 1983.

Marshall, I. Howard, and David Peterson, eds. *Witness to the Gospel: The Theology of Acts.* Grand Rapids, Mich.: Eerdmans, 1998.

Martin, Ralph P., and Peter H. Davids, eds. *Dictionary of the Later New Testament and Its Developments.* Downers Grove, Ill.: InterVarsity Press, 1997.

Miranda-Feliciano, Evelyn. *Filipino Values and Our Christian Faith.* Manila: OMF Literature, 1990.

Mitchell, Margaret M. *Paul and the Rhetoric of Reconciliation: An Exegetical Investigation of the Language and Composition of 1 Corinthians.* Louisville: Westminster John Knox, 1992.

Mulder, M. J., ed. *Mikra: Text, Translation, Reading and Interpretation of the Hebrew Bible in Ancient Judaism and Early Christianity.* Assen/Maastrict: Van Gorcum. Philadelphia: Fortress, 1988.

Newbigin, Lesslie. *The Gospel in a Pluralist Society.* Grand Rapids, Mich.: Eerdmans, 1989.

Newton, Derek. *Deity and Diet: The Dilemma of Sacrificial Food at Corinth.* Sheffield, U.K.: Sheffield Academic Press, 1998.

Niebuhr, H. Richard. *Christ and Culture.* New York: Harper and Row, 1951.

Nissen, Johannes. "Mission and Globalization in New Testament Perspective." In *For All People: Global Theologies in Contexts,* edited by E. M. W. Pedersen, H. Lam and P. Lodberg, pp. 32-51. Grand Rapids, Mich.: Eerdmans, 2002.

O'Brien, Peter T. *Colossians, Philemon.* Word Bible Commentary 44. Waco, Tex.: Word Books, 1982.

———. *Gospel and Mission in the Writings of Paul.* Grand Rapids, Mich.: Baker, 1993.

Okure, Teresa. "Inculturation: Biblical/theological Bases." In *32 Articles Evaluating Inculturation of Christianity in Africa,* edited by Teresa Okure et al., pp. 55-88. Eldoret, Kenya: Gaba Publications, 1990.

Osborne, Grant R. *Revelation.* Baker Exegetical Commentary on the New Testament. Grand Rapids, Mich.: Baker, 2002.

Padilla, C. René. *Mission Between the Times: Essays on the Kingdom.* Grand Rapids, Mich.: Eerdmans, 1985.

Parrott, John, ed. *Introduction to Third World Theologies.* Cambridge: Cambridge University Press, 2004.

Sanneh, Lamin. *Translating the Message: The Missionary Impact on Culture.* Maryknoll, N.Y.: Orbis, 1991.

Schnabel, Eckhard J. *Early Christian Mission.* 2 vols. Downers Grove, Ill.: InterVarsity Press, 2004.

Schreiter, Robert J. *Constructing Local Theologies.* Maryknoll, N.Y.: Orbis, 1985.

Sedmak, Clemens, *Doing Local Theology.* Maryknoll, N.Y.: Orbis, 2002.

Senior, Donald. *The Gospel of Matthew.* Nashville: Abingdon, 1997.

Shiner, Whitney. *Proclaiming the Gospel: First-Century Performance of Mark.* Harrisburg, Penn.: Trinity Press International, 2003.

Shorter, Aylward. *Toward a Theology of Inculturation.* Maryknoll, N.Y.: Orbis, 1988.

Soards, Marion L. *The Speeches in Acts: Their Content, Context, and Concerns.* Louisville: Westminster John Knox, 1994.

Spencer, F. Scott. *Journeying Through Acts: A Literary-Cultural Reading.* Peabody, Mass.: Hendrickson, 2004.

Stackhouse, Max L. *Apologia: Contextualization, Globalization, and Mission in Theological Education.* Grand Rapids, Mich.: Eerdmans, 1988.

Stanley, Christopher D. *Paul and the Language of Scripture: Citation Technique in the Pauline Epistles and Contemporary Literature.* Society for New Testament Studies Monograph Series 69. Cambridge: Cambridge University Press, 1992.

Strong, David K. "The Jerusalem Council: Some Implications for Contextualization. Acts 15:1-35. In *Mission in Acts: Ancient Narratives and Contemporary Context,* edited by Robert L. Gallagher and Paul Hertig, pp. 196-208. Maryknoll, N.Y.: Orbis, 2004.

Sugirtharajah, R. S., ed. *Dictionary of Third World Theologies.* Maryknoll, N.Y.: Orbis, 2000.

———. ed. *Voices from the Margin: Interpreting the Bible in the Third World.* Maryknoll, N.Y.: Orbis, 1991.

Tannehill, Robert C. *The Narrative Unity of Luke-Acts.* 2 vols. Philadelphia: Fortress, 1986-1990.

Thiselton, Anthony C. *The First Epistle to the Corinthians.* New International Greek Testament Commentary. Grand Rapids, Mich.: Eerdmans, 2000.

Thompson, Marianne Meye. "John, Gospel of." In *Dictionary of Jesus and the Gospels,* edited by Joel B. Green, Scot McKnight and I. Howard Marshall, pp. 368-83. Downers Grove, Ill.: InterVarsity Press, 1992.

Towner, Philip H. "Romans 13:1-7 and Paul's Missiological Perspective: A Call to Political Quietism or Transformation?" In *Romans and the People of God: Essays in Honor of Gordon D. Fee on the Occasion of His 65ᵗʰ Birthday,* edited by S. K. Soderlund and N. T. Wright, pp. 149-69. Grand Rapids, Mich.: Eerdmans, 1999.

Volf, Miroslav. *Exclusion and Embrace: A Theological Exploration of Identity, Otherness, and Reconciliation.* Nashville: Abingdon, 1996.

———. "When Gospel and Culture Intersect: Notes on the Nature of Christian Difference." In *Pentecostalism in Context: Essays in Honor of William W. Menzies,* edited by William M. Menzies and Robert Menzies, pp. 223-36. Sheffield, U.K.: Sheffield University Press, 1997.

Walsh, Brian J., and Sylvia C. Keesmat. *Colossians Remixed: Subverting the Empire.* Downers Grove, Ill.: InterVarsity Press, 2004.

Webber, Robert E. *The Younger Evangelicals: Facing the Challenges of the New World.* Grand Rapids, Mich.: Baker, 2002.

Willis, W. L. *Idol Meat in Corinth: The Pauline Argument in 1 Corinthians 8 and 10.* Chico, Calif.: Scholars Press, 1985.

Wilson, Walter T. *The Hope of Glory: Education and Exhortation in the Epistle to the Colossians.* Leiden: Brill, 1997.

Winter, Bruce W. "In Public and in Private: Early Christians and Religious Pluralism." In *One God, One Lord,* edited by Andrew D. Clarke and Bruce W. Winter, pp. 125-48. Grand Rapids, Mich.: Baker, 1992.

Winter, Bruce W., and Andrew D. Clarke, eds. *The Book of Acts in Its Ancient Literary Setting.* Vol. 1, The Book of Acts in Its First Century Setting. Grand Rapids, Mich.: Eerdmans, 1993.

Witherington, Ben, III. *The Acts of the Apostles: A Socio-Rhetorical Commentary*. Grand Rapids, Mich.: Eerdmans, 1998.

———. *Conflict and Community in Corinth: A Socio-Rhetorical Commentary on 1 and 2 Corinthians*. Grand Rapids, Mich.: Eerdmans, 1995.

———. *Grace in Galatia: A Commentary on Paul's Letter to the Galatians*. Grand Rapids, Mich.: Eerdmans, 1998.

———. *John's Wisdom: A Commentary on the Fourth Gospel*. Louisville: Westminster John Knox, 1995.

———. *The Paul Quest: The Renewed Search for the Jew of Tarsus*. Downers Grove, Ill.: InterVarsity Press, 1998.

———. *Paul's Narrative Thought World: The Tapestry of Tragedy and Triumph*. Louisville: Westminster John Knox, 1994.

Wright, N. T. *The Epistles of Paul to the Colossians and to Philemon: An Introduction and Commentary*. Tyndale New Testament Commentaries. Grand Rapids, Mich.: Eerdmans, 1986.

———. *The New Testament and the People of God*. Minneapolis: Fortress, 1992.

———. "One God, One Lord, One People: Incarnational Christology for a Church in a Pagan Environment," *Ex Auditu* 7 (1991): 45-58.

———. "Paul's Gospel and Caesar's Empire." In *Paul and Politics: Ekklesia, Israel, Imperium, Interpretation,* edited by R. A. Horsley, pp. 160-83. Harrisburg, Penn.: Trinity Press International, 2000.

———. *What Saint Paul Really Said: Was Paul of Tarsus the Real Founder of Christianity?* Grand Rapids, Mich.: Eerdmans, 1997.

Yeo Khiok-khng. *What Has Jerusalem to Do with Beijing? Biblical Interpretation from a Chinese Perspective*. Harrisburg, Penn.: Trinity Press International, 1998.

Zweck, Dean. "The *Exordium* of the Areopagus Speech, Acts 17.22,23." *New Testament Studies* 35 (1989): 94-103.

Subject Index

Acts of the Apostles
  audience of, 28
  as a cultural document,
    26-28
  genre of, 26
  historical basis of
    speeches in, 56n. 2
  Mosaic law in, 33, 35n. 30,
    36n. 33, 38, 43-47, 49,
    52, 58, 61, 63
  purpose of, 28-30
  speeches in, 32-33, 40-42,
    56-88
Adam/Christ typology, 205-
  6, 208, 212
allegory, 159-60, 168
already/not yet, 96, 101,
  115, 223-24, 226-27, 231
Antioch community, 43-44,
  47, 48, 51
apocalyptic
  literature and symbols,
    203, 206, 209, 219, 241-
    42, 269n. 7, 272-73, 278-
    79, 281, 291-92, 317
  perspective, 95-96, 120-
    22, 206, 219, 272, 283,
    291
apologetics, 77, 81, 237,
  247, 317-18, 321
apostolic decree, 46-47, 50
Areopagus, 66, 73-76, 81-
  82, 86, 185
Aristotle, 132-33, 147
asceticism, 216-17, 223, 225,
  228-29
Babylon, symbol of, 271-72,
  274, 276, 284-88, 290,
  292
catholic spirit, 314
chreia, 239
Christ
  conformity to, 104, 129,

174-76, 178-79, 193, 198,
  200, 212-13
death of. *See* death of
  Christ, contextualiza-
  tion of
as firstfruits, 203, 205
image of, 104, 151, 208
incarnation of, 18, 20-23,
  104, 159, 195, 196, 210,
  260, 262-63, 311
as Lord, 43-44, 147-48,
  228-29, 230
resurrection of. *See* resurrection of Christ
sufficiency of, 218, 219,
  221, 223-25, 230, 233
supremacy of, 218, 219-
  23, 230, 304
christological hymns, 97,
  173, 174-76, 195, 220-22,
  226, 229
church
  as agent of contextualiza-
    tion, 51, 318. *See also*
    contextualization, eccle-
    sial; contextualization,
    role of the community in
  as mission outpost, 320
  relationship to the culture.
    See culture, church's re-
    lationship to
  as resident alien, 320
  unity of, 49, 50-55, 175,
    177-78, 263, 309-10,
    319
citizenship
  dual, 143, 320
  heavenly, 143-44,
  Paul's Roman, 27, 124
Colossian "philosophy." *See*
  syncretism, Colossian
conscience, 126, 129, 185-
  86, 190-91
contextualism, 311
contextualization
  cruciform, 198, 322
  definition of, 19-20
  ecclesial, 51-52, 54, 264,
    304-5, 318-21
  evangelistic, 16, 20, 56-57,
    89-90, 110, 319, 321
    for educated Greeks in

Athens, 72-85, 86-88
for God-fearers, 35, 39-
  42
for Jews in Antioch, 57-
  66, 84, 86-88
Paul's practice of, 106,
  195-99, 198, 306-7
for polytheists in Lystra,
  66-72, 84-85, 86-88
for Samaritans, 34
example of Jesus for, 20-
  23, 261
incarnational, 20-23, 104,
  127, 170, 196, 211, 322
for Islamic people, 51,
  200, 307
of language and imagery,
  106-11, 128-31, 144-46,
  185-86, 188, 209, 219,
  222, 261, 265, 297-300
lifestyle, 182, 195-98, 200-
  201
limits of, 77, 172-73, 197,
  302-7
missional, 51-52, 90, 264,
  305, 319, 321-22
in multicultural settings,
  125, 150, 309-10, 312-15
New Testament models
  for, 15-16, 20-22, 54-55,
  71-72, 81-84, 85-86, 89-
  90, 116-17, 150-51, 161-
  63, 170-73, 199-201, 212-
  13, 230-33, 265, 266,
  291-95, 296-309, 311-13,
  316-19, 321-22
noncoercive, 82, 84, 185,
  230, 232
Old Testament, 16n. 3
for postmodern culture,
  14, 24n. 18, 49, 82, 201,
  265, 295, 299, 315-18
role of experience in, 39,
  48-49
role of the community in,
  40, 51-53, 318-19
role of the Holy Spirit in,
  30-31, 39, 48, 54, 151,
  170, 181, 200-201, 264,
  271, 292, 297, 302, 304-
  5, 318, 321-22
of Scripture, 17, 46, 49, 61-